POWER QUOTES

POWER QUOTES

4,000
TRENCHANT SOUNDBITES ON

Leadership & Liberty,
Treason & Triumph, Sacrifice & Scandal,
Risk & Rebellion, Weakness & War,
and Other Affaires Politiques

DANIEL B. BAKER

BARNES
&NOBLE
BOOKS
NEW YORK

Contents

Preface

Power Quotes assembles a collection of specifically chosen statements, from the very familiar to the lesser-known, ranging from historical to contemporary utterances. In compiling this book, I discovered no limit to the potential number of relevant and "quotable" quotations, and every foray into a new source typically turned up several, rather than one or two, possibilities.

Selection Criteria

My aim was to limit *Power Quotes* to specific topic areas, thus eliminating scores of other quotations on hundreds of subjects found in general quotation books. Moreover, these quotations were to be relevant to the modern world. This criterion does not eliminate historical quotations but, rather, involved searching out those with general and continuing application. Eliminated, then, were those quotations that referred to one historical event and those that may have made sense to a classically educated person of the nineteenth century but would be meaningless to a reader today.

Original Language and Reliable Translations Provided

To the extent possible, I have tracked down the original quotations in languages other than English. The English translations of these quotations can vary enormously. Typically, however, the variance is between a "literary" translation that reads well in English (and therefore is often best known), but has only a tenuous relationship to the original, and a "literal" translation that faithfully reproduces the meaning of the original, but is eminently "unquotable" in English. I tried to steer a middle course in choosing a translation or, in some cases, making my own. In any case, the most honest method seemed to be to include the original language version so readers, to the extent that their expertise might allow, can make their own choices.

Source Material

To ensure inclusion of well-known quotations on the subjects chosen, I consulted the following references:

> *Bartlett's Familiar Quotations,* 15th edition (Boston: Little, Brown and Company, 1980)
> *Classical and Foreign Quotations* (London: J. Whitaker & Sons, 1904)
> *Das Grosse Kruger Zitaten Buck* (Frankfurt: Wolfgang Kruger Verlag)
> *Dictionary of Contemporary Quotations* (John Gordon Burke Publisher, Inc., 1981)
> *A Dictionary of Political Quotations* (London: Europa Publications, 1984)
> *Dictionnaire de citations françaises* (Paris: Le Robert, 1978)
> *The Great Quotations* (Secaucus, N.J.: Lyle Stuart Inc., 1983)
> *The International Thesaurus of Quotations* (New York: Harper and Row, 1970)
> *The Oxford Dictionary of Quotations,* 2nd edition (London: Oxford University Press, 1955)
> *The Quotable Woman* (New York: Facts on File, 1982)
> *Quotations in Black* (Westport, Conn.: Greenwood Press, 1981)
> *Respectfully Quoted* (Washington, D.C.: Library of Congress, 1989)
> *Simpson's Contemporary Quotations* (Boston: Houghton Mifflin Company, 1988)
> *Treasury of Presidential Quotations* (Chicago: Follett Publishing Company, 1964)

For the initial legwork in tracking down and documenting famous quotations, I am very grateful to those editors who have gone before.

Using these well-known references as a base, I turned to the original sources and verified, as much as possible, the accuracy of the quotations themselves as well as related data. This search then turned up numerous other potential quotations that have been sifted through, and in many instances, included. Occasionally, two sources differed and an adjudication between them had to be made. In addition, misquotes and other errors in citation were identified through this search, and these have been corrected.

Introduction

Power is pleasure; and pleasure sweetens pain. —*William Hazlitt, 1926*

Next to enjoying ourselves, the next greatest pleasure consists in preventing others from enjoying themselves, or more generally, in the acquisition of power. —*Bertrand Russell, 1928*

Power makes you attractive; it even makes women love old men.
—*Joseph Joubert, 1842*

Power is the great aphrodisiac. —*Henry Kissinger, 1971*

We have, I fear, confused power with greatness.
—*Stewart L. Udall, 1965*

To be great is to be misunderstood. —*Ralph Waldo Emerson, 1841*

Power is ironic; power is comedic; power is seductive and dramatic; power is above criticism and beneath contempt. Power comes in many guises, from sheer military might to skillful diplomacy, from effective legislation to eloquent speech that moves or motivates. The more than four thousand trenchant soundbites you'll find in **Power Quotes** look at power from over fifty angles, ranging from **Business** to **Women.** Look up the category **Leadership/Statesmanship,** for example, and read why Niccolò Machiavelli concluded in 1532 that "It is far safer to be feared than loved."

Arranged topic-by-topic, **Power Quotes** brings together a broad range of citations on common themes, providing you with an overview of thinking on such concepts as **Economics, Government,** and **Public Opinion.** This arrangement allows you to find those perfectly appropriate motivational words on a given theme. Perhaps Oscar Wilde's 1892 comment on aspiration, also found in the **Leadership/Statesmanship** category, can inspire a demoralized audience: "We are all in the gutter, but some of us are looking at the stars."

I chose these quotations for their contemporary significance, whether they were originally uttered by Herodotus, Montaigne, Vince Lombardi, Groucho Marx, Gloria Steinem, or Desmond Tutu. Go back to the **Leadership/Statesmanship** category and you'll find Voltaire's 1751 declaration that "The history of the world's great leaders is often the story of human folly." But in 1930 Knut Rockne saw **Leadership/Statesmanship** this way: "You show me a good and gracious loser, and I'll show you a failure!"

About forty percent of the citations included in *Power Quotes* date from the post-World War II era. **Leadership/Statesmanship** in 1986 was summed up by Margaret Thatcher like this: "What is success? I think it is a mixture of having a flair for the thing that you are doing; knowing that it is not enough, that you have got to have hard work and a certain sense of purpose."

Within each subject category, quotations are arranged by date, allowing browsers to appreciate the development of thought on a given topic, from Classical times to the present. Under **War and Peace**, begin by reading the Greek poet Homer's thoughts on victory in 700 B.C., and conclude with General H. Norman Schwarzkopf's assessment of an adversary's competence in 1991.

Some surprises await the browser. Did you know that in 1968, when Lyndon B. Johnson announced that he would not run for a second term for president, he was echoing the 1884 declaration of William Tecumseh Sherman: "I will not accept if nominated and will not serve if elected"? And which American said that "Public opinion in this country is everything," and when did this cynical insight emerge? Would you have guessed Abraham Lincoln, in 1859?

And what about other famous words by Lincoln? The **Author Index** lets you find quotations by any of your favorite pundits. If you come across a quote you like but you don't recognize the speaker, the **Author Index**'s brief background description helps identify the person quoted and provides context for the quotation. If you know of a quote by a specific author or you're curious about who said what, this is the place to look.

Paging through *Power Quotes* you'll encounter old favorites, like "I have nothing to offer but blood, toil, tears and sweat" (Sir Winston S. Churchill, 1940), and "You see things; and you say, 'Why?' But I dream things that never were; and I say 'Why not?' " (George Bernard Shaw, 1921). From Michel de Montaigne's sixteenth-century observation that "Even on the highest throne in the world, we are still sitting on our ass" to Richard M. Nixon's 1972 assertion, "I never shoot blanks," many quotes cut to the chase. Wily advice from a Canadian, "Diplomacy is letting someone else have your way" (Lester B. Pearson, 1965), is intercut with paradoxical French introspection, "I respect only those who resist me, but I cannot tolerate them" (Charles De Gaulle, 1968), and leavened with

British pragmatism, "A little inaccuracy sometimes saves tons of explanation" (H. H. Munro [Saki], 1924).

Armed with the arsenal of distilled thought stockpiled in *Power Quotes,* you're bound to find that nugget of inspiration or snappy comeback you need to win your own personal skirmishes. While it's worth considering Herodotus' view, expressed in 430 B.C., that "the bitterest pain among men is to have much knowledge but no power," don't forget that, as Sir Francis Bacon wrote in 1597, "Knowledge is power." Turn the page, and become empowered.

POWER
QUOTES

Bureaucracy

It's all papers and forms, the entire Civil Service is like a fortress made of papers, forms, and red tape.

Alexander Ostrovsky
The Diary of a Scoundrel
1868

The bureaucracy is what we all suffer from.
Die Bürokratie ist es, an der wir alle kranken.

Prince Otto von Bismarck
comments in Friedrichsruh
Dec 12, 1891

I believe there are still some people who think that a democratic State is scarcely distinguishable from the people. This, however, is a delusion. The State is a collection of officials, different for different purposes, drawing comfortable incomes so long as the status quo is preserved. The only alteration they are likely to desire in the status quo is an increase of bureaucracy and of the power of the bureaucrats.

Bertrand Russell
Maurice Conaway lecture
1922

A statesman is judged by results. If his policy fails he goes. It may be unfair, but there is a kind of rough justice about it. Mr. Montagu Norman (Governor of the Bank of England), on the other hand, is never called upon to explain, justify or defend his policies. And it is his policies which have been carried out for the past ten years. Governments may come and governments may go, but the Governor of the Bank of England goes on for ever. It is a classic example of power without responsibility.

Robert, Baron Boothby
speech in the House of Commons
Apr 25, 1932

The power which a multiple millionaire, who may be my neighbor and perhaps my employer, has over me is very much less than that which the smallest fonctionnaire possesses who wields the coercive power of the state, and on whose discretion it depends whether and how I am to be allowed to live or to work.

Friedrich August von Hayek
The Road to Serfdom
1944

The nearest approach to immortality on earth is a government bureau.

James F. Byrnes
Speaking Frankly
1947

Bureaucracies are designed to perform public business. But as soon as a bureaucracy is established, it develops an autonomous spiritual life and comes to regard the public as its enemy.

Brooks Atkinson
"September 9"
Once Around the Sun
1951

Brooks Atkinson "September 9" *Once Around the Sun* 1951	The perfect bureaucrat everywhere is the man who manages to make no decisions and escape all responsibility.
Dwight D. Eisenhower speech in Peoria, Illinois Sep 25, J56	Farming looks mighty easy when your plow is a pencil, and you're a thousand miles from the corn field.
Mary McCarthy "The Vita Activa" *New Yorker* Oct 18, 1958	Bureaucracy, the rule of no one, has become the modern form of despotism.
Gore Vidal *Sex, Death and Money* 1968	There is something about a bureaucrat that does not like a poem.
Eugene J. McCarthy *Time* Feb 12, 1979	The only thing that saves us from the bureaucracy is inefficiency. An efficient bureaucracy is the greatest threat to liberty.
Charles Peters *How Washington Really Works* 1980	Bureaucrats write memoranda both because they appear to be busy when they are writing and because the memos, once written, immediately become proof they were busy.
Hyman G. Rickover quoted by William A. Clinkscales Jr. *The New York Times* Nov 3, 1986	If you're going to sin, sin against God, not the bureaucracy, God will forgive you but the bureaucracy won't.

Citizenship

Baruch (Benedictus de) Spinoza *Tractatus Politicus* 1676	Citizens are not born, but made. *Homines enim civiles non nascuntur, sed fiunt.*
Voltaire "Patrie" *Dictionnaire philosophique* 1764	He who would not wish his own country to be bigger or smaller, richer or poorer, would be a citizen of the universe. *Celui qui voudrait que sa patrie ne fût jamais ni plus grande ni plus petite, ni plus riche ni plus pauvre serait le citoyen de l'univers.*
Thomas Jefferson letter to John B. Colvin Sep 20, 1810	A strict observance of the written laws is doubtless one of the high virtues of a good citizen, but it is not the highest. The laws of necessity, of self-preservation, of saving our country when in danger, are of higher obligation.
Daniel Webster speech in Plymouth, Massachusetts Dec 22, 1820	Whatever makes men good Christians, makes them good citizens.
James Russell Lowell "On the Capture of Fugi- tive Slaves near Washington" 1845	Before Man made us citizens, great Nature made us men.

Everyone who receives the protection of society owes a return for the benefit.

John Stuart Mill
On Liberty
1859

Without a home their can be no good citizen. With a home there can be no bad one.

Andrew Johnson
quoted by George L. Tappan
Andrew Johnson, Not Guilty
May, 1872

The first requisite of a good citizen in this republic of ours is that he shall be able and willing to pull his weight.

Theodore Roosevelt
speech in New York City
Nov 11, 1902

To acquire immunity to eloquence is of the utmost importance to the citizens of a democracy.

Bertrand Russell
Power
1938

The Constitution does not provide for first and second class citizens.

Wendell Lewis Willkie
An American Program
1944

It is the duty of every citizen according to his best capacities to give validity to his convictions in political affairs.

Albert Einstein
Treasury for the Free World
1946

It is not the function of our Government to keep the citizen from falling into error; it is the function of the citizen to keep the Government from falling into error.

Robert H. Jackson
American Communications Association v. *Douds*
May, 1950

Politics ought to be the part-time profession of every citizen who would protect the rights and privileges of free people and who would preserve what is good and fruitful in our national heritage.

Dwight D. Eisenhower
broadcast speech
Jan 28, 1954

I deplore the need or the use of troops anywhere to get American citizens to obey the orders of constituted courts.

Dwight D. Eisenhower
on Arkansas' refusal to accept the Supreme Court's school desegregation ruling
May 14, 1958

The ignorance of one voter in a democracy impairs the security of all.

John F. Kennedy
speech at Vanderbilt Univ., Nashville, Tennessee
May 18, 1963

We will have to repent in this generation not merely for the vitriolic words and actions of the bad people, but for the appalling silence of the good people.

Martin Luther King Jr.
"Letter from the Birmingham Jail"
Jan 16, 1963

Because all Americans just must have the right to vote. And we are going to give them that right. All Americans must have the privileges of citizenship regardless of race. And they are going to have those privileges of citizenship regardless of race.

Lyndon Baines Johnson
speech to a joint session of U.S. Congress
Mar 15, 1965

J. William Fulbright
speech to the American
Newspaper Publishers
Association
Apr 28, 1966
The citizen who criticizes his country is paying it an implied tribute.

Class Divisions

Plato
The Republic
ca. 390 B.C.

Oligarchy: A government resting on a valuation of property, in which the rich have power and the poor man is deprived of it.

Aristotle
Politics
343 B.C.

The best political community is formed by citizens of the middle class.

Aristotle
Nicomachean Ethics
ca. 325 B.C.

When quarrels and complaints arise, it is when people who are equal have not got equal shares, or vice versa.

Juvenal
(Decimus Junius
Juvenalis)
Satires
ca. 100

It is not easy for men to rise whose qualities are thwarted by poverty.
Haud facile emergunt quorum virtutibus obstat.

Christopher Marlowe
The Jew of Malta
1589

Excess of wealth is cause of covetousness.

Thomas Fuller
Gnomologia
1732

He whose belly is full believes not him whose is empty.

Adam Smith
The Theory of Moral
Sentiments
1759

They (the rich) are led by an invisible hand to make nearly the same distribution of the necessaries of life, which would have been made, had the earth been divided into equal portions among all its inhabitants; and thus, without intending it, without knowing it, advance the interest of the society, and afford means to the multiplication of the species.

Alexander Hamilton
debate at the Constitu-
tional Convention
Jun 18, 1787

All communities divide themselves into the few and the many. The first are the rich and wellborn, the other the mass of the people. . . . The people are turbulent and changing; they seldom judge or determine right. Give therefore to the first class a distinct, perma-nent share in the government. They will check the unsteadiness of the second, and as they cannot receive any advantage by a change, they therefore will ever maintain good government.

Edmund Burke
Appeal from the New to the
Old Whigs
1791

A true natural aristocracy is not a separate interest in the state, or separable from it. It is an essential integrant part of any large body rightly constituted.

The freest government, if it could exist, would not be long acceptable, if the tendency of the laws were to create a rapid accumulation of property in few hands, and to render the great mass of the population dependent and penniless.

Daniel Webster
speech at Plymouth, Massachusetts on 200th anniversary of landing of Pilgrims
Dec 22, 1820

Distinctions in society will always exist under every just government. Equality of talents, of education, or of wealth can not be produced by human institutions.

Andrew Jackson
veto message
Jul 10, 1832

Nobility, say the aristocracy, is the intermedium between the king and the people—true; just as a sporting dog is the intermedium between the sportsman and the hare.

Honoré Gabriel, Comte de Mirabeau
"Apophthegms"
Mirabeau's Letters During His Residence in England
1832

Society is composed of two classes: they who have more dinners than appetite, and they who have more appetite than dinners.

Honoré Gabriel, Comte de Mirabeau
"Apophthegms"
Mirabeau's Letters During His Residence in England
1832

Aristocracy as a predominant element in a government, whether it be aristocracy of skin, of race, of wealth, of nobility, or of priesthood, has been to my mind the greatest source of evil throughout the world, because it has been the most universal and the most enduring.

Thomas Arnold
letter to T. Coolidge
May 18, 1838

The American aristocracy can be found in the lawyer's bar and the judge's bench.
L'aristocratie américaine est au banc des avocats et le siège des juges.

Alexis, Comte de Tocqueville
Democracy in America
1835-39

The English laborer does not find his worst enemy in the nobility, but in the middling class.

Orestes Augustus Brownson
Boston Quarterly Review
1840

I believe and I say it is true Democratic feeling, that all the measures of the government are directed to the purpose of making the rich richer and the poor poorer.

William Henry Harrison
speech
Oct 1, 1840

If trade unionists failed to register their protest by striking, their silence would be regarded as an admission that they acquiesced in the pre-eminence of economic forces over human welfare. Such acquiescence would be a recognition of the right of the middle classes to exploit the workers when business was flourishing and to let the workers go hungry when business was slack.

Friedrich Engels
The Condition of the Working Class in England in 1844
1844

Two nations between whom there is no intercourse and no sympathy; who are as ignorant of each other's habits, thoughts and feelings, as if they were dwellers in different zones or inhabitants of different planets . . . the rich and the poor.

Benjamin Disraeli
Sybil
1845

I was told that the Privileged and the People formed two nations.

Benjamin Disraeli
Sybil
1845

Karl Marx *The Communist Manifesto* 1848	The ruling ideas of each age have ever been the ideas of its ruling class.
Karl Marx *The Communist Manifesto* 1848	In proportion as the antagonism between classes within the nation vanishes, the hostility of one nation to another will come to an end.
Karl Marx *The Communist Manifesto* 1848	The history of all hitherto existing society is the history of class struggles.
Karl Marx *The Communist Manifesto* 1848	The executive of the modern state is but a committee for managing the common affairs of the whole bourgeoisie.
Karl Marx *The Communist Manifesto* 1848	Of all the classes that stand face to face with the bourgeoisie to-day, the proletariat alone is a really revolutionary class. The other classes decay and finally disappear in the face of modern industry; the proletariat is its special essential product.
Karl Marx *The Communist Manifesto* 1848	What the bourgeoisie, therefore, produces, above all, is its own grave-diggers. Its fall and the victory of the proletariat are equally inevitable.
Walter Savage Landor "Aristoteles and Callisthenes" *Imaginary Conversations* 1824-53	Wherever there is excessive wealth, there is also in the train of it excessive poverty; as, where the sun is brightest, the shade is deepest.
Andrew Johnson speech in the U.S. Senate May 20, 1858	The people are the safest, the best, and the most reliable lodgement of power. . . . Keep up the middle class; lop off an aristocracy on the one hand, and a rabble at the other; let the middle class . . . have the power, and your government is always secure.
Sojourner Truth attributed	The rich rob the poor and poor rob one another.
Elizabeth Cady Stanton speech to the New York state legislature Feb 18, 1860	You who have read the history of nations, from Moses down to our last election, where have you ever seen one class looking after the interests of another?
Wendell Phillips speech on Toussaint L'Ouverture 1861	Aristocracy is always cruel.
Victor Hugo *Les Misérables* 1862	There is always more misery among the lower classes than there is humanity in the higher. *Il y a toujours encore plus de misère en bas que de fraternité en haut.*
Karl Marx *The Civil War in France* 1871	The bourgeoisie of the whole world, which looks complacently upon the wholesale massacre after the battle, is convulsed by horror at the desecration of brick and mortar.

Inequality has the natural and necessary effect, under the present circumstances, of materializing our upper class, vulgarizing our middle class, and brutalizing our lower class.

Matthew Arnold
"Equality"
Mixed Essays
1879

So long as all the increased wealth which modern progress brings goes but to build up great fortunes, to increase luxury and make sharper the contrast between the House of Have and the House of Want, progress is not real and cannot be permanent.

Henry George
Progress and Povery
1879

Private ownership of land is the nether millstone. Material progress is the upper millstone. Between them, with increasing pressure, the working classes are being ground.

Henry George
Progress and Poverty
1879

The danger is not that a particular class is unfit to govern. Every class is unfit to govern.

Lord Acton
letter to Mary Gladstone
Apr 24, 1881

There are three ways by which an individual can get wealth— by work, by gift, and by theft. And, clearly, the reaons why the workers get so little is that the beggars and thieves get so much.

Henry George
Social Problems
1883

Capital is dead labor that, vampire-like, lives only by sucking living labor, and lives the more, the more labor it sucks.

Karl Marx
Das Kapital
1867-83

The most grinding poverty is a trifling evil compared with the inequality of classes.

William Morris
letter to Andreas Scheu
Sep 5, 1883

It is enough political economy for me to know that the idle rich class is rich and the working class is poor, and that the rich are rich because they rob the poor.

William Morris
lecture in Glasgow in 1884, quoted by J.B. Glasier
William Morris and the Early Days of the Socialist Movement
1921

It has become an article of the creed of modern morality that all labor is good in itself—a convenient belief to those who live on the labor of others.

William Morris
Useful Work Versus Useless Toil
1884

Where justice is denied, where poverty is enforced, where ignorance prevails, and where any one class is made to feel that society is in an organized conspiracy to oppress, rob, and degrade them, neither persons nor property will be safe.

Frederick Douglass
speech on twenty-fourth anniversary of emancipation in the District of Columbia
Apr, 1886

He mocks the people who proposes that the Government shall protect the rich and that they in turn will care for the laboring poor.

Grover Cleveland
fourth annual message to Congress
Dec 3, 1888

The state is nothing but an instrument of oppression of one class by another—no less so in a democratic republic than in a monarchy.

Friedrich Engels
preface to the 1891 edition of Karl Marx
The Civil War in France
1891

Leo XIII
encyclical
Rerum Novarum
1891

The great mistake made in regard to the matter now under consideration, is to take up the notion that class is naturally hostile to class, and that the wealthy and the working man are intended by nature to live in mutual conflict. So irrational and so false is this view, that the direct contrary is the truth. Just as the symmetry of the human frame is the result of the suitable arrangement of the different parts of the body, so in a state is it ordained by nature that these two classes should dwell in harmony and agreement, so as to maintain the balance of the body politic.

Oliver Wendell Holmes Sr.
Over the Teacups
1891

It is a very curious fact that, with all our boasted "free and equal" superiority over the communities of the Old World, our people have the most enormous appetite for Old World titles of distinction.

Henry Demarest Lloyd
Wealth Against Commonwealth
1894

For as true as that a house divided against itself cannot stand, and that a nation half-slave and half-free cannot permanently endure, it is true that a people who are slaves to market-tyrants will surely come to be their slaves in all else, that all liberty begins to be lost when one liberty is lost, that a people half democratic and half plutocratic cannot permanently endure.

William Jennings Bryan
"Cross of Gold" speech at the Democratic National Convention, Chicago, Illinois
Jul 8, 1896

Having behind us the producing masses of the nation and the world, supported by the commercial interests, the laboring interests and the toilers, everywhere, we will answer their demand for a gold standard by saying to them: You shall not press down upon the brow of labor this crown of thorns; you shall not crucify mankind upon a cross of gold.

Keir Hardie
quoted by Iain McLean
Keir Hardie
1975

For twenty-one years the Social Democratic Federation has based its propaganda on the class-war theory, and the result is dismal failure. How could it be otherwise? Mankind in the mass is not moved by hatred, but by love of what is right.

W.E.B. Du Bois
The Souls of Black Folk
1903

To be a poor man is hard, but to be a poor race in a land of dollars is the very bottom of hardships.

G.K. Chesterton
Heretics
1905

The oligarchic character of the modern English commonwealth does not rest, like many oligarchies, on the cruelty of the rich to the poor. It does not even rest on the kindness of the rich to the poor. It rests on the perennial and unfailing kindness of the poor to the rich.

David Lloyd George
speech at Mile End, London
Dec, 1910

An aristocracy is like cheese; the older it is the higher it becomes.

David Lloyd George
quoted by Martin Gilbert in introduction
Lloyd George
1968

All down History, nine-tenths of mankind have been grinding the corn for the remaining one-tenth, been paid with the husks— and bidden to thank God they had the husks.

Woodrow Wilson
speech
Oct 28, 1912

Energy in a nation is like sap in a tree; it rises from bottom up.

It's no disgrace t' be poor, but it might as well be.

"Kin" Hubbard
Abe Martin's Sayings and Sketches
1915

If capital an' labor ever do git t'gether it's good night fer th' rest of us.

"Kin" Hubbard
saying

A society without an aristocracy, without an elite minority, is not a society.
Una sociedad sin aristocracia, sin minoría egregia, no es una sociedad.

Jose Ortega y Gasset
Invertebrate Spain
1922

The government of the United States is a device for maintaining in perpetuity the rights of the people, with the ultimate extinction of all privileged classes.

Calvin Coolidge
speech in Philadelphia, Pennsylvania
Sep 25, 1924

(Its object was) to make working-class bees without a sting, who were to gather honey for the rich, but be deprived of the right to defend themselves.

Sir Oswald Mosley
on policies of British government during 1926 General Strike
The Star
Dec 15, 1926

Advocates of capitalism are very apt to appeal to the sacred principles of liberty, which are embodied in one maxim. The fortunate must not be restrained in the exercise of tyranny over the unfortunate.

Bertrand Russell
"Freedom in Society"
Skeptical Essays
1928

The conflict between capitalism and democracy is inherent and continuous; it is often hidden by misleading proaganda and by the outward forms of democracy, such as parliaments, and the sops that the owning classes throw to the other classes to keep them more or less contented.

Jawaharlal Nehru
Glimpses of World History
1933

The defeats and victories of the fellows at the top aren't defeats and victories for the fellows at the bottom.
Die Sieg und Niederlagen der Grossköpfigen oben und der von unten fallen nämlich nicht immer zusammen, durchaus nicht.

Bertolt Brecht
Mother Courage
1939

Civilization cannot survive if it rests upon a propertyless proletariat.

Ernest Bevin
speech to the annual conference of the Transport and General Workers' Union
Aug 18, 1941

The century on which we are entering can be and must be the century of the common man.

Henry Wallace
speech in New York City
May 8, 1942

A government which robs Peter to pay Paul can always depend on the support of Paul.

George Bernard Shaw
Everybody's Political What's What?
1944

Henry Miller
"Good News! God Is
Love!"
*The Air-Conditioned
Nightmare*
1945

We have two American flags always; one for the rich and one for the poor. When the rich fly it it means that things are under control; when the poor fly it it means danger, revolution.

T.S. Eliot
*Notes Towards the Defini-
tion of Culture*
1948

Numerous cross-divisions favour peace within a nation, by dispersing and confusing animosities; they favour peace between nations, by giving every man enough antagonism at home to exercise all his aggressiveness. . . . A nation which has gradations of class seems to me, other things being equal, likely to be more tolerant and pacific than one which is not so organised.

Jean-Paul Sartre
*The Devil and the Good
Lord*
1951

When the rich wage war it's the poor who die.

Nancy Mitford
Noblesse Oblige
1956

An aristocracy in a republic is like a chicken whose head has been cut off: it may run about in a lively way, but in fact it is dead.

Jawaharlal Nehru
The New York Times
Sep 7, 1958

The forces of a capitalist society, if left unchecked, tend to make the rich richer and the poor poorer.

John F. Kennedy
inaugural address
Jan 20, 1961

If a free society cannot help the many who are poor, it cannot save the few who are rich.

Michael Harrington
The Other America
1962

For the urban poor the police are those who arrest you. In almost any slum there is a vast conspiracy against the forces of law and order.

Michael Harrington
The Other America
1962

People who are much too sensitive to demand of cripples that they run races ask of the poor that they get up and act just like everyone else in the society.

John Kenneth
Galbraith
Made to Last
1964

Clearly the most unfortunate people are those who must do the same thing over and over again, every minute, or perhaps twenty to the minute. They deserve the shortest hours and the highest pay.

Adam Clayton Powell
Jr.
"Black Power: A Form of
Godly Power"
Keep the Faith, Baby!
1967

A man's respect for law and order exists in precise relationship to the size of his paycheck.

Calvin Trillin
"U.S. Journal: Resurrec-
tion City"
The New Yorker
Jun 15, 1968

The poor in Resurrection City have come to Washington to show that the poor in America are sick, dirty, disorganized, and powerless—and they are criticized daily for being sick, dirty, disorganized, and powerless.

David Frost
and Anthony Jay
The English
1968

The whole paraphernalia of the criminal law and the criminal courts is based on the need of the upper class to keep the lower class in its place.

Forgive us for pretending to care for the poor, when we do not like poor people and do not want them in our homes.

Church United Presbyterian
Litany for Holy Communion
1968

There is no need to feel pessimistic about this country. It is only the upper echelons who are licked.

Anthony Wedgwood Benn
Arguments for Socialism
1979

Anyone today who speaks of class in the context of politics runs the risk of excommunication and outlawry.

Anthony Wedgwood Benn
Marx Memorial Lecture in London
1982

Communism

What is a communist? One who hath yearnings/ For equal division of unequal earnings.

Ebenezer Elliott
"Epigram"
Poetical Works
1840

From each according to his abilities, to each according to his needs.

Louis Blanc
The Organization of Work
1840

Communism is inequality, but not as property is. Property is exploitation of the weak by the strong. Communism is exploitation of the strong by the weak.

Pierre Joseph Proudhon
Qu'est-ce la propriété?
1840

The earth is the first condition of our existence. To make it an object of trade was the last step towards making human beings an object of trade. To buy and sell land is an immorality surpassed only by the immorality of selling oneself into slavery.

Friedrich Engels
Outlines of a Critique of Political Economy
1844

It (Communism) is the solution of the riddle of history and knows itself to be the solution.

Karl Marx
"Private Property and Communism"
Economic and Philosophical Manuscripts
1844

In this sense, the theory of the communists may be summed up in the single sentence: Abolition of private property.

Karl Marx
The Communist Manifesto
1848

The communists disdain to conceal their views and aims. They openly declare that their ends can be obtained only be forcible overthrow of all existing social conditions.

Karl Marx
The Communist Manifesto
1848

A spectre is haunting Europe—the spectre of Communism. All the powers of old Europe have united in a holy alliance to exorcise this spectre.

Karl Marx
introduction
The Communist Manifesto
1848

Karl Marx
The Communist Manifesto
1848

Let the ruling classes tremble at a communist revolution. The proletarians have nothing to lose but their chains. They have a world to win. Working men of all countries, unite!

Alexander Ivanovich Herzen
The Development of Revolutionary Ideas in Russia
1851

Communism is a Russian autocracy turned upside down.

Karl Marx
letter to J. Wedemeyer
1852

What I did that was new was to demonstrate: (1) that the existence of classes is merely linked to particular phases in the development of production; (2) that class struggle necessarily leads to the dictatorship of the proletariat; (3) that this dictatorship itself constitutes the transition to the abolition of all classes and to a classless society.

Karl Marx
speech to English Chartists
1856

History is the judge;—its executioner, the proletarian.

Friedrich Engels
Socialism, Utopian and Scientific
1892

The first act by virtue of which the State really constitutes itself the representative of the whole of society—the taking possession of the means of production in the name of society—that is, at the same time, its last independent act as a State. State interference in social relations becomes, in one domain after another, superfluous, and then dies out of itself; the government of persons is replaced by the administration of things, and by the conduct of processes of production. The State is not "abolished." It dies out.

Friedrich Engels
Socialism, Utopian and Scientific
1892

These two great discoveries, the materialistic conception of history and the revelation of the secret of capitalistic produciton through surplus-value, we owe to Marx. With these discoveries socialism becomes a science.

Vladimir Ilyich Lenin
Imperialsm, The Highest Stage of Capitalism
1917

By its economic essence imperialism is monopolist capitalism. The fact alone determines the place of imperialism in history.

Maxim Gorky
New Life
Jan, 1918

The working class is for a Lenin what ore is for a metal worker.

Lincoln Steffens
reported conversation with Bernard Baruch following visit to the Soviet Union
1919

I have been over into the future, and it works.

George Bernard Shaw
interview
The Liberator
1919

A Bolshevik as far as I can tell is nothing but a socialist who wants to do something about it. To the best of my knowledge I am a Bolshevik myself.

Socialism is Soviet power plus the electrification of the whole country.

Vladimir Ilyich Lenin
Report to the Congress of Soviets
Dec 22, 1920

Marx's Capital is in essence a collection of atrocity stories designed to stimulate martial ardour against the enemy. Very naturally, it also stimulates the martial ardour of the enemy. It thus brings about the class-war which it prophesies.

Bertrand Russell
presidential address to the Students Union, London School of Economics
Oct 10, 1923

Print is the sharpest and the strongest weapon of our party.

Joseph Stalin
speech
Apr 19, 1923

The party in the last instance is always right, because it is the single historic instrument which the working class possesses for the solution of its fundamental problems. . . . I know that one must not be right against the party. One can be right only with the party, and through the party, because history has created no other road for the realization of what is right.

Leon Trotsky
speech to the congress of the Communist Party of the Soviet Union
May, 1924

The dictatorship of the Communist Party is maintained by recourse to every form of violence.

Leon Trotsky
Terrorism and Communism
1924

Marxian Socialism must always remain a portent to the historians of opinion—how a doctrine so illogical and so dull can have exercised so powerful and enduring an influence over the minds of men, and, through them, the events of history.

John Maynard Keynes
The End of Laissez-Faire
1925

It is impossible to build a socialist paradise as an oasis amid the inferno of world capitalism.

Leon Trotsky
Critique of the Programme of the Third International
1928

Whereas in Britain we are slaves to the past, in Russia they are slaves to the future.

Aneurin Bevan
remark on returning from the Soviet Union
1930

Leninism is a combination of two things which Europeans have kept for some centuries in different compartments of their soul—religion and business.

John Maynard Keynes
"A Short View of Russia"
Essays in Persuasion
1933

The more Communism, the more civilization.

George Bernard Shaw
The Intelligent Woman's Guide to Socialism, Capitalism, Sovietism and Fascism
1937

Every Communist must grasp the truth, "Political power grows out of the barrel of a gun."

Mao Tse-tung
"Problems of War and Strategy"
Nov 6, 1938

Mao Tse-tung
"Problems of War and
Strategy"
Nov 6, 1938

Our principle is that the Party commands the gun, and the gun must never be allowed to command the Party.

**Friedrich August von
Hayek**
*Freedom and the Econom-
ic System*
1940

The idea that a completely planned or directed economic system could and would be used to bring about distributive justice presupposes, in fact, the existence of something which does not exist and has never existed, a complete moral code in which the relative values of all human ends, the relative importance of all the needs of all the different people, are assigned a definite place and a definite quantitative significance.

Joseph Schumpeter
*Capitalism, Socialism and
Democracy*
1942

He who places his trust in the Marxian synthesis as a whole, in order to understand present situations and problems, is apt to be woefully wrong.

Joseph Schumpeter
*Capitalism, Socialism and
Democracy*
1942

There is little reason to believe that this socialism will mean the advent of the civilization of which orthodox socialists dream. It is much more likely to present fascist features. That would be a strange answer to Marx's prayer. But history sometimes indulges in jokes of questionable taste.

Joseph Schumpeter
*Capitalism, Socialism,
and Democracy*
1942

Marxism is essentially a product of the bourgeois mind.

Mao Tse-tung
"On the Chungking
Negotiations"
Oct 17, 1945

We Communists are like seeds and the people are like the soil. Wherever we go, we must unite with the people, take root and blossom among them.

**Sir Winston S.
Churchill**
telegram to President
Truman
May 12, 1945

What is to happen about Russia? . . . An iron curtain is drawn down upon their front. We do not know what is going on behind.

**Sir Winston S.
Churchill**
speech in Fulton,
Missouri
Mar 6, 1946

From Stettin in the Baltic to Trieste in the Adriatic an iron curtain has descended across the Continent.

Will Rogers
*The Autobiography of Will
Rogers*
1949

Communism is like Prohibition, it's a good idea, but it won't work.

Mao Tse-tung
Time
Dec 18, 1950

Communism is not love. Communism is a hammer which we use to crush the enemy.

Adlai E. Stevenson Jr.
speech in Urbana, Illinois
1951

Communism is the corruption of a dream of justice.

We must have faith in the masses and we must have faith in the Party. These are two cardinal principles. If we doubt these principles, we shall accomplish nothing.

Mao Tse-tung
On the Question of Agricultural Co-operation
Jul 31, 1955

The objection to a Communist always resolves itself into the fact that he is not a gentleman.

H.L. Mencken
Minority Report
1956

Whether you like it or not, history is on our side. We will bury you.

Nikita S. Khrushchev
reported remark at the Polish embassy in Moscow
Nov 18, 1956

A Communist has no right to be a mere onlooker.

Nikita S. Khrushchev
report to the Central Committee of the Communist party
Feb 14, 1956

Comrades! The cult of the individual acquired such monstrous size chiefly because Stalin himself, using all conceivable methods, supported the glorification of his own person.

Nikita S. Khrushchev
speech to a secret session of the 20th Congress of Communist party
Feb 23, 1956

Comrades! We must abolish the cult of the individual decisively, once and for all.

Nikita S. Khrushchev
speech to a secret session of the 20th Congress of the Communist party
Feb 23, 1956

Power is an end in itself and the essence of contemporary Communism.

Milovan Djilas
The New Class
1957

Letting a hundred flowers blossom and a hundred schools of thought contend is the policy for promoting the progress of the arts and the sciences and a flourishing socialist culture in our land.

Mao Tse-tung
speech at Beijing "On the Correct Handling of Contradictions Among the People"
Feb 27, 1957

The only vital political difference between Marx and Lenin is that Lenin had a revolution to practice on and Marx had not.

Max Eastman
letter
1958

Marxism is too uncertain of its grounds to be a science. I do not know a movement more self-centered and further removed from the facts than Marxism.

Boris Pasternak
Doctor Zhivago
1958

A strange, a perverted creed that has a queer attraction both for the most primitive and for the most sophisticated societies.

Harold Macmillan
remarks on Communism
New York Herald Tribune
Oct 15, 1961

I am a good friend to Communists abroad but I do not like them at home.

Souvanna Phouma
on his country's attempt to remain neutral
Life
Nov 3, 1961

Murray Kempton
"What Harvey Did"
America Comes of Middle Age
1963

As an organized political group, the Communists have done nothing to damage our society a fraction as much as what their enemies have done in the name of defending us against subversion.

Nikita S. Khrushchev
speaking of capitalists in a speech in Split, Yugoslavia
Aug 24, 1963

I once said, "We will bury you," and I got into trouble with it. Of course we will not bury you with a shovel. Your own working class will bury you.

Robert F. Kennedy
"Berlin East and West"
The Pursuit of Justice
1964

Far from being a classless society, Communism is governed by an elite as steadfast in its determination to maintain its prerogatives as any oligarchy known to history.

Graham Greene
The Comedians
1966

Communists have committed great crimes, but at least they have not stood aside, like an established society, and been indifferent. I would rather have blood on my hands than water like Pilate.

Charles E. Bohlen
The New York Times
Jan 2, 1966

In dealing with the Communists, remember that in their mind what is secret is serious, and what is public is merely propaganda.

Mao Tse-tung
quoted, "The Thoughts of Mao Tse-tung"
London Times
Oct 31, 1966

There may be thousands of principles of Marxism, but in the final analysis they can be summed up in one sentence. Rebellion is justified.

Edwin O. Reischauer
hearing before U.S. Senate Committee on Foreign Relations
Jan 31, 1967

They (communists) are not supermen at all. They are men with feet of clay which extend almost all the way up to their brains.

Régis Debray
Revolution in the Revolution?
1967

Guerilla warfare is to peasant uprisings what Marx is to Sorel.

Leonid Brezhnev
speech to the Congress of the Polish Communist Party
Nov 12, 1968

When internal and external forces which are hostile to Socialism try to turn the development of any Socialist country towards the restoration of a capitalist regime . . . it becomes not only a problem of the people concerned, but a common problem and concern of all Socialist countries.

Alexander Dubcek
frequently used slogan during the "Prague Spring"
1968

Give socialism back its human face.

Jean-François Ravel
Time
Feb 2, 1976

Stalinism is the essence of Communism.

The confrontation between a man—any man— and Communism is always over in two rounds. Communism nearly always wins the first round, like a wild beast that leaps at its adversary and bowls him over. But, if there is a second round, Communism nearly always loses. The man's eyes open and he sees that he admired a bundle of cast-offs, a semblance, an optical illusion. Then he's immunized, and for ever.

Alexander Solzhenitsyn
interview with Georges Suffert
Encounter
Apr, 1976

Communist countries never expel correspondents for telling lies.

Ross H. Munro
The New York Times
Nov 27, 1977

I don't like Communism because it hands out wealth through rationing books.

Omar Torrijos Herrera
The New York Times
Sep 7, 1977

No communist country has solved the problem of succession.

Henry A. Kissinger
Time
Mar 12, 1979

The terrible thing is that one cannot be a Communist and not let oneself in for the shameful act of recantation. One cannot be a Communist and preserve an iota of one's personal integrity.

Milovan Djilas
interview with George Urban
Encounter
Dec, 1979

The dictatorship of the proletetariat is an historically regressive idea for it makes the individual a servant of the state, robs him of his power of decision, and is thus at odds with the aspirations of mankind.

W. Averell Harriman
Encounter
Nov, 1981

It depends on the way you measure the concept of good, bad, better, worse, because, if you choose the example of what we Polish have in our pockets and in our shops, then I answer that Communism has done very little for us. If you choose the example of what is in our souls, instead, I answer that Communism has done very much for us. In fact our souls contain exactly the contrary of what they wanted. They wanted us not to believe in God and our churches are full. They wanted us to be materialistic and incapable of sacrifices: we are anti-materialistic, capable of sacrifice. They wanted us to be afraid of the tanks, of the guns, and instead we don't fear them at all.

Lech Walesa
interview with Oriana Fallaci
The Sunday Times
Mar 22, 1981

It doesn't matter if a cat is black or white, so long as it catches mice.

Deng Xiaoping
quoted on liberalization of Communist Party rules
Time
Jan 6, 1986

Without glasnost there is not, and there cannot be, democratism, the political creativity of the masses and their participation in management.

Mikhail S. Gorbachev
speech to the Communist Party Congress
The New York Times
Nov 9, 1986

Isn't it strange that . . . people build walls to keep an enemy out, and there's only one part of the world and one philosophy where they have to build walls to keep their people in?

Ronald Reagan
on the Berlin Wall
Aug 12, 1986

Conservatism

**2nd Viscount Falkland
(Lucius Cary)**
speech in the House of
Commons
Nov 22, 1641

When it is not necessary to change, it is necessary not to change.

Thomas Jefferson
letter to the Marquis de
Lafayette
Nov 4, 1823

The sickly, weakly, timid man fears the people, and is a Tory by nature.

Benjamin Disraeli
campaign speech at High
Wycombe, England
Nov 27, 1832

I am a Conservative to preserve all that is good in our constitution, a Radical to remove all that is bad. I seek to preserve property and to respect order, and I equally decry the appeal to the passions of the many or the prejudices of the few.

Thomas Arnold
letter to James Marshall
Jan 23, 1840

The principle of Conservatism has always appeared to me to be not only foolish, but to be actually felo de se: it destroys what it loves, because it will not mend it.

**Prince Clemens von
Metternich**
Autobiography
1880-83

This maxim, "to preserve is to act," has always served me as a line of conduct, while those who should have backed me up were confusing the duty of preservation with inactivity.

Ralph Waldo Emerson
lecture on "The Conser-
vative" in Boston,
Massachusetts
Dec 9, 1841

There is always a certain meanness in the argument of conservatism, joined with a certain superiority in its fact.

Benjamin Disraeli
Coningsby
1844

"A sound Conservative government," said Taper, musingly. "I understand: Tory men and Whig measures."

Benjamin Disraeli
Coningsby
1844

Conservatism discards Prescription, shrinks from Principle, disavows Progress; having rejected all respect for Antiquity, it offers no redress for the Present, and makes no preparation for the Future.

Ralph Waldo Emerson
"New England
Reformers"
1844

Men are conservatives when they are least vigorous, or when they are most luxurious. They are conservatives after dinner.

**Benjamin Disraeli
1st Earl of
Beaconsfield**
speech in the House of
Commons
Mar 3, 1845

A conservative government is an organized hypocrisy.

Henry David Thoreau
Journal
Mar 30, 1851

The man for whom law exists—the man of forms, the conservative—is a tame man.

It is not the metier of a Tory to have a policy, any more than it is that of a king to be a democrat. A tory government may do very well without a policy, just as a country gentleman may sit at home and live upon his rents.

Sir William Harcourt
"Pot and Kettle"
Saturday Review
Mar 21, 1857

What is conservatism? Is it not adherence to the old and tried against the new and untried?

Abraham Lincoln
speech at the Cooper Union, New York City
Feb 27, 1860

That man's the true Conservative/ Who lops the moulder'd branch away.

Alfred, Lord Tennyson
"Hands All Round"
1885

When a nation's young men are conservative, its funeral bell is already rung.

Henry Ward Beecher
Proverbs from Plymouth Pulpit
1887

Conservatism, I believe, is mainly due to want of imagination. In saying this, I do not for a moment mean to deny the other and equally obvious truth that Conservatism, in a lump, is a euphemism for selfishness.

Charles Grant Allen
"Imagination and Radicals"
Westminister Gazette
1894

Clearly to realise the condition of the unfortunate is the beginning of philanthropy. Clearly to realise the rights of others is the beginning of justice. "Put yourself in his place" strikes the keynote of ethics. Stupid people can only see their own side to a question: they cannot even imagine any other side possible. So, as a rule, stupid people are Conservative.

Charles Grant Allen
"Imagination and Radicals"
Westminster Gazette
1894

Come, come, my conservative friend, wipe the dew off your spectacles, and see that the world is moving.

Elizabeth Cady Stanton
The Woman's Bible
1895

The radical invents the views. When he has worn them out the conservative adopts them.

Mark Twain
Notebook
1935

The radical of one century is the conservative of the next.

Mark Twain
Notebook
1935

Conservative, n. A statesman who is enamored of existing evils, as distinguished from the Liberal, who wishes to replace them with others.

Ambrose Bierce
The Devil's Dictionary
1906

The healthy stomach is nothing if not conservative. Few radicals have good digestions.

Samuel Butler
Mind and Matter:
Indigestion
Notebooks
1912

Do the day's work. If it be to protect the rights of the weak, whoever objects, do it. If it be to help a powerful corporation better to serve the people, do that. Expect to be called a standpatter, but don't be a standpatter. Expect to be called a demagogue, but don't be a demagogue. Don't hesitate to be as reactionary as the multiplication table. Don't expect to build up the weak by pulling down the strong.

Calvin Coolidge
speech to the Massachusetts State Senate
Jan 7, 1914

Walter Lippmann
"Routineer and Inventor"
A Preface to Politics
1914

Success makes men rigid and they tend to exalt stability over all the other virtues; tired of the effort of willing they become fanatics about convesatism.

Sir Wilfrid Laurier
letter to Sir Allen
Aylesworth
May 15, 1917

Toryism . . . like the serpent sheds its skin, but ever remains the same repitle.

Suzanne LaFollette
"The Beginnings of
Emancipation"
Concerning Women
1926

All political and religious systems have their root and their strength in the innate conservatism of the human mind, and its intense fear of autonomy.

Franklin D. Roosevelt
speech in Syracuse, New
York
Sep 29, 1936

The true conservative is the man who has a real concern for injustices and takes thought against the day of reckoning.

Franklin D. Roosevelt
speech in Syracuse, New
York
Sep 29, 1936

Wise and prudent men—intelligent conservatives—have long known that in a changing world worthy institutions can be conserved only by adjusting them to the changing time.

Robert Frost
"Ten Mills"
A Further Range
1936

I never dared to be radical when young/ For fear it would make me conservative when old.

Franklin D. Roosevelt
radio address
Oct 26, 1939

A conservative is a man with two perfectly good legs who, however, has never learned how to walk forward.

**Sir Winston S.
Churchill**
speech in the House of
Commons
Nov 29, 1944

A love for tradition has never weakened a nation, indeed it has strengthened nations in their hour of peril; but the new view must come, the world must roll forward.

Aneurin Bevan
In Place of Fear
1952

How can wealth persuade poverty to use its political freedom to keep wealth in power? Here lies the whole art of Conservative politics in the twentieth century.

David Frost
BBC-TV
That Was The Year
Dec 31, 1962

Vote Labor and you build castles in the air. Vote Conservative and you can live in them.

Kingsley Amis
Sunday Telegraph
Jul 2, 1967

I am driven to grudging toleration of the Conservative Party because it is the party of non-politics, of resistance to politics.

Daniel P. Moynihan
The New York Post
May 14, 1969

Somehow liberals have been unable to acquire from life what conservatives seem to be endowed with at birth: namely, a healthy skepticism of the powers of government agencies to do good.

George F. Will
Newsweek
Sep 30, 1974

They (conservatives) define themselves in terms of what they oppose.

A conservative is a liberal who was mugged the night before.

Frank L. Rizzo
American Opinion
Nov, 1975

I've got money so I'm a Conservative.

Roy Herbert Thomson
Lord Thomson of Fleet
recalled on his death
Aug 4, 1976

Inflation is a great conservatizing issue.

George F. Will
Newsweek
Nov 7, 1977

Conservatives do not worship democracy. For them majority rule is a device. . . . And if it is leading to an end that is undesirable or is inconsistent with itself, then there is a theoretical case for ending it.

Sir Ian Gilmour
Inside Right
1977

A sharp Right turn . . . is likely to be followed by an even sharper Left turn. Hence Conservative moderation brings its own reward. The best way of safeguarding the future is by not trying to return to the past.

Sir Ian Gilmour
Inside Right
1977

Constitution

An act against the Constitution is void; an act against natural equity is void.

James Otis
Argument Against the Writs of Assistance
1761

Our chief danger arises from the democratic parts of our constitutions.

Edmund Jennings Randolph
attributed remark in debate at Constitutional Convention
May 29, 1787

Constitutions are the work of time, one cannot leave too large a space for improvements.
Les constitutions sont l'ouvrage du temps, on ne saurait laisser une trop large voie aux améliorations.

Napoleon I
remarks in the Council of State
Dec 1, 1803

Constitutions should be short and vague.
Il faut qu'une constitution soit courte et obscure.

Napoleon I
conference with the Swiss deputies
Jan 29, 1803

In questions of power . . . let no more be heard of confidence in men, but bind him down from mischief by the chains of the Constitution.

Thomas Jefferson
"Resolutions"
1803

Some men look at constitutions with sanctimonious reverence, and deem them like the ark of the covenant, too sacred to be touched.

Thomas Jefferson
letter to Samuel Kercheval
Jul 12, 1816

John Marshall quoted *New York Times* *Magazine* Oct 9, 1977	The peculiar circumstances of the moment may render a measure more or less wise, but cannot render it more or less constitutional.
William H. Seward speech in the U.S. Senate Mar 11, 1850	There is a higher law than the Constitution.
Henry Clay speech in the U.S. Senate Jan 29, 1850	The Constitution of the United States was made not merely for the generation that then existed, but for posterity—unlimited, undefined, endless, perpetual posterity.
Abraham Lincoln speech in Kalamazoo, Michigan Aug 27, 1856	Don't interfere with anything in the Constitution. That must be maintained, for it is the only safeguard of our liberties.
Lord Macaulay letter to Henry Randall May 23, 1857	Your Constitution is all sail and no anchor.
Andrew Johnson speech in Washington, D.C. Feb 22, 1866	Amendments to the Constitution ought to not be too frequently made; . . . (if) continually tinkered with it would lose all its prestige and dignity, and the old instrument would be lost sight of altogether in a short time.
James Bryce **Viscount Bryce** *The American* *Commonwealth* 1888	We have seen that the American Constitution has changed, is changing, and by the laws of its existence must continue to change, in its substance and practical working even when its words remain the same.
Calvin Coolidge acceptance speech as Re- publican nominee for president Aug 4, 1924	The Constitution is the sole source and guaranty of national freedom.
Zechariah Chaffee Jr. *The Nation* Jul 28, 1952	What is constitutional may still be unwise.
Potter Stewart majority opinion *Elkins v. United States* Jun 27, 1960	It must always be remembered that what the Constitution forbids is not all searches and seizures, but unreasonable searches and seizures.
Arthur J. Goldberg unanimous opinion May 27, 1963	The basic guarantees of our Constitution are warrants for the here and now, and unless there is an overwhelmingly compelling reason, they are to be promptly fulfilled.
John Marshall Harlan dissenting opinion *Reynolds, Judge et al.* v. *Sims et al.* 1964	The Constitution is not a panacea for every blot upon the public welfare, nor should this court, ordained as a judicial body, be thought of as a general haven for reform movements.
F. Lee Bailey *Newsweek* Apr 17, 1967	Can any of you seriously say the Bill of Rights could get through Congress today? It wouldn't even get out of committee.

Most faults are not in our Constitution, but in ourselves.

Ramsey Clark
Washington Post
Nov 12, 1970

It is indeed an odd business that it has taken this Court nearly two centuries to "discover" a constitutional mandate to have counsel at a preliminary hearing.

Warren E. Burger
dissenting opinion
Coleman v. *Alabama*
Jun 22, 1970

Our Constitution was not written in the sands to be washed away by each wave of new judges blown in by each successive political wind.

Hugo L. Black
dissenting opinion
Jan 20, 1970

Recalling that it is a Constitution intended to endure for ages to come we also remember that the Founders wisely provided the means for that endurance: Changes in the Constitution, when thought necessary, are to be proposed by Congress or conventions and ratified by the states. The Founders gave no such amending power to this Court.

Hugo L. Black
dissenting opinion
Jan 20, 1970

The layman's constitutional view is that what he likes is constitutional and that which he doesn't like is unconstitutional.

Hugo L. Black
The New York Times
Feb 26, 1971

Controversy over the meaning of our nation's most majestic guarantees frequently has been turbulent. . . . Abortion raises moral and spiritual questions over which honorable persons can disagree sincerely and profoundly. But those disagreements did not then and do not now relieve us of our duty to apply the Constitution faithfully.

Harry A. Blackmun
majority opinion
Roe v. *Wade; Doe* v. *Bolton*
Jan 22, 1973

My faith in the constitution is whole.

Barbara Jordan
statement at the House Judiciary Committee on impeachment of Richard Nixon
Jul 25, 1974

Our constitution works. Our great republic is a government of laws, not of men.

Gerald R. Ford
on succeeding Richard Nixon as president
Aug 9, 1974

"We, the people." It is a very eloquent beginning. But when that document was completed on the seventeenth of September in 1787 I was not included in that "We, the people." I felt somehow for many years that George Washington and Alexander Hamilton, just left me out by mistake. But through the process of amendment, interpretation and court decision I have finally been included in "We, the people."

Barbara Jordan
statement at the House Judiciary Committee on impeachment of Richard Nixon
Jul 25, 1974

The Constitution is not neutral. It was designed to take the government off the backs of people.

William O. Douglas
The Court Years 1939-75
1980

The Constitution requires that Congress treat similarly situated persons similarly, not that it engage in gestures of superficial equality.

William H. Rehnquist
majority opinion
Rostker v. *Goldberg*
Jun 25, 1981

William J. Brennan Jr. speech at Georgetown University *The New York Times* Oct 13, 1985	We look to the history of the time of framing and to intervening history of interpretation. But the ultimate question must be, what do the words of the text mean in our time.
William J. Brennan Jr. speech at Georgetown University *The New York Times* Oct 13, 1985	We current justices read the Constitution in the only way that we can: as 20th-century Americans.
Robert H. Bork *The New York Times* Jan 4, 1985	(Constitutional law): a ship with a great deal of sail but a very shallow keel.
Lewis F. Powell Jr. dissenting opinion Feb 19, 1985	The states' role in our system of government is a matter of constitutional law, not of legislative grace.
Antonin Scalia majority opinion *Arizona* v. *Hicks* Mar 3, 1987	There is nothing new in the realization that the Constitution sometimes insulates the criminality of a few in order to protect the privacy of us all.

Democracy

Plato *The Republic* ca. 390 B.C.	Democracy . . . is a charming form of government, full of variety and disorder, and dispensing a sort of equality to equals and unequals alike.
Aristotle *Politics* 343 B.C.	If liberty and equality, as is thought by some, are chiefly to be found in democracy, they will be best attained when all persons alike share the in the government to the utmost.
Aristotle *Politics* 343 B.C.	Democracy is the form of government in which the free are rulers.
Aristotle *Politics* 343 B.C.	The basis of a democratic state is liberty.
Aristotle *The Politics* 343 B.C.	A democracy exists whenever those who are free and are not well-off, being in the majority, are in sovereign control of government, an oligarchy when control lies with the rich and better-born, these being few.
Alcuin letter to Charlemagne *Works* 800	Nor should we listen to those who say, "The voice of the people is the voice of God" (vox populi, vox dei), for the turbulence of the mob is always close to insanity.
Edward I statement to the Model Parliament 1295	What touches all shall be approved by all. *Quod omnes tangit ab omnibus approbetur.*

Some to the common pulpits, and cry out,/ "Liberty, freedom, and enfranchisement."

William Shakespeare
Julius Caesar
1599

What is the city but the people?

William Shakespeare
Coriolanus
1607-08

The power of Kings and Magistrates is nothing else, but what is only derivative, transferr'd and committed to them in trust from the People, to the Common good of them all, in whom the power yet remianes fundamentally, and cannot be tak'n from them, without a violation of their natural birthright.

John Milton
The Tenure of Kings and Magistrates
1649

The majority is the best way, because it is visible, and has strength to make itself obeyed. Yet it is the opinion of the least able.
La pluralité est la meilleure voie, parce qu'elle est visible et qu'elle a la force pour se faire obéir. Cependant c'est l'avis des moins habiles.

Blaise Pascal
Pensées
1670

The most may err as grossly as the few.

John Dryden
Absalom and Achitophel
1681

Any government is free to the people under it where the laws rule and the people are a party to the laws.

William Penn
The Frame of Government of Pennsylvania
1682

Every Man, by consenting with others to make one Body Politick under one Government, puts himself under an obligation to every one of that Society, to submit to the determination of the majority, and to be concluded by it; or else this original Compact, whereby he and other incorporates into one Society, would signifie nothing.

John Locke
The Second Treatise on Government
1690

Men being . . . by Nature, all free, equal and independent, no one can be put out of this Estate, and subjected to the Political Power of another, without his own Consent.

John Locke
The Second Treatise on Government
1690

The Liberty of Man, in Society, is to be under no other Legislative Power, but that established, by consent, in the Commonwealth, nor under the Dominion of any will, or Restraint of any Law, but what the Legislative shall enact, according to the Trust put in it.

John Locke
The Second Treatise on Government
1690

Our supreme governors, the mob.

Horace Walpole
4th Earl of Orford
letter to Horace Mann
Sep 7, 1743

Were there a people of gods, their government would be democratic. So perfect a government is not for men.
S'il y avait un peuple de dieux, il se gouvernerait démocratiquement. Un gouvernement si parfait ne convient pas à des hommes.

Jean Jacques Rousseau
The Social Contract
1762

In the strict sense of the term, a true democracy has never existed and never will exist.
A prendre le terme dans la rigueur de l'acception, il n'a jamais existé de véritable démocratie, et il n'en existera jamais.

Jean Jacques Rousseau
The Social Contract
1762

Joseph Priestly
The First Principles of Government
1771

Governments will never be awed by the voice of the people, so long as it is a mere voice, without overt acts.

John Adams
handwritten notes for a speech in Braintree, Massachusetts
1772

There is danger from all men. The only maxim of a free government ought to be to trust no man living with power to endanger the public liberty.

John Adams
proclamation to the Massachusetts Bay Council
1774

As the happiness of the people is the sole end of government, so the consent of the people is the only foundation of it.

George Washington
letter to Lt. General Thomas Gage
Aug 20, 1775

I cannot conceive a rank more honorable, than that which flows from the uncorrupted choice of a brave and free people, the purest source and original fountain of all power.

George Mason
Virginia Bill of Rights
Jun 12, 1776

That all men are by nature equally free and independent, and have certain inherent rights, of which, when they enter into a state of society, they cannot by any compact deprive or divest their posterity; namely, the enjoyment of life and liberty, with the means of acquiring and possessing property, and pursuing and obtaining happiness and safety.

Thomas Jefferson
Declaration Of Independence
Jul 4, 1776

When, in the course of human events, it becomes necessary for one people to dissolve political bands which have connected them with another, and to assume among the powers of the earth the separate and equal station to which the Laws of Nature and of Nature's God entitle them, a decent respect to the opinions of mankind requires that they should declare the causes which impel them to the separation.

Thomas Jefferson
Declaration of Independence
Jul 4, 1776

Governments . . . deriv(e) their just powers from the consent of the governed.

Jeremy Bentham
"A Fragment on Government"
1776

It is the greatest happiness of the greatest number that is the measure of right and wrong.

Edmund Burke
Letter to the Sheriffs of Bristol
Apr 3, 1777

If any ask me what a free government is, I answer, that, for any practical purpose, it is what the people think so,—and that they, and not I, are the natural, lawful, and competent judges of this matter.

John Adams
letter to Abigail Adams
June 2, 1777

I am persuaded there is among the mass of our people a fund of wisdom, integrity, and humanity which will preserve their happiness in a tolerable measure.

Samuel Johnson
The Lives of the Most Eminent English Poets: Addison
1779-81

About things on which the public thinks long it commonly attains to think right.

Every government degenerates when trusted to the rulers of the people alone. The people themselves therefore are its only safe depositories.

Thomas Jefferson
Notes on the State of Virginia
1782

The good sense of the people is the strongest army our government can ever have . . . it will not fail them.

Thomas Jefferson
letter to William Carmichael
Dec 26, 1786

We are now forming a republican government. Real liberty is neither found in despotism or the extremes of democracy, but in moderate governments.

Alexander Hamilton
debate at the Constitutional Convention
Jun 26, 1787

Mobs will never do to govern states or command armies.

John Adams
letter to Benjamin Hichborn
Jan 27, 1787

Nothing but a permanent body can check the imprudence of democracy.

Alexander Hamilton
speech to the Constitutional Convention
Jun 18, 1787

We may define a republic . . . as a government which derives all its powers directly or indirectly from the great body of the people, and is administered by persons holding their offices during pleasure, for a limited period, or during good behavior. It is essential to such a government that it be derived from the great body of the society, not from an inconsiderable proportion, or a favored class of it.

James Madison
The Federalist
Jan 16, 1788

The essence of a free government consists in an effectual control of rivalries.

John Adams
Discourses on Davila
1789

What is the Third Estate? Everything. What has it hitherto been in the political order? Nothing. What does it ask? To be something.
Qu'est-ce que le Tiers Etat? Tout. Qu'a-t-il été jusqu'à présent dans l'ordre politique? Rien. Que demande-t-il? A devenir quelque chose.

Abbé (Emmanuel) Siéyès
Qu'est-ce que le Tiers Etat?
1789

The republican is the only form of government which is not eternally at open or secret war with the rights of mankind.

Thomas Jefferson
letter to William Hunter
Mar 11, 1790

If government be founded in the consent of the people, it can have no power over any individual by whom that consent is refused.

William Godwin
An Enquiry Concerning Political Justice
1793

The basis of our political system is the right of the people to make and to alter their constitutions of government.

George Washington
Farewell Address to the People of the United States
Sep 17, 1796

The very idea of the power and the right of the people to establish Government, presupposes the duty of every individual to obey the established Government.

George Washington
Farewell Address to the People of the United States
Sep 19, 1796

William Hazlitt
Free Thoughts in Public Affairs, or Advice to a Patriot
1806

No kingdom can be secure in its independence against a greater power that is not free in its spirit, as well as in its institutions.

Thomas Jefferson
letter to Gov. H. D. Tiffin
Feb 2, 1807

That government is the strongest of which every man feels himself a part.

John Adams
letter to John Tyler
1814

There is but one element of government, and that is the people. From this element spring all governments. "For a nation to be free, it is only necessary that she will it." For a nation to be a slave, it is only necessary that she will it.

Napoleon I
message to the Cour de Cassation
Mar 26, 1815

Sovereignty resides in the French People in the sense that everything, everything without exception, must be done in their interest, for their happiness, and for their glory.
La souveraineté réside dans le Peuple français, en ce sens que tout, tout sans exception, doit être fait pour son intérêt, pour son bonheur et pour sa gloire.

Claude Henri, Comte de Saint-Simon
Industry
1817

A state may prosper under any form of government, provided it is well administered. . . . If political freedom is more advantageous for the development of wealth, it is indirectly because it is more favorable to learning.

Thomas Jefferson
letter to John Adams
Dec 10, 1819

No government can continue good but under the control of the people.

John Marshall
Cohens v. Virginia
1821

The people made the Constitution, and the people can unmake it. It is the creature of their own will, and lives only by their will.

James Mill
Essay on Government
1821

The benefits of the Representative system are lost, in all cases in which the interests of the choosing body are not the same with those of the community.

Benjamin Disraeli
Vivian Grey
1826

I repeat . . . that all power is a trust; that we are accountable for its exercise; that, from the people, and for the people, all springs, and all must exist.

Ebenezer Elliott
Corn Law Rhymes
1828

Not kings and lords, but nations!/ Not thrones and crowns, but men!

Henry Clay
speech in Lexington, Kentucky
May 16, 1829

Government is a trust, and the officers of the government are trustees; and both the trust and the trustees are created for the benefit of the people.

Andrew Jackson
first annual message to Congress
Dec 8, 1829

I now commend you, fellow-citizens, to the guidance of Almighty God, with a full reliance on His merciful providence for the maintenance of our free institutions, and with an earnest supplication that whatever errors it may be my lot to commit in discharging the arduous duties which have devolved on me will find a remedy in the harmony and wisdom of your counsels.

The people's government, made for the people, made by the people, and answerable to the people.

Daniel Webster
second speech on Foote's
Resolution
Jan 26, 1830

Despotism accomplishes great things illegally; liberty doesn't even go to the trouble of accomplishing small things legally.
Le despotisme fait illégalement de grandes choses, la liberté ne se donne même pas la peine d'en faire légalement de très-petites.

Honoré de Balzac
La Peau de chagrin
1831

Compact is the basis and essence of free government. . . . No right to disregard it belongs to a party till released by causes of which the other parties have an equal right to judge.

James Madison
letter to Nicholas P. Trist
Jan 18, 1833

Where the people possess no authority, their rights obtain no respect.

George Bancroft
"To the Workingmen of
Northampton"
Boston Courier
Oct 22, 1834

The very essence of a free government consists in considering offices as public trusts, bestowed for the good of the country, and not for the benefit of an individual or a party.

John C. Calhoun
speech
Feb 13, 1835

Democratic institutions generally give men a lofty notion of their country and themselves.
Les institutions démocratiques donnent en général aux hommes une vaste idée de leur patrie et d'eux-mêmes.

Alexis, Comte de Tocqueville
Democracy in America
1839

One can change human institutions but not man. However energetically society in general may strive to make all citizens equal and alike, the personal pride of individuals will always seek to rise above the common level, and to form somewhere an inequality to their own advantage.
On peut changer les institutions humaines, mais non l'homme: quel que soit l'effort général d'une société pour rendre les citoyens égaux et semblables, l'orgueil particulier des individus cherchera toujours à échapper au niveau, et voudra former quelque part une inégalité dont il profite.

Alexis, Comte de Tocqueville
Democracy in America
1839

The taste for well-being is the prominent and indelible feature of democratic times.
Le goût du bien-être forme comme le trait saillant et indélébile des âges démocratiques.

Alexis, Comte de Tocqueville
Democracy in America
1839

Men living in democratic times have many passions, but most of their passions either end in the love of riches, or proceed from it.
Les hommes qui vivent dans les temps démocratiques ont beaucoup de passions; mais la plupart de leurs passions aboutissent à l'amour de la richesse ou en sortent.

Alexis, Comte de Tocqueville
Democracy in America
1839

The only legitimate right to govern is an express grant of power from the governed.

William Henry Harrison
inaugural address
Mar 4, 1841

Truth no more relies for success on ballot boxes than it does on cartridge boxes. . . . Political action is not moral action, anymore than a box on the ear is an argument.

William Lloyd Garrison
The Liberator
Mar 13, 1846

Ralph Waldo Emerson *Journals* 1846	Democracy becomes a government of bullies tempered by editors.
John Stuart Mill *Principles of Political Economy* 1848	A democratic constitution, not supported by democratic institutions in detail, but confined to the central government, not only is not political freedom, but often creates a spirit precisely the reverse, carrying down to the lowest grade in society the desire and ambition of political domination.
Theodore Parker speech in Boston, Massachusetts May 29, 1850	The American idea . . . is a democracy, that is a government of all the people, by all the people, and for all the people.
Theodore Parker quoted by Daniel Aaron *Men of Good Hope* 1951	Democracy is not possible except in a nation where there is so much property, and that so widely distributed, that the whole people can have considerable education—intellectual, moral, affectional, and religious. So much property, widely distributed, judiciously applied, is the indispensable material basis of a democracy.
Franklin Pierce inaugural address Mar 4, 1853	The dangers of a concentration of all power in the general government of a confederacy so vast as ours are too obvious to be disregarded.
Abraham Lincoln speech in Peoria, Illinois Oct 16, 1854	No man is good enough to govern another man without that other's consent.
William Ewart Gladstone speech in the House of Commons 1858	Decision by majorities is as much an expedient as lighting by gas.
Abraham Lincoln written fragment ca. Aug 1, 1858	As I would not be a slave, so I would not be a master. This expresses my idea of democracy. Whatever differs from this, to the extent of the difference, is no democracy.
3rd Marquess of Salisbury "The Theories of Parliamentary Reform" *Oxford Essays* 1858	The best form of Government (setting aside the question of morality) is one where the masses have little power, and seem to have a great deal.
Abraham Lincoln notes for speeches in Ohio Sep 16, 1859	The people—the people are the rightful masters of both congresses and courts—not to overthrow the Constitution, but to overthrow the men who pervert it.
Ralph Waldo Emerson "Power" *Conduct of Life* 1860	The evils of popular government appear greater than they are; there is compensation for them in the spirit and energy it awakens.
Ralph Waldo Emerson "Power" *The Conduct of Life* 1860	The instinct of the people is right.

This country, with its institutions, belongs to the people who inhabit it. Whenever they shall grow weary of the existing government, they can exercise their constitutional right of amending it, or their revolutionary right to dismember or overthrow it.

Abraham Lincoln
first inaugural address
Mar 4, 1861

Why should there not be a patient confidence in the ultimate justice of the people? Is there any better or equal hope in the world?

Abraham Lincoln
first inaugural address
Mar 4, 1861

While the people retain their virtue and vigilance, no administration, by any extreme of wickedness or folly, can very seriously injure the government in the short space of four years.

Abraham Lincoln
first inaugural address
Mar 4, 1861

Vox populi, vox humbug.

William Tecumseh Sherman
letter to his wife
Jun 2, 1863

We here highly resolve . . . that this nation, under God, shall have a new birth of freedom, and that government of the people, by the people, and for the people, shall not perish from the earth.

Abraham Lincoln
from the Gettysburg address
Nov 19, 1863

The principle of our Government is that of equal laws and freedom of industry.

Andrew Johnson
first annual message to Congress
Dec 4, 1865

Our government springs from and was made for the people—not the people for the Government. To them it owes allegiance; from them it must derive its courage, strength, and wisdom.

Andrew Johnson
first annual message to Congress
Dec 4, 1865

It is the multiplication table which furnishes in the last resort the essential test that distinguishes right from wrong in the government of a nation. If one man imprisons you, that is tyranny; if two men, or a number of men imprison you, that is freedom.

3rd Marquess of Salisbury
"Parliamentary Reform"
Quarterly Review
Jul, 1865

All the world over, I will back the masses against the classes.

William Ewart Gladstone
speech in Liverpool, England
Jan 21, 1866

The mass of the English people are politically contented as well as politically deferential.

Walter Bagehot
The English Constitution
1867

I shall on all subjects have a policy to recommend, but none to enforce against the will of the people.

Ulysses S. Grant
first inaugural address
Mar 4, 1869

Political democracy, as it exists and practically works in America, with all its threatening evils, supplies a training school for making first-class men. It is life's gymnasium, not of good only, but of all.

Walt Whitman
"Democratic Vistas"
1871

I have always been of the mind that in a democracy manners are the only effective weapons against the bowie-knife.

James Russell Lowell
letter to Miss Norton
Mar 4, 1873

Sir James Fitzjames Stephen *Liberty, Equality, Fraternity* 1873	In a pure democracy the ruling men will be the wirepullers and their friends.
Matthew Arnold "Democracy" *Mixed Essays* 1879	Nations are not truly great solely because the individuals composing them are numerous, free, and active; but they are great when these numbers, this freedom, this activity are employed in the service of an ideal higher than that of an ordinary man, taken by himself.
James A. Garfield letter Apr 21, 1880	All free governments are managed by the combined wisdom and folly of the people.
Prince Otto von Bismarck speech to the Reichstag May 8, 1880	To fight against the government with any means is a basic right and sport of every German. *Gegen die Regierung mit allen Mitteln zu kämpfen, ist ja ein Grundrecht und Sport eines jeden Deutschen.*
Joseph Chamberlain on opposition to extending British suffrage to agricultural workers Oct 18, 1882	Macaulay's illustration of the man who would not go into the water until he had learned to swim is the type of all the objections raised to the extension of self-government amongst the people.
Henry George *Social Problems* 1883	We cannot safely leave politics to politicians, or political economy to college professors. The people themselves must think, because the people alone can act.
Rutherford B. Hayes letter Nov 25, 1885	Politics and law are (or rather, should be)—merely results, merely the expression of what the people wish.
Henry Ward Beecher *Proverbs from Plymouth Pulpit* 1887	The real democratic American ideal is, not that every man shall be on a level with every other man, but that every man shall have liberty to be what god made him, without hindrance.
Henry Ward Beecher *Proverbs from Plymouth Pulpit* 1887	It is for men to choose whether they will govern themselves or be governed.
Friedrich Nietzsche *The Will to Power* 1888	Democracy represents the disbelief in all great men and in all elite societies: everybody is everybody's equal. *Die Demokratie repräsentirt den Unglauben an grosse Menschen und an Elite-Gesellschaft: Jeder ist jedem gleich.*
Benjamin Harrison speech in Detroit, Michigan Feb 22, 1888	The bottom principle . . . of our structure of government—is the principle of control by the majority. Everything else about our government is appendage, it is ornamentation.
William McKinley speech to the House of Representatives May 18, 1888	The majority voice should be controlling, but it must be after a full, fair, and candid expression.

If this nation is not truly democratic, then she must die.

Alexander Crummell
speech to the Protestant
Episcopal Church
Congress, Buffalo, New
York
Nov 20, 1888

Democratic institutions are never done—they are, like the living tissue, always a-making. It is a strenuous thing this of living the life of a free people: and we cannot escape the burden of our inheritance.

Woodrow Wilson
speech in Middletown,
Connecticut
Apr 30, 1889

Democracy means simply the bludgeoning of the people by the people for the people.

Oscar Wilde
"The Soul of Man Under
Socialism"
Fortnightly Review
Feb, 1891

The Republican form of government is the highest form of government: but because of this it requires the highest type of human nature—a type nowhere at present existing.

Herbert Spencer
"The Americans"
Essays
1891

My plan cannot fail if the people are with us and we ought not to succeed unless we do have the people with us.

William Jennings Bryan
letter to Andrew Carnegie
Jan 13, 1899

I know of no better or safer human tribunal than the people.

William McKinley
speech in Boston,
Massachusetts
Feb 16, 1899

Democracy is only an experiment in government, and it has the obvious disadvantage of merely counting votes instead of weighing them.

William Ralph Inge
Possible Recovery?

Democracy is not so much a form of government as a set of principles.

Woodrow Wilson
Atlantic Monthly
Mar, 1901

If Despotism failed only for want of a capable benevolent despot, what chance has Democracy, which requires a whole population of capable voters.

George Bernard Shaw
"Epistle Dedicatory"
Man and Superman
1902

Democracy substitutes election by the incompetent many for appointment by the corrupt few.

George Bernard Shaw
"Maxims for
Revolutionists"
Man and Superman
1902

The government is us; we are the government, you and I.

Theodore Roosevelt
speech in Asheville,
North Carolina
Sep 9, 1902

The noblest of all forms of government is self-government; but it is also the most difficult.

Theodore Roosevelt
fifth annual message to
Congress
Dec 5, 1905

Theodore Roosevelt eighth annual message to Congress Dec 8, 1908	The danger to American democracy lies not in the least in the concentration of administrative power in responsible and accountable hands. It lies in having the power insufficiently concentrated, so that no one can be held responsible to the people for its use. Concentrated power is palpable, visible, responsible, easily reached, quickly held to account.
Theodore Roosevelt speech in Cleveland, Ohio Nov 5, 1910	A great democracy must be progressive or it will soon cease to be great or a democracy.
Theodore Roosevelt letter to Edward Grey Nov 15, 1913	There is something to be said for government by a great aristocracy which has furnished leaders to the nation in peace and war for generations; even a democrat like myself must admit this.
Walter Lippmann "The Golden Rule and After" *A Preface to Politics* 1914	"The consent of the governed" is more than a safeguard against ignorant tyrants: it is an insurance against benevolent despots as well.
Woodrow Wilson speech in Washington, D.C. Sep 28, 1915	Democracy is the most difficult form of government, because it is the form under which you have to persuade the largest number of persons to do anything in particular.
John Dewey *Democracy and Education* 1916	A democracy is more than a form of government; it is primarily a mode of associated living, of conjoint communicated experience.
Woodrow Wilson interview Nov 5, 1916	Only governments and not people initiate wars. . . . Democracy, therefore, is the best preventive of such jealousies and suspicions and secret intrigues as produce wars among nations where small groups control rather than the great body of public opinion.
Calvin Coolidge speech in Springfield, Massachusetts Jul 4, 1916	Democracy is not a tearing-down; it is a building-up. . . . It does not destroy; it fulfills. . . . It is the alpha and omega of man's relation to man. . . . Its foundation lays hold upon eternity.
Vladimir Ilyich Lenin *The State and the* *Revolution* 1917	A democracy is a state which recognizes the subjection of the minority to the majority, that is, an organization for the systematic use of violence by one class against the other, by one part of the population against another.
Woodrow Wilson speech to Congress Apr 2, 1917	The world must be made safe for democracy. Its peace must be planted on the tested foundations of political liberty.
David Lloyd George **1st Earl Lloyd-George** speech in London Jan 18, 1918	No democracy has ever long survived the failure of its adherents to be ready to die for it. . . . My own conviction is this, the people must either go on or go under.
Woodrow Wilson speech in Columbus, Ohio Sep 4, 1919	In the last analysis, my fellow countrymen, as we in America would be the first to claim, a people are responsible for the acts of their government.

Democracy is a form of government which may be rationally defended, not as being good, but as being less bad than any other.

It was the bitter experience of all public men from George Washington down that democracies are at least contemporarily fickle and heartless.

Democracy is the theory that the common people know what they want, and deserve to get it good and hard.

The most valuable of all human possessions, next to a superior and disdainful air, is the reputation of being well to do. Nothing else so neatly eases one's way through life, especially in democratic countries.

It would be folly to argue that the people cannot make political mistakes. They can and do make mistakes. But compared with the mistakes which have been made by every kind of autocracy they are unimportant.

Americans ought ever be asking themselves about their concept of the ideal republic.

Whatever democracy may be theoretically, one is sometimes tempted to define it practically as standardized and commercial melodrama.

There is one thing better than good government, and that is government in which all people have a part.

It is evident that our whole political machinery pre-supposes a people so fundamentally at one that they can safely afford to bicker; and so sure of their own moderation that they are not dangerously disturbed by the never-ending din of political conflict. May it always be so.

We have not got democratic government today. We have never had it and I venture to suggest to Honourable Members opposite that we shall never have it. What we have done in all the progress of reform and evolution is to broaden the basis of oligarchy.

The health of any democracy, no matter what its type or status, depends on a small technical detail: the conduct of elections. Everything else is secondary.
La salud de las democracias, cualesquiera que sean su tipo y su grado, depende de un mísero detalle técnico: el procedimiento electoral. Todo lo demás es secundario.

William Ralph Inge
"Our Present Discontents"
Outspoken Essays: First Series
1919

Herbert Hoover
in 1919 as quoted
Memoirs
1952

H.L. Mencken
"Sententiae"
A Book of Burlesques
1920

H.L. Mencken
Prejudices: Third Series
1922

Calvin Coolidge
speech in Evanston, Illinois
Jan 21, 1923

Warren G. Harding
speech in Kansas City, Missouri
Jun 22, 1923

Irving Babbitt
Democracy and Leadership
1924

Walter Hines Page
Life and Letters
1922-25

**Arthur Balfour
1st Earl of Balfour**
introduction to
Walter Bagehot
The English Constitution
Nov, 1927

**Anthony Eden
1st Earl of Avon**
speech in the House of Commons
Mar 29, 1928

José Ortega y Gasset
The Revolt of the Masses
1930

Huey P. Long
speech in the U.S. Senate
May 16, 1932

I do not want the voice of the people shut out.

Learned Hand
speech to the Federal Bar
Association
Mar 8, 1932

Even though counting heads is not an ideal way to govern, at least it is better than breaking them.

Franklin D. Roosevelt
speech in San Francisco,
California
Sep 23, 1932

Democracy . . . is a quest, a never-ending seeking for better things, and in the seeking . . . and the striving for them there are many roads to follow.

Alfred E. Smith
speech in Albany,
New York
Jun 27, 1933

All the ills of democracy can be cured by more democracy.

Franklin D. Roosevelt
speech to Conference of
Catholic Charities
Oct 4, 1933

A democracy, the right kind of democracy, is bound together by the ties of neighborliness.

Franklin D. Roosevelt
speech in Los Angeles,
California
Oct 1, 1935

Democracy is not a static thing. It is an everlasting march.

Franklin D. Roosevelt
annual message to
Congress
Jan 3, 1936

They realize that in thirty-four months we have built up new instruments of public power. In the hands of a people's Government this power is wholesome and proper. But in the hands of political puppets of an economic autocracy such power would provide the shackles for the liberties of the people.

Jayaprakash Narayan
Why Socialism?
1936

What the masses vote or do not vote for is not important— their opinion depends wholly on the extent to which they have been made conscious of their rights and potentialities. All the problems of society would have disappeared immediately if the masses really knew what was good for them.

Franklin D. Roosevelt
speech at Roanoke Island,
North Carolina
Aug 18, 1937

My anchor is democracy—and more democracy.

Franklin D. Roosevelt
annual message to
Congress
Jan 6, 1937

The deeper purpose of democratic government is to assist as many of its citizens as possible . . . to improve their conditions of life, to retain all personal liberty which does not adversely affect their neighbors, and to pursue the happiness which comes with security and an opportunity for recreation and culture.

Franklin D. Roosevelt
speech to the Pan-
American Union,
Washington, D.C.
Apr 14, 1937

The continued maintenance and improvement of democracy constitute the most important guarantee of international peace.

In the transition to political democracy, this country . . . underwent . . . no inner conversion. She accepted it as a convenience, like an improved system of telephones. . . . She changed her political garments, but not her heart. She carried into the democratic era, not only the institutions, but the social habits and mentality of the oldest and toughest plutocracy in the world. . . . She went to the ballot-box touching her hat.

Richard Tawney
"The Realities of Democracy"
The Highway
Jan, 1937

Democracy: a mockery that mouths the words and obstructs every effort of an honest people to establish a government for the welfare of the people.

Father Charles E. Coughlin
Social Justice
Aug 1, 1938

Let us never forget that government is ourselves and not an alien power over us. The ultimate rulers of our democracy are not a President and senators and congressmen and government officials, but the voters of this country.

Franklin D. Roosevelt
speech in Marietta, Ohio
Jul 8, 1938

In a social system in which power is open to all, the posts which confer power will, as a rule, be occupied by men who differ from the average in being exceptionally power-loving.

Bertrand Russell
Power
1938

Democracy, the practice of self-government, is a covenant among free men to respect the rights and liberties of their fellows.

Franklin D. Roosevelt
State of the Union
message
Jan 4, 1939

For democrats in troubled countries, the height of the art of governing seems to consist in accepting slaps so as to avoid kicks. . . . The enemies of democracy take advantage of this and grow daily more insolent.
Il colmo dell'arte di governo per i democratici dei paesi in crisi sembra consistere nell'incassare degli schiaffi per non ricevere dei calci. . . . Gli avversari della democrazia ne approfittano e diventano sempre più insolenti.

Ignazio Silone
The School for Dictatorships
1939

I'm tired of hearing it said that democracy doesn't work. Of course it doesn't work. It isn't supposed to work. We are supposed to work it.

Alexander Woollcott
quoted
Kansas City Times
Jan 4, 1977

Democracy is the superior form of government, because it is based on a respect for man as a reasonable being.

John F. Kennedy
Why England Slept
1940

Democracy is not just a word, to be shouted at political rallies and then put back in the dictionary after election day.

Franklin D. Roosevelt
presidential campaign
speech
Nov 4, 1940

It is one of the characteristics of a free and democratic nation that it have free and independent labor unions.

Franklin D. Roosevelt
speech to the Teamsters
Union, Washington, D.C.
Sep 11, 1940

The increasing discredit into which democratic government has fallen is due to democracy having been burdened with tasks for which it is not suited.

Friedrich August von Hayek
Freedom and the Economic System
1940

Friedrich August von Hayek
Freedom and the Economic System
1940

If a democratic people comes under the sway of an anti-capitalistic creed, this means that democracy will inevitably destroy itself.

Felix Frankfurter
Minersville School District v. Gobitis
1940

The ultimate foundation of a free society is the binding tie of cohesive sentiment.

Louis D. Brandeis
Labor
Oct 17, 1941

We can have democracy in this country or we can have great wealth concentrated in the hands of a few, but we can't have both.

Sir Winston S. Churchill
speech to a joint session of U.S. Congress
Dec 26, 1941

I am a child of the House of Commons. I was brought up in my father's house to believe in democracy. "Trust the people"—that was his message.

Henry Miller
"Raimu"
The Wisdom of the Heart
1941

It is the American vice, the democratic disease which expresses its tyranny by reducing everything unique to the level of the herd.

Jacques Maritain
"La Tragédie de la démocratie"
Christianisme et démocratie
1942

The tragedy of modern democracies is that they have not yet succeeded in effecting democracy.

Joseph Schumpeter
Capitalism, Socialism and Democracy
1942

Democracy is a political method, that is to say, a certain type of institutional arrangement for arriving at political—legal and administrative—decisions and hence incapable of being an end in itself.

George C. Marshall
Yank
Jan 28, 1943

In a democracy such as ours military policy is dependent on public opinion.

Langston Hughes
The Black Man Speaks
1943

I swear to the Lord/ I still can't see/ Why Democracy means/ Everybody but me.

Sir Winston S. Churchill
letter to Herbert Morrison
Nov 21, 1943

Nothing can be more abhorrent to democracy than to imprison a person or keep him in prison because he is unpopular. This is really the test of civilisation.

Franklin D. Roosevelt
radio address
Feb 12, 1943

The whole cornerstone of our democratic edifice was the principle that from the people and the people alone flows the authority of government.

Reinhold Niebuhr
foreword
The Children of Light and the Children of Darkness
1944

Man's capacity for justice makes democracy possible, but man's inclination to injustice makes democracy necessary.

Democracy is not tolerance. Democracy is a prescribed way of life erected on the premise that all men are created equal.

Chester Bomar Himes
If You're Scared, Go Home!
1944

The blind lead the blind. It's the democratic way.

Henry Miller
"With Edgar Varese in the Gobi Desert"
The Air-Conditioned Nightmare
1945

To define democracy in one word, we must use the word "cooperation."

Dwight D. Eisenhower
speech in Abilene, Kansas
Jun, 1945

There is no indispensable man in a democracy. When a republic comes to a point where a man is indispensable, then we have a Caesar.

Harry S Truman
interview
ca. 1946

The constant danger to democracy lies in the tendency of the individual to hide himself in the crowd—to defend his own failure to act forthrightly according to conviction under the false excuse that the effort of one in one hundred forty million has no significance.

Dwight D. Eisenhower
speech in Northfield, Vermont
Jun 9, 1946

Democracy is the recurrent suspicion that more than half of the people are right more than half of the time.

E.B. White
The Wild Flag
1946

Many forms of Government have been tried, and will be tried in this world of sin and woe. No one pretends that democracy is perfect or all-wise. Indeed, it has been said that democracy is the worst form of Government except all those other forms that have been tried from time to time.

Sir Winston S. Churchill
speech in the House of Commons
Nov 11, 1947

Human dignity, economic freedom, individual responsibility, these are the characteristics that distinguish democracy from all other forms devised by man.

Dwight D. Eisenhower
speech at the Univ. of West Virginia
Sep 24, 1947

Those who worry about radicalism in our schools and colleges are often either reactionaries who themselves do not bear allegiance to the traditional American principles, or defeatists who despair of the success of our own philosophy in an open competition.

James Bryant Conant
Education in a Divided World
1948

My notion of democracy is that under it the weakest should have the same opportunity as the strongest. This can never happen except through non-violence.

Mohandas K. Gandhi
Non-Violence in Peace and War
1948

I believe that the foundation of democratic liberty is a willingness to believe that other people may perhaps be wiser than oneself.

Clement Attlee
speech to the Labour Party annual conference
Oct, 1948

A democracy in which everybody had an equal responsibility in everything would be oppressive for the conscientious and licentious for the rest.

T.S. Eliot
Notes Toward The Definition of Culture
1948

Max Lerner
"The Negroes and the Draft"
Actions and Passions
1949

The taste of democracy becomes a bitter taste when the fullness of democracy is denied.

Will Rogers
The Autobiography of Will Rogers
1949

One of the evils of democracy is, you have to put up with the man you elect whether you want him or not.

Max Lerner
"The Negroes and the Draft"
Actions and Passions
1949

It is not the armed forces which can protect our democracy. It is the moral strength of democracy which alone can give any meaning to the efforts at military security.

Harry S Truman
inaugural address
Jan 20, 1949

Democracy is based on the conviction that man has the moral and intellectual capacity, as well as the inalienable right, to govern himself with reason and justice.

Albert Einstein
Out of My Later Years
1950

In a healthy nation there is a kind of balance between the will of the people and the government, which prevents its degeneration into tyranny.

Carl Sandburg
"I Am the People, the Mob"
Complete Poems
1950

I am the people—the mob—the crowd—the mass./ Do you know that all the great work of the world is done through me?

E.M. Forster
Two Cheers for Democracy
1951

Two Cheers for Democracy: one because it admits variety and two because it permits criticism. Two cheers are quite enough: there is no occasion to give three. Only Love, the Beloved Republic, deserves that.

J. William Fulbright
speech in the U.S. Senate
Mar 27, 1951

A democracy can recover quickly from physical or economic disaster, but when its moral convictions weaken it becomes easy prey for the demagogue and the charlatan. Tyranny and oppression then become the order of the day.

Adlai E. Stevenson Jr.
speech in Springfield, Illinois
Aug 14, 1952

The essence of a republican government is not command. It is consent.

Aneurin Bevan
In Place of Fear
1952

The issue . . . in a capitalist democracy resolves itself into this: either poverty will use democracy to win the struggle against property, or property, in fear of poverty, will destroy democracy.

Adlai E. Stevenson Jr.
speech in Chicago, Illinois
Sep 29, 1952

As citizens of this democracy, you are the rulers and the ruled, the lawgivers and the law-abiding, the beginning and the end.

Robert Maynard Hutchins
Great Books
1954

The death of democracy is not likely to be an assassination from ambush. It will be a slow extinction from apathy, indifference, and undernourishment.

Democracy is clearly most appropriate for countries which enjoy an economic surplus and least appropriate for countries where there is an economic insufficiency.

David Morris Potter
People of Plenty: Economic Abundance and the American Character
1954

The upward course of a nation's history is due in the long run to the soundness of heart of its average men and women.

Elizabeth II
Christmas address
Dec 25, 1954

A free society is one where it is safe to be unpopular.

Adlai E. Stevenson Jr.
quoted
Human Behavior
May, 1978

Since the beginning of time, governments have been mainly engaged in kicking people around. The astonishing achievement of modern times in the Western world is the idea that the citizens should do the kicking.

Adlai E. Stevenson Jr.
quoted
Human Behavior
May, 1978

Popular government has not yet been proved to guarantee, always and every where, good government.

Walter Lippmann
The Public Philosophy
1955

Democracy cannot be saved by supermen, but only by the unswerving devotion and goodness of millions of little men.

Adlai E. Stevenson Jr.
speech
1955

If I were to attempt to put my political philosophy tonight into a single phrase, it would be this: Trust the people.

Adlai E. Stevenson Jr.
speech in Harrisburg, Pennsylvania
Sep 13, 1956

The history of free men is never really written by chance but by choice—their choice.

Dwight D. Eisenhower
speech in Pittsburgh, Pennsylvania
Oct 9, 1956

The function of parliamentary democracy, under universal suffrage, historically considered, is to expose wealth-privilege to the attacks of the people.

Aneurin Bevan
New York Times Magazine
Oct 27, 1957

If one man offers you democracy and another offers you a bag of grain, at what stage of starvation will you prefer the grain to the vote?

Bertrand Russell
Silhouettes in Satire
1958

We hold the view that the people make the best judgment in the long run.

John F. Kennedy
campaign speech, Greensboro, North Carolina
Sep 17, 1960

Democracy is good. I say this because other systems are worse.

Jawaharlal Nehru
The New York Times
Jan 25, 1961

We have no greater asset than the willingness of a free and determined people, through its elected officials, to face all problems frankly and meet all dangers free from panic or fear.

John F. Kennedy
State of the Union message
Jan 29, 1961

Margaret Chase Smith
speech in the U.S. Senate
Sep 21, 1961

In these perilous hours, I fear that the American people are ahead of their leaders in realism and courage—but behind them in knowledge of the facts because the facts have not been given to them.

Felix Frankfurter
Baker v. Carr
1962

In a democratic society like ours, relief must come through an aroused popular conscience that sears the conscience of the people's representatives.

John F. Kennedy
speech in San Jose, Costa Rica
Mar 19, 1963

Democracy is never a final achievement. It is a call to untiring effort, to continual sacrifice and to the willingness, if necessary, to die in its defense.

J. William Fulbright
speech in the U.S. Senate
Mar 27, 1964

We are inclined to confuse freedom and democracy, which we regard as moral principles, with the way in which these are practiced in America—with capitalism, federalism and the two-party system, which are not moral principles, but simply the accepted practices of the American people.

Lyndon Baines Johnson
commencement address,
National Cathedral School,
Washington, D.C.
Jun 1, 1965

Let no one think for a moment that national debate means national division.

Edmund S. Muskie
speech in South Bend, Indiana
Sep 11, 1968

You have the God-given right to kick the government around—don't hesitate to do so.

Richard M. Nixon
televised speech
Nov 3, 1969

And so tonight—to you, the great silent majority of my fellow Americans—I ask for your support.

Shirley Chisholm
Unbought and Unbossed
1970

Everyone else is represented in Washington by a rich and powerful lobby, it seems. But there is no lobby for the people.

Gerald R. Ford
address at Jacksonville Univ., Jacksonville, Florida
Dec 16, 1971

In a political sense, there is one problem that currently underlies all of the others. That problem is making Government sufficiently responsive to the people. If we don't make government responsive to the people, we don't make it believable. And we must make government believable if we are to have a functioning democracy.

Walter E. Washington
attributed
1971

People are not an interruption of our business. People are our business.

Sam Ervin
news conference during Watergate investigation
Time
Apr 16, 1973

Divine right went out with the American Revolution and doesn't belong to the White House aides. What meat do they eat that makes them grow so great?

Sovereignty remains at all times with the people and they do not forfeit through elections the rights to have the law construed against and applied to every citizen.

Court of Appeals United States
ruling that President Nixon had to turn over presidential tapes
The New York Times
Oct 14, 1973

Secrecy and a free, democratic government don't mix.

Harry S Truman
quoted by Merle Miller
Plain Speaking: An Oral Biography of Harry S Truman
1974

Television is democracy at its ugliest.

Paddy Chayefsky
The New York Times
Nov 14, 1976

That's what the American system is all about: to keep power divided, to prevent a small core from either pole suddenly thrusting its decisions on the country.

Charles M. Mathias Jr.
Time
Aug 23, 1976

The stakes . . . are too high for government to be a spectator sport.

Barbara Jordan
commencement address, Harvard Univ.
Jun 16, 1977.

I would rather trust twelve jurors with all their prejudices and biases than I would a judge. I think the reason democracy works is because as you multiply judgements, you reduce the incidence of errors.

Louis Nizer
Chicago Tribune Magazine
Feb 5, 1978

The experience of democracy is like the experience of life itself—always changing, infinite in its variety, sometimes turbulent and all the more valuable for having been tested by adversity.

Jimmy Carter
speech to the Indian Parliament
Jan 2, 1978

Most people's opinions are of no value at all.

A.L. Rowse
The Observer
Aug 26, 1979

(Our goal is) a society with a minimum of compulsion, a maximum of individual freedom and of voluntary association and the abolition of exploitation and poverty.

Roger N. Baldwin
recalled on his death
Aug 26, 1981

A government is not in power; it is in office, put there by the will of the people.

Stanley Baldwin
quoted by his daughter, Lorna Howard, in a letter
The Times
Jan 23, 1982

Democracy is not a fragile flower; still it needs cultivating.

Ronald Reagan
speech to British parliament
Jun 8, 1982

I don't run democracy. I train troops to defend democracy.

Lt. Gen. Alfred M. Gray
speech to new officers
Newsweek
Jul 9, 1984

Norman Thomas
quoted on the 30th anniversary of U.S. Senate's censure of Joseph McCarthy
The New York Times
Dec 2, 1984

The struggle is confused; our knight wins by no clean thrust of lance or sword, but the dragon somehow poops out, and decent democracy is victor.

Pericles
quoted by Sir Karl Popper, "Popper on Democracy"
The Economist
Apr 23, 1988

Although only a few may originate a policy, we are all able to judge it.

Sir Karl Popper
"Popper on Democracy"
The Economist
Apr 23, 1988

Decisions arrived at democratically, and even the powers conveyed upon a government by a democratic vote, may be wrong. It is hard, if not impossible, to construct a constitution that safeguards against mistakes.

Sir Karl Popper
"Popper on Democracy"
The Economist
Apr 23, 1988

How can we best avoid situations in which a bad ruler causes too much harm? When we say that the best solution known to us is a constitution that allows a majority vote to dismiss the government, then we do not say the majority vote will always be right. We do not even say that it will usually be right. We say only that this very imperfect procedure is the best so far invented.

Ronald Reagan
farewell address
Jan 11, 1989

The moral way of government is the practical way of government. Democracy, the profoundly good, is also the profoundly productive.

Ronald Reagan
farewell address
Jan 11, 1989

"We the People" tell the government what to do, it doesn't tell us. "We the people" are the driver—the government is the car. And we decide where it should go, and by what route, and how fast.

Democratic Party

Ignatius Donnelly
speech to the Minnesota state legislature
Sep 13, 1860

The Democratic Party is like a mule. It has neither pride of ancestry nor hope of posterity.

Finley Peter Dunne
Mr. Dooley's Opinions
1900

Th' dimmycratic party ain't on speakin' terms with itsilf.

Woodrow Wilson
speech in Indianapolis, Indiana
Jan 8, 1915

I love the Democratic Party; but I love America a great deal more. . . . When the Democratic Party thinks that it is an end in itself, then I rise up and dissent.

The Democrats today trust in the people, the plain, ordinary, everyday citizen, neither superlatively rich nor distressingly poor, not one of the "best minds" but the average mind. The Socialists believe in making the Government the people's master; the Republicans believe that the moneyed "aristocracy", the few great financial minds, should rule the Government; the Democrats believe that the whole people should govern.

Eleanor Roosevelt
"Jeffersonian Principles the Issue in 1928"
Current History
Jun, 1928

We can make this thing into a Party, instead of a Memory.

Will Rogers
letter to Al Smith on the Democratic party
Jan 19, 1929

Let it be . . . the task of our party to break with foolish traditions.

Franklin D. Roosevelt
quoted by Frank Kingdon
As FDR Said
1932

You've got to be (an) optimist to be a Democrat, and you've got to be a humorist to stay one.

Will Rogers
Good Gulf radio show
Jun 24, 1934

I am not a member of any organized party—I am a Democrat.

Will Rogers
quoted by P.J. O'Brien
Will Rogers, Ambassador of Good Will, Prince of Wit and Wisdom
1935

Every Harvard class should have one Democrat to rescue it from oblivion.

Will Rogers
The Autobiography of Will Rogers
1949

The Democratic Party at its worst is better for the country than the Republican Party at its best.

Lyndon Baines Johnson
speech
1955

Have you ever tried to split sawdust?

Eugene J. McCarthy
on accusation he had split Democratic Party,
NBC-TV
Oct 23, 1969

A new Government took office in Washington, not via bayonets and tanks as is the custom in some of the world's capitals (but) in the Democratic Way . . . via hyperbole, sham, melodrama and public-spirited mendacity.

R. Emmett Tyrrell Jr.
on Carter's inauguration
Time
Mar 7, 1977

The Democratic Party is a party in name only, not in shared belief.

Ramsey Clark
Time
Aug 25, 1980

There were so many candidates on the platform that there were not enough promises to go around.

Ronald Reagan
on Democratic presidential primary debate in New Hampshire
Newsweek
Feb 6, 1984

Lance Morrow
"All Right, What Kind of
People Are We?"
Time
Jul 30, 1984

In the pageant of unity (at the Democratic National Convention), one speaker after another recited a Whitmanesque litany of races and classes and minorities and interests and occupations—or unemployments. Some speakers, in fact, made the nation sound like an immense ingathering of victims—terrorized senior citizens, forsaken minorities, Dickensian children—warmed by the party's Frank Capra version of America: Say, it's a wonderful life!

Jeane J. Kirkpatrick
Time
Jun 17, 1985

(Democrats) can't get elected unless things get worse—and things won't get worse unless they get elected.

Dictatorship/Tyranny

Aesop
"The Wolf and the Lamb"
Fables
ca. 550 B.C.

Any excuse will serve a tyrant.

Aeschylus
Prometheus Bound
ca. 478 B.C.

This is a sickness rooted and inherent/ in the nature of a tyranny:/ that he that holds it does not trust his friends.

Aeschylus
Agamemnon
458 B.C.

Death is better, a milder fate than tyranny.

Plato
The Republic
ca. 390 B.C.

When the tyrant has disposed of foreign enemies by conquest or treaty, and there is nothing to fear from them, then he is always stirring up some war or other, in order that the people may require a leader.

Plato
The Republic
ca. 390 B.C.

The people have always some champion whom they set over them and nurse into greatness. . . . This and no other is the root from which a tyrant springs; when he first appears he is a protector.

Lucius Accius
fragment from a lost
tragedy

Let them hate me, so they but fear me.
Oderint, dum metuant.

Benvenuto Cellini
Autobiography
1558-66

The laws can't be enforced against the man who is the laws' master.

William Shakespeare
*King Henry the Sixth,
Part III*
1591

For how can tyrants safely govern home,/ Unless abroad they purchase great alliance?

William Shakespeare
Julius Caesar
1599

The abuse of greatness is when it disjoins/ Remorse from power.

For the people, I desire their liberty and freedom as much as anybody whatever. But I must tell you that their liberty and freedom consists in having of government those laws by which their life and their goods may be most their own. It is not having a share in government; that is nothing pertaining to them. A subject and a sovereign are clean different things.

Charles I
speech on the scaffold
Jan 30, 1649

The face of tyranny / Is always mild at first.
Toujours la tyrannie a d'heureuses prémices.

Jean Racine
Britannicus
1669

Of all the tyrannies on humankind, / The worst is that which persecutes the mind.

John Dryden
The Hind and the Panther
1687

You need neither art nor science to be a tyrant.
Il ne faut ni art ni science pour exercer la tyrannie.

Jean de La Bruyère
"Du souverain ou de la république"
Les Caractères
1688

All men would be tyrants if they could.

Daniel Defoe
The Kentish Petition
1712-13

The tyranny of the many would be when one body takes over the rights of the others, and then exercises its power to change the laws in its favor. . . . One despot always has a few good moments, but an assembly of despots never does.
Cette tyrannie de plusieurs serait celle d'un corps qui envahirait les droits des autres corps, et qui exercerait le despotisme à la faveur des lois corrompues par lui. . . . Un despote a toujours quelques bons moments; une assemblée de despotes n'en a jamais.

Voltaire
"Tyrannie"
Dictionnaire philosophique
1764

We call a tyrant the leader whose only law is that of his own whim, who expropriates the property of his subjects, and then drafts them to go take that of their neighbors.
On appelle tyran le souverain qui ne connaît de lois que son caprice, qui prend le bien de ses sujets, et qui ensuite les enrôle pour aller prendre celui des voisins.

Voltaire
"Tyrannie"
Dictionnaire philosophique
1764

Under which kind of tyranny would you rather live? Neither, but if a choice must be made I would prefer the tyranny of one to that of the many.
Sous quelle tyrannie aimeriez-vous mieux vivre? Sous aucune; mais, s'il fallait choisir, je détesterais moins la tyrannie d'un seul que celle de plusieurs.

Voltaire
"Tyrannie"
Dictionnaire philosophique
1764

Whoever has power in his hands wants to be despotic; the craze for domination is an incurable disease.

Voltaire
letter to M. Damilaville
Oct 16, 1765

Pure despotism is the punishment for men's bad conduct. If a community of men is subdued by an individual or by a few, that is obviously because it has neither the courage nor the ability to govern itself.

Voltaire
Republican Ideas
1765

William Pitt **1st Earl of Chatham** speech in the House of Lords in defense of John Wilkes Jan 9, 1770	Where law ends, tyranny begins.
Edmund Burke speech, "On Conciliation with the American Colonies" Mar 22, 1775	The use of force alone is temporary. It may subdue for a moment, but it does not remove the necessity of subduing again: and a nation is not governed which is perpetually conquered.
Edmund Burke speech, "On Conciliation with the American Colonies" Mar 22, 1775	Slavery they can have anywhere. It is a weed that grows in every soil.
Thomas Paine *The American Crisis* Dec. 23, 1776	Tyranny, like hell, is not easily conquered; yet we have this consolation with us, that the harder the conflict, the more glorious the triumph. What we obtain too cheap, we esteem too lightly: it is dearness only that gives everything its value.
Samuel Johnson quoted by James Boswell *Life of Samuel Johnson* Apr 14, 1778	A country governed by a despot is an inverted cone.
William Pitt **the Younger** speech in the House of Commons Nov 18, 1783	Necessity is the plea for every infringement of human freedom. It is the argument of tyrants, it is the creed of slaves.
William Pitt **the Younger** speech on the India Bill Nov, 1783	Necessity is the argument of tyrants, it is the creed of slaves.
George Washington letter to the Marquis de Lafayette Apr 28, 1788	When a people shall have become incapable of governing themselves, and fit for a master, it is of little consequence from what quarter he comes.
Edmund Burke *Reflections on the Revolution in France* 1790	Kings will be tyrants from policy, when subjects are rebels from principle.
Denis Diderot *Supplement to Bougainville's "Voyage"* 1796	Watch out for the fellow who talks about putting things in order! Putting things in order always means getting other people under your control.
Thomas Jefferson letter to Philip Mazzei Jan 1, 1797	Timid men who prefer the calm of despotism to the tempestuous sea of liberty.
Thomas Jefferson letter to Benjamin Rush Sep 23, 1800	I have sworn upon the altar of God, eternal hostility against every form of tyranny over the mind of man.

Force is the vital principle and immediate parent of despotism.

Thomas Jefferson
first inaugural address
Mar 4, 1801

Great ambition, unchecked by principle or the love of glory, is an unruly tyrant.

Alexander Hamilton
letter to James Bayard
Jan 16, 1801

What has always made the state a hell on earth has been precisely that man has tried to make it his heaven.

Friedrich Hölderlin
quoted by Friedrich
von Hayek
The Road to Serfdom
1944

The people are always in the wrong when they are faced by the armed forces.
Le peuple a toujours tort, quand il s'oppose à la force armée.

Napoleon I
letter to Gen. Clarke,
duc de Feltre
Oct 2, 1810

Power, like a desolating pestilence,/ Pollutes whate'er it touches; and obedience,/ Bane of all genius, virtue, freedom, truth,/ Makes slaves of men, and, of the human frame,/ A mechanized automaton.

Percy Bysshe Shelley
Queen Mab
1813

Anarchy always brings about absolute power.
L'anarchie ramène toujours au gouvernement absolu.

Napoleon I
speech at the opening of
the legislature
Jun 7, 1815

Among the several cloudy appellatives which have been commonly employed as cloaks for misgovernment, there is none more conspicuous in this atmosphere of illusion than the word Order.

Jeremy Bentham
The Book of Fallacies
1824

Whatever government is not a government of laws, is a despotism, let it be called what it may.

Daniel Webster
remarks in Bangor, Maine
Aug 25, 1835

Slavery always has, and always will, produce insurrections wherever it exists, because it is a violation of the natural order of things, and no human power can much longer perpetuate it.

Angelina Grimké
"Appeal to the Christian
Women of the South"
*The Anti-Slavery
Examiner*
Sep, 1836

Our fathers waged a bloody conflict with England, because they were taxed without being represented. . . . They were not willing to be governed by laws which they had no voice in making; but this is the way in which women are governed in this Republic.

Angelina Grimké
*Letters to Catherine
Beecher*
1836

France was long a despotism tempered by epigrams.

Thomas Carlyle
*History of the French
Revolution*
1837

Tyrants are but the spawn of Ignorance,/ Begotten by the slaves they trample on.

James Russell Lowell
"Prometheus"
1843

The nose of a mob is its imagination. By this, at any time, it can be quietly led.

Edgar Allan Poe
Marginalia
1844–49

Pierre Joseph Proudhon
Confessions of a Revolutionary
1849

Whoever puts his hand on me to govern me is a usurper and a tyrant; I declare him my enemy.

William Ewart Gladstone
letter to the Earl of Aberdeen referring to the Kingdom of the Two Sicilies
1851

This is the negation of God erected into a system of Government.

Frederick Douglass
speech on "The Meaning of July Fourth for the Negro" in Rochester, New York
Jul 5, 1852

Oppression makes a wise man mad.

Walter Savage Landor
"Anacreon and Polycrates"
Imaginary Conversations
1824-53

Tyrants never perish from tryanny, but always from folly.

Abraham Lincoln
speech in Peoria, Illinois
Oct 16, 1854

When the white man governs himself, that is self-government; but when he governs himself and also governs another man, that is more than self-government—that is despotism.

Abraham Lincoln
letter to Joshua Speed
Aug 24, 1855

As a nation, we began by declaring that all men are created equal. We now practically read it, all men are created equal except Negroes. When the know-nothings get control, it will read, all men are created equal except the negroes and foreigners and Catholics. When it comes to this I shall prefer emigrating to some country where they make no pretense of loving liberty—to Russia, for instance, where despotism can be pure, and without the base alloy of hypocrisy.

John Stuart Mill
On Liberty
1859

Whatever crushes individuality is despotism, by whatever name it may be called.

John Stuart Mill
On Liberty
1859

A State which dwarfs its men, in order that they may be more docile instruments in its hand even for beneficial purposes—will find that with small men no great thing can really be accomplished.

Frederick Douglass
speech in Geneva, New York
Aug 1, 1860

They who study mankind with a whip in their hands will always go wrong.

Fyodor Dostoevsky
The House of The Dead
1862

Tyranny is a habit; it may develop, and it does develop at last, into a disease.

Andrew Johnson
speech in Washington, D.C.
Feb 22, 1866

It is a fact attested in history that sometimes revolutions most disastrous to freedom are effected without the shedding of blood. The substance of your government may be taken away, while the form and the shadow remain to you.

Was there ever any domination which did not appear natural to those who possessed it?

John Stuart Mill
The Subjection of Women
1869

You have not converted a man because you have silenced him.

John Morley
(1st Viscount Morley
of Blackburn)
Rousseau
1876

The more complete the despotism, the more smoothly all things move on the surface.

Elizabeth Cady
Stanton
History of Woman
Suffrage
1881

The prolonged slavery of women is the darkest page in human history.

Elizabeth Cady
Stanton
History of Woman
Suffrage
1881

Make men large and strong, and tyranny will bankrupt itself in making shackles for them.

Henry Ward Beecher
Proverbs from Plymouth
Pulpit
1887

The Austrian government . . . is a system of despotism tempered by casualness.

Victor Adler
speech to the International Socialist Congress
in Paris
Jul 17, 1889

There are three kinds of despots. There is the despot who tyrannizes over the body. There is the despot who tyrannizes over the soul. There is the despot who tyrannizes over soul and body alike. The first is called the Prince. The second is called the Pope. The third is called the People.

Oscar Wilde
"The Soul of Man Under
Socialism"
Fortnightly Review
Feb, 1891

A man may build himself a throne of bayonets, but he cannot sit on it.

William Ralph Inge
Wit and Wisdom of Dean
Inge

The State is still, after individual despots have been largely modified or eliminated, a collective despot, mostly inexorable, almost irresponsible, and entirely inaccessible to those personal appeals which have sometimes moved the obsolete or obsolescent tyrants to pity. In its selfishness and meanness, it is largely the legislated and organized ideal of the lowest and stupidest of its citizens, whose daily life is nearest the level of barbarism.

William Dean Howells
quoted by Daniel Aaron
Men of Good Hope
1951

The possession of unlimited power will make a despot of almost any man. There is a possible Nero in the gentlest human creature that walks.

Thomas Bailey Aldrich
"Leaves from a
Notebook"
Ponkapog Papers
1903

No man is good enough to be another man's master.

George Bernard Shaw
Major Barbara
1905

Maxim Gorky *Enemies* 1906	What can you do by killing? Nothing. You kill one dog, the master buys another—that's all there is to it.
Edgar Watson Howe *Country Town Sayings* 1911	People tolerate those they fear further than those they love.
Woodrow Wilson speech in New York City Sep 4, 1912	The concentration of power is what always precedes the destruction of human initiative, and, therefore of human energy.
W.E.B. Du Bois "Our Own Consent" *Crisis* Jan, 1913	Oppression costs the oppressor too much if the oppressed stand up and protest. The protest need not be merely physical—the throwing of stones and bullets—if it is mental, spiritual; if it expresses itself in silent, persistent dissatisfaction, the cost to the oppressor is terrific.
John Morley *Recollections* 1917	Excess of severity is not the path to order. On the contrary, it is the path to the bomb.
Adolf Hitler *Mein Kampf* 1924	The one means that wins the easiest victory over reason: terror and force. *Das freilich die Vernunft am leichtesten besiegt: der Terror, die Gewahlt.*
Adolf Hitler *Mein Kampf* 1924	The great masses of the people . . . will more easily fall victims to a big lie than to a small one. *Die breite Masse eines Volkes . . . einer grossen Lüge leichten zum Opfer fällt als einer kleinen.*
Adolf Hitler speech at his trial for sedition in Munich Mar 22, 1924	The man who is born to be a dictator is not compelled; he wills it. . . . The man who feels called upon to govern a people has no right to say, If you want me or summon me, I will cooperate. No, it is his duty to step forward.
Upton Sinclair *Singing Jailbirds* 1924	Fascism is Capitalism plus Murder.
Mohandas K. Gandhi *Young India* Feb 12, 1925	The willing sacrifice of the innocents is the most powerful retort to insolent tyranny that has yet been conceived by God or man.
Joseph Goebbels speech to Nazi party con- gress, Nuremberg, Germany Aug, 1927	Whoever can conquer the street will one day conquer the state, for every form of power politics and any dictatorially-run state has its roots in the street.
Joseph Goebbels *Der Angriff* Apr 30, 1928	We (the Nazi members) enter parliament in order to supply ourselves, in the arsenal of democracy, with its own weapons. . . . If democracy is so stupid as to give us free tickets and salaries for this bear's work, that is its affair.

Under the species of Syndicalism and Fascism there appears for the first time in Europe a type of man who does not want to give reasons or to be right, but simply shows himself resolved to impose his opinions.

Bajo las especies de sindicalismo y fascismo aparece por primera vez en Europa un tipo de hombre que no quiere dar razones ni quiere tener razón, sino, sencillamente, se muestra resuelto a imponer sus opiniones.

José Ortega y Gasset
The Revolt of the Masses
1930

We shall never secure emancipation from the tyranny of the white oppressor until we have achieved it in our own souls.

W.E.B. Du Bois
"Patient Asses"
Crisis
Mar, 1930

If the nineteenth centruy was a century of individualism . . . it may be expected that this will be the century of collectivism, and hence the century of the State.

Benito Mussolini
The Political and Social Doctrine of Fascism
1932

Dictators ride to and fro upon tigers which they dare not dismount. And the tigers are getting hungry.

Sir Winston S. Churchill
While England Slept
1936

So long as men worship the Caesars and Napoleons, Caesars and Napoleons will duly rise and make them miserable.

Aldous Huxley
Ends and Means
1937

History proves that dictatorships do not grow out of strong and successful governments, but out of weak and helpless ones.

Franklin D. Roosevelt
fireside chat
Apr 14, 1938

You cannot organize civilization around the core of militarism and at the same time expect reason to control human destinies.

Franklin D. Roosevelt
radio address
Oct 26, 1938

The dictator, in all his pride, is held in the grip of his party machine. He can go forward; he cannot go back. He must blood his hounds and show them sport, or else, like Actaeon of old, be devoured by them. All strong without, he is all-weak within.

Sir Winston S. Churchill
radio address to the United States
Oct 16, 1938

A dictatorship is a regime in which people quote instead of thinking.

Una dittatura è un regime in cui, invece di pensare, gli uomini citano.

Ignazio Silone
The School for Dictatorships
1939

I suspect that in our loathing of totalitarianism, there is infused a good deal of admiration for its efficiency.

T.S. Eliot
"The Idea of a Christian Society"
1939

When a nation has alllowed itself to fall under a tyrannical regime, it cannot be absolved from the faults due to the guilt of the regime.

Sir Winston S. Churchill
message sent following a visit to Italy
Jul 28, 1944

Antoine de Saint- **Exupéry** *Citadelle* 1948	True, it is evil that a single man should crush the herd, but see not there the worst form of slavery, which is when the herd crushes out the man. *Il est certes mauvais que l'homme écrase le troupeau. Mais ne cherche point là le grand esclavage: il se montre quand le troupeau écrase l'homme.*
Aneurin Bevan *Tribune* Feb 3, 1950	You cannot educate a man to be a trained technician inside a factory and ask him to accept the status of a political robot outside. . . . A totalitarian state or a one-party state is a persistent contradiction with the needs of a thriving industrial community.
Albert Camus "Metaphysical Rebellion" *The Rebel* 1951	The slave begins by demanding justice and ends by wanting to wear a crown. He must dominate in his turn. *L'esclave commence par réclamer justice et finit par vouloir la royauté. Il lui faut dominer à son tour.*
Jean-Paul Sartre reported remarks on the execution of Julius and Ethel Rosenberg Jun 22, 1953	Fascism is not defined by the number of its victims, but by the way it kills them.
Dwight D. Eisenhower State of the Union address Jan 7, 1954	From behind the Iron Curtain, there are signs that tyranny is in trouble and reminders that its structure is as brittle as its surface is hard.
Eric Hoffer *The Passionate State of* *Mind* 1954	Radicalism itself ceases to be radical when absorbed mainly in preserving its control over a society or an economy.
Bernard Baruch *A Philosphy of Time* 1954	So efficient are the available instruments of slavery—finger-prints, lie detectors, brainwashings, gas chambers—that we shiver at the thought of political change which might put these instruments in the hands of men of hate.
Simone Weil *Oppression and Liberty* 1958	Man alone can enslave man.
Harry S Truman speech at Columbia Univ. Apr 28, 1959	Whenever you have an efficient government you have a dictatorship.
John F. Kennedy State of the Union address Jan 14, 1963	A police state finds it cannot command the grain to grow.
John F. Kennedy State of the Union address Jan 14, 1963	Nothing more exactly identifies the totalitarian or closed socie-ty than the rigid and, more often than not, brutish direction of labor at all levels.
Eric Hoffer *The Ordeal of Change* 1964	The benevolent despot who sees himself as a shepherd of the people still demands from others the submissiveness of sheep.

Totalitarianism spells simplification: an enormous reduction in the variety of aims, motives, interests, human types, and, above all, in the categories and units of power.

Eric Hoffer
The Ordeal of Change
1964

When men are ruled by fear, they strive to prevent the very changes that will abate it.

Alan Paton
"The Challenge of Fear"
Saturday Review
Sep 9, 1967

It is the common failing of totalitarian regimes that they cannot really understand the nature of our democracy. They mistake dissent for disloyalty. They mistake restlessness for a rejection of policy. They mistake a few committees for a country. They misjudge individual speeches for public policy.

Lyndon Baines Johnson
speech
Sep 29, 1967

The trouble with military rule is that every colonel or general is soon full of ambition. The navy takes over today and the army tomorrow.

Yakubu Gowon
Chicago Daily News
Aug 29, 1970

There are similarities between absolute power and absolute faith: a demand for absolute obedience, a readiness to attempt the impossible, a bias for simple solutions—to cut the knot rather than unravel it, the viewing of compromise as surrender. Both absolute power and absolute faith are instruments of dehumanization. Hence, absolute faith corrupts as absolutely as absolute power.

Eric Hoffer
"Thoughts of Eric Hoffer"
The New York Times Magazine
Apr 25, 1971

The most potent weapon in the hands of the oppressor is the mind of the oppressed.

Steve Biko
speech in Cape Town
1971

We are no longer interested in elections except as a means to reach our objectives.

Juan Peron
The New York Times
Jul 14, 1973

I don't mind dictatorships abroad provided they are pro-American.

George C. Wallace
Time
Oct 27, 1975

The totalitarian state is not power unchained it is truth chained.
L'Etat totalitaire . . . ce n'est pas la force déchainée, c'est la vérité enchainée.

Bernard-Henri Lévy
La Barbarie à visage humain
1977

The more a regime claims to be the embodiment of liberty the more tyrannical it is likely to be.

Sir Ian Gilmour
Inside Right
1977

Ours is not yet a totalitarian government, but it is an elitist democracy—and becoming more so every year.

Victor L. Marchetti
Inquiry
Feb 6, 1978

When you stop a dictator there are always risks. But there are greater risks in not stopping a dictator.

Margaret Thatcher
interview on BBC-TV during the Falklands War
Apr 5, 1982

Anybody who has ever lived . . . under a dictatorship which cannot be removed without bloodshed will know that a democracy, imperfect though it is, is worth fighting for and, I believe, worth dying for.

Sir Karl Popper
"Popper on Democracy"
The Economist
Apr 23, 1988

We do not base a choice on the goodness of democracy, which may be doubtful, but solely on the evilness of a dictatorship, which is certain. Not only because the dictator is bound to make bad use of his power, but because a dictator, even if he were benevolent, would rob all others of their responsibility, and thus of their human rights and duties.

Economics/The Economy

Voltaire
Lettres philosophiques
1734

Commerce, which has made the citizens of England rich, also helped to make them free, and this freedom has encouraged commerce even more.

Le commerce, qui a enrichi les citoyens en Angleterre, a contribué à les rendre libres, et cette liberté a étendu le commerce à son tour.

Adam Smith
An Inquiry Into the Nature and Causes of The Wealth of Nations
1776

Labour, therefore, it appears evidently, is the only universal, as well as the only accurate, measure of value, or the only standard by which we can compare the values of different commodities, at all times, and at all places.

Benjamin Franklin
Thoughts on Commercial Subjects
ca. 1780

No nation was ever ruined by trade.

Napoleon I
quoted by Emmanuel de Las Cases
Mémorial de Ste. Hélène
Jun 17, 1816

If there ever existed a monarchy strong as granite, it would only take the ideas of the economists to reduce it to powder.

S'il existait une monarchie de granit, il suffirait des idéalités des économistes pour la réduire en poudre.

Lord Macaulay
"Essay on Mitford's History of Greece"
1824

Free trade, one of the greatest blessings which a government can confer on a people, is in almost every country unpopular.

Victor Hugo
Les Misérables
1862

Social prosperity means man happy, the citizen free, the nation great.

Prospérité sociale, cela veut dire l'homme heureux, le citoyen libre, la nation grande.

William Morris
Art Under Plutocracy
1883

The very essence of competitive commerce is waste, the waste that comes from the anarchy of war.

William Jennings Bryan
"Cross of Gold" speech at the Democratic National Convention, Chicago, Illinois
Jul 8, 1896

Burn down your cities and leave our farms, and your cities will spring up again as if by magic; but destroy our farms and the grass will grow in the streets of every city in the country.

Joseph Chamberlain
speech in Birmingham, England
Nov 13, 1896

Commerce is the greatest of all political interests.

Political institutions are a superstructure resting on an economic foundation.

Vladimir Ilyich Lenin
The Three Sources and Three Constituent Parts of Marxism
1913

There is no subtler, no surer means of overturning the existing basis of society than to debauch the currency. The process engages all the hidden forces of economic law on the side of destruction, and does it in a manner which not one man in a million is able to diagnose.

John Maynard Keynes
The Economic Consequences of the Peace
1919

Unionism seldom, if ever, uses such power as it has to insure better work; almost always it devotes a large part of that power to safeguarding bad work.

H.L. Mencken
Prejudices: Third Series
1922

When more and more people are thrown out of work, unemployment results.

Calvin Coolidge
attributed
New York Herald Tribune
Sep 29, 1954

The slogan of progress is changing from the full dinner pail to the full garage.

Herbert Hoover
The New Day
1928

Prosperity is only an instrument to be used, not a deity to be worshiped.

Calvin Coolidge
speech
Jun 11, 1928

If the unemployed could eat plans and promises they would be able to spend the winter on the Riviera.

W.E.B. Du Bois
"As the Crow Flies"
Crisis
Jan, 1931

True wealth is not a static thing. It is a living thing made out of the disposition of men to create and to distribute the good things of life and rising standards of living.

Franklin D. Roosevelt
speech in Washington, D.C.
Oct 24, 1934

Practical men, who believe themselves to be quite exempt from any intellectual influences, are usually the slaves of some defunct economist. . . . It is ideas, not vested interests, which are dangerous for good or evil.

John Maynard Keynes
The General Theory of Employment, Interest and Money
1936

We have always known that heedless self-interest was bad morals; we know now that it is bad economics.

Franklin D. Roosevelt
second inaugural address
Jan 20, 1937

Economic progress, in capitalist society, means turmoil.

Joseph Schumpeter
Capitalism, Socialism and Democracy
1942

There is inherent in the capitalist system a tendency toward self-destruction.

Joseph Schumpeter
Capitalism, Socialism and Democracy
1942

True individual freedom cannot exist without economic security and independence. People who are hungry and out of a job are the stuff of which dictatorships are made.

Franklin D. Roosevelt
message to Congress
Jan 11, 1944

John Kenneth Galbraith *The Affluent Society* 1958	Nothing so weakens government as persistent inflation.
John Kenneth Galbraith *The Affluent Society* 1958	In a community where public services have failed to keep abreast of private consumption things are very different. Here, in an atmosphere of private opulence and public squalor, the private goods have full sway.
John F. Kennedy campaign speech in Sioux Falls, South Dakota Sep 22, 1960	The farmer is the only man in our economy who buys everything at retail, sells everything he sells at wholesale, and pays the freight both ways.
Milton Friedman *Capitalism and Freedom* 1962	The Great Depression, like most other periods of severe unemployment, was produced by government mismanagement rather than by any inherent instability of the private economy.
Luther H. Hodges *Wall Street Journal* Mar 14, 1962	If ignorance paid dividends, most Americans could make a fortune out of what they don't know about economics.
Sir Winston S. Churchill quoted *To the Point International* Nov 1, 1976	You don't make the poor richer by making the rich poorer.
Jimmy Carter (James Earl, Jr.) *Time* Mar 26, 1979	The corrosive effects of inflation eat away at ties that bind us together as a people.
Dixy Lee Ray speech to Scientists and Engineers for Secure Energy 1980	The reality is that zero defects in products plus zero pollution plus zero risk on the job is equivalent to maximum growth of government plus zero economic growth plus runaway inflation.
Ronald Reagan his recollection of a 1980 campaign remark Oct 2, 1986	Recession is when your neighbor loses his job. Depression is when you lose yours. And recovery is when Jimmy Carter loses his.
Lloyd Bentsen on Reagan administration's economic policies, televised campaign debate Oct 5, 1988	If you let me write $200 billion worth of hot checks every year, I could give you an illusion of prosperity, too.
a Senate staffer remarks on the resounding rejection of a deal to reduce the federal deficit quoted in *Newsweek* Oct 15, 1990	We pulled a rabbit out of the hat and it mooned us.

Education

The people may be made to follow a path of action, but they may not be made to understand it.

Confucius
The Analects
ca. 480 B.C.

Liberty cannot be preserved without general knowledge among the people.

John Adams
"Dissertation on the Canon and the Feudal Law"
Aug, 1765

It is an axiom in my mind that our liberty can never be safe but in the hands of the people themselves, and that, too, of the people with a certain degree of instruction.

Thomas Jefferson
letter to George Washington
Jan 4, 1786

Educate and inform the whole mass of people. Enable them to see that it is to their interest to preserve peace and order. . . . They are the only sure reliance for the preservation of our liberty.

Thomas Jefferson
letter to James Madison
Dec 20, 1787

The project of a national education ought uniformly to be discouraged, on account of its obvious alliance with national government. This is an alliance of a more formidable nature than the old and much contested alliance of church and state.

William Godwin
An Enquiry Concerning Political Justice
1793

Enlighten the people generally, and tyranny and oppressions of body and mind will vanish like the evil spirits at the dawn of day.

Thomas Jefferson
letter to Pierre S. du Pont de Nemours
Apr 24, 1816

If a nation expects to be ignorant and free, in a state of civilization, it expects what never was and never will be.

Thomas Jefferson
letter to Col. Charles Yancey
Jan 6, 1816

Let us by all wise and constitutional measures promote intelligence among the people as the best means of preserving our liberties.

James Monroe
first inaugural address
Mar 4, 1817

I know no safe depository of the ultimate powers of the society but the people themselves; and if we think them not enlightened enough to exercise their control with a wholesome discretion, the remedy is not to take it from them, but to inform their discretion by education. This is the true corrective of abuses of constitutional power.

Thomas Jefferson
letter to William Charles Jarvis
Sep 28, 1820

Learned Institutions ought to be favorite objects with every free people. They throw that light over the public mind which is the best security against crafty & dangerous encroachments on the public liberty.

James Madison
letter to W.T. Barry
Aug 4, 1822

What spectacle can be more edifying or more seasonable, than that of Liberty & Learning, each leaning on the other for their mutual & surest support?

James Madison
letter to W.T. Barry
Aug 4, 1822

James Madison letter to W.T. Barry Aug 4, 1822	A popular government without popular information or the means of acquiring it is but a prologue to a farce or a tragedy or perhaps both.
Henry Brougham **Baron Brougham** attributed	Education makes a people easy to lead, but difficult to drive; easy to govern, but impossible to enslave.
Alexis, Comte de **Tocqueville** *Democracy in America* 1839	It is obvious that in democratic societies it is in the interest of the individual as well as that of the state that the education of the greatest number should be in scientific, commercial, and industrial subjects rather than literary ones. *Il est évident que, dans les sociétés démocratiques, l'intérêt des individus, aussi bien que la sûreté de l'Etat, exigent que l'éducation du plus grand nombre soit scientifique, commerciale et industrielle plutôt que litteraire.*
Frederick Douglass "Bibles for the Slaves" Jun, 1847	Give a hungry man a stone and tell him what beautiful houses are made of it; give ice to a freezing man and tell him of its good properties in hot weather; throw a drowning man a dollar, as a mark of your good will; but do not mock the bondman in his misery by giving him a Bible when he cannot read it.
Horace Mann *Twelfth Annual Report to* *the Massachusetts State* *Board of Education* 1848	Education, then, beyond all other devices of human origin, is the great equalizer of the conditions of men,—the balance-wheel of the social machinery.
Robert Lowe speech in the House of Commons on grant of franchise to non-proper- tied men Jul 15, 1867	I believe it will be absolutely necessary that you should prevail on our future masters to learn their letters.
Benjamin Disraeli speech in the House of Commons Jun 15, 1874	Upon the education of the people of this country the fate of this country depends.
James A. Garfield *Maxims* 1880	Liberty can be safe only when Suffrage is illuminated by Education.
Frederick Douglass speech at the Colored High School Commence- ment, Baltimore, Maryland Jun 22, 1894	A little learning, indeed, may be a dangerous thing, but the want of learning is a calamity to any people.
William McKinley speech in Pittsburgh, Pennsylvania Nov 3, 1897	The free man cannot be long an ignorant man.
John Dewey "Democracy in Education" *The Elementary School* *Teacher* Dec, 1903	We naturally associate democracy, to be sure, with freedom of action, but freedom of action without freed capacity of thought behind it is only chaos.

The highest result of education is tolerance.

Hellen Keller
Optimism
1903

No amount of charters, direct primaries, or short ballots will make a democracy out of an illiterate people.

Walter Lippmann
"Revolution and Culture"
A Preface to Politics
1914

Human history becomes more and more a race between education and catastrophe.

H.G. Wells
The Outline of History
1920

By educating the young generation along the right lines, the People's State will have to see to it that a generation of mankind is formed which will be adequate to this supreme combat that will decide the destinies of the world.

Adolf Hitler
Mein Kampf
1924

Democracy has arrived at a gallop in England and I feel all the time that it is a race for life; can we educate them before the crash comes?

Stanley Baldwin
letter to Edward Wood
1928

Knowledge—that is, education in its true sense—is our best protection against unreasoning prejudice and panic-making fear, whether engendered by special interest, illiberal minorities, or panic-stricken leaders.

Franklin D. Roosevelt
speech in Boston,
Massachusetts
Oct 31, 1932

A democratic form of government, a democratic way of life, presupposes free public education over a long period; it presupposes also an education for personal responsibility that too often is neglected.

Eleanor Roosevelt
"Let Us Have Faith in Democracy"
Land Policy Review, Department of Agriculture
Jan, 1942

If we value the pursuit of knowledge, we must be free to follow wherever that search may lead us. The free mind is no barking dog, to be tethered on a ten-foot chain.

Adlai E. Stevenson Jr.
speech at the Univ. of Wisconsin, Madison
Oct 8, 1952

In history it is always those with little learning who overthrow those with much learning. . . . When young people grasp a truth they are invincible and old people cannot compete with them.

Mao Tse-tung
address to the Chengtu conference
Mar 22, 1958

Liberty without learning is always in peril, and learning without liberty is always in vain.

John F. Kennedy
speech at Vanderbilt Univ., Nashville, Tennessee
May 18, 1963

Leadership and learning are indispensable to each other.

John F. Kennedy
speech prepared for delivery in Dallas the day of his assassination
Nov 22, 1963

Poverty has many roots, but the tap root is ignorance.

Lyndon Baines Johnson
message to Congress
Jan 12, 1965

Elections and Voting

Thomas Paine
Dissertation on First Principles of Government
1795

The right of voting for representatives is the primary right by which other rights are protected. To take away this right is to reduce a man to slavery, for slavery consists in being subject to the will of another, and he that has not a vote in the election of representatives is in this case.

Lord Macaulay
letter to an unnamed correspondent
Aug 3, 1832

To request an honest man to vote according to his conscience is superfluous. To request him to vote against his conscience is an insult. The practice of canvassing is quite reasonable under a system in which men are sent to Parliament to serve themselves. It is the height of absurdity under a system in which men are sent to Parliament to serve the public.

Benjamin Disraeli
Tancred
1847

A majority is always the best repartee.

Henry David Thoreau
Civil Disobedience
1849

All voting is a sort of gaming, like chequers of backgammon, with a slight moral tinge to it.

Abraham Lincoln
speech
May 19, 1856

The ballot is stronger than the bullet.

William Porcher Miles
speech in the House of Representatives
Mar 31, 1858

"Vote early and vote often," the advice openly displayed on the election banners in one of our northern cities.

Abraham Lincoln
speech to his supporters following his re-election
Nov 10, 1864

We cannot have free government without elections; and if the rebellion could force us to forego or postpone a national election, it might fairly claim to have already conquered and ruined us.

George Eliot
(Mary Ann Evans)
Felix Holt, the Radical
1866

An election is coming. Universal peace is declared, and the foxes have a sincere interest in prolonging the lives of the poultry.

Elizabeth Cady Stanton
letter to Thomas Wentworth Higginson
Jan 13, 1868

Our "pathway" is straight to the ballot box, with no variableness nor shadow of turning. . . . We demand in the Reconstruction suffrage for all the citizens of the Republic. I would not talk of Negroes or women, but of citizens.

Walt Whitman
"Democratic Vistas"
1871

I know nothing grander, better exercise, better digestion, more positive proof of the past, the triumphant result of faith in human kind, than a well-contested American national election.

Benjamin Harrison
second annual address to Congress
Dec 1, 1890

If any intelligent and loyal company of American citizens were required to catalogue the essential human conditions of national life, I do not doubt that with absolute unanimity they would begin with "free and honest elections."

Vote, n. The instrument and symbol of a freeman's power to make a fool of himself and a wreck of his country.

Ambrose Bierce
The Devil's Dictionary
1906

A rayformer thinks he was ilicted because he was a rayformer, whin th' thruth iv th' matther is he was ilicted because no wan knew him.

Finley Peter Dunne
Observations by Mr. Dooley
1906

We'd all like t'vote fer th'best man, but he's never a candidate.

"Kin" Hubbard
The Best of Kin Hubbard
1984

Inside the polling booth every American man and woman stands as the equal of every other American man and woman. There they have no superiors. There they have no masters save their own minds and consciences.

Franklin D. Roosevelt
speech in Worcester, Massachusetts
Oct 21, 1936

Elections are won by men and women chiefly because most people vote against somebody, rather than for somebody.

Franklin P. Adams
Nods and Becks
1944

I could not consent to the introduction into our national life of a device so alien to all our traditions as the referendum, which has only too often been the instrument of Nazism and Fascism.

Clement Attlee
1st Earl Attlee
letter to Winston Churchill
May 21, 1945

Voting is merely a handy device; it is not to be identified with democracy, which is a mental and moral relation of man to man.

George Douglas Cole
Essays in Social Theory
1950

Vote for the man who promises least; he'll be the least disappointing.

Bernard Baruch
quoted by Meyer Berger
Meyer Berger's New York
1960

A whore's vote is just as good as a debutante's.

Sam Rayburn
quoted
D Magazine
Jun, 1979

The margin is narrow, but the responsibility is clear.

John F. Kennedy
press conference following a close congressional election
Nov 11, 1963

People only leave (Washington) by way of the box—ballot or coffin.

Claiborne Pell
Vogue
Aug 1, 1963

The vote is the most powerful instrument ever devised by man for breaking down injustice and destroying the terrible walls which imprison men because they are different from other men.

Lyndon Baines Johnson
speech on signing the Voting Rights Bill
Aug 6, 1965

The first step toward liberation for any group is to use the power in hand. . . . And the power in hand is the vote.

Helen Gahagan Douglas
quoted by Lee Israel
Ms.
Oct, 1973

Morris K. Udall anecdote about politician used to console campaign workers on defeat in primary *Chicago Sun–Times* Jul 14, 1976	The voters are the people who have spoken—the bastards.
George F. Will on conservatives *Newsweek* Mar 8, 1976	Voters don't decide issues, they decide who will decide issues.
Theodore M. Hesburgh *Reader's Digest* Oct, 1984	Voting is a civic sacrament.
James Reston *The New York Times* Oct 10, 1984	An election is a bet on the future, not a popularity test of the past.
William E. Simon quoted *A Guide to the 99th Congress* 1985	Bad politicians are sent to Washington by good people who don't vote.
Michael Dukakis acceptance speech as Democratic nominee for president Jul 21, 1988	This election is not about ideology; it's about competence.

Environment

Thomas Jefferson letter to James Madison Sep 6, 1789	The earth belongs always to the living generation: they may manage it, then and what proceeds from it, as they please, during their usufruct.
Theodore Roosevelt seventh annual message to Congress Dec 3, 1907	To waste, to destroy, our natural resources, to skin and exhaust the land instead of using it so as to increase its usefulness, will result in undermining in the days of our children the very prosperity which we ought by right to hand down to them amplified and developed.
Theodore Roosevelt speech to Colorado Live Stock Association Aug 29, 1910	The nation behaves well if it treats the natural resources as assets which it must turn over to the next generation increased, and not impaired, in value.
Theodore Roosevelt *The Outlook* Aug 27, 1910	This policy (conservation) rests upon the fundamental law that neither man nor nation can prosper unless, in dealing with the present, thought is steadily taken for the future.
Joseph G. Cannon attributed by Blair Bolles *Tyrant from Illinois* 1951	Not one cent for scenery.

The greatest domestic problem facing our country is saving our soil and water. Our soil belongs also to unborn generations.

Sam Rayburn
quoted by Valton J. Young
The Speaker's Agent
1956

It is our task in our time and in our generation to hand down undiminished to those who come after us, as was handed down to us by those who went before, the natural wealth and beauty which is ours.

John F. Kennedy
speech dedicating the National Wildlife Federation Building
Mar 3, 1961

Once you've seen one redwood, you've seen them all.

Ronald Reagan
The New York Times Magazine
Jul 4, 1976

For this generation, ours, life is nuclear survival, liberty is human rights, the pursuit of happiness is a planet whose resources are devoted to the physical and spiritual nourishment of its inhabitants.

Jimmy Carter
farewell address
Jan 14, 1981

Equality

Democracy arises out of the notion that those who are equal in any respect are equal in all respects; because men are equally free, they claim to be absolutely equal.

Aristotle
Politics
343 B.C.

For what people have always sought is equality before the law. For rights that were not open to all alike would be no rights.
Ius enim semper est quaesitum aequabile; neque enim aliter esset ius.

Marcus Tullius Cicero
De Officiis
44 B.C.

The poorest he that is in England hath a life to live as the greatest he.

Thomas Rainborowe
at the army debates at Putney, quoted by Thomas Love Peacock
Life of Rainborowe
Oct 29, 1647

It is better that some should be unhappy than that none should be happy, which would be the case in a general state of equality.

Samuel Johnson
quoted by James Boswell
Life of Samuel Johnson
Apr 7, 1776

The foundation on which all our constitutions are built is the natural equality of man.

Thomas Jefferson
letter to George Washington
Apr 16, 1784

There can be no truer principle than this—that every individual of the community at large has an equal right to the protection of government.

Alexander Hamilton
speech to the Constitutional Convention
Jun 29, 1787

Equal laws protecting equal rights . . . the best guarantee of loyalty & love of country.

James Madison
letter to Jacob De La Motta
Aug, 1820

3rd Viscount Palmerston
speech in the House of Commons on Catholic emancipation
Mar 18, 1829

Under a pure despotism, a people may be contented, because all are slaves alike; but those who, under a free government, are refused equal participation, must be discontented.

Andrew Jackson
veto message
Jul 10, 1832

It is to be regretted that the rich and powerful all too often bend the acts of government to their selfish purpose. . . . In the full enjoyment of the gifts of Heaven and the fruits of superior industry, economy, and virtue, every man is equally entitled to protection by law.

Alexis, Comte de Tocqueville
speech in the Constituent Assembly
Sep 12, 1848

Democracy and socialism have nothing in common but one word: equality. But notice the difference: while democracy seeks equality in liberty, socialism seeks equality in restraint and servitude.

Elizabeth Cady Stanton
First Women's Rights Convention, Seneca, New York
Declaration of Sentiments
Jul 19-20, 1848

We hold these truths to be self-evident, that all men and women are created equal.

Frederick Douglass
speech in Boston, Massachusetts
Jun 8, 1849

It's a poor rule that won't work both ways.

Abraham Lincoln
speech in Bloomington, Illinois
May 19, 1856

Be not deceived. Revolutions do not go backward. The founder of the Democratic party declared that all men were created equal.

Abraham Lincoln
speech in Springfield, Illinois
Jun 27, 1857

I think the authors of that notable instrument (the Declaration of Independence) intended to include all men, but they did not intend to declare all men equal in all respects. They did not mean to say all were equal in color, size, intellect, moral developments, or social capacity. They defined with tolerable distinctness in what respects they did consider all men equal—equal with "certain inalienable rights, among which are life, liberty, and the pursuit of happiness." This they said, and this they meant.

Abraham Lincoln
speech in Chicago, Illinois
Jul 10, 1858

Let us discard all this quibbling about this man or the other man, this race or that race and the other race being inferior and therefore they must be placed in an inferior position—discarding our standard that we have left us! Let us discard all these things and unite as one people throughout this land until we shall once more stand up declaring that all men are created equal.

Susan B. Anthony
The Revolution
Mar 18, 1869

Join the union, girls, and together say Equal Pay for Equal Work.

Michael Bakunin
Anarchist Declaration
1870

We wish, in a word, equality — equality in fact as corollary, or, rather, as primordial condition of liberty. From each according to his faculties, to each according to his needs; that is what we wish sincerely and energetically.

Choose equality.

Matthew Arnold
"Equality"
Mixed Essays
1879

Equality—the informing soul of Freedom!

James A. Garfield
Maxims
1880

The yearning after equality is the offspring of covetousness, and there is no possible plan for satisfying that yearning which can do aught else than rob A to give to B; consequently all such plans nourish some of the meanest vices of human nature, waste capital, and overthrow civilization.

William Graham Sumner
conclusion
What Social Classes Owe to Each Other
1883

Emperors, kings, artisans, peasants, big people, little people—at the bottom we are all alike and all the same; all just alike on the inside, and when our clothes are off, nobody can tell which of us is which.

Mark Twain
"Does the Race of Man Love a Lord?"
North American Review
Apr, 1902

Our aim is to recognize what Lincoln pointed out: The fact that there are some respects in which men are obviously not equal: but also insist that there should be an equality of self-respect and of mutual respect, an equality of rights before the law, and at least an approximate equality in the conditions under which each man obtains the chance to show the stuff that is in him when compared to his fellows.

Theodore Roosevelt
seventh annual message to Congress
Dec 3, 1907

Liberty without equality is a name of noble sound and squalid result.

Leonard Hobhouse
Liberalism
1911

Couldn't we even argue that it is because men are unequal that they have that much more need to be brothers?

Charles Du Bos
Journal
Feb 27, 1918

All animals are equal/ But some animals are more equal than others.

George Orwell
Animal Farm
1946

It is a wise man who said that there is no greater inequality than the equal treatment of unequals.

Felix Frankfurter
dissenting opinion
Dennis v. United States
1949

We clamor for equality chiefly in matters in which we ourselves cannot hope to obtain excellence.

Eric Hoffer
The Passionate State of Mind
1954

Legislation to apply the principle of equal pay for equal work without discrimination because of sex is a matter of simple justice.

Dwight D. Eisenhower
State of the Union message
Jan 5, 1956

There is always inequity in life. Some men are killed in war and some men are wounded, and some men are stationed in the Antarctic and some are stationed in San Francisco. It's very hard in military or personal life to assure complete equality. Life is unfair.

John F. Kennedy
letter to a reservist on active duty
Mar 21, 1962

John F. Kennedy speech at San Diego State College, San Diego, California Jun 6, 1963	All of us do not have equal talent, but all of us should have an equal opportunity to develop our talents.
Lyndon Baines **Johnson** speech at Wayne State Univ., Detroit, Michigan Jan 6, 1963	A government conceived and dedicated to the purpose that all men are born free and equal cannot pervert its mission by rephrasing the purpose to suggest that men shall be free today—but shall be equal a little later.
William Faulkner "On Fear: Deep South in Labor: Mississippi" *Essays, Speeches &* *Public Letters* 1965	To live anywhere in the world today and be against equality because of race or color, is like living in Alaska and being against snow.
Lewis F. Powell Jr. majority opinion *Regents of the University* *of California* v. *Bakke* Jun 28, 1978	The guarantee of equal protection cannot mean one thing when applied to one individual and something else when applied to a person of another color. If both are not accorded the same protection, then it is not equal.

Ethics in Politics

Bible *1 Samuel* ca. 800 B.C.	Righteousness exalteth a nation.
Aristotle *Nicomachean Ethics* ca. 325 B.C.	It is not always the same thing to be a good man and a good citizen.
Sallust *Jugurthine War* ca. 41 B.C.	A good man would prefer to be defeated than to defeat injustice by evil means. *Sed bono vinci satius est quam malo more iniuriam vincere.*
Juvenal *Satires* ca. 115	But who is to guard the guards themselves? *Sed quis custodiet ipsos Custodes?*
Niccolò Machiavelli *Il Principe* 1532	The prince must not mind incurring the scandal of those vices, without which it would be difficult to save the state, for if one considers well, it will be found that some things which seem virtues would, if followed, lead to one's ruin, and some others which appear vices result in one's greater security and wellbeing. *Et etiam non si curi di incorrere nella infamia di quelli vizii, sanza quali e' possa difficilmente saluare lo stato; perché, se si considerrà bene tutto, si troverrà qualque cosa che parrà virtù, e seguendola sarebbe la ruina sua, e qualcuna altra che parrà vizio, e seguendola ne riesce la securtà e il bene essere suo.*
Edmund Burke *Thoughts on the Cause of* *the Present Discontents* 1770	Public life is a situation of power and energy; he trespasses against his duty who sleeps over his watch, as well as he that goes over to the enemy.

The whole art of government consists in the art of being honest.

Thomas Jefferson
"Draft of Instructions to the Virginia Delegates in the Continental Congress"
Aug, 1774

Conscience has no more to do with gallantry than it has with politics.

Richard Brinsley Sheridan
The Duenna
1775

Corruption, the most infallible symptom of constitutional liberty.

Edward Gibbon
The History of the Decline and Fall of the Roman Empire
1776-88

I have the consolation of having added nothing to my private fortune during my public service, and of retiring with hands as clean as they are empty.

Thomas Jefferson
letter to Count Diodati
1807

He (Edward Livingston) is a man of splendid abilities, but utterly corrupt. He shines and stinks like rotten mackerel by moonlight.

John Randolph of Roanoke
quoted by W. Cabell Bruce
John Randolph of Roanoke, 1773-1833
1922

A marciful Providunce fashioned us holler/ O' purpose thet we might our princerples swaller.

James Russell Lowell
The Biglow Papers: First Series
1848

It is, when strictly judged, an act of public immorality to form and lead an opposition on a certain plea, to succeed, and then in office to abandon it.

William Ewart Gladstone
letter to Lord Aberdeen
Aug 5, 1852

Moral principle is a looser bond than pecuniary interest.

Abraham Lincoln
speech
Oct, 1856

Most of the great results of history are brought about by discreditable means.

Ralph Waldo Emerson
"Considerations by the Way"
The Conduct of Life
1860

I think I can say, and say with pride, that we have some legislatures that bring higher prices than any in the world.

Mark Twain (Samuel L. Clemens)
Sketches, New and Old
1875

When I want to buy up any politician I always find the anti-monopolists the most purchasable—they don't come so high.

William Vanderbilt
interview
Chicago Daily News
Oct 9, 1882

The principles of public morality are as definite as those of the morality of private life; but they are not identical.

Lord Acton
letter to Bishop Mandell Creighton
Apr 5, 1887

George Bernard Shaw *The Man of Destiny* 1897	There is nothing so bad or so good that you will not find Englishmen doing it; but you will never find an Englishman in the wrong. He does everything on principle. He fights you on patriotic principles; he robs you on business principles; he enslaves you on imperial principles.
Mark Twain "Corn Pone Opinions" *Europe and Elsewhere* 1925	You tell me whar a man gits his corn pone, en I'll tell you what his 'pinions is.
Theodore Roosevelt "The Strenuous Life" *The Strenuous Life: Essays and Addresses* 1900	No man is justified in doing evil on the ground of expediency.
Theodore Roosevelt on investigative journalists, in speech in Washington, D.C. Apr 14, 1906	The men with the muck-rakes are often indispensable to the well-being of society, but only if they know when to stop raking the muck.
Emma Goldman "The Tragedy of Women's Emancipation" *Anarchism and Other Essays* 1911	Corruption of politics has nothing to do with the morals, or the laxity of morals, of various political personalities. Its cause is altogether a material one.
Woodrow Wilson speech in Minneapolis, Minnesota Sep 18, 1912	The cure for bad politics is the same as the cure for tuberculosis. It is living in the open space.
Woodrow Wilson quoted by William B. Hale *The New Freedom* 1913	Publicity is one of the purifying elements of politics. . . . Nothing checks all the bad practices of politics as public exposure. . . . An Irishman, seen digging around the wall of a house, was asked what he was doing. He answered, "Faith, I am letting the dark out of the cellar." Now, that's exactly what we want to do.
John Morley *Recollections* 1917	In my creed, waste of public money is like the sin against the Holy Ghost.
Bertrand Russell presidential address to the Students Union, London School of Economics Oct 10, 1923	But even a politician who is honest in the highest sense may be very harmful; one may take George III as an illustration. Stupidity and unconscious bias often work more damage than venality.
Bertrand Russell presidential address to the Students Union, London School of Economics Oct 10, 1923	The conception of an "honest" politician is not altogether a simple one. The most tolerant definition is one whose political actions are not dictated by a desire to increase his own income.
H.L. Mencken *Prejudices: Fourth Series* 1924	The difference between a moral man and a man of honor is that the latter regrets a discreditable act, even when it has worked and he has not been caught.

When a fellow says it hain't the money but the principle o' the thing, it's th' money.

"Kin" Hubbard
Hoss Sense and Nonsense
1926

You cannot adopt politics as a profession and remain honest.

Louis McHenry Howe
speech
Jan 17, 1933

Shrewdness in Public Life all over the World is always honored, while honesty in Public Men is generally attributed to Dumbness and is seldom rewarded.

Will Rogers
The Autobiography of Will Rogers
1949

A lie is an abomination unto the Lord, and a very present help in trouble.

Adlai E. Stevenson Jr.
speech in Springfield,
Illinois
Jan, 1951

I cannot and will not cut my conscience to fit this year's fashions.

Lillian Hellman
letter to Committee on
Un-American Activities of
the House of
Representatives
May 19, 1952

Those who corrupt the public mind are just as evil as those who steal from the public purse.

Adlai E. Stevenson Jr.
speech in Albuquerque,
New Mexico
Sep 12, 1952

This Administration intends to be candid about its errors; for, as a wise man once said: "An error doesn't become a mistake until you refuse to correct it." We intend to accept full responsibility for our errors.

John F. Kennedy
speech in New York City,
New York
Apr 27, 1961

The basis of effective government is public confidence, and that confidence is endangered when ethical standards falter or appear to falter.

John F. Kennedy
message to Congress
Apr 27, 1961

Congress—these, for the most part, illiterate hacks whose fancy vests are spotted with gravy and whose speeches, hypocritical, unctuous and slovenly, are spotted also with the gravy of political patronage.

Mary McCarthy
On the Contrary
1961

When there is a lack of honor in government, the morals of the whole people are poisoned.

Herbert Hoover
recalled on his 90th
birthday
The New York Times
Aug 9, 1964

The citizen is influenced by principle in direct proportion to his distance from the political situation.

Milton Rakove
The Virginia Quarterly Review
Summer, 1965

Most of us are honest at all time, and all of us are honest most of the time.

Charles M. Mathias Jr.
on ethics among
congressmen and senators
Time
Mar 31, 1967

Lyndon Baines Johnson speech at a Democratic fundraising dinner Sep 30, 1967	There are plenty of recommendations on how to get out of trouble cheaply and fast. Most of them come down to this: Deny your responsibility.
Shirley Chisholm *Unbought and Unbossed* 1970	When morality comes up against profit, it is seldom that profit loses.
Lawton M. Chiles Jr. *Christian Science Monitor* Nov 4, 1975	Secrecy in government has become synonymous, in the public mind, with deception by the government.
Peter Lisagor *Time* Dec 20, 1976	Washington is a place where the truth is not necessarily the best defense. It surely runs a poor second to the statute of limitations.
William Proxmire *The New York Times* Sep 9, 1977	Sunlight remains the world's best disinfectant.
William Safire *Book Digest* Jul, 1977	I think that one of Nixon's great contributions to civil liberties was getting caught doing what the two presidents before him got away with.
Edward I. Koch *The New York Times* Oct 23, 1979	It happens that intellectual honesty is not the coin of the realm in politics.
Walter Lippmann quoted *Newsweek* May 12, 1980	Certainly he (Richard Nixon) is not of the generation that regards honesty as the best policy. However, he does regard it as a policy.
Theodore H. White *Time* Nov 19, 1984	The flood of money that gushes into politics today is a pollution of democracy.
Jerome Krutz *Wall Street Journal* Apr 10, 1984	If a person is an economic being and figures out the odds, then there is a very high incentive to cheat. That is, of course, putting aside honor, duty and patriotism.
Donald T. Regan *The New York Times* Aug 25, 1986	We do many things at the federal level that would be considered dishonest and illegal if done in the private sector.

Expressions and Phrases

Homer *Iliad* ca. 700 B.C.	There is strength in the union even of very sorry men.
Euripides *Ion* ca. 415 B.C.	Authority is never without hate.

A sword never kills anybody; it's a tool in the killer's hand.
Quemadmodum gladius neminem occidit; occidentis telum est.

Seneca (the Younger)
Letters to Lucilius
ca. 63-65

If a house be divided against itself, that house cannot stand.

Bible
Mark
ca. 70

Even on the highest throne in the world, we are still sitting on our ass.
Et au plus eslevé throne du monde, si ne sommes assis que sus nostre cul.

Michel de Montaigne
"De l'experiénce"
Essais
1580-88

I will follow the right side even to the fire, but excluding the fire if I can.
Je suivrai le bon parti jusques au feu, mais exclusivement si je puis.

Michel de Montaigne
"De l'utile et de l'honnête"
Essais
1580-88

To win without risk is to triumph without glory.
A vaincre sans péril on triomphe sans gloire.

Pierre Corneille
The Cid
1636

Many . . . have too rashly charged the troops of error, and remain as trophies unto the enemies of truth.

Sir Thomas Browne
Religio Medici
1642

If a donkey bray at you, don't bray at him.

George Herbert
Jacula Prudentum
1651

Everyone complains about his memory, but no one complains about his judgement.
Tout le monde se plaint de sa mémoire, et personne ne se plaint de son jugement.

François, Duc de La Rochefoucauld
Réflexions, ou Sentences et maximes morales
1665

Nothing is as dangerous for the state as those who would govern kingdoms with maxims found in books.
Il n'y a rien de plus dangereux pour l'Etat que ceux qui veulent gouverner les Royaumes par les maximes, qu'ils tirent de leurs livres.

Cardinal Richelieu
Political Testament part I, chap. 8, sec. 2
1687

Changing Hands without changing Measures, is as if a Drunkard in a Dropsey should change his Doctors, and not his Dyet.

1st Marquess of Halifax
Maxims of State
1700

The mob has many heads but no brains.

Thomas Fuller
Gnomologia
1732

From fanaticism to barbarism is only one step.

Denis Diderot
Essai sur le merite de la vertu
1745

The first man who, having enclosed a piece of ground, thought to himself to say, This is mine, and found people simple enough to believe him, was the true founder of civil society.

Jean Jacques Rousseau
Discourse on the Origin of Inequality Among Men
1755

Edmund Burke *Thoughts on the Cause of the Present Discontents* 1770	When bad men combine, the good must associate; else they will fall one by one, an unpitied sacrifice in a contemptible struggle.
John Adams "Argument in Defense of the Soldiers in the Boston Massacre Trials" Dec, 1770	Facts are stubborn things; and whatever may be our wishes, our inclinations, or the dictates of our passions, they cannot alter the state of facts and evidence.
Voltaire letter to M. le Riche Feb 6, 1770	The number of wise men will always be small. It is true that it has increased; but that is nothing compared with the fools, and unfortunately it is said that God is always on the side of the big battalions.
Thomas Jefferson "Draft of Instructions to the Virginia Delegates in the Continental Congress" Aug, 1774	Force cannot give right.
Edmund Burke speech, "On Conciliation with the American Colonies" Mar 22, 1775	I do not know the method of drawing up an indictment against a whole people.
Benjamin Franklin at the signing of the Declaration of Independence Jul 4, 1776	We must all hang together, or assuredly we shall all hang separately.
John Paul Jones letter to the American commissioners in France Feb 10, 1778	Whoever can surprize well must Conquer.
Edmund Burke *Reflections on the Revolution in France* 1790	Good order is the foundation of all things.
Thomas Paine *The Rights of Man* 1791	No man is prejudiced in favor of a thing knowing it to be wrong. He is attached to it on the belief of its being right.
Georges Jacques Danton speech to the Legislative Committee of General Defence Sep 2, 1792	Boldness, more boldness, and always boldness! *De l'audace, et encore de l'audace, et toujours de l'audace!*
Thomas Jefferson letter to George Washington May 16, 1792	Delay is preferable to error.
Mary Wollstonecraft *The French Revolution* 1794	Every political good carried to the extreme must be productive of evil.

The outcome of the greatest events is always determined by a trifle.

Napoleon I
letter to the foreign
secretary
Oct 7, 1797

If our house be on fire, without inquiring whether it was fired from within or without, we must try to extinguish it.

Thomas Jefferson
letter to James Lewis, Jr.
May 9, 1798

The state is the divine idea as it exists on earth. . . . We must therefore worship the state as the manifestation of the divine on earth. . . . The march of God in the world, that is what the state is.

Georg Wilhelm Friedrich Hegel
The German Constitution
1802

It's worse than a crime, it's a blunder.
C'est plus qu'un crime, c'est une faute.

Charles-Maurice de Talleyrand
attributed remark following the murder of the Duc d'Enghien by Napoleon's agents
Mar 21, 1804

This is the beginning of the end.
Voilà le commencement de la fin.

Charles-Maurice de Talleyrand
attributed remark on the announcement of Napoleon's defeat at Borodino
1812

My toast would be, may our country be always successful, but whether successful or otherwise, always right.

John Quincy Adams
letter to John Adams
Aug 1, 1816

Political truth is a libel—religious truth blasphemy.

William Hazlitt
"Commonplaces"
The Round Table
1817

Poets and philosophers are the unacknowledged legislators of the world.

Percy Bysshe Shelley
A Philosophical View of Reform
1819–20

Any plan conceived in moderation must fail when the circumstances are set in extremes.

Prince Clemens von Metternich
letter to General de Vincent
Dec 2, 1822

We uniformly applaud what is right and condemn what is wrong, when it costs us nothing but the sentiment.

William Hazlitt
"Characteristics"
The Literary Examiner
1823

I called a New World into existence to redress the balance of the Old.

George Canning
speech in the House of Commons
Dec 12, 1826

In an age that is so full of dangers for the very foundations and safeguards of social order, the only good policy is to pursue no policy.

Prince Clemens von Metternich
letter to Count d'Apponyi
Jan 27, 1826

Lord Macaulay "On Machiavelli" 1827	Nothing is so useless as a general maxim.
Andrew Jackson toast at a Jefferson Day dinner Apr 13, 1830	Our Union: It must be preserved.
William Lloyd Garrison prospectus *The Liberator* 1830	My country is the world; my countrymen are mankind.
John C. Calhoun toast in reply to President Jackson's at Jefferson Day dinner Apr 13, 1830	The Union, next to our liberty, most dear. May we all remember that it can only be preserved by respecting the rights of the States and by distributing equally the benefits and burdens of the Union.
Daniel Webster second speech on Foote's Resolution Jan 26, 1830	Liberty and Union, now and forever, one and inseparable.
Lord Macaulay review of Moore's Life of Lord Byron *Edinburgh Review* Jun, 1831	We know no spectacle so ridiculous as the British public in one of its periodical fits of morality.
Andrew Jackson veto message Jul 10, 1832	Mere precedent is a dangerous source of authority.
Georg Wilhelm Friedrich Hegel *Introduction to the Philosophy of History* 1832	Amid the pressure of great events, a general principle gives no help.
Honore Gabriel, Comte de Mirabeau "Apophthegms" *Mirabeau's Letters During His Residence in England* 1832	The body politic is like a tree; as it proceeds upwards, it stands as much in need of heaven as of earth.
Benjamin Disraeli speech at High Wycombe, England Dec 16, 1834	It is the fashion to style the present moment an extraordinary crisis.
David Crockett *Autobiography* 1834	Be always sure you are right—then go ahead.
Ralph Waldo Emerson *Journals* 1836	Sometimes a scream is better than a thesis.

One country, one constitution, one destiny.

Daniel Webster
speech
Mar 15, 1837

Nothing astonishes men so much as common sense and plain dealing.

Ralph Waldo Emerson
"Art"
Essays: First Series
1841

One must, if one can, kill one's opponent, but never rouse him by contempt and the whiplash.

Prince Clemens von Metternich
letter to Count d'Apponyi
Sep 10, 1842

The right hon. Gentleman caught the Whigs bathing, and walked away with their clothes.

Benjamin Disraeli
remarks in the House of Commons on the Tory government of Sir Robert Peel
Feb 28, 1845

I glory in conflict, that I may hereafter exult in victory.

Frederick Douglass
"Farewell Speech to the British People" in London
Mar 30, 1847

America cannot always sit as a queen in peace and repose. Prouder and stronger governments than hers have been shattered by the bolts of a just God.

Frederick Douglass
"Government and Its Subjects"
The North Star
Nov 9, 1849

An invasion of armies can be resisted, but not an idea whose time has come.
On résiste à l'invasion des armées; on ne résiste pas à l'invasion des idées.

Victor Hugo
Histoire d'un crime
1852

The assailant is often in the right; the assailed is always.

Walter Savage Landor
"John of Gaunt and Joanna of Kent"
Imaginary Conversations
1824-53

The mass of men lead lives of quiet desperation.

Henry David Thoreau
"Economy"
Walden
1854

Better to abolish serfdom from above than to wait till it begins to abolish itself from below.

Alexander II
speech in Moscow
Mar 30, 1856

He said that he felt "like the boy that stumped his toe,—'it hurt too bad to laugh, and he was too big to cry.' "

Abraham Lincoln
attributed by John T. Morse
Abraham Lincoln
1893

Abraham Lincoln speech at the Illinois Republican state convention, quoting Mark 3:25 Jun 16, 1858	"A house divided against itself cannot stand." I believe this government cannot endure, permanently half slave and half free. I do not expect the Union to be dissolved—I do not expect the house to fall—but I do expect it will cease to be divided. It will become all one thing, or all the other.
Abraham Lincoln attributed to a speech given at Clinton, Illinois Sep 2, 1858	You can fool some of the people all of the time, and all of the people some of the time, but you cannot fool all of the people all of the time.
John Bright speech in Birmingham, England Oct 29, 1858	This regard for the liberties of Europe, this care at one time for the Protestant interest, this excessive love for the balance of power, is neither more nor less than a gigantic system of outdoor relief for the aristocracy of Great Britain.
Lord John Russell speech to the electors of the City of London Apr, 1859	Among the defects of the bill, which were numerous, one provision was conspicuous by its presence and another by its absence.
Benjamin Disraeli speech Jan 24, 1860	How much easier it is to be critical than to be correct.
Abraham Lincoln speech at the Cooper Union, New York City Feb 27, 1860	Let us have faith that right makes might, and in that faith let us to the end do our duty as we understand it.
3rd Marquess of Salisbury "The Budget and the Reform Bill" *Quarterly Review* Apr, 1860	The leap which the House of Commons is taking with such philosophic calmness is a leap absolutely in the dark.
Jefferson Davis inaugural address as president of the Confederate States of America Feb 18, 1861	All we ask is to be let alone.
Abraham Lincoln letter to Horace Greeley Aug 22, 1862	I shall try to correct errors when shown to be errors, and I shall adopt new views so fast as they shall appear to be true views.
Prince Otto von Bismarck speech to the Prussian House of Delegates Sep 30, 1862	Not by speech-making and the decisions of majorities will the great questions of the day be settled—that was the great mistake of 1848 and 1849—but by iron and blood. *Nicht durch reden und Majoritätsbeschlüsse werden die grossen Fragen der Zeit entschieden—das ist der Fehler von 1848 und 1849 gewesen—sondern durch Eisen und Blut.*
Abraham Lincoln attributed by General James B. Fry in Allen Thorndyke Rice *Reminiscences of Abraham Lincoln* 1886	I could as easily bail out the Potomac River with a teaspoon as attend to all the details of the army.

It is not best to swap horses while crossing the river.

Abraham Lincoln
reply to National Union
League
Jun 9, 1864

Truth is generally the best vindication against slander.

Abraham Lincoln
letter to Secretary of War
Edwin Stanton
Jul 18, 1864

Fellow-citizens! God reigns and the government at Washington still lives.

James A. Garfield
speech in New York City
following assassination of
Abraham Lincoln
Apr 17, 1865

Assassination has never changed the history of the world.

Benjamin Disraeli
speech
May, 1865

As scarce as truth is, the supply has always been in excess of the demand.

**Josh Billings
(Henry Wheeler Shaw)**
Affurisms from Josh Billings: His Sayings
1865

England is the mother of parliaments.

John Bright
speech in Birmingham,
England
Jan 18, 1865

No doubt we are making a great experiment and taking a leap in the dark.

14th Earl of Derby
speech on the Reform Act
in the House of Lords
Aug 6, 1867

I have climbed to the top of the greasy pole.

Benjamin Disraeli
remarks on being made
prime minister
1868

Humanity is only I write large, and love for Humanity generally means zeal for MY notions as to what men should be and how they should live.

**Sir James Fitzjames
Stephen**
*Liberty, Equality,
Fraternity*
1873

I am grateful for even the sharpest criticism, as long as it sticks to the point.
Ich bin dankbar fur die schärfste Kritik, wenn sie nur sachlich bleibt.

**Prince Otto von
Bismarck**
speech to the Reichstag
Nov 30, 1874

The freethinking of one age is the common sense of the next.

Matthew Arnold
God and the Bible
1875

Force is not a remedy.

John Bright
speech in Birmingham,
England
Nov 16, 1880

Anatole France *The Crime of Sylvestre Bonnard* 1881	Those who have given themselves the most concern about the happiness of peoples have made their neighbors very miserable.
Alexander Crummell speeech to the Freedmen's Aid Society, Ocean Grove, New Jersey Aug 15, 1883	Error moves with quick feet . . . and truth must never be lagging behind.
Karl Marx *Das Kapital* 1867-83	If money, according to Augier, "comes into the world with a congenital bloodstain on one cheek," capital comes dripping from head to foot, from every pore, with blood and dirt.
William Tecumseh Sherman message to the Republican National Convention Jun 5, 1884	I will not accept if nominated and will not serve if elected.
Edward Stuyvesant Bragg speech seconding the Democratic nomination of Grover Cleveland for president Jul 9, 1884	They love him most for the enemies he has made.
Oscar Wilde *The Picture of Dorian Gray* 1891	A man cannot be too careful in the choice of his enemies.
Oscar Wilde *Lady Windermere's Fan* 1892	What is a cynic? A man who knows the price of everything, and the value of nothing.
Oscar Wilde *Lady Windermere's Fan* 1892	Experience is the name everyone gives to their mistakes.
Henry Demarest Lloyd *Wealth Against Commonwealth* 1894	Nature is rich; but everywhere man, the heir of nature, is poor.
William Jennings Bryan "Cross of Gold" speech at the Democratic National Convention, Chicago, Illinois Jul 8, 1896	The humblest citizen of all the land, when clad in the armor of a righteous cause, is stronger than all the hosts of error.
Theodore Roosevelt *Thomas Hart Benton* 1897	After the war, and until the day of his death, his (Wendell Phillips) position on almost every public question was either mischievous or ridiculous, and usually both.
Clifford K. Berryman cartoon caption *The Washington Post* Apr 3, 1898	Stout hearts, my laddies! If the row comes, REMEMBER THE MAINE, and show the world how American sailors can fight.

Half-heartedness never won a battle.

William McKinley
speech in New York City
Jan 27, 1898

Life'd not be worth livin' if we didn't keep our inimies.

Finley Peter Dunne
*Mr. Dooley in Peace and
in War*
1898

Among men, Hinnissy, wet eye manes dhry heart.

Finley Peter Dunne
"Casual Observations"
Mr. Dooley's Opinions
1900

Herein lies the tragedy of the age: not that men are poor—all men know something of poverty; not that men are wicked—who is good? Not that men are ignorant—what is truth? Nay, but that men know so little of men.

W.E.B. Du Bois
The Souls of Black Folk
1903

The foes from whom we pray to be delivered are our own passions, appetites, and follies; and against these there is always need that we should war.

Theodore Roosevelt
proclamation
Nov 2, 1905

Compromise, n. Such an adjustment of conflicting interests as gives each adversary the satisfaction of thinking he has got what he ought not to have, and is deprived of nothing except what was unjustly his due.

Ambrose Bierce
The Devil's Dictionary
1906

Abuse a man unjustly, and you will make friends for him.

Edgar Watson Howe
Country Town Sayings
1911

There is nothing I love as much as a good fight.

Franklin D. Roosevelt
interview
The New York Times
Jan 22, 1911

The motto should not be: Forgive one another; rather, Understand one another.

Emma Goldman
"The Tragedy of Women's Emancipation"
Anarchism and Other Essays
1911

The Army will hear nothing of politics from me, and in return I expect to hear nothing of politics from the Army.

Herbert Asquith
speech at Ladybank,
England
Apr 4, 1914

The lamps are going out all over Europe, we shall not see them lit again in our lifetime.

**Edward Grey
1st Viscount Grey of Fallodon**
remark on the outbreak of
World War I
Twenty-Five Years
Aug 3, 1914

To die for an idea is to place a pretty high price upon conjectures.

Anatole France
The Revolt of the Angels
1914

George Bernard Shaw
The Rejected Statement
1916

Assassination is the extreme form of censorship.

William Allen White
referring to Progressive
party in 1916, after Theodore Roosevelt declined
to run
1916

All dressed up, with nowhere to go.

Vladimir Ilyich Lenin
Letter from Afar
1917

Capitalists are no more capable of self-sacrifice than a man is capable of lifting himself by his bootstraps.

David Lloyd George
speech at
Wolverhampton, England
Nov 24, 1918

What is our task? To make Britain a fit country for heroes to live in.

Edgar Watson Howe
Ventures in Common Sense
1919

Instead of loving your enemy, treat your friend a little better.

Mohandas K. Gandhi
Satyagraha Leaflet No. 13
May 3, 1919

Victory attained by violence is tantamount to a defeat, for it is momentary.

H.G. Wells
The Outline of History
1920

Our true nationality is mankind.

Warren G. Harding
speech in Boston,
Massachusetts
June, 1920

America's present need is not heroics, but healing; not nostrums, but normalcy; not revolution, but restoration.

George Bernard Shaw
Back to Methuselah
1921

You see things; and you say, "Why?" But I dream things that never were; and I say "Why not?"

Mohandas K. Gandhi
letter to the general
secretary of the
Congress party
Mar 8, 1922

A policy is a temporary creed liable to be changed, but while it holds good it has got to be pursued with apostolic zeal.

Joseph G. Cannon
quoted on his retirement
The Baltimore Sun
Mar 4, 1923

The pendulum will swing back.

Warren G. Harding
address at Arlington Na-
tional Cemetery
May 30, 1923

I wish we might have less condemnation of error and more commendation of right.

W.E.B. Du Bois
The Gift of Black Folk
1924

If there is anybody in this land who thoroughly believes that the meek shall inherit the earth, they have not often let their presence be known.

A little inaccuracy sometimes saves tons of explanation.

Hector Hugh Munro (Saki)
"The Comments of Moung Ka"
The Square Egg
1924

Rumor travels faster, but it don't say put as long as truth.

Will Rogers
"Politics Getting Ready to Jell"
The Illiterate Digest
1924

I do not choose to run.

Calvin Coolidge
public statement
Aug 2, 1927

A man always has two reasons for what he does—a good one, and the real one.

J.P. Morgan
attributed by Owen Wister
Roosevelt: The Story of a Friendship
1930

Nothing is more dangerous than an idea, when it's the only one we have.
Rien n'est plus dangereux qu'une idée quand on n'a qu'une idée.

Emile Auguste Chartier
La Lumiere
Jul 5, 1930

If you can't lick 'em, jine 'em.

James E. Watson
attributed, in article, "Senator James E. Watson"
The Atlantic Monthly
Feb, 1932

I pledge you, I pledge myself, to a new deal for the American people.

Franklin D. Roosevelt
acceptance speech as Democratic nominee for president
Jul 2, 1932

People don't eat in the long run—they eat every day.

Harry L. Hopkins
attributed by Robert E. Sherwood
Roosevelt and Hopkins: An Intimate History
1933

The only thing we have to fear is fear itself—nameless, unreasoning, unjustified terror which paralyzes needed efforts to convert retreat into advance.

Franklin D. Roosevelt
first inaugural address
Mar 4, 1933

(Hoover was the greatest engineer in the world since) he had drained, ditched, and damned the United States in three years.

Anonymous
attributed to a Kansas farmer by Roy Victor Peel
The 1932 Campaign
1935

We have earned the hatred of entrenched greed.

Franklin D. Roosevelt
message to Congress
Jan 3, 1936

Georges Bernanos *The Diary of a Country* *Priest* 1936	A poor man with nothing in his belly needs hope, illusion, more than bread.
Heywood Broun "'Jam-Tomorrow' Progressives" *New Republic* Dec 15, 1937	A technical objection is the first refuge of a scoundrel.
Franklin D. Roosevelt radio address Oct 26, 1939	Repetition does not transform a lie into a truth.
Sir Winston S. **Churchill** BBC radio broadcast Oct 1, 1939	I cannot forecast to you the action of Russia. It is a riddle wrapped in a mystery inside an enigma; but perhaps there is a key. That key is Russian national interest.
Franklin D. Roosevelt Pan American Day address Apr 15, 1939	Men are not prisoners of fate, but only prisoners of their own minds.
Franklin D. Roosevelt quoted *Kansas City Times* Jan 14, 1977	If you treat people right they will treat you right—90 percent of the time.
Franklin D. Roosevelt quoted *Kansas City Star* Jun 5, 1977	When you get to the end of your rope, tie a knot and hang on.
Franklin D. Roosevelt speech in Dayton, Ohio Oct 12, 1940	The core of our defense is the faith we have in the institutions we defend.
Franklin D. Roosevelt fireside chat Dec 29, 1940	We must be the great arsenal of democracy.
Sir Winston S. **Churchill** speech in the House of Commons May 13, 1940	I have nothing to offer but blood, toil, tears and sweat.
Sir Winston S. **Churchill** speech in the House of Commons Jul 14, 1940	We shall show mercy, but we shall not ask for it.
Sir Winston S. **Churchill** speech in the House of Commons Jun 18, 1940	Let us . . . brace ourselves to our duties, and so bear ourselves that if the British Empire and its Commonwealth last for a thousand years, men will still say: "This was their finest hour."

Eternal truths will be neither true nor eternal unless they have fresh meaning for every new social situation.

Franklin D. Roosevelt
speech at the Univ. of Pennsylvania
Sep 20, 1940

We shall not fail or falter; we shall not weaken or tire. . . . Give us the tools and we will finish the job.

Sir Winston S. Churchill
BBC radio broadcast
Feb 9, 1941

When I warned them (the French government) that Britain would fight on alone whatever they did, their Generals told their Prime Minister and his divided Cabinet: "In three weeks England will have her neck wrung like a chicken." Some chicken! Some neck!

Sir Winston S. Churchill
speech to the Canadian parliament
Dec 30, 1941

Never give in, never give in, never, never, never, never,—in nothing, great or small, large or petty—never give in except to convictions of honor and good sense.

Sir Winston S. Churchill
address at Harrow School
Oct 29, 1941

This is one of those cases in which the imagination is baffled by the facts.

Sir Winston S. Churchill
remark in the House of Commons following the defection of Rudolf Hess
May 13, 1941

This is not the end. It is not even the beginning of the end. But it is, perhaps, the end of the beginning.

Sir Winston S. Churchill
speech in London following Montgomery's victory in North Africa
Nov 10, 1942

As always, victory finds a hundred fathers but defeat is an orphan.

Count Galeazzo Ciano
The Ciano Diaries, 1939-1943
Sep 9, 1942

I always avoid prophesying beforehand, because it is a much better policy to prophesy after the event has already taken place.

Sir Winston S. Churchill
press conference in Cairo
Feb 1, 1943

If this is a blessing, it is certainly very well disguised.

Sir Winston S. Churchill
remark to his wife following defeat in 1945 election, quoted
Memoirs of Richard Nixon
Jun 4, 1945

Every segment of our population, and every individual, has a right to expect from his government a Fair Deal.

Harry S Truman
speech to Congress
Sep 6, 1945

Any man's coward who won't die for what he believes.

Chester Bomar Himes
If He Hollers Let Him Go
1945

Douglas MacArthur on the signing of the Japanese surrender in Tokyo Bay Sep 2, 1945	These proceedings are closed.
Mao Tse-tung "On Coalition Government" Apr 24, 1945	The people, and the people alone, are the motive force in the making of world history.
Franklin D. Roosevelt message for Jefferson Day Apr 13, 1945	The only limit to our realization of tomorrow will be our doubts of today.
Mao Tse-tung "Talk with the American Correspondent Anna Louise Strong" Aug, 1946	All reactionaries are paper tigers.
Bernard Baruch speech in Columbia, South Carolina Apr 16, 1947	Let us not be deceived—we are today in the midst of a cold war.
Mohandas K. Gandhi *Non-Violence in Peace and War* 1948	Non-violence is not a garment to be put on and off at will. Its seat is in the heart, and it must be an inseparable part of our very being.
Harry S Truman quoted *Time* Jun 9, 1975	I never did give anybody hell. I just told the truth, and they thought it was hell.
Bertrand Russell "An Outline of Intellectual Rubbish" *Unpopular Essays* 1950	Neither a man nor a crowd nor a nation can be trusted to act humanely or to think sanely under the influence of a great fear.
Sir Winston S. Churchill *The Second World War* 1950	If Hitler invaded hell I would make at least a favorable reference to the devil in the House of Commons.
Eric Hoffer *The True Believer* 1951	A grievance is most poignant when almost redressed.
Douglas MacArthur address to Congress Apr 19, 1951	The world has turned over many times since I took the oath on the plain at West Point, and the hopes and dreams have long since vanished; but I still remember the refrain of one of the most popular barracks ballads of that day which proclaimed most proudly that old soldiers never die; they just fade away. And like the old soldier in that ballad, I now close my military career and just fade away, an old soldier who tried to do his duty as God gave him the sight to see that duty.

A nation without dregs and malcontents, is orderly, decent, peaceful and pleasant, but perhaps without the seed of things to come.

Eric Hoffer
The True Believer
1951

For it is often easier to fight for principles than to live up to them.

Adlai E. Stevenson Jr.
speech in New York City
Aug 27, 1952

Words calculated to catch everyone may catch no one.

Adlai E. Stevenson Jr.
speech to Democratic National Convention, Chicago, Illinois
Jul 21, 1952

Nature is neutral. Man has wrested from nature the power to make the world a desert or to make the deserts bloom. There is no evil in the atom; only in men's souls.

Adlai E. Stevenson Jr.
speech in Hartford, Connecticut
Sep 18, 1952

The general has dedicated himself so many times, he must feel like the cornerstone of a public building.

Adlai E. Stevenson Jr.
on Dwight D. Eisenhower
The New York Times
Nov, 1952

Let's talk sense to the American people. Let's tell them the truth, that there are no gains without pains.

Adlai E. Stevenson Jr.
acceptance speech as Democratic nominee for president
Jul 26, 1952

No people on earth can be held, as a people, to be an enemy, for all humanity shares the common hunger for peace and fellowship and justice.

Dwight D. Eisenhower
address to the American Society of Newspaper Editors
Apr 16, 1953

For myself I am an optimist—it does not seem to be much use being anything else.

Sir Winston S. Churchill
speech at the Lord Mayor's banquet, London
Nov 9, 1954

A fanatic is one who can't change his mind and won't change the subject.

Sir Winston S. Churchill
quoted
The New York Times
Jul 5, 1954

You have a row of dominoes set up. You knock over the first one, and what will happen to the last one is a certainty that it will go over very quickly.

Dwight D. Eisenhower
on the strategic importance of Indochina, at a press conference
Apr 7, 1954

This organization (the United Nations) is created to prevent you from going to hell. It isn't created to take you to heaven.

Henry Cabot Lodge Jr.
The New York Times
Jan 28, 1954

An editor is someone who separates the wheat from the chaff and then prints the chaff.

Adlai E. Stevenson Jr.
quoted
Texas Observer
Dec 24, 1976

Adlai E. Stevenson Jr. quoted *Human Behavior* May, 1978	Man does not live by words alone, despite the fact that sometimes he has to eat them.
Charles De Gaulle *Mémoires de guerre:* *L'Appel* 1955	France cannot be France without greatness. *La France ne peut être la France sans la grandeur.*
Dag Hammarskjold *The New York Times* Jun 27, 1955	Everything will be all right—you know when? When people, just people, stop thinking of the United Nations as a weird Picasso abstraction and see it as a drawing they made themselves.
Georges Bernanos *Why Freedom?* 1955	The first sign of corruption in a society that is still alive is that the end justifies the means.
Douglas MacArthur quoted by Courtney Whitney *MacArthur: His Rendez-* *Vous with History* 1955	There is no security on this earth; there is only opportunity.
Adlai E. Stevenson Jr. speech in Oakland, California Feb 1, 1956	Eggheads of the the world arise—I was even going to add that you have nothing to lose but your yolks.
Edwin O'Connor title of novel 1956	The Last Hurrah.
John Mason Brown *Through These Men* 1956	The more I observed Washington, the more frequently I visited it, and the more people I interviewed there, the more I understood how prophetic L'Enfant was when he laid it out as a city that goes around in circles.
Nikita S. Khrushchev on invasion of Hungary, quoted by Veljko Micunovich *Moscow Diary* Oct, 1956	What is there left for us to do? If we let things take their course the West would say we were either stupid or weak, and that's one and the same thing.
Sir Winston S. **Churchill** quoted by Hugh Thomas *The Suez Affair* 1967	I am not sure I should have dared to start; but I am sure I should not have dared to stop.
Dwight D. Eisenhower second inaugural address Jan 21, 1957	May we know unity—without conformity.
Harold Macmillan speech in Bedford, England Jul 20, 1957	Indeed let us be frank about it: most of our people have never had it so good.

Believe in life! Always human beings will live and progress to greater, broader, and fuller life.

W.E.B. Du Bois
last message to the world
1957

Support by United States rulers is rather in the nature of the support that the rope gives to a hanged man.

Nikita S. Khrushchev
interview in Egyptian
newspaper
Nov 25, 1957

What counts is not necessarily the size of the dog in the fight— it's the size of the fight in the dog.

Dwight D. Eisenhower
speech to the Republican
National Committee
Jan 31, 1958

He (Sen. Joseph McCarthy) stamped with his name a tendency, a whole cluster of tendencies in American life. The name survives. To many Americans, whatever is illiberal, anti-intellectual, repressive, reactionary, totalitarian or merely swinish will hereafter be McCarthyism. The word is imprecise, but it conveys a meaning and a powerful image.

Richard H. Rovere
"The Frivolous
Demagogue"
Esquire
Jun, 1958

If you want to get along, go along.

Sam Rayburn
quoted
Washingtonian
Nov, 1978

Son, always tell the truth. Then you'll never have to remember what you said the last time.

Sam Rayburn
quoted
Chicago Sun–Times
Jun 28, 1979

The most striking of all the impressions I have formed since I left London a month ago is of the strength of African national consciousness. . . . The wind of change is blowing through the continent. Whether we like it or not, the growth of national consciousness is a political fact.

Harold Macmillan
speech to the South
African parliament
Feb 3, 1960

We stand today on the edge of a new frontier—the frontier of the 1960s—a frontier of unknown opportunities and perils—a frontier of unfulfilled hopes and threats.

John F. Kennedy
acceptance speech for the
Democratic presidential
nomination
Jul 15,1960

The Assembly has witnessed over the last weeks how historical truth is established; once an allegation has been repeated a few times, it is no longer an allegation, it is an established fact, even if no evidence has been brought out in order to support it.

Dag Hammarskjold
on attacks by Soviet
Premier Nikita S.
Khrushchev in the U.N.
General Assembly
The New York Times
Oct 4, 1960

In battling evil, excess is good; for he who is moderate in announcing the truth is presenting half-truth. He conceals the other half out of fear of the people's wrath.

Kahlil Gibran
"Narcotics and Dissecting
Knives"
Thoughts and Meditations
1960

The opinions that are held with passion are always those for which no good ground exists; indeed the passion is the measure of the holder's lack of rational conviction. Opinions in politics and religion are almost always held passionately.

Bertrand Russell
introduction
Sceptical Essays
1961

John F. Kennedy inaugural address Jan 20, 1961	Let the word go forth from this time and place, to friend and foe alike, that the torch has been passed to a new generation of Americans.
John F. Kennedy inaugural address Jan 20, 1961	All this will not be finished in the first hundred days. Nor will it be finished in the first thousand days, nor in the life of this administration, nor even perhaps in our lifetime on this planet. But let us begin.
John F. Kennedy *The New York Times* Dec 24, 1961	Khrushchev reminds me of the tiger hunter who has picked a place on the wall to hang the tiger's skin long before he has caught the tiger. This tiger has other ideas.
David Brinkley on the 1960 Democratic National Convention *Newsweek* Mar 13, 1961	This is the first convention of the space age—where a candidate can promise the moon and mean it.
Learned Hand recalled on his death Aug 16, 1961	There is no surer way to misread any document than to read it literally.
John F. Kennedy inaugural address Jan 20, 1961	With a good conscience our only sure reward, with history the final judge of our deeds, let us go forth to lead the land we love, asking His blessing and His help, but knowing that here on earth God's work must truly be our own.
John F. Kennedy speech at a dinner on his 44th birthday, Washington D.C. May 27, 1961	When we got into office, the thing that surprised me most was to find that things were just as bad as we'd been saying they were.
John F. Kennedy remarks at a dinner hon- oring American Nobel Prize winners Apr 29, 1962	I think this is the most extraordinary collection of talent, of human knowledge, that has ever been gathered together at the White House, with the possible exception of when Thomas Jefferson dined alone.
Dean Rusk on the Cuban missile cirsis *Saturday Evening Post* Dec 8, 1962	We were eyeball-to-eyeball and the other fellow just blinked.
Adlai E. Stevenson Jr. to Soviet ambassador Valerian Zorin at the United Nations Oct 25, 1962	This is the first time I ever heard it said that the crime is not the burglary, but the discovery of the burglary.
John F. Kennedy quoted by William Manchester *Portrait of a President* 1962	Washington is a city of Southern efficiency and Northern charm.
Jo Grimond speech at the Liberal par- ty annual conference Sep 15, 1963	And in bygone days, commanders were taught that, when in doubt, they should march their troops towards the sound of gunfire. I intend to march my trooper towards the sound of gunfire.

I believe in the forgiveness of sin and the redemption of ignorance.

Adlai E. Stevenson Jr.
retort to a heckler asking him to state his beliefs
Time
Nov 1, 1963

All progress is precarious, and the solution of one problem brings us face to face with another problem.

Martin Luther King Jr.
Strength to Love
1963

Our problems are man-made, therefore they may be solved by man. And man can be as big as he wants. No problem of human destiny is beyond human beings.

John F. Kennedy
speech at The American Univ., Washington, D.C.
Jun 10, 1963

The price of eternal vigilance is indifference.

Marshall McLuhan
Understanding Media
1964

What is objectionable, what is dangerous about extremists is not that they are extreme, but that they are intolerant. The evil is not what they say about their cause, but what they say about their opponents.

Robert F. Kennedy
"Extremism, Left and Right"
The Pursuit of Justice
1964

I would remind you that extremism in the defense of liberty is no vice. And let me remind you also that moderation in the pursuit of justice is no virtue.

Barry Goldwater
speech accepting Republican nomination as president
Jul 16, 1964

I just want to do God's will. And he's allowed me to go up to the mountain. And I've looked over, and I've seen the Promised Land.

Martin Luther King Jr.
speech in Memphis, Tennessee
Apr 3, 1964

A great writer is, so to speak, a second government in his country. And for that reason no regime has ever loved great writers, only minor ones.

Alexander Solzhenitsyn
The First Circle
1964

There are two problems in my life. The political ones are insoluble and the economic ones are incomprehensible.

Sir Alec Douglas-Home
The New York Times
Jan 9, 1964

Where there are two PhDs in a developing country, one is head of state and the other is in exile.

Lord Samuel
The New York Times
Jul 5, 1964

The Liberals talk about a stable government, but we don't know how bad the stable is going to smell.

Thomas Douglas
campaign speech
Oct, 1965

You show me a black man who isn't an extremist and I'll show you one who needs psychiatric attention.

Malcolm X
introduction by Alex Haley
Autobiography of Malcolm X
1965

You may be sure that the Americans will commit all the stupidities they can think of, plus some that are beyond imagination.

Charles De Gaulle
Time
Dec 17, 1965

George Brown quoted *Christian Science Monitor* Aug 19, 1966	I've got nothing against men wearing striped pants and black jackets if they want to, and they can wear Anthony Eden hats to their hearts' content. It's the wearing of striped pants in the soul that I object to, and having a Homburg hat where your heart ought to be.
Adam Clayton Powell Jr. "Minimum Living— Minimum Religion" *Keep the Faith, Baby!* 1967	Mix a conviction with a man and something happens.
Abba Eban on being asked if Israel's policy was hawkish or dovish *The New York Post* Jul 8, 1967	Israel is not an aviary.
Adam Clayton Powell Jr. "The Temptations of Modernity" *Keep the Faith, Baby!* 1967	We have produced a world of contented bodies and discontented minds.
Clark M. Clifford on being asked if he was a hawk or a dove *The New York Times* Jan 2, 1968	I am not conscious of falling under any of those ornithological divisions.
Eldridge Cleaver attributed 1968	You're either part of the solution or part of the problem.
Spiro T. Agnew reported *The New York Times* Oct 20, 1969	A spirit of national masochism prevails, encouraged by an effete corps of impudent snobs who characterize themselves as intellectuals.
Gamal Abdel Nasser on refusing Western economic assistance *Réalités* Jan 20, 1969	We're a sentimental people. We like a few kind words better than millions of dollars given in a humiliating way.
Spiro T. Agnew speech in San Diego, California Sep 11, 1970	In the United States today, we have more than our share of the nattering nabobs of negativism.
Walt Kelly cartoon strip 1971	We have met the enemy and he is us.
Juan Peron *The New York Times* Jul 14, 1973	It is not that we were so good, but those who followed us were so bad that they made us seem better than we were.

The experience may have been costly, but it was also priceless.

Peter G. Peterson
on his experience in the Nixon administration
Quote
Jan 18, 1973

I think we ought to let him hang there, let him twist slowly, slowly in the wind.

John Ehrlichman
to presidential counsel John Dean, referring to FBI Director L. Patrick Gray
Mar 7, 1973

Always give your best, never get discouraged, never be petty; always remember, others may hate you. Those who hate you don't win unless you hate them. And then you destroy yourself.

Richard M. Nixon
speech to members of his administration following his resignation
Aug 9, 1974

My fellow Americans, our long national nightmare is over.

Gerald R. Ford
on succeeding Richard Nixon as president
Aug 9, 1974

We are making remarkable progress toward an agreement— and toward a nervous breakdown. It's going to be a race to see which will be achieved first.

Henry A. Kissinger
on Middle East peace negotiations
Time
Sep 8, 1975

We Americans are a peculiar people. We are for the underdog no matter how much of a dog he is.

**A.B. Chandler
("Happy")**
Reader's Digest
Nov, 1975

If this is a Great Society, I'd hate to see a bad one.

Fannie Lou Hamer
The Worker
Jul 13, 1975

Totalitarianism is bad, gangsterism is worse, but capitulationism is the worst of all.

Daniel P. Moynihan
Time
Jan 26, 1976

For God's sake, how many swan songs can a lame duck deliver?

Henry A. Kissinger
commenting on the number of his farewell ceremonies
Rolling Stone
Mar 10, 1977

There cannot be a crisis next week. My schedule is already full.

Henry A. Kissinger
Time
Jan 24, 1977

Our decision about energy will test the character of the American people and the ability of the President and the Congress to govern this Nation. This difficult effort will be the "moral equivalent of war," except that we will be uniting our efforts to build and not to destroy.

Jimmy Carter
televised address to the nation
Apr 18, 1977

Barbara Jordan commencement address, Harvard Univ. Jun 16, 1977	What the people want is very simple. They want an America as good as its promise.
Barbara Jordan interview *Senior Scholastic* Oct, 1977	When do any of us ever do enough?
Peter C. Goldmark Jr. *The New York Times* May 24, 1977	Welfare is hated by those who administer it, mistrusted by those who pay for it and held in contempt by those who receive it.
Elizabeth II Silver Jubilee address Jun 7, 1977	It is easy enough to define what the Commonwealth is not. Indeed this is quite a popular pastime.
Wade Hampton McCree Jr. *Chicago Sun–Times* Jun 20, 1978	Washington is the only town in the world where sound travels faster than light.
Groucho Marx *San Francisco Chronicle* Jan 29, 1978	Military intelligence is a contradiction in terms.
Richard M. Nixon *The Observer* Dec 3, 1978	(Watergate) was worse than a crime, it was a blunder.
Robert S. Strauss on being asked when he planned to quit as chair- man of the Democratic Party *Chicago Tribune* Feb 5, 1978	It's a little like makin' love to a gorilla. You don't quit when you're tired—you quit when the gorilla's tired.
Ronald Reagan speech to Conservative Political Action Conference Mar 17, 1978	With our eyes fixed on the future, but recognizing the realities of today . . . we will achieve our destiny to be as a shining city on a hill for all mankind to see.
Henry A. Kissinger *Wilson Library Bulletin* Mar, 1979	Each success only buys an admission ticket to a more difficult problem.
Vince Lombardi *Newsweek* Nov 19, 1979	Winning isn't everything. It is the only thing.
Eric Sevareid *Town & Country* May, 1979	The chief cause of problems is solutions.
Henry A. Kissinger *White House Years* 1979	History knows no resting places and no plateaus.

One point has already been proved. Everything that happened once can happen again.

Jacobo Timerman
*Prisoner Without a Name,
Cell Without a Number*
1981

Of course it's the same old story. Truth usually is the same old story.

Margaret Thatcher
Time
Feb 16, 1981

You cannot shake hands with a clenched fist.

Indira Gandhi
quoted
Christian Science Monitor
May 17, 1982

In crises the most daring course is often safest.

Henry A. Kissinger
Years of Upheaval
1982

Platitudes? Yes, there are platitudes. Platitudes are there because they are true.

Margaret Thatcher
London Times
Jun 1, 1984

It is human nature that rules the world, not governments and regimes.

Svetlana Alliluyeva
The New York Times
Nov 3, 1984

I cast my bread on the waters long ago. Now it's time for you to send it back to me—toasted and buttered on both sides.

Jesse Jackson
speech to African-
American voters in
New York City
Jan 30, 1984

I'm not the type to get ulcers. I give them.

Edward I. Koch
The New York Times
Jan 20, 1984

(Their) insatiable lust for power is only equaled by their incurable impotence in exercising it.

**Sir Winston S.
Churchill**
on Labour Party, quoted
by John Colville
The Fringes of Power
1985

Rarely have so many people been so wrong about so much.

Richard M. Nixon
on war in Vietnam
No More Vietnams
1985

If you don't like the president, it costs you 90 bucks to fly to Washington to picket. If you don't like the governor, it costs you 60 bucks to fly to Albany to picket. If you don't like me, 90 cents.

Edward I. Koch
The New York Times
Feb 28, 1985

I think he is an entertainer. I would prefer if he were a performer.

Carol Bellamy
on New York City Mayor
Edward Koch
The New York Times
Jan 31, 1985

There are more secrets, but there is not more secrecy.

Steven Garfinkel
The New York Times
Apr 15, 1986

Donald R. Manes statement on radio on reports he called Mayor Koch a crook Feb 3, 1986	I apologize for what was said even though I didn't say it.
Jim Hightower on instructions to his staff, speech to the Dallas Chamber of Commerce *The New York Times* Mar 9, 1986	Do something. It it doesn't work, do something else. No idea is too crazy.
George C. Marshall favorite advice, quoted by Walter Isaacson and Evan Thomas *The Wise Men* 1986	Don't fight the problem, decide it.
Margaret Thatcher interview with Barbara Walters on ABC-TV Mar 18, 1987	To wear your heart on your sleeve isn't a very good plan; you should wear it inside, where it functions best.
James A. McClure on why there were no leaks from a closed Con- gressional hearing *The New York Times* Jan 24, 1987	In that hearing, we didn't hear anything.
Jesse Jackson speech to the Democratic National Convention, At- lanta, Georgia Jul 18, 1988	Keep hope alive.
George Bush inaugural address Jan 20, 1989	We have more will than wallet; but will is what we need.
George Bush inaugural address Jan 20, 1989	America is never wholly herself unless she is engaged in high moral principle. We as a people have such a purpose today. It is to make kinder the face of the nation and gentler the face of the world.

Freedom of Speech

Confucius *The Analects* ca. 480 B.C.	When law and order prevail in the land, a man may be bold in speech and bold in action; but when the land lacks law and order, though he may take bold action, he should lay restraint on his speech.
Euripides *The Phoenician Women* 411-409 B.C.	But this is slavery, not to speak one's thought.

Reason and free inquiry are the only effectual agents against error.

Thomas Jefferson
Notes on the State of Virginia
1782

Opinions become dangerous to a state only when persecution makes it necessary for the people to communicate their ideas under the bond of secrecy.

Charles James Fox
speech in the House of Commons
May 1797

When people talk of the freedom of writing, speaking or thinking I cannot choose but laugh. No such thing ever existed. No such thing now exists; but I hope it will exist. But it must be hundreds of years after you and I shall write and speak no more.

John Adams
letter to Thomas Jefferson
Jul 15, 1818

Free Discussion is the only necessary Constitution—the only necessary Law of the Constitution.

Richard Carlile
The Republican
1823

Men are never so likely to settle a question rightly as when they discuss it freely.

Lord Macaulay
"Southey's Coloquies on Society"
1830

When a country is tolerably quiet, it is better for a Government to be hard of hearing in respect of seditious language than to be very agile in prosecuting.

Sir Robert Peel
letter to Sir James Graham
Dec, 1841

If all mankind, minus one, were of one opinion, and only one person were of the contrary opinion, mankind would be no more justified in silencing that one person, than he, if he had the power, would be justified in silencing mankind.

John Stuart Mill
On Liberty
1859

He who knows only his own side of the case, knows little of that.

John Stuart Mill
On Liberty
1859

We can never be sure that the opinion we are endeavoring to stifle is a false opinion; and if we are sure, stifling it would be an evil still.

John Stuart Mill
On Liberty
1859

The very aim and end of our institutions is just this: that we may think what we like and say what we think.

Oliver Wendell Holmes Sr.
The Professor at the Breakfast Table
1860

Was Pilate right in crucifying Christ? I reply, Pilate's paramount duty was to preserve the peace in Palestine, to form the best judgment he could as to the means required for that purpose, and to act upon it when it was formed. Therefore, if and in so far as he believed, in good faith and on reasonable grounds, that what he did was necessary for the preservation of the peace of Palestine, he was right. It was his duty to run the risk of being mistaken, notwithstanding Mr. Mill's principle as to liberty, and particularly as to liberty in the expression of opinion.

Sir James Fitzjames Stephen
Liberty, Equality, Fraternity
1873

The wisest thing to do with a fool is to encourage him to hire a hall and discourse to his fellow-citizens. Nothing chills nonsense like exposure to the air.

Woodrow Wilson
Constitutional Government
1908

William Howard Taft speech in Denver, Colorado Sep 21, 1909	Where the people rule, discussion is necessary.
Theodore Roosevelt *Kiplinger Washington Letter* Apr 23, 1918	Free speech, exercised both individually and through a free press, is a necessity in any country where people are themselves free.
Oliver Wendell Holmes Jr. *Schenck v. United States; Baer v. United States* 1919	But the character of every act depends upon the circumstances in which it is done. . . . The most stringent protection of free speech would not protect a man in falsely shouting fire in a theatre and causing a panic. It does not even protect a man from an injunction against uttering words that may have all the effect of force. . . . The question in every case is whether the words are used in such circumstances and are of such a nature as to create a clear and present danger that they will bring about the substantive evils that Congress has a right to prevent. It is a question of proximity and degree.
Oliver Wendell Holmes Jr. *Gitlow v. New York* 1925	It is said that this manifesto is more than a theory, that it was an incitement. Every idea is an incitement.
Heywood Broun "The Miracle of Debs" *New York World* Oct 23, 1926	Free speech is about as good a cause as the world has ever known. But, like the poor, it is always with us and gets shoved aside in favor of things more vital.
Heywood Broun "The Miracle of Debs" *New York World* Oct 23, 1926	Almost nobody means precisely what he says when he makes the declaration, "I'm in favor of free speech."
Emile Auguste Chartier ("Alain") *Le Citoyen contre les pouvoirs* 1926	To think is to say no.
Louis D. Brandeis concurring opinion *Whitney v. California* 1927	Fear of serious injury cannot alone justify suppression of free speech and assembly. Men feared witches and burned women. It is the function of speech to free men from the bondage of irrational fears.
Oliver Wendell Holmes Jr. *United States v. Schwimmer* 1928	If there is any principle of the constitution that more imperatively calls for attachment than any other it is the principle of free thought—not free thought for those who agree with us but freedom for the thought that we hate.
Herbert Hoover campaign speech in New York City Oct 22, 1928	Free speech does not live many hours after free industry and free commerce die.
Benjamin N. Cardozo *Palko v. Connecticut* 1937	Freedom of expression is the matrix, the indispensable condition, of nearly every other form of freedom.

Everyone is in favour of free speech. Hardly a day passes without its being extolled, but some people's idea of it is that they are free to say what they like, but if anyone says anything back, that is an outrage.

Sir Winston S. Churchill
speech in the House of Commons
Oct 13, 1943

The problem of freedom in America is that of maintaining a competition of ideas, and you do not achieve that by silencing one brand of idea.

Max Lerner
"The Muzzling of the Movies"
Actions and Passions
1949

Laws alone cannot secure freedom of expression; in order that every man present his views without penalty there must be a spirit of tolerance in the entire population.

Albert Einstein
Out of My Later Years
1950

Every man has the right to be heard; but no man has the right to strangle democracy with a single set of vocal cords.

Adlai E. Stevenson Jr.
speech in New York City
Aug 28, 1952

Don't join the book burners. Don't think you are going to conceal faults by concealing evidence that they ever existed.

Dwight D. Eisenhower
speech at Dartmouth College
Jun 14, 1953

Here in America we are descended in blood and in spirit from revolutionists and rebels—men and women who dared to dissent from accepted doctrine. As their heirs, we may never confuse honest dissent with disloyal subversion.

Dwight D. Eisenhower
speech at Columbia Univ. bicentennial dinner
May 31, 1954

Free speech is not to be regulated like diseased cattle and impure butter. The audience . . . that hissed yesterday may applaud today, even for the same performance.

William O. Douglas
dissenting opinion
Roth v. *United States*
Jun 24, 1957

In the end it is worse to suppress dissent than to run the risk of heresy.

Learned Hand
Oliver Wendell Holmes lecture, Harvard Univ.
1958

I am not so much concerned with the right of everyone to say anything he pleases as I am about our need as a self-governing people to hear everything relevant.

John F. Kennedy
speech to the National Civil Liberties Conference
Apr 16, 1959

The censor's sword pierces deeply into the heart of free expression.

Earl Warren
dissenting opinion
Times Film Corp. v. *City of Chicago*
Jan 23, 1961

Criticism of government finds sanctuary in several portions of the 1st Amendment. It is part of the right of free speech. It embraces freedom of the press.

Hugo L. Black
dissenting opinion
Feb 27, 1961

The first principle of a free society is an untrammeled flow of words in an open forum.

Adlai E. Stevenson Jr.
The New York Times
Jan 19, 1962

Mao Tse-tung speech to a Central Work Conference Jan 30, 1962	Let other people speak out. The heavens will not fall and you will not be thrown out. If you do not let others speak, then the day will surely come when you will be thrown out.
Hugo L. Black at the American Jewish Congress Apr 14, 1962	My view is, without deviation, without exception, without any ifs, buts, or whereases that freedom of speech means that you shall not do something to people either for the views they have or the views they express or the words they speak or write.
Hugo L. Black *New York Times Company* v. *Sullivan* 1964	An unconditional right to say what one pleases about public affairs is what I consider to be the minimum guarantee of the First Amendment.
Matthew Tobriner ruling that Henry Miller's Tropic of Cancer was not pornographic *Wall Street Journal* Feb 3, 1964	Man's drive for self-expression, which over the centuries has built his monuments, does not stay within set bounds; the creations which yesterday were the detested and the obscene become the classics of today.
Hubert H. Humphrey speech in Madison, Wisconsin Aug 23, 1965	The right to be heard does not automatically include the right to be taken seriously.
Thurgood Marshall unanimous opinion *Stanley* v. *Georgia* Apr 7, 1969	If the 1st Amendment means anything, it means that a state has no business telling a man, sitting alone in his own house, what books he may read or what films he may watch.
Eleanor Holmes **Norton** *The New York Post* Mar 28, 1970	The only way to make sure people you agree with can speak is to support the rights of people you don't agree with.
Harry A. Blackmun majority opinion *Roe* v. *Wade; Doe* v. *Bolton* Jan 22, 1973	By placing discretion in the hands of an official to grant or deny a license, such a statute creates a threat of censorship that by its very existence chills free speech.
Daniel P. Moynihan *Time* Jan 26, 1976	There is no nation so poor that it cannot afford free speech, but there are few elites which will put up with the bother of it.
Sir Stephen Spender *The Thirties and After* 1978	What we call the freedom of the individual is not just the luxury of one intellectual to write what he likes to write, but his being a voice which can speak for those who are silent. And if he permits his freedom of expression to be abolished, then he has abolished their freedom to find in his voice a voice for their wrongs.
William O. Douglas *The Court Years 1939-75* 1980	One who comes to the Court must come to adore, not to protest. That's the new gloss on the 1st Amendment.
Warren E. Burger majority opinion Jul 2, 1980	Free speech carries with it some freedom to listen.

(To restrict political spending) is much like allowing a speaker in a public hall to express his views while denying him the use of an amplifying system.

William H. Rehnquist
majority opinion
Jun 18, 1986

Freedom of the Press

It is the characteristic of the most stringent censorships that they give credibility to the opinions they attack.
C'est le propre des censures violentes d'accréditer les opinions qu'elles attaquent.

Voltaire
preface, "Poème sur le désastre de Lisbonne"
1758

The abuses of the press are notorious. . . . License of the press is no proof of liberty. When a people are corrupted, the press may be made an engine to complete their ruin.

John Adams
"Novanglus"
Boston Gazette
Feb 6, 1775

The freedom of the press is one of the great bulwarks of liberty, and can never be restrained but by despotic governments.

George Mason
Virginia Bill of Rights
Jun 12, 1776

The basis of our government being the opinion of the people, the very first object should be to keep that right; and were it left to me to decide whether we should have a government without newspapers, or newspapers without a government, I should not hesitate a moment to prefer the latter. But I should mean that every man should receive those papers, and be capable of reading them.

Thomas Jefferson
letter to Col. Edward Carrington
Jan 16, 1787

To the press alone, chequered as it is with abuses, the world is indebted for all the triumphs which have been gained by reason and humanity over error and oppression.

James Madison
"Report on the Resolutions" of the Virginia House of Delegates
1799

Let them say, if they want, that the sun revolves around the earth, that the melting of the ice causes the tides, and that we are charlatans: complete liberty must prevail.
Qu'on dise, si l'on veut, que le soleil tourne, que c'est la fonte des glaces qui produit le flux et le reflux, et que nous sommes des charlatans; il doit régner la plus grande liberté.

Napoleon I
letter to the Consuls of the Republic
Jun 7, 1800

I want a situation without censorship, because I do not want to be responsible for whatever they may say.
Je voudrais une organisation sans censure, car je ne veux pas être responsable de tout ce qu'ils peuvent dire.

Napoleon I
letter to M. Fouché
Jun 1, 1805

The man who never looks into a newspaper is better informed than he who reads them, inasmuch as he who knows nothing is nearer the truth than he whose mind is filled with falsehoods and errors.

Thomas Jefferson
letter to John Norvell
Jun 11, 1807

Give them a corrupt House of Lords, give them a venal House of Commons, give them a tyrannical Prince, give them a truckling court, and let me have but an unfettered Press. I will defy them to encroach a hair's breadth upon the liberties of England.

Richard Brinsley Sheridan
speech in the House of Commons
Feb 6, 1810

Thomas Jefferson letter to Col. Charles Yancey Jan 6, 1816	The functionaries of every government have propensities to command at will the liberty and property of their constituents. There is no safe deposit for these but with the people themselves; nor can they be safe with them without information. Where the press is free, and every man able to read, all is safe.
Alexis, Comte de Tocqueville *Democracy in America* 1835	In order to enjoy the inestimable benefits that the liberty of the press ensures, it is necessary to submit to the inevitable evils that it creates. *Pour recueillir les biens inestimables qu'assure la liberté de la presse, il faut savoir se soumettre aux maux inévitables qu'elle fait naître.*
Alexis, Comte de Tocqueville *Democracy in America* 1835	Sovereignty of the people and freedom of the press are each necessary to the other while censorship and universal suffrage are contradictory. *La souveraineté du peuple et la liberté de la presse sont donc deux choses entièrement corrélatives: la censure et le vote universel sont au contraire deux choses qui se contredisent.*
Thomas Carlyle *On Heros, Hero-Worship, and the Heroic in History* 1841	Burke said there were Three Estates in Parliament; but, in the Reporters' Gallery yonder, there sat a Fourth Estate, more important by far than they all.
Wendell Phillips speech Jan 28, 1852	We live under a government of men and morning newspapers.
James A. Garfield speech to the Ohio Editorial Association Jul 11, 1878	The chief danger which threatens the influence and honor of the press is the tendency of its liberty to degenerate into license.
Theodore Roosevelt speech to the New York state assembly Mar 27, 1883	We have all of us at times suffered from the liberty of the press, but we have to take the good with the bad.
Oscar Wilde "The Soul of Man Under Socialism" *Fortnightly Review* Feb, 1891	In old days men had the rack. Now they have the press.
Theodore Roosevelt letter to Henry Cabot Lodge Jun 16, 1905	The more I see of the Czar, Kaiser, and the Mikado, the better I am content with democracy, even if we have to include the American newspapers as one of its assets—liability would be a better term.
Edgar Watson Howe *Country Town Sayings* 1911	The liberty of the press is most generally approved when it takes liberties with the other fellow, and leaves us alone.

The papers conducted by Lord Rothermere and Lord Beaverbrook are not newspapers in the ordinary acceptance of the term. They are engines of propaganda, for the constantly changing policies, desires, personal wishes, personal likes and dislikes of two men. . . . What the proprietorship of these papers is aiming at is power, and power without responsibility—the prerogative of the harlot throughout the ages.

Stanley Baldwin
speech in London
Mar 18, 1931

A free press stands as one of the great interpreters between the government and the people. To allow it to be fettered is to be fettered ourselves.

George Sutherland
Grosjean v. *American Press Co.*
1935

Freedom of conscience, of education, of speech, of assembly are among the very fundamentals of democracy and all of them would be nullified should freedom of the press ever be successfully challenged.

Franklin D. Roosevelt
letter to W.N. Hardy
Sep 4, 1940

The hand that rules the press, the radio, the screen and the far-spread magazine, rules the country.

Learned Hand
memorial address for Justice Brandeis
Dec 21, 1942

I . . . will die for the freedom of the press, even for the freedom of newspapers that call me everything that is a good deal less than . . . a gentleman.

Dwight D. Eisenhower
press conference in Moscow
Aug 14, 1945

It is very difficult to have a free, fair and honest press anywhere in the world. In the first place, as a rule, papers are largely supported by advertising, and that immediately gives the advertisers a certain hold over the medium which they use.

Eleanor Roosevelt
If You Ask Me
1946

Freedom from something is not enough. It should also be freedom for something. Freedom is not safety but opportunity. Freedom ought to be a means to enable the press to serve the proper functions of communication in a free society.

Zechariah Chaffee Jr.
"The Press Under Pressure"
Nieman Reports
Apr, 1948

A politician wouldn't dream of being allowed to call a columnist the things a columnist is allowed to call a politician.

Max Lerner
"Love and Hate in Politics"
Actions and Passions
1949

Freedom of the press is not an end in itself but a means to the end of a free society.

Felix Frankfurter
The New York Times
Nov 28, 1954

Whenever the press quits abusing me I know I'm in the wrong pew. I don't mind it because when they throw bricks at me—I'm a pretty good shot myself and I usually throw 'em back at 'em.

Harry S Truman
speech in Washington, D.C.
Feb 22, 1958

A free press can of course be good or bad, but, most certainly, without freedom it will never be anything but bad. . . . Freedom is nothing else but a chance to be better, whereas enslavement is a certainty of the worse.

Albert Camus
Resistance, Rebellion, and Death
1960

Walter Lippmann speech at the International- al Press Institute Assemby, London May 27, 1965	Responsible journalism is journalism responsible in the last analysis to the editor's own conviction of what, whether interesting or only important, is in the public interest.
Walter Lippmann speech at the International- al Press Institute Assem- bly, London May 24, 1965	Without criticism and reliable and intelligent reporting, the government cannot govern.
Hugo L. Black concurring opinion, Penta- gon Papers case *New York Times Co.* v. *U.S.; U.S.* v. *The Wash- ington Post* Jun 30, 1971	Paramount among the responsibilities of a free press is the duty to prevent any part of the government from deceiving the people and sending them off to distant lands to die of foreign fevers and foreign shot and shell.
Hugo L. Black concurring opinion, Penta- gon Papers case *New York Times Co.* v. *U.S.; U.S.* v. *The Wash- ington Post* Jun 30, 1971	In revealing the workings of government that led to the Vietnam War, the newspapers nobly did precisely that which the Founders hoped and trusted they would do.
Hugo L. Black concurring opinion, Penta- gon Papers case *New York Times Co.* v. *U.S.; U.S.* v. *The Wash- ington Post* Jun 30, 1971	In my view, far from deserving condemnation for their courageous reporting, the New York Times, the Washington Post and other newspapers should be commended for serving the purpose that the Founding Fathers saw so clearly.
Nelson A. Rockefeller speech in Syracuse, New York Nov 29, 1972	I'm convinced that if reporters should ever lose the right to protect the confidentiality of their sources then serious investigative reporting will simply dry up. The kind of resourceful, probing journalism that first exposed most of the serious scandals, corruption and injustice in our nation's history would simply disappear.
Daniel P. Moynihan *University Daily Kansan* Feb 16, 1977	When a person goes to a country and finds their newspapers filled with nothing but good news, he can bet there are good men in jail.
A.J. Liebling *American Film* Jul/Aug, 1978	Freedom of the press belongs to those who own one.
I.F. Stone *Chicago Tribune* Jan 26, 1978	The First Amendment gives newspapermen a status and a mandate, an honored place in society, that cannot be matched in England, much less on the European continent. It is peculiarly American. I feel as though I survived an Ice Age and helped to keep this heritage intact.
Gen. William C. **Westmoreland** *Time* Apr 5, 1982	Vietnam was the first war ever fought without any censorship. Without censorship, things can get terribly confused in the public mind.

If you can manipulate news, a judge can manipulate the law. A smart lawyer can keep a killer out of jail, a smart accountant can keep a thief from paying taxes, a smart reporter could ruin your reputation—unfairly.

Mario Cuomo
NBC-TV
Aug 21, 1986

If we had had the technology back then, you would have seen Eva Braun on the "Donahue" show and Hitler on "Meet the Press."

Ed Turner
response to criticism of live television coverage of Saddam Hussein quoted in *Newsweek*
Sep 17, 1990

Freedom/Liberty

Proclaim liberty throughout all the land unto all the inhabitants thereof.

Bible
inscribed on the Liberty Bell, Philadelphia, Pennsylvania
ca. 500 B.C.

Freedom suppressed and again regained bites with keener fangs than freedom never endangered.
Acriores autem morsus sunt intermissae libertatis quam retentae.

Marcus Tullius Cicero
De Officiis
44 B.C.

Freedom can't be kept for nothing. If you set a high value on liberty, you must set a low value on everything else.
Non potest gratis constare libertas. Hanc si magno aestimas, omnia parvo aestimanda sunt.

Lucius Annaeus Seneca (the Younger)
Letters to Lucilius
ca. 63-65

Every subject's duty is the king's; but every subject's soul is his own.

William Shakespeare
Henry V
1599

I confess it cannot be thought, but that men should fly from oppression, but disorder will give them but an incommodious sanctuary.

John Locke
preface
First Tract on Government
1660

A man cannot part with his liberty and have it too, convey it by compact to the magistrate, and retain it himself.

John Locke
First Tract on Government
1660

He that complies against his will is of his opinion still.

Samuel Butler (1)
Hudibras
1664

Without Freedom of Thought, there can be no such Thing as Wisdom; and no such Thing as publick Liberty, without Freedom of Speech.

Benjamin Franklin
The New England Courant
Jul 9, 1722

Liberty of thought is the life of the soul.

Voltaire
Essay on Epic Poetry
1727

Thomas Fuller *Gnomologia* 1732	Lean liberty is better than fat slavery.
4th Earl of Chesterfield speech in the House of Lords Jun 2, 1737	One of the greatest blessings a people, my Lords, can enjoy is liberty; but every good in this life has its alloy of evil. . . . Like a changeable silk, we cannot easily discover where the one ends, or where the other begins.
Charles Louis de Montesquieu *De l'Esprit des lois* 1748	Liberty is the right of doing whatever the laws permit. *La liberté est le droit de faire tout ce que les lois permettent.*
Benjamin Franklin reply of the Pennsylvania Assembly to the governor Nov 11, 1755	Those who would give up essential Liberty, to purchase a little temporary Safety, deserve neither Liberty nor Safety.
Jean Jacques Rousseau *The Social Contract* 1762	What man loses by the social contract is his natural liberty and an unlimited right to everything he tries to get and succeeds in getting; what he gains is civil liberty and the proprietorship of all he possesses. *Ce que l'homme perd par le contrat social, c'est sa liberté naturelle et un droit illimité à tout ce qui le tente et qu'il peut atteindre; ce qu'il gagne, c'est la liberté civile et la propriété de tout ce qu'il possède.*
Jean Jacques Rousseau *The Social Contract* 1762	Man is born free; and everywhere he is in chains. *L'homme est né libre, et partout il est dans les fers.*
Jean Jacques Rousseau *The Social Contract* 1762	To renounce liberty is to renounce being a man, to surrender the rights of humanity and even its duties. *Renoncer à sa liberté c'est renoncer à sa qualité d'homme, aux droits de l'humanité, même à ses devoirs.*
John Adams "Dissertation on the Canon and the Feudal Law" Aug, 1765	The jaws of power are always open to devour, and her arm is always stretched out, if possible, to destroy the freedom of thinking, speaking, and writing.
William Pitt **1st Earl of Chatham** speech in the House of Commons Jan 14, 1766	I rejoice that America has resisted. Three millions of people, so dead to all the feelings of liberty, as voluntarily to submit to be slaves, would have been fit instruments to make slaves of the rest.
John Dickinson *Letters from a Farmer in Pennsylvania* 1768	The cause of Liberty is a cause of too much dignity to be sullied by turbulence and tumult. It ought to be maintained in a manner suitable to her nature.
Joseph Priestly *Essay on Government* 1768	It is an universal maxim, that the more liberty is given to everything which is in a state of growth, the more perfect it will become.

The God who gave us life, gave us liberty at the same time.

Thomas Jefferson
"Draft of Instructions to the Virginia Delegates in the Continental Congress"
Aug, 1774

Is life so dear, or peace so sweet, as to be purchased at the price of chains and slavery? Forbid it, Almighty God!—I know not what course others may take, but as for me, give me liberty, or give me death!

Patrick Henry
speech to the Virginia Convention
Mar 23, 1775

Liberty can no more exist without virtue and independence, than the body can live and move without a soul.

John Adams
"Novanglus"
Boston Gazette
Feb 6, 1775

Abstract liberty, like other mere abstractions, is not to be found.

Edmund Burke
speech, "On Conciliation with the American Colonies"
Mar 22, 1775

Freedom and not servitude is the cure of anarchy; as religion, and not atheism, is the true remedy for superstition.

Edmund Burke
speech, "On Conciliation with the American Colonies"
Mar 22, 1775

The arms we have been compelled by our enemies to assume we will, in defiance of every hazard, with unabating firmness and perseverance, employ for the preservation of our liberties; being with one mind resolved to die free rather than live slaves.

Thomas Jefferson
"Declaration of the Causes of Taking Up Arms"
Jul 6, 1775

Nip the shoots of arbitrary power in the bud, is the only maxim which can ever preserve the liberties of any people.

John Adams
"Novanglus"
Boston Gazette
Feb 6, 1775

How is it that we hear the loudest yelps for liberty among the drivers of negroes.

Samuel Johnson
"On the American Revolutionaries"
Taxation No Tyranny
1775

Those who expect to reap the blessing of freedom must, like men, undergo the fatigue of supporting it.

Thomas Paine
The American Crisis
Dec 23, 1776

Though the flame of liberty may sometimes cease to shine, the coal can never expire.

Thomas Paine
The American Crisis
Dec 23, 1776

For the support of this Declaration, with a firm reliance on the protection of Divine Providence, we mutually pledge to each other our Lives, our Fortunes, and our sacred Honor.

Thomas Jefferson
closing lines
Declaration of Independence
1776

Liberty must be limited in order to be possessed.

Edmund Burke
Letter to the Sheriffs of Bristol
Apr 3, 1777

Edmund Burke *Letter to the Sheriffs of Bristol* Apr 3, 1777	The true danger is when liberty is nibbled away, for expedients, and by parts.
John Adams letter to Abigail Adams Apr 26, 1777	Posterity! You will never know how much it cost the present generation to preserve your freedom! I hope you will make good use of it! If you do not, I shall repent it in Heaven that I ever took half the pains to preserve it!
Edmund Burke speech in Buckinghamshire, England 1784	The people never give up their liberties but under some delusion.
Frederick the Great on his deathbed Apr 1, 1786	I am tired of ruling over slaves.
Thomas Jefferson letter to William Stephens Smith Nov 13, 1787	The tree of liberty must be refreshed from time to time with the blood of patriots and tyrants. It is its natural manure.
Thomas Jefferson letter to Col. William S. Smith Nov 13, 1787	What country can preserve its liberties, if its rulers are not warned from time to time, that this people preserve the spirt of resistance?
James Madison speech to the Virginia Convention on adoption of the U.S. Constitution Jun 6, 1788	Since the general civilization of mankind, I believe there are more instances of the abridgment of freedom of the people, by gradual and silent encroachments of those in power, than by violent and sudden usurpations.
Thomas Jefferson letter to Edward Carrington May 27, 1788	The natural progress of things is for liberty to yield and government to gain ground.
Charles James Fox speech in the House of Commons May 8, 1789	No human government has a right to enquire into private opinions, to presume that it knows them, or to act on that presumption. Men are the best judges of the consequences of their own opinions, and how far they are likely to influence their actions; and it is most unnatural and tyrannical to say, "As you think, so must you act. I will collect the evidence of your future conduct from what I know to be your opinions."
Thomas Jefferson letter to the Marquis de Lafayette Apr 2, 1790	We are not to expect to be translated from despotism to liberty in a feather bed.
Thomas Jefferson letter to Rev. Charles Clay Jan 27, 1790	The ground of liberty is to be gained in inches.
John Philpot Curran speech in Dublin, Ireland Jul 10, 1790	The condition upon which God hath given liberty to men is eternal vigilance.

To erect and concentrate and perpetuate a large monied interest . . . must in the course of human events produce one or other of two evils, the prostration of agriculture at the feet of commerce, or a change in the present form of federal government, fatal to the existence of American liberty.

Patrick Henry
speech to the Virginia
House of Representatives
Dec, 23, 1790

I would rather be exposed to the inconveniencies attending too much liberty than those attending too small a degree of it.

Thomas Jefferson
letter to Archibald Stuart
Dec 23, 1791

It is ordained in the eternal constitution of things that men of intemperate minds cannot be free. Their passions forge their fetters.

Edmund Burke
*Letter to a Member of the
French National Assembly*
1791

It is not because we have been free, but because we have a right to be free, that we ought to demand freedom. Justice and liberty have neither birth nor race, youth nor age. It would be the same absurdity to assert, that we have a right to freedom, because the Englishmen of Alfred's reign were free, as that three and three are six, because they were so in the camps of Genghis Khan.

Sir James Mackintosh
Vindicae Gallicae
1791

O liberty! O liberty! what crimes are committed in thy name!
O liberté! O liberté! que de crimes on commet en ton nom!

**Mme. Roland
(Marie-Jeanne)**
quoted by Alphonse
de Lamartine
Histoire des Girondins
1847

As for me, I think anyone, whoever he may be, who has done nothing for liberty, or has not done all he could deserves to be counted as an enemy to it.

Joseph-Pierre Fayau
speech to the National
Convention
Nov 26, 1793

He that would make his own liberty secure, must guard even his enemy from oppression; for if he violates this duty, he establishes a precedent that will reach to himself.

Thomas Paine
Dissertation on First Principles of Government
1795

A people are free in proportion as they form their own opinions.

**Samuel Taylor
Coleridge**
Prospectus
The Watchman
1796

With what deep worship I have still adored/ The spirit of divinest Liberty.

**Samuel Taylor
Coleridge**
"France: An Ode"
1798

Freedom of religion, freedom of the press, freedom of person under the protection of habeas corpus; and trial by juries impartially selected,—these principles form the bright constellation which has gone before us.

Thomas Jefferson
first inaugural address
Mar 4, 1801

The love of liberty is the love of others; the love of power is the love of ourselves.

William Hazlitt
"The Times Newspaper"
Political Essays
1819

Thomas Jefferson letter to Richard Rush Oct 20, 1820	The boisterous sea of liberty is never without a wave.
John Quincy Adams letter to James Lloyd Oct 1, 1822	Individual liberty is individual power, and as the power of a community is a mass compounded of individual powers, the nation which enjoys the most freedom must necessarily be in proportion to its numbers the most powerful nation.
Lord Macaulay "On Milton" 1825	There is only one cure for the evils which newly acquired freedom produces, and that cure is freedom.
William Lloyd Garrison prospectus *The Liberator* Jan 1, 1831	Tell a man whose house is on fire, to give a moderate alarm; tell him to moderately rescue his wife from the hands of the ravisher; tell the mother to gradually extricate her babe from the fire into which it has fallen; but urge me not to use moderation in a cause like the present. I am in earnest—I will not equivocate —I will not excuse—I will not retreat a single inch—AND I WILL BE HEARD.
Georg Wilhelm Friedrich Hegel *Introduction to the Philosophy of History* 1832	The history of the world is none other than the progress of the consciousness of freedom. *Die Weltgeschichte ist der Fortschritt im Bewusstsein der Freiheit.*
Daniel Webster speech in the U.S. Senate May 27, 1834	The contest, for ages, has been to rescue Liberty from the grasp of executive power.
Daniel Webster speech in the U.S. Senate Jun 3, 1834	God grants liberty only to those who love it, and are always ready to guard and defend it.
William Henry Harrison speech in Dayton, Ohio Sep 10, 1840	In America, a glorious fire has been lighted upon the alter of liberty. . . . Keep it burning, and let the sparks that continually go up from it fall on other altars, and light up in distant lands the fire of freedom.
William Henry Harrison speech during presidential campaign 1840	See to the government. See that the government does not acquire too much power. Keep a check upon your rulers. Do this, and liberty is safe.
Pierre Joseph Proudhon *Qu'est-ce la propriéte?* 1840	At the moment that man inquires into the motives which govern the will of his sovereign—at that moment man revolts. If he obeys, no longer because the king commands, but because the king demonstrates the wisdom of his commands, it may be said that henceforth he will recognize no authority, and that he has become his own king.
James Russell Lowell "Stanzas on Freedom" 1843	True freedom is to share/ All the chains our brothers wear,/ And, with heart and hand, to be/ Earnest to make others free!

Let your motto be resistance, resistance, RESISTANCE! No oppressed people have ever secured their liberty without resistance.

Henry Highland Garnet
"Address to the Slaves of the United States"
1843

They are slaves who dare not be/ In the right with two or three.

James Russell Lowell
"Stanzas on Freedom"
1843

I didn't know I was a slave until I found out I couldn't do the things I wanted.

Frederick Douglass
Narrative of the Life of Frederick Douglass
1845

Liberty exists in proportion to wholesome restraint.

Daniel Webster
speech at the Charleston Bar
May 10, 1847

It is harder to preserve than to obtain liberty.

John C. Calhoun
speech in the U.S. Senate
Jan, 1848

The liberty of the individual is the greatest thing of all, it is on this and on this alone that the true will of the people can develop.

Alexander Ivanovich Herzen
introduction, "To My Son Alexander"
From The Other Shore
1848-49

The word "liberty" in the mouth of Mr. Webster sounds like the word "love" in the mouth of a courtesan.

Ralph Waldo Emerson
Journal
Feb 12, 1851

No one can be perfectly free till all are free; no one can be perfectly moral till all are moral; no one can be perfectly happy till all are happy.

Herbert Spencer
Social Statics
1851

Eternal vigilance is the price of liberty.

Wendell Phillips
speech
1852

Liberty unregulated by law degenerates into anarchy, which soon becomes the most horrid of all despotisms.

Millard Fillmore
third annual message to Congress
Dec 5, 1852

Let us remember that revolutions do not always establish freedom. Our own free institutions were not the offspring of our Revolution. They existed before.

Millard Fillmore
third annual message to Congress
Dec 5, 1852

True liberty acknowledges and defends the equal rights of all men, and all nations.

Gerrit Smith
speech in U.S. House of Representatives
Jun 27, 1854

My faith in the proposition that each man should do precisely as he pleases with all which is exclusively his own lies at the foundation of the sense of justice there is in me. I extend the principle to communities of men as well as to individuals.

Abraham Lincoln
speech in Peoria, Illinois
Oct 16, 1854

Abraham Lincoln speech in Peoria, Illinois Oct 16, 1854	Let us readopt the Declaration of Independence, and with it the practices and policy which harmonize with it. Let North and South— let all Americans—let all lovers of liberty everywhere join in the great and good work. If we do this, we shall not only save the Union, but we shall have so saved it that the succeeding millions of free, happy people, the world over, shall rise up and call us blessed to the latest generations.
Frederick Douglass *My Bondage and My Freedom* 1855	He who would be free must strike the first blow.
Frederick Douglass speech at Canandaigua, New York Aug 4, 1857	If there is no struggle there is no progress. Those who profess to favor freedom and yet deprecate agitation, are men who want crops without plowing up the ground, they want rain without thunder and lightning. They want the ocean without the awful roar of its many waters. This struggle may be a moral one, or it may be a physical one, and it may be both moral and physical, but it must be a struggle. Power concedes nothing without a demand. It never did and it never will.
Frederick Douglass speech in Canandaigua, New York Aug 4, 1857	The whole history of the progress of human liberty shows that all concessions yet made to her august claims have been born of earnest struggle.
Abraham Lincoln letter to H. Asbury Nov 19, 1858	The fight must go on. The cause of civil liberty must not be surrendered at the end of one or even one hundred defeats.
John Stuart Mill *On Liberty* 1859	The struggle between liberty and authority is the most conspicuous feature in the portions of history with which we are earliest familiar, particularly in that of Greece, Rome and England.
John Stuart Mill *On Liberty* 1859	The only freedom which deserves the name, is that of pursuing our own good in our own way, so long as we do not attempt to deprive others of theirs, or impede their efforts to obtain it.
John Stuart Mill *On Liberty* 1859	There is a limit to the legitimate interference of collective opinion with individual independence: and to find that limit, and maintain it against encroachment, is as indispensable to a good condition of human affairs, as protection against political despotism.
John Stuart Mill *On Liberty* 1859	The sole end for which mankind are warranted, individually or collectively, in interfering with the liberty of action of any of their number is self-protection.
John Stuart Mill *On Liberty* 1859	The individual is not accountable to society for his actions, insofar as these concern the interests of no person but himself.
John Stuart Mill *On Liberty* 1859	The liberty of the individual must be thus far limited; he must not make himself a nuisance to other people.
John Stuart Mill *On Liberty* 1859	Liberty consists in doing what one desires.

The only purpose for which power can be rightfully exercised over any member of a civilised community, against his will, is to prevent harm to others. His own good, either physical or moral, is not a sufficient warrant.

John Stuart Mill
On Liberty
1859

A person should be free to do as he likes in his own concerns; but he ought not to be free to do as he likes in acting for another, under the pretext that the affairs of the other are his own affairs.

John Stuart Mill
On Liberty
1859

The spirit of improvement is not always a spirit of liberty, for it may aim at forcing improvements on an unwilling people.

John Staurt Mill
On Liberty
1859

This is a world of compensation; and he who would be no slave must consent to have no slave. Those who deny freedom to others deserve it not for themselves, and under a just God, cannot long retain it.

Abraham Lincoln
letter to H.L. Pierce
Apr 6, 1859

Mankind are greater gainers by suffering each other to live as seems good to themselves, than by compelling each to live as seems good to the rest.

John Stuart Mill
On Liberty
1859

Whether in chains or in laurels, liberty knows nothing but victories.

Wendell Phillips
speech at Harper's Ferry, Virginia
Nov 1, 1859

If this country cannot be saved without giving up the principle . . . (of the Declaration of Independence), I would rather be assassinated on this spot than surrender it.

Abraham Lincoln
speech in Philadelphia, Pennsylvania
Feb 22, 1861

I am the son of Liberty and to her I owe all that I am. If it is necessary to veil her statue it is not for me to do it.

Camillo, Conte di Cavour
letter to the Countess of Circourt
Jan, 1861

Liberty, misunderstood by materialists as the right to do or not to do anything not directly injurious to others, we understand as the faculty of choosing, among the various modes of fulfilling duty, those most in harmony with our own tendencies.

Giuseppe Mazzini
On the Unity of Italy
1861

A man who has nothing which he is willing to fight for, nothing which he cares more about than he does about his personal safety, is a miserable creature who has no chance of being free, unless made and kept so by the exertions of better men than himself.

John Stuart Mill
"The Contest in America"
Fraser's Magazine
Feb, 1862

In giving freedom to the slave, we assure freedom to the free. . . . We shall nobly save or meanly lose the last, best hope of earth.

Abraham Lincoln
message to Congress
Dec 1, 1862

Liberation is not deliverance.
Libération n'est pas délivrance.

Victor Hugo
Les Misérables
1862

Human liberty, the only true foundation of human government.

Ulysses S. Grant
message to the citizens of Memphis, Tennessee
1863

Charles Sumner
speech, "Slavery and the
Rebellion" delivered at
the Cooper Union, New
York City
Nov 5, 1864

Where Slavery is, there Liberty cannot be; and where Liberty is, there Slavery cannot be.

Abraham Lincoln
speech in Baltimore,
Maryland
Apr 18, 1864

The shepherd drives the wolf from the sheep's throat, for which the sheep thanks the shepherd as his liberator, while the wolf denounces him for the same act, as the destroyer of liberty, especially as the sheep was a black one.

Abraham Lincoln
speech to the 140th
Indiana regiment
Mar 17, 1865

Whenever (I) hear any one, arguing for slavery I feel a strong impulse to see it tried on him personally.

Ralph Waldo Emerson
"Boston"
*May-Day and Other
Pieces*
1867

For what avail the plow or sail,/ Or land or life, if freedom fail?

Michael Bakunin
*Federalism, Socialism and
Anti-Theologism*
1868

Where the State begins, individual liberty ceases, and vice versa.

Michael Bakunin
*Federalism, Socialism and
Anti-Theologism*
1868

Intellectual slavery, of whatever nature it may be, will always have as a natural result both political and social slavery.

Harriet Tubman
quoted by Sarah H.
Bradford
*Harriet, the Moses of
Her People*
1869

When I found I had crossed that line, I looked at my hands to see if I was the same person. There was such a glory over everything.

Harriet Tubman
quoted by Sarah H.
Bradford
*Harriet, the Moses of
]Her People*
1869

There was one of two things I had a right to, liberty or death. If I could not have one, I would have the other, for no man should take me alive. I should fight for my liberty as long as my strength lasted, and when the time came for me to go, the Lord would let them take me.

Lord Acton
lecture on "The History
of Freedom in Antiquity"
at Bridgnorth, England
Feb 26, 1877

Liberty is not a means to a higher political end. It is itself the highest political end.

Henrik Ibsen
Pillars of Society
1877

The spirit of truth and the spirit of freedom—they are the pillars of society.
Sandhedens og frihedens and—det er samfundets stotter.

Lord Acton
lecture on "The History
of Freedom in Antiquity"
at Bridgnorth, England
Feb 26, 1877

Liberty, next to religion, has been the motive of good deeds and the common pretext of crime.

If the perpetual oscillation of nations between anarchy and despotism is to be replaced by the steady march of self-restraining freedom, it will be because men will gradually bring themselves to deal with political, as they now deal with scientific questions.

Thomas Henry Huxley
"Science and Culture"
1880

The shallow consider liberty a release from all law, from every constraint. The wise see in it, on the contrary, the potent Law of Laws.

Walt Whitman
"Freedom"
Notes Left Over
1881

Keep, ancient lands, your storied pomp! cries she/ With silent lips. Give me your tired, your poor,/ Your huddled masses yearning to breathe free,/ The wretched refuse of your teeming shore./ Send these, the homeless, tempest-tossed to me;/ I lift my lamp beside the golden door.

Emma Lazarus
The New Colossus
1886

Liberty cannot live apart from from constitutional principle.

Woodrow Wilson
Political Science Quarterly
Jun, 1887

When liberty becomes license, some form of one-man power is not far distant.

Theodore Roosevelt
Works
1887

Liberty is the soul's right to breathe, and, when it can not take a long breath, laws are girdled too tight.

Henry Ward Beecher
Proverbs from Plymouth Pulpit
1887

Then what is freedom? It is the will to be responsible to ourselves.
Denn was ist Freiheit? Dasz man den Willen zur Selbstverantwortlichkeit hat.

Friedrich Nietzsche
"Skirmishes in a War with the Age"
Twilight of the Idols
1888

The demand of the Labour party is for economic freedom. It is the natural outcome of political enfranchisement.

Keir Hardie
speech to the inaugural conference of the Independent Labour party
Jan 13, 1893

Liberty recast the old forms of government into the Republic, and it must remould our institutions of wealth into the Commonwealth.

Henry Demarest Lloyd
Wealth Against Commonwealth
1894

Liberty produces wealth and wealth destroys liberty.

Henry Demarest Lloyd
Wealth Against Commonwealth
1894

Liberty and monopoly cannot live together.

Henry Demarest Lloyd
Wealth Against Commonwealth
1894

It is by the goodness of God that in our country we have those three unspeakably precious things: freedom of speech, freedom of conscience, and the prudence never to practice either of them.

Mark Twain
Following the Equator
1897

Mark Twain letter to the Reverend Joseph Twichell 1898	It is a worthy thing to fight for one's freedom; it is another sight finer to fight for another man's.
Prince Peter Kropotkin *Memoirs of a Revolutionist* 1899	Freedom remains still the wisest cure for freedom's temporary inconveniences.
Mark Twain *Notebook* 1935	Irreverence is the champion of liberty and its only sure defense.
Clarence S. Darrow funeral oration for John P. Altgeld Mar 14, 1902	Liberty is the most jealous and exacting mistress that can beguile the brain and soul of man.
George Bernard Shaw "Maxims for Revolutionists" *Man and Superman* 1902	Liberty means responsibility. That is why most men dread it.
Ambrose Bierce *The Devil's Dictionary* 1906	Freedom, n. The distinction between freedom and liberty is not accurately known; naturalists have never been able to find a living specimen of either.
Ambrose Bierce *The Devil's Dictionary* 1906	Liberty, n. One of Imagination's most precious possessions.
Woodrow Wilson *Constitutional Government* 1908	The ideals of liberty cannot be fixed from generation to generation; only its conception can be, the large image of what it is. Liberty fixed in unalterable law would be no liberty at all.
William Howard Taft speech in Fresno, California Oct 10, 1909	Liberty is the means in the pursuit of happiness.
W.E.B. Du Bois "The Legacy of John Brown" *John Brown* 1909	Liberty trains for liberty. Responsibility is the first step in responsibility.
W.E.B. Du Bois "The Legacy of John Brown" *John Brown* 1909	The cost of liberty is less than the price of repression.

No man can be just who is not free.

Woodrow Wilson
speech to the Democratic
National Convention
Jul 7, 1912

There will be no greater burden in our generation than to organize the forces of liberty on our time, in order to make conquest of a new freedom for America.

Woodrow Wilson
speech in Indianapolis,
Indiana
Oct 3, 1912

The only freedom consists in the people taking care of the government.

Woodrow Wilson
speech in New York City
Sep 4, 1912

Liberty has never come from the government. Liberty has always come from the subjects of it. The history of liberty is a history of resistance. The history of liberty is a history of limitations of governmental power, not the increase in it.

Woodrow Wilson
speech at the New York
Press Club
Sep 9, 1912

Liberty is its own reward.

Woodrow Wilson
speech
Sep 12, 1912

You cannot tear up ancient rootages and safely plant the tree of liberty in soil that is not native to it.

Woodrow Wilson
speech
Sep 25, 1912

I would rather belong to a poor nation that was free than to a rich nation that had ceased to be in love with liberty.

Woodrow Wilson
speech in Mobile,
Alabama
Oct 27, 1913

Most men, after a little freedom, have preferred authority with the consoling assurances and the economy of effort which it brings.

Walter Lippmann
A Preface to Morals
1913

A thing that stands demonstrable is that nationhood is not achieved otherwise than in arms. . . . We may make mistakes in the beginning and shoot the wrong people; but bloodshed is a cleansing and a sanctifying thing, and the nation which regards it as the final horror has lost its manhood. There are many things more horrible than bloodshed; and slavery is one of them.

Padraic Pearse
The Coming Revolution
1913

Liberty does not consist . . . in mere general declarations of the rights of man. It consists in the translation of those declarations into definite action.

Woodrow Wilson
speech in Philadelphia,
Pennsylvania
Jul 4, 1914

Those men and women are fortunate who are born at a time when a great struggle for human freedom is in progress.

Emmeline Pankhurst
My Own Story
1914

There are two good things in life—freedom of thought and freedom of action.

W. Somerset Maugham
Of Human Bondage
1915

Liberty is often a fierce and intractable thing, to which no bounds can be set, and to which no bounds of a few men's choosing ought ever be set.

Woodrow Wilson
third annual message
to Congress
Dec 7, 1915

Vladimir Ilyich Lenin *The State and the* *Revolution* 1917	While the state exists there is no freedom; when there is freedom there will be no state.
Eugene V. Debs speech in Cleveland, Ohio Sep 9, 1917	While there is a lower class I am in it, while there is a criminal class I am of it; while there is a soul in prison, I am not free.
Woodrow Wilson speech to Congress Apr 2, 1917	Only free peoples can hold their purpose and their honor steady to a common end, and prefer the interests of mankind to any narrow interest of their own.
Woodrow Wilson speech in Indianapolis, Indiana Sep 4, 1919	We do not profess to be the champions of liberty, and then consent to see liberty destroyed.
Calvin Coolidge speech in Washington, D.C. Apr 27, 1922	There is no substitute for a militant freedom.
Marcus Moziah Garvey *Philosophy and Opinions* 1923	Radicalism is a label that is always applied to people who are endeavoring to get freedom.
Calvin Coolidge speech in Washington, D.C. Sep 21, 1924	Liberty is not collective, it is personal. All liberty is individual liberty.
Charles Evans Hughes speech in Faneuil Hall, Boston, Massachusetts Jun 17, 1925	When we lose the right to be different, we lose the privilege to be free.
Suzanne LaFollette "Women and Marriage" *Concerning Women* 1926	It is necessary to grow accustomed to freedom before one may walk in it sure-footedly.
Louis D. Brandeis concurring opinion *Whitney* v. *California* 1927	Those who won our independence believed that the final end of the State was to make men free to develop their faculties; and that in its government the deliberative forces should prevail over the arbitrary. They valued liberty both as an end and as a means. They believed liberty to be the secret of happiness and courage to be the secret of liberty.
Will Rogers *There's Not a Bathing* *Suit in Russia* 1927	Liberty don't work as good in practice as it does in Speech.
Louis D. Brandeis dissenting opinion *Olmstead* v. *United States* 1928	Men born to freedom are naturally alert to repel invasion of their liberty by evil-minded rulers. The greatest dangers to liberty lurk in insidious encroachment by men of zeal, well-meaning but without understanding.

Freedom is a very great reality. But it means, above all things, freedom from lies.

D.H. Lawrence
Pornography and Obscenity
1930

Liberty is so much latitude as the powerful choose to accord to the weak.

Learned Hand
speech, Univ. of Pennsylvania Law School
Jun 1930

It must be admitted that liberty is the hardest test that one can inflict on a people. To know how to be free is not given equally to all men and all nations.

Paul Valéry
"On the Subject of Dictatorship"
Reflections on the World Today
1931

It is a good thing to demand liberty for ourselves and for those who agree with us, but it is a better thing and a rarer thing to give liberty to others who do not agree with us.

Franklin D. Roosevelt
radio address
Nov 22, 1933

Liberty is not just an idea, an abstract principle. It is power, effective power to do specific things. There is no such thing as liberty in general; liberty, so to speak, at large.

John Dewey
"Liberty and Social Control"
The Social Frontier
Nov, 1935

Freedom belongs to the strong.

Richard Wright
Long Black Song
1936

The truth is found when men are free to pursue it.

Franklin D. Roosevelt
speech at Temple Univ., Philadelphia
Feb 22, 1936

The hungry and the homeless don't care about liberty any more than they care about cultural heritage. To pretend that they do care is cant.

E.M. Forster
"Liberty in England"
Abinger Harvest
1936

The greater the importance of safeguarding the community from incitements to the overthrow of our institutions by force and violence, the more imperative is the need to preserve inviolate the constitutional rights of free speech, free press and free assembly in order to maintain the opportunity for free political discussion, to the end that government may be responsive to the will of the people and that changes, if desired, may be obtained by peaceful means. Therein lies the security of the Republic, the very foundation of constitutional government.

Charles Evans Hughes
DeJonge v. *Oregon*
1937

We hear about constitutional rights, free speech and the free press. Every time I hear these words I say to myself, "That man is a Red, that man is a Communist." You never hear a real American talk like that.

Frank Hague
New York World–Telegram
Apr 2, 1938

For the saddest epitaph which can be carved in memory of a vanished liberty is that it was lost because its possessors failed to stretch forth a saving hand while yet there was time.

George Sutherland
dissenting opinion
Associated Press v. *National Labor Relations Board*
1938

Franklin D. Roosevelt speech in New York City Jun 30, 1938	Freedom to learn is the first necessity of guaranteeing that man himself shall be self-reliant enough to be free.
Dorothy Canfield Fisher *Seasoned Timber* 1939	Freedom is not worth fighting for if it means no more than license for everyone to get as much as he can for himself.
Benedetto Croce *Freedom* 1940	Morality, and the ideal of freedom which is the political expression of morality, are not the property of a given party or group, but a value that is fundamentally and universally human, to diffuse and enhance which all of us must devote our efforts and good will. . . . No people will be truly free till all are free.
Franklin D. Roosevelt radio address Oct 13, 1940	Human kindness has never weakened the stamina or softened the fiber of a free people. A nation does not have to be cruel to be tough.
Franklin D. Roosevelt campaign speech in Cleveland, Ohio Nov 2, 1940	We have learned that freedom in itself is not enough. Freedom of speech is of no use to a man who has nothing to say. Freedom of worship is of no use to a man who has lost his God.
Franklin D. Roosevelt speech at the dedication of the Great Smokey Mts. National Park Sep 2, 1940	We believe that the only whole man is a free man.
Ernest Bevin speech in Cardiff, Wales, urging maximum war production Nov, 1940	Do not worry about what it costs. . . . You can easily rebuild wealth, but you cannot create liberty when it has gone. Once a nation is put under another, it takes years and generations of struggle to get liberty back.
W. Somerset Maugham *Strictly Personal* 1941	If a nation values anything more than freedom, it will lose its freedom; and the irony of it is that if it is comfort or money that it values more, it will lose that too.
José Martí *Granos de oro:* *pensamientos seleccionados* *en las Obras de Jose Martí* 1942	The dagger plunged in the name of Freedom is plunged into the breast of Freedom.
Philip Wylie introduction *Generation of Vipers* 1942	If liberty has any meaning it means freedom to improve.
Felix Frankfurter *McNabb* v. *United States* 1943	The history of liberty has largely been the history of the observance of procedural safeguards.
Wendell Lewis Willkie *One World* 1943	Freedom is an indivisible word. If we want to enjoy it, and fight for it, we must be prepared to extend it to everyone, whether they qre rich or poor, whether they agree with us or not, no matter what their race or the color of their skin.

None who have always been free can understand the terrible fascinating power of the hope of freedom to those who are not free.

Pearl S. Buck
What America Means to Me
1943

Men would rather be starving and free than fed in bonds.

Pearl S. Buck
What America Means to Me
1943

A nation which makes the final sacrifice for life and freedom does not get beaten.

Kemal Atatürk
quoted by M.M. Mousharrafa
Ataturk
1944

Liberty lies in the hearts of men and women; when it dies there, no constitution, no law, no court can save it; no constitution, no law, no court can even do much to help it.

Learned Hand
speech in New York City
May 21, 1944

The winning of freedom is not to be compared to the winning of a game—with the victory recorded forever in history. Freedom has its life in the hearts, the actions, the spirits of men and so it must be daily earned and refreshed—else like a flower cut from its life-giving roots, it will wither and die.

Dwight D. Eisenhower
speech to the English Speaking Union, London, England
1944

The ruling class or race must share their freedom with everyone in order to preserve it; or they must give it up.

Chester Bomar Himes
"Negro Martyrs are Needed"
Crisis
May, 1944

The system of private property is the most important guaranty of freedom, not only for those who own property, but scarcely less for those who do not.

Friedrich August von Hayek
The Road to Serfdom
1944

The spirit of liberty is the spirit which is not too sure it is right.

Learned Hand
speech in New York City
May 21, 1944

I wish that every human life might be pure transparent freedom.

Simone de Beauvoir
The Blood of Others
1946

Political liberty is nothing else but the diffusion of power.

Lord Hailsham (Quinton Hogg)
The Case for Conversatism
1947

When poems stop talking about the moon and begin to mention poverty, trade unions, color, color lines and colonies, somebody tells the police.

Langston Hughes
My Adventures as a Social Poet
1947

No man is entitled to the blessings of freedom unless he be vigilant in its preservation.

Douglas MacArthur
title of a speech to the Japanese people
May 3, 1948

Mohandas K. Gandhi *Non-Violence in Peace* *and War* 1948	The moment the slave resolves that he will no longer be a slave, his fetters fall. He frees himself and shows the way to others. Freedom and slavery are mental states.
Dwight D. Eisenhower speech at Columbia Univ. Oct 12, 1948	It is not enough merely to realize how freedom has been won. Essential also is it that we be ever alert to all threats to that freedom. . . . One danger arises from too great a concentration of power in the hands of any individual or group: The power of concentrated finance, the power of selfish pressure groups, the power of any class organized in opposition to the whole—any one of these, when allowed to dominate, is fully capable of destroying individual freedom as is power concentrated in the political head of state.
James Bryant Conant *Education in a Divided* *World* 1948	Diversity of opinion within the framework of loyalty to our free society is not only basic to a university but to the entire nation.
Mohandas K. Gandhi *Non-Violence in Peace* *and War* 1948	The cause of liberty becomes a mockery if the price to be paid is the wholesale destruction of those who are to enjoy liberty.
W.E.B. Du Bois "Freedom to Learn" *Midwest Journal* Winter, 1949	Freedom always entails danger.
Bertrand Russell "The Role of Individuality" *Authority and the* *Individual* 1949	Too little liberty brings stagnation, and too much brings chaos.
Will Rogers *The Autobiography of* *Will Rogers* 1949	A Country can get more real joy out of just Hollering for their Freedom than they can if they get it.
Albert Einstein *Impact* 1950	While it is true that an inherently free and scrupulous person may be destroyed, such an individual can never be enslaved or used as a blind tool.
David Riesman *The Lonely Crowd* 1950	Men are created different; they lose their social freedom and their individual autonomy in seeking to become like each other.
Erik H. Erikson *Childhood and Society* 1950	The American feels so rich in his opportunities for free expression that he often no longer knows what he is free from. Neither does he know where he is not free; he does not recognize his native autocrats when he sees them.
Albert Einstein *Out of My Later Years* 1950	Everything that is really great and inspiring is created by the individual who can labor in freedom.
George Douglas Cole *Essays in Social Theory* 1950	Man in Society is not free where there is no law; he is most free where he cooperates best with his equals in the making of laws.

Liberty is the possibility of doubting, the possibility of making a mistake, the possibility of searching and experimenting, the possibility of saying "No" to any authority—literary, artistic, philosophic, religious, social, and even political.

Ignazio Silone
The God That Failed
1950

A hungry man is not a free man.

Adlai E. Stevenson Jr.
speech in Kasson,
Minnesota
Sep 6, 1952

The mind is the expression of the soul, which belongs to God and must be let alone by government.

Adlai E. Stevenson Jr.
speech in Salt Lake City,
Utah
Oct 14, 1952

Carelessness about our security is dangerous; carelessness about our freedom is also dangerous.

Adlai E. Stevenson Jr.
speech in Detroit,
Michigan
Oct 7, 1952

The right to be let alone is indeed the beginning of all freedoms.

William O. Douglas
dissenting opinion
Public Utilities Commission v. *Pollak*
May 26, 1952

We can afford no liberties with liberty itself.

Robert H. Jackson
dissenting opinion
Zorach v. *Clausor*
Apr 7, 1952

Shouting is not a substitute for thinking and reason is not the subversion but the salvation of freedom.

Adlai E. Stevenson Jr.
Godkin Lectures, Harvard Univ.
Mar, 1954

The 5th Amendment is an old friend and a good friend . . . one of the great landmarks in men's struggle to be free of tyranny, to be decent and civilized.

William O. Douglas
An Almanac of Liberty
1954

Not for the flag/ Of any land because myself was born there/ Will I give up my life./ But I will love that land where man is free,/ And that will I defend.

Edna St. Vincent Millay
"Not for a Nation"
Mine the Harvest
1954

The real guarantee of freedom is an equilibrium of social forces in conflict, not the triumph of any one force.

Max Eastman
Reflections on the Failure of Socialism
1955

It has been well said that a hungry man is more interested in four sandwiches than four freedoms.

Henry Cabot Lodge Jr.
The New York Times
Mar 29, 1955

Civilization exists precisely so that there may be no masses but rather men alert enough never to constitute masses.

Georges Bernanos
Why Freedom?
1955

Liberty is always unfinished business.

**ACLU
(American Civil Liberties Union)**
Annual Report, 1955–56

William Faulkner *Harper's Magazine* Jun, 1956	We cannot choose freedom established on a hierarchy of degrees of freedom, on a caste system of equality like military rank. We must be free not because we claim freedom, but because we practice it.
Salvador de Madariaga *The New York Times* Jan 29, 1957	He is free . . . who knows how to keep in his own hands the power to decide, at each step, the course of his life, and who lives in a society which does not block the exercise of that power.
John F. Kennedy speech in Washington, D.C. Jul 2, 1957	The most powerful single force in the world today is neither Communism nor capitalism, neither the H-bomb nor the guided missile—it is man's eternal desire to be free and independent.
Dwight D. Eisenhower fifth annual message to Congress Jan 10, 1957	Freedom has been defined as the opportunity for self-discipline. . . . Should we persistently fail to discipline ourselves, eventually there will be increasing pressure on government to redress the failure. By that process freedom will step by step disappear.
Dwight D. Eisenhower remarks in Washington, D.C. May 1, 1957	In my opinion, you can't take freedom and allow freedom finally to be pushed back to the shores of the United States and maintain it in the United States. It can't be done. There's too much interdependence in the world.
Paul Robeson *Here I Stand* 1958	Freedom is a hard-bought thing.
Mohandas K. Gandhi quoted *Saturday Review* Mar 1, 1959	Freedom is not worth having if it does not connote freedom to err.
John F. Kennedy campaign speech in Washington, D.C. Oct 2, 1960	If men and women are in chains, anywhere in the world, then freedom is endangered everywhere.
Adlai E. Stevenson Jr. *Putting First Things First* 1960	We have confused the free with the free and easy.
E.B. White "Letter from the West" *The Points of My Compass* 1960	Liberty is never out of bounds or off limits; it spreads wherever it can capture the imagination of men.
John F. Kennedy inaugural address Jan 20, 1961	In the long history of the world, only a few generations have been granted the role of defending freedom in its hour of maximum danger. I do not shrink from this responsibility—I welcome it.
John F. Kennedy speech to the United Nations General Assembly Sep 25, 1961	Conformity is the jailer of freedom and the enemy of growth.

Freedom is not something that anybody can be given; freedom is something people take and people are as free as they want to be.

James Baldwin
"Notes for a Hypothetical Novel"
Nobody Knows My Name
1961

We stand for freedom. That is our conviction for ourselves; that is our only commitment to others.

John F. Kennedy
message to Congress
May 25, 1961

If the self-discipline of the free cannot match the iron discipline of the mailed fist, in economic, political, scientific, and all the other kinds of struggles, as well as the military, then the peril to freedom will continue to rise.

John F. Kennedy
speech to the American Society of Newspaper Editors
Apr 20, 1961

The best road to progress is freedom's road.

John F. Kennedy
message to Congress
Mar 14, 1961

The cost of freedom is always high, but Americans have always paid it.

John F. Kennedy
radio and television address
Oct 12, 1962

History suggests that capitalism is a necessary condition for political freedom. Clearly it is not a sufficient condition.

Milton Friedman
Capitalism and Freedom
1962

The kind of economic organization that provides economic freedom directly, namely, competitive capitalism, also promotes political freedom because it separates economic power from political power and in this way enables the one to offset the other.

Milton Friedman
Capitalism and Freedom
1962

Freedom in economic arrangements is itself a component of freedom broadly understood, so economic freedom is an end in itself . . . Economic freedom is also an indispensable means toward the achievement of political freedom.

Milton Friedman
Capitalism and Freedom
1962

The wave of the future is not the conquest of the world by a single dogmatic creed but the liberation of the diverse energies of free nations and free men.

John F. Kennedy
speech at the Univ. of California, Berkeley
Mar 23, 1962

Two thousand years ago the proudest boast was "Civis Romanus sum." Today, in the world of freedom, the proudest boast is "Ich bin ein Berliner." . . . All free men, wherever they may live, are citizens of Berlin, and, therefore, as a free man, I take pride in the words, "Ich bin ein Berliner."

John F. Kennedy
speech in West Berlin
Jun 26, 1963

Oppressed people cannot remain oppressed forever.

Martin Luther King Jr.
"Letter from the Birmingham Jail"
Jan 16, 1963

No cause is left but the most ancient of all, the one, in fact, that from the beginning of our history has determined the very existence of politics, the cause of freedom versus tyranny.

Hannah Arendt
"Introduction"
On Revolution
1963

John F. Kennedy speech in West Berlin Jun 26, 1963	Freedom is indivisible, and when one man is enslaved, all are not free.
Robert F. Kennedy "Berlin East and West" *The Pursuit of Justice* 1964	The free way of life proposes ends, but it does not prescribe means.
Eric Hoffer *The Ordeal of Change* 1964	There can be no real freedom without the freedom to fail.
J. William Fulbright speech in the U.S. Senate Mar 25, 1964	We must dare to think about "unthinkable things," because when things become "unthinkable," thinking stops and action becomes mindless. If we are to disabuse ourselves of old myths and to act wisely and creatively upon the new realities of our time, we must think about our problems with perfect freedom.
Mao Tse-tung reported remarks Aug 18, 1964	Freedom is the understanding of necessity and the transformation of necessity.
Malcolm X speech at the Militant Labor Forum Symposium in New York City May 29, 1964	Truth is on the side of the oppressed.
Malcolm X speech in New York City Dec 31, 1964	After you get your freedom, your enemy will respect you.
Julius K. Nyerere *Time* Apr 9, 1964	Freedom to many means immediate betterment, as if by magic. . . . Unless I can meet at least some of these aspirations, my support will wane and my head will roll just as surely as the tickbird follows the rhino.
Marya Mannes "A Time for Change" *But Will It Sell?* 1964	The suppression of civil liberties is to many less a matter of horror than the curtailment of the freedom to profit.
Malcolm X speech to the Militant Labor Forum Symposium in New York City Jan 7, 1965	You can't separate peace from freedom because no one can be at peace unless he has his freedom.
Edward Kennedy **Ellington** **"Duke"** "Sacred Concert" 1965	Freedom is sweet, on the beat/ Freedom is sweet to the reet complete/ It's got zestness and bestness/ Sugar and cream on the blessedness,/ No more pains, no more chains,/ To keep free from being free./ Freedom is sweet fat, and that's for me.
Malcolm X *Malcolm X Speaks* 1965	Time is on the side of the oppressed today, it's against the oppressor. Truth is on the side of the oppressed today, it's against the oppressor. You don't need anything else.
J. William Fulbright speech in the U.S. Senate Apr 21, 1966	In a democracy dissent is an act of faith. Like medicine, the test of its value is not in its taste, but its effects.

Freedom is an internal achievement rather than an external judgment.

Adam Clayton Powell Jr.
"Man's Debt to God"
Keep the Faith, Baby!
1967

In the act of resistance the rudiments of freedom are already present.

Angela Yvonne Davis
Lectures on Liberation, I
1968

May God prevent us from becoming "right-thinking men"—that is to say men who agree perfectly with their own police.

Thomas Merton
quoted in his obituary
The New York Times
Dec 11, 1968

We have to talk about liberating minds as well as liberating society.

Angela Yvonne Davis
open forum discussion
with Herbert Marcuse at
the University of
California
Oct 24, 1969

There are men—now in power in this country—who do not respect dissent, who cannot cope with turmoil, and who believe that the people of America are ready to support repression as long as it is done with a quiet voice and a business suit. And it is up to us to prove they are wrong.

John V. Lindsay
speech at the Univ. of
California, Berkeley
Apr 2, 1970

Yet we can maintain a free society only if we recognize that in a free society no one can win all the time. No one can have his own way all the time, and no one is right all the time.

Richard M. Nixon
Alfred M. Landon lecture
at Kansas State Univ.
Sep 16, 1970

If you use words for political purposes, they soon lose whatever meaning they may have had. If you are tempted to brandish the word "free," remember that over the gates of Auschwitz there stretched—and still stretches—the inscription "Arbeit Macht Frei."

C.P. Snow
Baron Snow
speech at Loyola Univ.,
Chicago
1970

We know that the road to freedom has always been stalked by death.

Angela Yvonne Davis
"Tribute to George
Jackson"
Daily World
Aug 25, 1971

The essence of a free life is being able to choose the style of living you prefer free from exclusion and without the compulsion of conformity or law.

Eleanor Holmes Norton
commencement address
at Barnard College, New
York City
Jun 6, 1972

Since when have we Americans been expected to bow submissively to authority and speak with awe and reverence to those who represent us?

William O. Douglas
recalled on his retirement,
concerning unjust arrests
for disorderly conduct
Nov 12, 1975

The biggest menace to American freedom is the intelligence community.

I.F. Stone
Wilson Library Bulletin
Sep, 1976

Alan K. Simpson *The New York Times* Sep 26, 1982	There is no "slippery slope" toward loss of liberties, only a long staircase where each step downward must first be tolerated by the American people and their leaders.
Nelson Mandela *Time* Feb 25, 1985	Only free men can negotiate; prisoners cannot enter into contracts.
Jon Newman *The New York Times* Nov 29, 1986	(American liberty) is premised on the accountability of free men and women for what they have done, not for what they may do.
George Bush inaugural address Jan 20, 1989	We know what works: Freedom works. We know what's right: Freedom is right. We know how to secure a more just and prosperous life for man on earth: through free markets, free speech, free elections and the exercise of free will unhampered by the state.
Ronald Reagan farewell address Jan 11, 1989	I hope we have once again reminded people that man is not free unless government is limited. There's a clear cause and effect here that is as neat and predictable as a law of physics: as government expands, liberty contracts.

Government

Confucius *The Analects* ca 480 B.C.	Good government obtains when those who are near are made happy, and those who are far off are attracted.
Confucius *The Analects* ca. 480 B.C.	Tzu-kung asked about government. The Master said, "Give them enough food, give them enough arms, and the common people will have trust in you."
Confucius *The Analects* ca. 480 B.C.	The Master said, "Guide them by edicts, keep them in line with punishments, and the common people will stay out of trouble but will have no sense of shame. Guide them by virtue, keep them in line with the rites, and they will, besides having a sense of shame, reform themselves."
Phaedrus "The Ass and the Old Shepherd" *Fables* 1st cent. A.D.	In a change of government, the poor change nothing beyond the change of their master. *In principatu commutando saepius/ nil praeter domini nomen mutant pauperes.*
Michel de Montaigne "De la présomption" *Essais* 1580-88	It is very easy to accuse a government of imperfection, for all mortal things are full of it. *Il est bien aisé d'accuser d'imperfection une police, car toutes choses mortelles en sont pleines.*
William Penn "Preface" *The Frame of Government of Pennsylvania* 1682	Governments, like clocks, go from the motions men give them, and as governments are made and moved by men, so by them are they ruined too. Wherefore governments rather depend upon men than men upon governments.

Let the people think they govern and they will be governed.

William Penn
Some Fruits of Solitude in Reflections and Maxims
1693

I speak of this incontestable truth: the social world is certainly the work of man.

Giovanni Battista Vico
Scienza Nuova
1725

Governments must be conformable to the nature of the governed; governments are even a result of that nature.

Giovanni Battista Vico
Scienza Nuova
1725

For forms of government let fools contest;/ Whate'er is best administer'd is best.

Alexander Pope
Essay on Man
1733

If it's true that you can't abolish vice, the science of those who govern is to at least see that it competes with the public good.
S'il est vrai qu'on ne peut anéantir le vice, la science du ceux qui gouvernent est de le faire concourir au bien public.

Marquis de Vauvenargues
Réflexions et maximes
1746

For a state to be strong either the people must have freedom based on law or the sovereign must be all-powerful without any contradiction.
Il faut, pour qu'un Etat soit puissant, ou que le peuple ait une liberté fondée sur les lois, ou que l'autorité souveraine soit affermie sans contradiction.

Voltaire
Le Siècle de Louis XIV
1751

Lawful and settled authority is very seldom resisted when it is well employed.

Samuel Johnson
The Rambler
1750-52

The body politic, as well as the human body, begins to die as soon as it is born, and carries in itself the causes of its destruction.
Le corps politique, aussi bien que le corps de l'homme, commence à mourir dès sa naissance et porte en lui-même les causes de sa déstruction.

Jean Jacques Rousseau
The Social Contract
1762

In several countries it is maintained that citizens do not have the right to leave the country where they happened to have been born. What this says is clear: "This country is so bad and so misgoverned that we can't let anyone leave or everyone would want to." How much better to make it so the citizens want to stay and foreigners want to come.
On a prétendu dans plusieurs pays qu'il n'était pas permis à un citoyen de sortir de la contrée ou le hasard l'a fait naître; le sens de cette loi est visiblement: "Ce pays est si mauvais et si mal gouverné que nous défendons à chaque individu d'en sortir, de peur que tout le monde n'en sorte." Faites mieux: donnez à tous vos sujets envie de demeurer chez vous, et aux étrangers d'y venir.

Voltaire
"Egalité"
Dictionnaire philosophique
1764

A wise government knows how to enforce with temper or to conciliate with dignity.

George Grenville
speech during the Wilkes debate in the House of Commons
1769

Samuel Johnson quoted by James Boswell *Life of Samuel Johnson* Mar 31, 1772	I would not give half a guinea to live under one form of government rather than another. It is of no moment to the happiness of an individual.
John Adams "Novanglus" *Boston Gazette* 1774	A government of laws, and not of men.
Edmund Burke speech, "On Conciliation with the American Colonies" Mar 22, 1775	All government,—indeed, every human benefit and enjoyment, every virtue and every prudent act,—is founded on compromise and barter.
Edmund Burke speech, "On Conciliation with the American Colonies" Mar 22, 1775	Refined policy ever had been the parent of confusion, and ever will be so long as the world endures. Plain good intention, which is as easily discovered at the first view as fraud is surely detected at last, is, let me say, of no mean force in the government of mankind.
Samuel Johnson "On the American Revolutionaries" *Taxation No Tyranny* 1775	All government is ultimately and essentially absolute.
Thomas Paine "Of the Origin and Design of Government in General" *Common Sense* 1776	Society in every state is a blessing, but government, even in its best state is but a necessary evil; in its worst state, an intolerable one.
Thomas Paine "Of the Origin and Design of Government in General" *Common Sense* 1776	Society is produced by our wants, and government by our wickedness; the former promotes our happiness positively by uniting our affections, the latter negatively be restraining our vices.
Thomas Jefferson *Notes on the State of Virginia* 1782	It is error alone which needs the support of government. Truth can stand by itself.
George Washington letter to John Jay Aug 1, 1786	Experience has taught us that men will not adopt and carry into execution measures the best calculated for their own good without the intervention of a coercive power.
Alexander Hamilton *The Federalist* Dec 1, 1787	Why has government been instituted at all? Because the passions of men will not conform to the dictates of reason and justice, without constraint.
Thomas Jefferson *Autobiography* 1787	It is not by consolidation, or concentration of powers, but by their distribution, that good government is effected.

No man is a warmer advocate for proper restraints and wholesome checks in every department of government than I am; but I have never yet been able to discover the propriety of placing it absolutely out of the power of men to render essential services, because a possibility remains of their doing ill.

George Washington
letter to Bushrod Washington
Nov 10. 1787

But what is government itself, but the greatest of all reflections on human nature? If men were angels, no government would be necessary. If angels were to govern men, neither external nor internal controls on government would be necessary.

James Madison
The Federalist
Feb 6, 1788

Energy in government is essential to that security against external and internal danger, and to that prompt and salutary execution of the laws which enter into the very definition of good government.

James Madison
Federalist
Jan. 11, 1788

Governments destitute of energy, will ever produce anarchy.

James Madison
speech to the Virginia Convention on adoption of the U.S. Constitution
Jun 7, 1788

To model our political system upon speculations of lasting tranquility, is to calculate on the weaker springs of the human character.

Alexander Hamilton
The Federalist
Jan 5, 1788

Governments arise either out of the people or over the people.

Thomas Paine
The Rights of Man
1791

The circumstances of the world are continually changing, and the opinions of men change also; and as Government is for the living, and not for the dead, it is the living only that have any right in it.

Thomas Paine
The Rights of Man
1791

Since government, even in its best state is an evil, the object principally to be aimed at is that we should have as little of it as the general peace of human society will permit.

William Godwin
An Enquiry Concerning Political Justice
1793

(Liberty) is indeed little less than a name, where the Government is too feeble to withstand the enterprises of faction, to confine each member of society within the limits prescribed by the law, and to maintain all in the secure and tranquil enjoyment of the rights of persons and property.

George Washington
Farewell Address to the People of the United States
Sep 19, 1796

Without an army, authority, and discipline there is no political independence or civil liberty.
Sans armée, sans force, sans discipline, il n'est ni indépendance politique ni liberté civil.

Napoleon I
speech to the National Guard of the Cisalpine Republic
May 14, 1797

Governments are more the effect than the cause of that which we are.

Samuel Taylor Coleridge
letter to George Coleridge
Apr, 1798

Napoleon I
letter to Gen. Commes
Mar 19, 1800

Don't forget that weakness produces civil wars, and that vigor maintains peace and prosperity in a state.

N'oubliez pas que la faiblesse produit des guerres civiles, et que l'énergie maintient la tranquillité et la prospérité des Etats.

Napoleon I
remarks quoted by
Roederer
Aug 2, 1800

It is in no one's interest to overturn a government in which everyone with ability can find a place.

Personne n'a intérêt a renverser un gouvernement dans lequel tout ce qui a du mérite est placé.

Thomas Jefferson
first inaugural address
Mar 4, 1801

A wise and frugal Government, which shall restrain men from injuring one another, shall leave them otherwise free to regulate their own pursuits of industry and improvement, and shall not take from the mouth of labor the bread it has earned—this is the sum of good government.

Thomas Jefferson
letter to Thomas Cooper
Nov 29, 1802

If we can prevent the government from wasting the labors of the people, under the pretence of taking care of them, they must become happy.

Napoleon I
letter to Count Fouché,
minister of police
Jan 1, 1809

See that government weighs as little as possible and does not unnecessarily burden the people.

Veillez à ce que l'autorité se fasse sentir le moins possible et ne pèse pas inutilement sur les peuples.

Joseph de Maistre
Lettres et opuscules inédits
Aug 15, 1811

Every country has the government it deserves.

Toute nation a le gouvernement qu'elle mérite.

**1st Duke of
Wellington
(Arthur Wellesley)**
letter to Lord William
Bentinck
Dec 24, 1811

Trust nothing to the enthusiasm of the people. Give them a strong and a just, and, if possible, a good, government; but, above all, a strong one.

Napoleon I
imperial séance
Jun 7, 1813

Men are powerless to secure the future; institutions alone fix the destinies of nations.

Thomas Jefferson
letter to John Wayle
Eppes
Sep 9, 1814

No government can be maintained without the principle of fear as well as of duty. Good men will obey the last, but bad ones the former only.

Thomas Jefferson
letter to Joseph C. Cabell
Feb 2, 1816

The way to have good and safe government, is not to trust it all to one, but to divide it among the many, distributing to every one exactly the functions he is competent to (perform).

Napoleon I
reported remarks
Feb 16, 1817

Governments only keep their word when they are forced to, or when it is to their advantage.

Les gouvernements ne tiennent leur parole que quand ils y sont forcés, ou que cela leur est avantageux.

Which is the best government? That which teaches us to govern ourselves.

Welche Regierung die beste sei? Diejenige, die uns lehrt, uns selbst zu regieren.

Johann Wolfgang von Goethe
quoted by Bailey Saunders
The Maxims and Reflections of Goethe
1893

There are no necessary evils in government. Its evils exist only in its abuses.

Andrew Jackson
veto of Bank Bill
Jul 10, 1832

Peoples and governments never have learned anything from history, or acted on principles deduced from it.

Georg Wilhelm Friedrich Hegel
Introduction to the Philosophy of History
1832

If the government would confine itself to equal protection, and, as Heaven does its rains, shower its favors alike on the high and the low, the rich and the poor, it would be an unqualified blessing.

Andrew Jackson
veto message
Jul 10, 1832

What would happen if only the middle classes were involved in making the laws? One could be sure that they would not be extravagant with taxes, because there is nothing so disastrous for a small fortune as a large tax. . . . Therefore, government by the middle classes would seem to be the most economical.

Admettez, au contraire, que ce soient les classes moyennes qui seules fassent la loi. L'on peut compter qu'elles ne prodigueront pas les impôts, parce qu'il n'y a rien de si désastreux qu'une grosse taxe venant à frapper une petite fortune. . . . Le gouvernement des classes moyennes me semble devoir être . . . le plus economique.

Alexis, Comte de Tocqueville
Democracy in America
1835

Every central government worships uniformity: uniformity relieves it from inquiry into an infinity of details, which must be attended to if rules have to be adapted to different men, instead of indiscriminately subjecting all men to the same rule.

Tout gouvernement central adore l'uniformité; l'uniformité lui évite l'examen d'une infinité de détails dont il devrait s'occuper, s'il fallait faire la règle pour les hommes, au lieu de faire passer indistinctement tous les hommes sous la meme règle.

Alexis, Comte de Tocqueville
Democracy in America
1839

A decent and manly examination of the acts of Government should be not only tolerated, but encouraged.

William Henry Harrison
inaugural address
Mar 4, 1841

The greatest need a people have is for government; their greatest happiness is having good government.

Le plus grand besoin d'un peuple est d'être gouverné; son plus grand bonheur, d'etre bien gouverné.

Joseph Joubert
Pensées
1842

In the long-run every Government is the exact symbol of its People, with their wisdom and unwisdom; we have to say, Like People like Government.

Thomas Carlyle
Past and Present
1843

Government is at best but an expedient; but most governments are usually, and all governments are sometimes, inexpedient.

Henry David Thoreau
Civil Disobedience
1849

Henry David Thoreau *Civil Disobedience* 1849	The objections which have been brought against a standing army, and they are many and weighty, and deserve to prevail, may also at last be brought against a standing government.
Pierre Joseph Proudhon *Idée Générale de la Révolution au XIXe Siècle* 1851	To be governed is to be watched over, inspected, spied on, directed, legislated at, regulated, docketed, indoctrinated, preached at, controlled, assessed, weighed, censored, ordered about, by men who have neither the right nor the knowledge nor the virtue.
Henri Frederic Amiel *Journal* Jun 17, 1852	The test of every religious, political, or educational system, is the man which it forms. If a system injures the intelligence it is bad. If it injures the character it is vicious, if it injures the conscience it is criminal.
Abraham Lincoln first inaugural address Mar 4, 1861	It is safe to assert that no government proper ever had a provision in its organic law for its own termination.
Abraham Lincoln first inaugural address Mar 4, 1861	Perpetuity is implied, if not expressed, in the fundamental law of all national governments.
John Ruskin *Unto This Last* 1862	Government and co-operation are in all things the laws of life; anarchy and competition the laws of death.
Abraham Lincoln "Response to a Serenade" Nov 10, 1864	It has long been a grave question whether any government not too strong for the liberties of its people, can be strong enough to maintain its own existence?
Benjamin Disraeli speech on "Conservative Principles" Apr 3, 1872	The test of political institutions is the condition of the country whose future they regulate.
Walt Whitman "Democracy in the New World" *Notes Left Over* 1881	Man is about the same, in the main, whether with despotism, or whether with freedom.
Prince Otto von Bismarck speech in the Reichstag Feb 24, 1881	There are times when one must govern liberally and times when one must be dictatorial; everything changes, there is no eternity here. *Es gibt Zeiten, wo man liberal regieren muss, und Zeiten, wo man diktatorisch regieren muss; es wechselt alles, hier gibt es keine Ewigkeit.*
Henry Ward Beecher *Proverbs from Plymouth Pulpit* 1887	The worst thing in this world, next to anarchy, is government.
John James Ingalls *The New York World* 1890	The purification of politics is an iridescent dream. Government is force.
Ellen Glasgow *The Voice of the People* 1900	The government's like a mule, it's slow and it's sure; it's slow to turn, and it's sure to turn the way you don't want it.

Government is a matter of insight and of sympathy. If you don't know what the great body of men are up against how are you going to help them?

Woodrow Wilson
speech in Buffalo,
New York
Sep 2, 1912

What is a Government for except to dictate! If it does not dictate, then it is not a Government.

David Lloyd George
War Memoirs
1933-36

In anarchy it's not just the king who loses his rights but the worker as well.
Wo nichts ist, da hat nicht nur der Kaiser, sondern auch der Proletarier sein Recht verloren.

Max Weber
Politik als Beruf
1918-19

Government is a very natural thing and in most instances ought to be a very normal and deliberate proceeding.

Warren G. Harding
speech in Marion, Ohio
Jul 5, 1920

A good government remains the greatest of human blessings, and no nation has ever enjoyed it.

William Ralph Inge
"The State, Visible
and Invisible"
*Outspoken Essays: Second
Series*
1922

The experience of Russia, more than any theories, has demonstrated that all government, whatever its forms or pretenses, is a dead weight that paralyzes the free spirit and activities of the masses.

Emma Goldman
*My Disillusionment in
Russia*
1923

Order is not pressure which is imposed on society from without, but an equilibrium which is set up from within.
Orden no es una presión que desde fuera se ejerce sobre la sociedad, sino un equilibro que se suscita en su interior.

José Ortega y Gasset
Mirabeau o el político
1927

We get the fundamental confusion that government, since it can correct much abuse, can also create righteousness.

Herbert Hoover
letter to William O.
Thompson
Dec 30, 1929

Governments are best classified by considering who are the "somebodies" they are in fact endeavoring to satisfy.

**Alfred North
Whitehead**
Adventures in Ideas
1933

That government which thinks in terms of humanity will continue.

Franklin D. Roosevelt
campaign speech in
Rochester, New York
Oct 17, 1936

Mankind needs government, but in regions where anarchy has prevailed they will, at first, submit only to despotism. We must therefore seek first to secure government, even though despotic, and only when government has become habitual can we hope successfully to make it democratic.

Bertrand Russell
Power
1938

Any system of government will work when everything is going well. It's the system that functions in the pinches that survives.

John F. Kennedy
Why England Slept
1940

Adlai E. Stevenson Jr. speech in Bloomington, Illinois 1948	Government is more than the sum of all the interests; it is the paramount interest, the public interest. It must be the efficient, effective agent of a responsible citizenry, not the shelter of the incompetent and the corrupt.
Bertrand Russell "Control and Initiative" *Authority and the Individual* 1949	In our complex world, there cannot be fruitful initiative without government, but unfortunately there can be government without initiative.
Adlai E. Stevenson Jr. speech in Los Angeles, California Sep 11, 1952	The really basic thing in government is policy. Bad administration, to be sure, can destroy good policy, but good administration can never save bad policy.
Adlai E. Stevenson Jr. speech in Chicago, Illinois Sep 29, 1952	Government cannot be stronger or more tough-minded than its people. It cannot be more inflexibly committed to the task than they.
Eric Hoffer *The Passionate State of Mind* 1954	No matter how noble the objectives of a government, if it blurs decency and kindness, cheapens human life, and breeds ill will and suspicion—it is an evil government.
John F. Kennedy message to Congress Apr 27, 1961	The basis of effective government is public confidence.
Arthur Sylvester speech in New York City Dec 6, 1962	I think the inherent right of the Government to lie to save itself when faced with nuclear disaster is basic.
Murray Kempton "Academic Pride" *America Comes of Middle Age* 1963	It is a function of government to invent philosophies to explain the demands of its own convenience.
Bernard Baruch press conference in New York City Aug 18, 1964	You talk about capitalism and communism and all that sort of thing, but the important thing is the struggle everybody is engaged in to get better living conditions, and they are not interested too much in the form of government.
Ronald Reagan quoted *The New York Times Magazine* Nov 14, 1965	Government is like a big baby—an alimentary canal with a big appetite at one end and no sense of responsibility at the other.
Charles De Gaulle *The New York Times* Nov 14, 1965	To govern is always to choose among disadvantages.
Daniel P. Moynihan *The New York Times* Mar 2, 1976	The single most exciting thing you encounter in government is competence, because it's so rare.
Ronald Reagan *Washington Post* Apr 20, 1976	I believe that government is the problem, not the answer.

The problem isn't a shortage of fuel, it's a surplus of government.

Ronald Reagan
Newsweek
Oct 1, 1979

A government is not legitimate merely because it exists.

Jeane J. Kirkpatrick
on Sandinista government
in Nicaragua
Time
Jun 17, 1985

The nine most terrifying words in the English language are, "I'm from the government and I'm here to help."

Ronald Reagan
speech
Aug 12, 1986

An entirely new problem should be recognised as the fundamental problem of a rational political theory: how is the state to be constituted so that bad rulers can be got rid of without bloodshed, without violence?

Sir Karl Popper
"Popper on Democracy"
The Economist
Apr 23, 1988

Government and Business

Money is, with propriety, considered as the vital principle of the body politic; as that which sustains its life and motion, and enables it to perform its most essential functions.

Alexander Hamilton
The Federalist
Dec 28, 1787

It is in the interests of those who govern and those who are governed to extend the political importance of the industrialists, since, on the one hand, they are always inclined to support the existing government and, on the other, they work ceaselessly to limit power and to decrease taxation.

Claude Henri, Comte de Saint-Simon
Industry
1817

In democracies, nothing is more great or more brilliant than commerce.
Dans les démocraties, il n'y a rien de plus grand ni de plus brillant que le commerce.

Alexis, Comte de Tocqueville
Democracy in America
1839

Trade and commerce, if they were not made of Indian rubber, would never manage to bounce over the obstacles which legislators are continually putting in their way.

Henry David Thoreau
Civil Disobedience
1849

Property is a god. This god already has its theology (called state politics and juridical right) and also its morality, the most adequate expression of which is summed up in the phrase: "That man is worth so much!"

Michael Bakunin
The Knouto-Germanic Empire and the Social Revolution
1871

Glory be, whin business gets above sellin' tinpinny nails in a brown paper cornucopy, 't is hard to tell it fr'm murther.

Finley Peter Dunne
"On Wall Street"
Mr. Dooley's Opinions
1900

The biggest corporation, like the humblest private citizen, must be held to strict compliance with the will of the people as expressed in the fundamental law.

Theodore Roosevelt
speech in Cincinnati, Ohio
1902

Theodore Roosevelt speech at Osawatomie, Kansas Aug 31, 1910	The man who wrongly holds that every human right is secondary to his profit must now give way to the advocate of human welfare, who rightly maintains that every man holds his property subject to the general right of the community to regulate its use to whatever degree the public welfare may require it.
Emma Goldman "The Tragedy of Women's Emancipation" *Anarchism and Other Essays* 1911	Politics is the reflex of the business and industrial world.
Woodrow Wilson speech in Chicago, Illinois Feb 12, 1912	Sound business need have no fear of progressive government. It is only the business that thrives on special privilege that is in danger.
Theodore Roosevelt *Autobiography* 1913	We demand that big business give the people a square deal; in return we must insist that when anyone engaged in big business honestly endeavors to do right he shall himself be given a square deal.
Calvin Coolidge speech in New York City Nov 20, 1920	Civilization and profits go hand in hand.
Calvin Coolidge speech in Washington, D.C. Jan 17, 1924	We want wealth, but there are many other things we want very much more. Among them are peace, honor, charity, and idealism.
Calvin Coolidge speech to the American Society of Newspaper Editors Jan 17, 1925	The chief business of the American people is business.
Richard Tawney *Religion and The Rise of Capitalism* 1926	An organised money market has many advantages. But it is not a school of social ethics or of political responsibility.
Henry Stimson *Diary* Aug 26, 1940	If you are going to try to go to war, or to prepare for war, in a capitalist country, you have got to let business make money out of the process or business won't work.
Charles E. Wilson remarks to the press Jan 23, 1953	What is good for the country is good for General Motors, and vice versa.
John F. Kennedy reported remarks on steel industry executives who increased prices Apr 11, 1962	My father always told me that all business men were sons of bitches, but I never believed it till now.
Lyndon Baines Johnson speech to the Houston Chamber of Commerce Aug 12, 1963	No political party can be a friend of the American people which is not a friend of American business.

Nothing is illegal if one hundred businessmen decide to do it, and that's true anywhere in the world.

Andrew Young
Rolling Stone
Mar 24, 1977

I learned in business that you had to be very careful when you told somebody that's working for you to do something, because the chances are very high he'd do it. In government, you don't have to worry about that.

George P. Shultz
The New York Times
Oct 14, 1984

Little ol'boy in the Panhandle told me the other day you can still make a small fortune in agriculture. Problem is, you got to start with a large one.

Jim Hightower
speech to the Dallas Chamber of Commerce
The New York Times
Mar 9, 1986

The only difference between a pigeon and the American farmer today is that a pigeon can still make a deposit on a John Deere.

Jim Hightower
speech to the Dallas Chamber of Commerce
The New York Times
Mar 9, 1986

International Affairs/Diplomacy

The rulers of the state are the only ones who should have the privilege of lying, either at home or abroad; they may be allowed to lie for the good of the state.

Plato
The Republic
ca. 390 B.C.

Wisdom is better than weapons of war.

Bible
Ecclesiates
ca. 180 B.C.

An ambassador is an honest man sent to lie abroad for the good of his country.

Sir Henry Wotton
written in the autograph album of Christopher Fleckmore
1604

If a man be gracious and courteous to strangers, it shows he is a citizen of the world, and that his heart is no island cut off from other lands, but a continent that joins to them.

Sir Francis Bacon
"Of Goodness and Goodness of Nature"
Essays
1625

The problem of establishing a perfect civil constitution is subordinate to the problem of a law-governed external relationship with other states, and cannot be solved unless the latter is also solved.

Immanuel Kant
Idea for a Universal History with a Cosmopolitan Purpose
1784

Even to observe neutrality you must have a strong government.

Alexander Hamilton
speech to the Constitutional Convention
Jun 29, 1787

I think every nation has a right to establish that form of government, under which it conceives it may live most happy; provided it infracts no right, or is not dangerous to others; and that no governments ought to interfere with the internal concerns of another, except for the security of what is due to themselves.

George Washington
letter to the Marquis de Lafayette
Dec 25, 1789

Thomas Jefferson letter to Mr. Dumas Mar 24, 1793	Peace with all nations, and the right which that gives us with respect to all nations, are our object.
George Washington *Farewell Address to the People of the United States* Sep 17, 1796	It is our true policy to steer clear of permanent alliance with any portion of the foreign world.
George Washington *Farewell Address to the People of the United States* Sep 17, 1796	There can be no greater error than to expect or calculate upon real favors from nation to nation.
George Washington letter to James Monroe Aug 25, 1796	I have always given it as my decided opinion that no nation had a right to intermeddle in the internal concerns of another; that every one had a right to form and adopt whatever government they liked best to live under themselves; and that, if this country could, consistently with its engagements, maintain a strict neutrality and thereby preserve peace, it was bound to do so by motives of policy, interest, and every other considerations.
Thomas Jefferson first inaugural address Mar 4, 1801	Peace, commerce, and honest friendship with all nations— entangling alliances with none.
Washington Irving "English Writers on America" *The Sketch Book of Geoffrey Crayon, Gent.* 1819-20	It is but seldom that any one overt act produces hostilities between two nations; there exists, more commonly, a previous jealousy and ill will, a predisposition to take offense.
Andrew Jackson second inaugural address Mar 4, 1833	The foreign policy adopted by our government is to do justice to all, and to submit to wrong by none.
Andrew Jackson sixth annual message to Congress Dec 1, 1834	Our institutions are essentially pacific. Peace and friendly intercourse with all nations are as much the desire of our Government as they are the interest of the people.
Martin Van Buren fourth annual message to Congress Dec 5, 1840	A faithful observance in the management of our foreign relations of the practice of speaking plainly, dealing justly, and requiring truth and justice in return (are) the best conservatives of the peace of nations.
3rd Viscount Palmerston speech in the House of Commons Mar 1, 1843	The sun never sets upon the interests of this country.
James K. Polk inaugural address Mar 4, 1845	In the management of our foreign relations it will be my aim to observe a careful respect for the rights of other nations, while our own will be the subject of constant watchfulness. Equal and exact justice should characterize all our intercourse with foreign countries.

We have no eternal allies, and we have no perpetual enemies. Our interests are eternal and perpetual, and those interests it is our duty to follow.

3rd Viscount Palmerston (Henry John Temple)
speech in the House of Commons
Mar 1, 1848

Tranquility at home and peaceful relations abroad constitute the true permanent policy of our country.

James K. Polk
fourth annual message to Congress
Dec 5, 1848

As the Roman in days of old held himself free from indignity when he could say Civis Romanus sum, so also a British subject, in whatever land he may be, shall feel confident that the watchful eye and the strong arm of England will protect him against injustice and wrong.

3rd Viscount Palmerston
speech in the House of Commons
Jun 25, 1850

In ninety-nine cases out of a hundred, when there is a quarrel between two states, it is generally occasioned by some blunder of a ministry.

Benjamin Disraeli
speech in the House of Commons
Feb 19, 1858

Colonies do not cease to be colonies because they are independent.

Benjamin Disraeli
speech in the House of Commons
Feb 5, 1863

The foreign policy of the noble Earl (Russell, foreign secretary) . . . may be summed up in two short homely but expressive words, "meddle" and "muddle."

14th Earl of Derby
speech in the House of Lords
Feb, 1864

The old-world diplomacy of Europe was largely carried on in drawing rooms, and, to a great extent, of necessity still is so. Nations touch at their summits.

Walter Bagehot
The English Constitution
1867

If we are to negotiate peace . . . I imagine an essentially modest role . . . that of an honest broker who means to do business.

Prince Otto von Bismarck
speech to the Reichstag
Feb 19, 1878

Lord Salisbury and myself have brought you back peace—but a peace, I hope, with honour.

Benjamin Disraeli
speech in the House of Lords
Jul 16, 1878

Vacillation and inconsistency are as incompatible with successful diplomacy as they are with the national dignity.

Benjamin Harrison
speech in Indianapolis, Indiana
Sep 11, 1888

We Americans have no commission from God to police the world.

Benjamin Harrison
campaign speech
1888

I asked Tom if countries always apologized when they had done wrong, and he says: "Yes; the little ones does."

Mark Twain
Tom Sawyer Abroad
1894

Benjamin Harrison *North American Review* Mar, 1901	Will it not be wise to allow the friendship between nations to rest upon deep and permanent things? . . . Irritations of the cuticle must not be confounded with heart failure.
Theodore Roosevelt speech in Chicago, Illinois Apr 2, 1903	There is a homely old adage which runs: "Speak softly and carry a big stick; you will go far." If the American Nation will speak softly, and yet build, and keep at a pitch of the highest training, a thoroughly efficient navy, the Monroe Doctrine will go far.
Theodore Roosevelt directive to government officials Mar 10, 1904	Courtesy, moderation, and self-restraint should mark international, no less than private, intercourse.
Ambrose Bierce *The Devil's Dictionary* 1906	Diplomacy, n. The patriotic art of lying for one's country.
Ambrose Bierce *The Devil's Dictionary* 1906	Consul, n. In American politics, a person who having failed to secure an office from the people is given one by the Administration on condition that he leave the country.
Woodrow Wilson message to Congress Aug 27, 1913	We can afford to exercise the self-restraint of a really great nation which realizes its own strength and scorns to misuse it.
Woodrow Wilson speech in Philadelphia, Pennsylvania Jul 4, 1914	When I have made a promise as a man I try to keep it, and I know no other rule permissible to a nation.
Woodrow Wilson "Proclamation" Aug 19, 1914	The United States must be neutral in fact as well as in name. We must be impartial in thought as well as in action.
Woodrow Wilson speech in Philadelphia, Pennsylvania May 10, 1915	There is such a thing as man being too proud to fight. There is such a thing as a nation being so right that it does not need to convince others by force that it is right.
Woodrow Wilson speech to the U.S. Senate Jan 22, 1917	There must be, not a balance of power, but a community of power; not organized rivalries, but an organized common peace.
Woodrow Wilson first of the "Fourteen Points" given in a speech to Congress Jan 18, 1918	Open covenants of peace, openly arrived at, after which there shall be no private international understandings of any kind but diplomacy shall proceed always frankly and in the public view.
Hans von Seeckt at the Rapallo Confer- ence, quoted by Erich Eyck *Geschichte der Weimarer* *Republik* Apr, 1922	Whenever our policy in the West has run aground, it has always been wise to try something in the East. *In Zeiten, in denen unsere Politik im Westen festgefahren war, ist es immer richtig gewesen, aktiv im Osten zu werden.*
Agnes Repplier "Allies" *Under Dispute* 1924	The friendships of nations, built on common interests, cannot survive the mutability of those interests.

The foreign policy of America can best be described by one word—peace.

Calvin Coolidge
acceptance speech as
Republican nominee
for president
Aug 14, 1924

Our foreign policy has one primary object, and that is peace.

Herbert Hoover
speech at Palo Alto,
California
Aug 11, 1928

We never lost a war and we never won a conference in our lives. I believe that we could without any degree of egotism, single-handed lick any nation in the world. But we can't confer with Costa Rica and come home with our shirts on.

Will Rogers
quoted by Paula
McSpadden Love
The Will Rogers Book
1972

Diplomacy is to do and say the nastiest thing in the nicest way.

Isaac Goldberg
The Reflex
1930

If our civilization is to be perpetuated, the great causes of world peace, world disarmament and world recovery must prevail. They cannot prevail until a path to their attainment is built upon honest friendship, mutual confidence, and proper co-operation among the nations.

Herbert Hoover
statement to the press
Nov 23, 1932

In the field of foreign policy I would dedicate this nation to the policy of the good neighbor.

Franklin D. Roosevelt
acceptance speech as the
Democratic nominee for
president
Jul 2, 1932

I have always said that a conference was held for one reason only, to give everybody a chance to get sore at everybody else. Sometimes it takes two or three conferences to scare up a war, but generally one will do it.

Will Rogers
syndicated column
The New York Times
Jul 6, 1933

Time is the very material commodity which the Foreign Office is expected to provide in the same way as other departments provide other war material.

**Robert, 1st Baron
Vansittart**
memorandum
Dec 31, 1936

Outside the kingdom of the Lord there is no nation which is greater than any other. God and history will remember your judgment.

Haile Selassie
speech at the League of
Nations
1936

Much of what Mr. Wallace calls his global thinking is, no matter how you slice it, still globaloney. Mr. Wallace's warp of sense and his woof of nonsense is very tricky cloth out of which to cut the pattern of a postwar world.

Clare Boothe Luce
speech to the House of
Representatives
Feb, 1943

In foreign relations, as in all other relations, a policy has been formed only when commitments and power have been brought into balance.

Walter Lippmann
U.S. Foreign Policy
1943

There is nothing more likely to start disagreement among people or countries than an agreement.

E.B. White
"My Day"
One Man's Meat
1944

Harry S Truman speech in Kansas City, Missouri Apr, 1945	When Kansas and Colorado have a quarrel over the water in the Arkansas River they don't call out the National Guard in each state and go to war over it. They bring a suit in the Supreme Court of the United States and abide by the decision. There isn't a reason in the world why we cannot do that internationally.
Ernest Bevin *The Spectator* Apr 20, 1951	My (foreign) policy is to be able to take a ticket at Victoria Station and go anywhere I damn well please.
Dwight D. Eisenhower State of the Union message Feb 2, 1953	Foreign policy must be clear, consistent and confident.
Dwight D. Eisenhower first inaugural address Jan 20, 1953	Whatever America hopes to bring to pass in the world must first come to pass in the heart of America.
George F. Kennan Stafford Little Lectures, Princeton Univ. Mar, 1954	By this I mean that a political society does not live to conduct foreign policy; it would be more correct to say that it conducts foreign policy in order to live.
Adlai E. Stevenson Jr. *Call to Greatness* 1954	For the nation's purposes always exceed its means, and it is finding a balance between means and ends that is the heart of foreign policy and that makes it such a speculative, uncertain business.
Chou En-lai *Saturday Evening Post* Mar 27, 1954	All diplomacy is a continuation of war by other means.
Harold Macmillan speech in the House of Commons Jul 27, 1955	A Foreign Secretary . . . is always faced with this cruel dilemma. Nothing he can say can do very much good, and almost anything he may say may do a great deal of harm. Anything he says that is not obvious is dangerous; whatever is not trite is risky. He is forever poised between the cliche and the indiscretion.
Dag Hammarskjold after talks with Soviet leaders *Look* Sep 19, 1956	I never discuss discussions.
Dwight D. Eisenhower remarks to League of Women Voters, Washington. D.C. May 1, 1957	A foreign policy is not difficult to state. We are for peace, first, last and always, for very simple reasons. We know that it is only in a peaceful atmosphere, a peace with justice, one in which we can be confident, that America can prosper as we have known prosperity in the past.
Dwight D. Eisenhower news conference Jan 30, 1957	You don't promote the cause of peace by talking only to people with whom you agree.
George F. Kennan Reith Lectures on BBC radio 1957	Until we stop pushing the Kremlin against a closed door, we shall never learn whether it would be prepared to go through an open one.

The true end of political action is, after all, to affect the deeper convictions of men; this the atomic bomb cannot do. The suicidal nature of this weapon renders it unsuitable both as a sanction of diplomacy and as the basis of an alliance.

George F. Kennan
Reith Lectures on
BBC radio
1957

What we call foreign affairs is no longer foreign affairs. It's a local affair. Whatever happens in Indonesia is important to Indiana. . . . We must understand people. As long as any . . . cannot enjoy the blessings of peace with justice, then indeed there is no peace anywhere.

Dwight D. Eisenhower
speech in Arlington,
Virginia
Jun 12, 1959

Let every nation know, whether it wishes us well or ill, that we shall pay any price, bear any burden, meet any hardship, support any friend, oppose any foe, to assure the survival and the success of liberty.

John F. Kennedy
inaugural address
Jan 20, 1961

Diplomacy and defense are not substitutes for one another. Either alone would fail.

John F. Kennedy
speech at Univ. of
Washington, Seattle
Nov 16, 1961

So let us begin anew—remembering on both sides (Soviet and American) that civility is not a sign of weakness, and sincerity is always subject to proof. Let us never negotiate out of fear, but let us never fear to negotiate.

John F. Kennedy
inaugural address
Jan 20, 1961

Every government is in some respects a problem for every other government, and it will always be this way so long as the sovereign state, with its supremely self-centered rationale, remains the basis of international life.

George F. Kennan
Russia and the West under Lenin and Stalin
1961

The freedom of the city is not negotiable. We cannot negotiate with those who say, "What's mine is mine and what's yours is negotiable."

John F. Kennedy
televised speech
Jul 25, 1961

A state worthy of the name has no friends—only interests.

Charles De Gaulle
quoted by former aide
Constantin Melnick
Newsweek
Oct 1, 1962

Great Britain has lost an Empire and has not yet found a role.

Dean Acheson
speech at the U.S. Military Academy, West Point, New York
Dec 5, 1962

Diplomats are useful only in fair weather. As soon as it rains they drown in every drop.

Charles De Gaulle
quoted by former aide
Constantin Melnick
Newsweek
Oct 1, 1962

The purpose of foreign policy is not to provide an outlet for our own sentiments of hope or indignation; it is to shape real events in a real world.

John F. Kennedy
speech at the Mormon Tabernacle, Salt Lake City
Sep 26, 1963

John F. Kennedy State of the Union address Jan 14, 1963	We shall be judged more by what we do at home than what we preach abroad.
Lyndon Baines Johnson speech to the United Nations General Assembly Dec 17, 1963	Any man and any nation that seeks peace—and hates war—and is willing to fight the good fight against hunger, and disease and ignorance and misery will find the United States of America by their side, willing to walk with them—walk with them every step of the way.
Lyndon Baines Johnson speech in Gettysburg, Pennsylvania May 30, 1963	We keep a vigil of peace around the world.
John F. Kennedy speech at the Mormon Tabernacle, Salt Lake City Sep 26, 1963	We must recognize that every nation determines its policies in terms of its own interests.
John F. Kennedy speech prepared for delivery in Dallas the day of his assassination Nov 22, 1963	A nation can be no stronger abroad than she is at home. Only an America which practices what it preaches about equal rights and social justice will be respected by those whose choice affects our future.
James Reston *The New York Times* Dec 16, 1964	This is the devilish thing about foreign affairs: they are foreign and will not always conform to our whim.
John F. Kennedy quoted *Saturday Review* Mar 7, 1964	You can always survive a mistake in domestic affairs but you can get killed by one made in foreign policy.
Lyndon Baines Johnson State of the Union address Jan 8, 1964	Our ultimate goal is a world without war. A world made safe for diversity, in which all good men, goods and ideas can freely move across every border and every boundary.
J. William Fulbright speech in the U.S. Senate Mar 27, 1964	We are handicapped by (foreign) policies based on old myths rather than current realities.
Julius K. Nyerere *Reporter* Apr 9, 1964	Small nations are like indecently dressed women. They tempt the evil-minded.
Adlai E. Stevenson Jr. *The New York Times* Aug 14, 1964	After four years at the United Nations I sometimes yearn for the peace and tranquility of a political convention.
Lester B. Pearson *Vancouver Sun* Mar 18, 1965	Diplomacy is letting someone else have your way.
Alex Quaison-Sackey *Quote* Jun 27, 1965	There is now a balance of terror.

Men and nations do behave wisely, once all other alternatives have been exhausted.

Abba Eban
Vogue
Aug 1, 1967

Foreign relations are like human relations. They are endless. The solution of one problem usually leads to another.

James Reston
Sketches in the Sand
1967

Men may be linked in friendship. Nations are linked only by interests.

Rolf Hochhuth
The Soldiers
1967

Nations, like individuals, have to limit their objectives, or take the consequences.

James Reston
Sketches in the Sand
1967

If there ever was in the history of humanity an enemy who was truly universal, an enemy whose acts and moves trouble the entire world, threaten the entire world, attack the entire world in any way or another, that real and really universal enemy is precisely Yankee imperialism.

Fidel Castro
speech to the International Cultural Congress in Havana
Jan 12, 1968

I report to you that our country is challenged at home and abroad: that it is our will that is being tried and not our strength; our sense of purpose and not our ability to achieve a better America.

Lyndon Baines Johnson
State of the Union address
Jan 17, 1968

Why employ intelligent and highly paid ambassadors and then go and do their work for them? You don't buy a canary and sing yourself.

Sir Alec Douglas-Home
The New York Times
Apr 21, 1969

If, when the chips are down, the world's most powerful nation, the United States of America, acts like a pitiful, helpless giant, the forces of totalitarianism and anarchy will threaten free nations and free institutions throughout the world.

Richard M. Nixon
televised speech
Apr 30, 1970

Diplomacy . . . means the art of nearly deceiving all your friends, but not quite deceiving all your enemies.

Kofi Busia
interview
Feb 2, 1970

I don't like hypocrisy—even in international relations.

Kofi Busia
interview
Feb 2, 1970

Our idea is to create a situation in which those lands to which we have obligations or in which we have interests, if they are ready to fight a fire, should be able to count on us to furnish the hose and water.

Richard M. Nixon
The New York Times
Mar 10, 1971

No foreign policy—no matter how ingenious—has any chance of success if it is born in the minds of a few and carried in the hearts of none.

Henry A. Kissinger
speech to the International Platform Association
Aug 2, 1973

Making foreign policy is a little bit like making pornographic movies. It's more fun doing it than watching it.

William P. Rogers
Chicago Sun–Times
Jun 29, 1976

Henry A. Kissinger speech to the Boston World Affairs Council Mar 11, 1976	Our greatest foreign policy problem is our divisions at home. Our greatest foreign policy need is national cohesion and a return to the awareness that in foreign policy we are all engaged in a common national endeavor.
Ronald Reagan *U.S. News & World* *Report* May 7, 1979	The (Carter) administration doesn't know the difference between being a diplomat and a doormat.
George S. McGovern *The Observer* Nov 25, 1979	He who tugs Uncle Sam's beard too hard risks reprisal from the mightiest nation on the face of this earth.
Henry A. Kissinger *White House Years* 1979	The management of a balance of power is a permanent undertaking, not an exertion that has a foreseeable end.
Michael Stewart *Life and Labour* 1980	It was . . . a Foreign Office joke that I could never make a speech of any length without using the word "mankind"; it seems to me a good word for a Foreign Secretary to have firmly fixed in his head.
Ronald Reagan speech to British parliament Jun 8, 1982	The ultimate determinant in the struggle now going on for the world will not be bombs and rockets but a test of wills and ideas—a trial of spiritual resolve; the values we hold, the beliefs we cherish and the ideas to which we are dedicated.
Ronald Reagan speech to the United Nations General Assembly Sep 26, 1983	What has happened to the dreams of the United Nations's founders? What has happened to the spirit which created the United Nations? The answer is clear: Governments got in the way of the dreams of the people.
Margaret Thatcher *London Times* Jun 1, 1984	I have a habit of comparing the phraseology of communiques, one with another across the years, and nohing a certain similarity of words, a certain similarity of optimism in the reports which followed the summit meetings and a certain similarity in the lack of practical results during the ensuing years.
Henry A. Kissinger commencement address at Univ. of South Carolina *Time* Jun 17, 1985	(The) American temptation (is) to believe that foreign policy is a subdivision of psychiatry.
Margaret Thatcher discussing talks with Mikhail Gorbachev, CBS-TV Mar 11, 1985	We didn't have to do the minuets of diplomacy. We got down to business.
Dean Rusk on 10th anniversary of fall of Saigon *The New York Times* Apr 30, 1985	The fidelity of the United States to security treaties is not just an empty matter. It is a pillar of peace in the world.
Conor Cruise O'Brien *New Republic* Nov 4, 1985	You can safely appeal to the United Nations in the comfortable certainty that it will let you down.

If the United Nations is a country unto itself, then the commodity it exports most is words.

Esther B. Fein
The New York Times
Oct 14, 1985

Can you imagine a policeman being required to secure the assent of parties to a street fight before breaking up the conflict?

Carlos P. Romulo
on the role of the United Nations, recalled on his death
Dec 15, 1985

We said nonsense but it was important nonsense.

Nora Astorga
on conversations at the United Nations with the U.S. ambassador
The New York Times
Sep 28, 1986

It it better to discuss things, to argue and engage in polemics than make perfidious plans of mutual destruction.

Mikhail S. Gorbachev
following discussions with U.S. Secretary of State George Shultz
The New York Times
Apr 19, 1987

A world without nuclear weapons would be less stable and more dangerous for all of us.

Margaret Thatcher
reported remarks to Mikhail Gorbachev
Time
Apr 27, 1987

Watching foreign affairs is sometimes like watching a magician; the eye is drawn to the hand performing the dramatic flourishes, leaving the other hand—the one doing the important job—unnoticed.

David K. Shipler
"For Israel and U.S., a Growing Military Partnership"
The New York Times
Mar 15, 1987

You don't negotiate with someone who marches into another country, devastates it, killing whoever stands in his way. You get him out, make him pay and see that he is never in a position to do these things again.

Margaret Thatcher
quoted in
Newsweek
Oct 29, 1990

We have before us the opportunity to forge for ourselves and for future generations a new world order, a world where the rule of law, not the law of the jungle, governs the conduct of nations.

George Bush
speech to the nation following the outbreak of war in the Persian Gulf, quoted in
Newsweek
Jan 28, 1991

What is at stake is more than one small country. It is a big idea, a new world order, where diverse nations are drawn together in common cause to achieve the universal aspirations of mankind: peace and security, freedom and the rule of law.

George Bush
State of the Union address quoted in
Time
Mar 18, 1991

Judiciary and Judges

Judges must beware of hard constructions and strained inferences, for there is no worse torture than the torture of laws.

Sir Francis Bacon
"Of Judicature"
Essays
1625

Jean de La Bruyère
"De quelques usages"
Les Caractères
1688

The duty of judges is to render justice; their profession is to discern it. There are some who know their duty and who practice their profession.

Le devoir des juges est de rendre justice; leur métier de la différer: Quelques-uns savent leur devoir, et font leur métier.

1st Earl of Mansfield (William Murray)
trial of John Wilkes to appeal his earlier conviction for non-appearance
1768

We must not regard political consequences, however formidable they may be; if rebellion was the certain consequence, we are bound to say, "Justitia fiat, ruat coelum" ("Let justice be done, though the sky falls").

John Marshall
Marbury v. *Madison*
1803

It is emphatically the province and duty of the judicial department to say what the law is. . . . If two laws conflict with each other, the courts must decide on the operation of each. . . . This is the very essence of judicial duty.

Thomas Jefferson
letter to Thomas Ritchie
Dec 25, 1820

The judiciary of the United States is the subtle corps of sappers and miners constantly working under ground to undermine the foundations of our confederated fabric. . . . A judiciary independent of a king or executive alone, is a good thing; but independent of the will of the nation is a solecism, at least in a republican government.

Thomas Jefferson
letter to W.C. Jarvis
Sep 28, 1820

It is a very dangerous doctrine to consider the judges as the ultimate arbiters of all constitutional questions. It is one which would place us under the despotism of an oligarchy.

Alexis, Comte de Tocqueville
Democracy in America
1835

There is hardly a political question in the United States which does not sooner or later turn into a judicial one.

Il n'est presque pas de question politique, aux Etats-Unis, qui ne se résolve tôt ou tard en question judiciaire.

Finley Peter Dunne
"The Supreme Court's Decisions"
Mr. Dooley's Opinions
1901

No matter whether th' constitution follows th' flag or not, th' supreme coort follows th' iliction returns.

Charles Evans Hughes
speech to the Elmira, New York, Chamber of Commerce
May 3, 1907

We are under a Constitution, but the Constitution is what the judges say it is, and the judiciary is the safeguard of our liberty and of our property under the Constitution.

Emma Goldman
"The Social Aspects of Birth Control"
Mother Earth
Apr, 1916

But even judges sometimes progress.

Benjamin F. Fairless
speech in Boston, Massachusetts
May 18, 1950

What five members of the Supreme Court say the law is may be something vastly different from what Congress intended the law to be.

We do not sit as a superlegislature to weigh the wisdom of legislation.

William O. Douglas
majority opinion
Day-Brite Lighting, Inc.
v. *Missouri*
Mar 3, 1952

We are not unaware that we are not final because we are infallible; we know that we are infallible only because we are final.

Robert H. Jackson
concurring opinion
Feb 9, 1953

Whenever you put a man on the Supreme Court he ceases to be your friend.

Harry S Truman
recalled on his 75th
birthday
The New York Times
May 8, 1959

As a member of this court I am not justified in writing my private notions of policy into the Constitution, no matter how deeply I may cherish them or how mischievous I may deem their disregard.

Felix Frankfurter
The New York Times
Aug 9, 1964

Our chief justices have probably had more profound and lasting influence on their times and on the direction of the nation than most presidents.

Richard M. Nixon
on appointment of chief
justice Warren Burger
May 21, 1969

You sit up there, and you see the whole gamut of human nature. Even if the case being argued involves only a little fellow and $50, it involves justice. That's what is important.

Earl Warren
recalled on his death
Time
Jul 22, 1974

The judicial system is the most expensive machine ever invented for finding out what happened and what to do about it.

Irving R. Kaufman
quoted
San Francisco Chronicle
Apr 17, 1977

Presidents come and go, but the Supreme Court, through its decisions, goes on forever.

Richard M. Nixon
Playboy
Apr, 1979

At the constitutional level where we work, 90 percent of any decision is emotional. The rational part of us supplies the reasons for supporting our predilections.

William O. Douglas
The Court Years 1939-75
1980

It is not our job to apply laws that have not yet been written.

John Paul Stevens
majority opinion
Sony v. *Universal City
Studios*
Jan 17, 1984

(The judiciary is) the least dangerous branch of our government.

Alexander M. Bickel
quoted
Christian Science Monitor
Feb 11, 1986

Somewhere "out there," beyond the walls of the courthouse, run currents and tides of public opinion which lap at the courtroom door.

William H. Rehnquist
speech at the Suffolk University Law School,
Boston, Massachusetts
Apr 17, 1986

Byron R. White majority opinion *Bowers* v. *Hardwick* Jun 30, 1986	The Court is most vulnerable and comes nearest to illegitimacy when it deals with judge-made constitutional law having little or no cognizable roots in the language or design of the Constitution.

Justice

Hammurabi *Code of Hammurabi* ca. 1760 B.C.	If a man destroy the eye of another man, they shall destroy his eye.
Plato *The Republic* ca. 390 B.C.	Mankind censures injustice, fearing that they may be victims of it and not because they shrink from committing it.
Plato *The Republic* ca. 390 B.C.	Everywhere there is one principle of justice, which is the interest of the stronger.
Aristotle *Nicomachean Ethics* ca. 325 B.C.	All virtue is summed up in dealing justly.
Epicurus *Principal Doctrines* ca. 300 B.C.	There is no such thing as justice in the abstract; it is merely a compact between men.
Marcus Tullius Cicero *De Legibus* ca. 52 B.C.	Let the punishment match the offense. *Noxiae poena par esto.*
Marcus Tullius Cicero *De Officiis* 44 B.C.	More law, less justice. *Summum ius summa iniuria.*
Horace *Satires* 38 B.C.	If you study the history and records of the world you must admit that the source of justice was the fear of injustice. *Iura inventa metu iniusti fateare necesse est, tempora si fastosque velis evolvere mundi.*
Saint Augustine *De Civitate Dei* 413-426	Justice is that virtue that assigns to every man his due. *Quae igitur iustitia est hominis quae ipsum hominem.*
Saint Augustine *De Civitate Dei* 413-426	Consequently, if the republic is the weal of the people, and there is no people if it be not associated by a common acknowledgment of right, and if there is no right where there is no justice, then most certainly it follows that there is no republic where there is no justice. *Ac per hoc, si res publica est populi et populus non est qui consensu non sociatus est iuris, non est autem ius ubi nulla iustitia est, procul dubio colligitur, ubi iustitia non est, non esse rem publicam.*

One of the uses of our system of justice is to warn others. . . . We are reforming, not the hanged man, but everyone else.

C'est un usage de notre justice d'en condamner aucuns pour l'avertissement des autres. . . . On ne corrige pas celui qu'on pend, on corrige les autres par lui.

Michel de Montaigne
"De l'art de conférer"
Essais
1580-88

Even the laws of justice themselves cannot subsist without mixture of injustice.

Les lois mêmes de la justice ne peuvent subsister sans quelque mélange d'injustice.

Michel de Montaigne
"Nous ne goûtons rien de pur"
Essais
1580-88

There are in nature certain fountains of justice, whence all civil laws are derived but as streams.

**Sir Francis Bacon
1st Viscount St. Albans**
Advancement of Learning
1605

Extreme justice is often unjust.
Une extrême justice est souvent une injure.

Jean Racine
The Thebaid
1664

The love of justice in most men is simply the fear of suffering injustice.

L'amour de la justice n'est, en la plupart des hommes, que la crainte de souffrir l'injustice.

Francois, Duc de La Rochefoucauld
Réflexions, ou Sentences et maximes morales
1665

Justice without strength is powerless, strength without justice is tyrannical. . . . Therefore, unable to make what is just strong, we have made what is strong just.

La justice sans la force est impuissante. La force sans la justice est tyrannique. . . . Et ainsi ne pouvant faire que ce qui est juste fût fort, on a fait que ce qui est fort fût juste.

Blaise Pascal
Pensées
1670

A guilty man punished is an example for the mob; an innocent man convicted is the business of every honest person.

Un coupable puni est un exemple pour la canaille; un innocent condamné est l'affaire de tous les honnêtes gens.

Jean de La Bruyère
"De quelques usages"
Les Caractères
1688

They have a Right to censure, that have a Heart to help: the rest is Cruelty, not Justice.

William Penn
Some Fruits of Solitude in Reflections & Maxims
1693

Rigid justice is the greatest injustice.

Thomas Fuller
Gnomologia
1732

One can't be just if one is not human at the same time.
On ne peut être juste si on n'est pas humain.

**Marquis de Vauvenargues
(Luc de Clapier)**
Réflexions et maximes
1746

Be just before you're generous.

Richard Brinsley Sheridan
The School for Scandal
1777

Sir William Blackstone *Commentaries on the* *Laws of England* 1783	For the law holds, that it is better that ten guilty persons escape, than that one innocent suffer.
Immanuel Kant *Idea for a Universal History with a Cosmopolitan Purpose* 1784	The greatest problem for the human species, the solution of which nature compels him to seek, is that of attaining a civil society which can administer justice universially.
Benjamin Franklin letter to Benjamin Vaughan Mar 14, 1785	That it is better 100 guilty Persons should escape than that one innocent Person should suffer, is a Maxim that has been long and generally approved.
George Washington letter to Edmund Randolph Sep 27, 1789	The administration of justice is the firmest pillar of Government.
Jeremy Bentham *Introduction to the Principles of Morals and Legislation* 1789	All punishment is mischief. All punishment in itself is evil.
Edmund Burke *Reflections on the Revolution in France* 1790	Justice is itself the great standing policy of civil society; and any eminent departure from it, under any circumstances, lies under the suspicion of being no policy at all.
Mary Wollstonecraft *A Vindication of the Rights of Women* 1792	It is justice, not charity, that is wanting in the world.
Thomas Jefferson first inaugural address Mar 4, 1801	Equal and exact justice to all men of whatever state or persuasion, religious or political.
Napoleon I remarks in the Council of State Mar 12, 1803	To be just is not simply doing right, the governed must be convinced that it is right. *Il ne suffit pas pour être juste de faire le bien, il faut encore que les administres soient convaincus.*
Napoleon I remarks in the Council of State Mar 12, 1803	There is no authority without justice. *Il n'y a point de force sans justice.*
Napoleon I letter to M. Fouché Jun 20, 1805	The art of policing is, in order not to punish often, to punish severely. *L'art de la police, afin de ne pas punir souvent, est de punir sévèrement.*
Napoleon I letter to M. Lebrun, quoted by Thibaudeau *Le Consulat et l'Empire* 1834	In matters of government, justice means force as well as virtue. *En fait de gouvernement, justice veut dire force comme vertu.*

I believe that justice is instinct and innate, that the moral sense is as much a part of our constitution as that of feeling, seeing, or hearing.

Thomas Jefferson
letter to John Adams
Oct 14, 1816

It is the feeling of injustice that is insupportable to all men.

Thomas Carlyle
Chartism
1839

When I refuse to obey an unjust law, I do not contest the right of the majority to command, but I simply appeal from the sovereignty of the people to the sovereignty of mankind.
Quand donc je réfuse d'obéir à une loi injuste, je ne dénie point à la majorité le droit de commander; j'en appelle seulement de la souveraineté du peuple à la souveraineté du genre humain.

Alexis, Comte de Tocqueville
Democracy in America
1835-39

Justice is truth in action.
La justice est la vérité en action.

Joseph Joubert
Pensées
1842

Justice is the great interest of man on earth.

Daniel Webster
speaking on Supreme
Court justice Joseph Story
Sep 12, 1845

Sir, I say that justice is truth in action.

Benjamin Disraeli
speech in the House of
Commons
Feb 11, 1851

As long as justice and injustice have not terminated their ever-renewing fight for ascendancy in the affairs of mankind, human beings must be willing, when need is, to do battle for the one against the other.

John Stuart Mill
"The Contest in America"
Fraser's Magazine
Feb, 1862

The severest justice may not always be the best policy.

Abraham Lincoln
message to Congress
Jul 17, 1862

"No, no!" said the Queen. "Sentence first—verdict afterwards."

**Lewis Carroll
(Charles L. Dodgson)**
Alice in Wonderland
1865

I have always found that mercy bears richer fruits than strict justice.

Abraham Lincoln
speech in Washington,
D.C.
1865

National injustice is the surest road to national downfall.

**William Ewart
Gladstone**
speech in Plumstead,
England
1878

Justice and good will will outlast passion.

James A. Garfield
letter accepting the
Republican nomination
for president
Jul 12, 1880

Robert G. Ingersoll *Prose-Poems and* *Selections* 1884	Justice should remove the bandage from her eyes long enough to distinguish between the vicious and the unfortunate.
Anatole France *Monsieur Bergeret à Paris* 1900	Once the laws are just, then men will be just. *Quand les lois seront justes, les hommes seront justes.*
Finley Peter Dunne "Cross-Examinations" *Mr. Dooley's Opinions* 1901	I tell ye Hogan's r-right whin he says: "Justice is blind." Blind she is, an' deef an' dumb an' has a wooden leg!
Anatole France "Crainquebille" 1905	Justice is the sanction used to support established injustices. *La justice est la sanction des injustices établies.*
Finley Peter Dunne "The Food We Eat" *Dissertations by Mr.* *Dooley* 1906	This home iv opporchunity where ivry man is th' equal iv ivry other man befure th' law if he isn't careful.
Samuel Butler *Notebooks* 1912	Justice is my being allowed to do whatever I like. Injustice is whatever prevents my doing so.
Woodrow Wilson first inaugural address Mar 4, 1913	The firm basis of government is justice, not pity.
Theodore Roosevelt *Autobiography* 1913	The only kinds of courage and honesty which are permanently useful to good institutions anywhere are those shown by men who decide all cases with impartial justice on grounds of conduct and not on grounds of class.
Emmeline Pankhurst *My Own Story* 1914	I was transfixed with horror, and over me there swept the sudden conviction that hanging was a mistake—worse, a crime. It was my awakening to one of the most terrible facts of life—that justice and judgment lie often a world apart.
Sir Max Beerbohm "Servants" *And Even Now* 1920	Somehow, our sense of justice never turns in its sleep till long after the sense of injustice in others has been thoroughly aroused.
H.L. Mencken *Prejudices: Third Series* 1922	Injustice is relatively easy to bear; what stings is justice.
Oliver Wendell Holmes Jr. *Olmstead* v. *United States* 1928	For my part I think it a less evil that some criminals should escape, than that the government should play an ignoble part.
Learned Hand speech to the New York Legal Aide Society Feb 16, 1951	If we are to keep our democracy, there must be one commandment: Thou shall not ration justice.

Peace and justice are two sides of the same coin.

Dwight D. Eisenhower
radio and television
address
Feb 20, 1957

Fairness is what justice really is.

Potter Stewart
Time
Oct 20, 1958

Swift justice demands more than just swiftness.

Potter Stewart
Time
Oct 20, 1958

We will not be satisfied until justice rolls down like waters and righteousness like a mighty stream.

Martin Luther King Jr.
speech in Washington,
D.C.
Jun 15, 1963

Justice is like a train that's nearly always late.

Yevgeny Yevtushenko
*A Precocious
Autobiography*
1963

We will demonstrate anew that the strong can be just in the use strength—and the just can be strong in the defense of justice.

**Lyndon Baines
Johnson**
speech to Congress
Nov 27, 1963

Injustice anywhere is a threat to justice everywhere.

Martin Luther King Jr.
"Letter from the Birming-
ham Jail"
Jan 16, 1963

Justice delayed is democracy denied.

Robert F. Kennedy
"To Secure These
Rights"
The Pursuit of Justice
1964

Get out of the way of Justice. She is blind.

Stanislaw Lec
More Unkempt thoughts
1968

White folks don't want peace; they want quiet. The price you pay for peace is justice. Until there is justice, there will be no peace and quiet.

Jesse Jackson
interview
Playboy
Nov, 1969

We have accumulated a wealth of historical experience which confirms our belief that the scales of American justice are out of balance.

Angela Yvonne Davis
statement to the court,
Marin County, California
Jan 5, 1971

The criminal justice system is breaking down because we, as a nation, have for too long neglected to nourish its heart—the court systems of our country.

G. Gordon Liddy
Connecticut
Feb, 1977

Before going to prison I believed that criticism of the criminal justice system for its treatment of the poor was so much liberal bleating and bunk. I was wrong.

G. Gordon Liddy
Connecticut
Feb, 1977

Law

Aeschylus *The Eumenides* 458 B.C.	Wrong must not win by technicalities.
Aristotle *Politics* 343 B.C.	Law is order, and good law is good order.
Aristotle *Politics* 343 B.C.	Even when laws have been written down, they ought not always to remain unaltered.
Aristotle *Politics* 343 B.C.	Whereas the law is passionless, passion must ever sway the heart of man.
Aristotle *Politics* 343 B.C.	Good laws if they are not obeyed, do not constitute good government.
Terence *Heauton Timoroumenos* ca. 163 B.C.	Extreme law is often extreme injustice. *Ius summum saepe summa est malitia.*
Marcus Tullius Cicero *De Legibus* ca. 52 B.C.	The good of the people is the supreme law. *Salus populi suprema est lex.*
Livy *Ab Urbe Condita* ca. 29 B.C.	No law is quite appropriate for all. *Nulla lex satis commoda omnibus est.*
Lucius Annaeus Seneca (the Elder) *Controversiae* ca. 40	Certain laws have not been written, but they are more fixed than all the written laws. *Quaedam iura non scripta, sed omnibus scriptis certiora sunt.*
Bible *1 Timothy* ca. 100	The law is good, if a man use it lawfully.
Solon quoted by Diogenes Laërtius *Lives and Opinions of Eminent Philosophers* 3rd cent. A.D.	Laws are like spider's webs which, if anything small falls into them they ensnare it, but large things break through and escape.
Magna Carta Clause 39 1215	No freeman shall be taken, or imprisoned, or outlawed, or exiled, or in any way harmed, nor will we go upon him nor will we send upon him, except by the legal judgment of his peers or by the law of the land.

To none will we sell, to none deny or delay, right or justice.

Magna Carta
Clause 40
1215

Law: an ordinance of reason for the common good, made by him who has care of the community.

Legis, quae nihil est aliud quam quaedam rationis ordinatio ad bonum commune, ab eo qui curam communitatis habet, promulgata.

St. Thomas Aquinas
Summa Theologiae
1273

The highest and ultimate instrument of political power is capital punishment.

Nervus potestatis politicae praecipuus et summus est supplicium capitale.

Philip Melanchthon
Philosophiae Moralis Epitomes
ca. 1530

Whoever desires to found a state and give it laws, must start with assuming that all men are bad and ever ready to display their vicious nature, whenever they may find occasion for it.

E necessario a chi dispone una republica e ordina leggi in quella, presupporre tutti gli uomini rei, e che li abbiano sempre a usare la malignità dello animo loro qualunque volta ne abbiano libera occasione.

Niccolò Machiavelli
Discourses on the First Ten Books of Titus Livius
1531

When it is a question of saving the fatherland, one should not stop for a moment to consider whether something is lawful or unlawful, gentle or cruel, laudable or shameful; but, putting aside every other consideration, one ought to follow to the end whatever resolve will save the life of the state and preserve the freedom of one's country.

La quale cosa merita de essere notata et osservata da qualunque cittadino si truova a consigliare la patria sua; perché dove si dilibera al tutto della salute della patria, non vi debbe cadere alcuna considerazione né di giusto né d'ingiusto, né di piatoso né di crudele, né di laudabile né d'ignominioso; anzi, posposto ogni altre rispetto, seguire al tutto quel partito che le salvi la vita e mantenghile la libertà.

Niccolò Machiavelli
Discourses on the First Ten Books of Titus Livius
1531

Because just as good morals, if they are to be maintained, have need of the laws, so the laws, if they are to be observed, have need of good morals.

Perché così come gli buoni costumi per mantenersi hanno bisogno delle leggi, così le leggi per osservarsi hanno bisogno de' buoni costumi.

Niccolò Machiavelli
Discourses on the First Ten Books of Titus Livius
1531

The chief foundations of all states, new as well as old or composite, are good laws and good arms; and as there cannot be good laws where the state is not well armed, it follows that where they are well armed they have good laws.

E principali fondamenti che abbino tutti li stati, così nuovi, comme vecchi o misti, sono le buone legge e le buone arme. E perché non può essere buone legge dove non sono buone arme, e dove sono buone arme conviene sieno buone legge.

Niccolò Machiavelli
Il Principe
1532

If we insist, however, that sovereign power means exemption from all law whatsoever, there is no prince who can be regarded as sovereign, since all the princes of the earth are subject to the laws of God and of nature, and even to certain human laws common to all nations.

Jean Bodin
Six Books of the Commonwealth
1576

Michel de Montaigne "Apologie de Raimond Sebond" *Essais* 1580-88	Nothing is more subject to change than the laws. *Il n'est rien sujet à plus continuelle agitation que les lois.*
William Shakespeare *Henry VI, Part II* 1591	The first thing we do, let's kill all the lawyers.
William Shakespeare *The Merchant of Venice* 1595	In law, what plea so tainted and corrupt/ But, being seasoned with a gracious voice,/ Obscures the show of evil?
William Shakespeare *Measure for Measure* 1604-05	We must not make a scarecrow of the law,/ Setting it up to fear the birds of prey,/ And let it keep one shape, till custom make it/ Their perch, and not their terror.
Miguel de Cervantes *Don Quixote* 1605-15	Laws that only threaten, and are not kept, become like the log that was given to the frogs to be their king, which they feared at first, but soon scorned and trampled on. *Las leyes que atemorizan y no se ejecutan, vienen á ser como la viga, rey de las ranas: que al principio las espantó, y con el tiempo, la menospreciaron y se subieron sobre ella.*
Robert Burton *The Anatomy of Melancholy* 1621	No rule is so general, which admits not some exception.
Sir Edward Coke *Institutes: Commentary upon Littleton* 1628	A man's house is his castle.
John Locke *The Second Treatise on Government* 1690	Where-ever Law ends, Tyranny begins.
1st Marquess of Halifax (George Savile) *The Character of a Trimmer* 1700	No prince is so Great, as not to think fit, for his own Credit at least, to give an outward, when he refuseth a real, worship to the laws.
1st Marquess of Halifax *Political Thoughts and Reflections* 1750	Men are not hanged for stealing Horses, but that Horses may not be stolen.
John Locke *Some Thoughts Concern- ing Education* 1693	Good and evil, reward and punishment, are the only motives to a rational creature; these are the spur and reins whereby all mankind are set on work and guided.
Jonathan Swift *A Critical Essay upon the Faculties of the Mind* 1707	Laws are like cobwebs, which may catch small flies, but let wasps and hornets break through.

The more laws, the more offenders.

Thomas Fuller
Gnomologia
1732

Law cannot persuade where it cannot punish.

Thomas Fuller
Gnomologia
1732

It is better to risk saving a guilty man than to condemn an innocent one.
Il vaut mieux hasarder de sauver un coupable que de condamner un innocent.

Voltaire
Zadig
1747

The wording of laws should mean the same thing to all men.
Il est essentiel que les paroles des lois réveillent chez tous les hommes les mêmes idées.

Charles Louis de Montesquieu
De l'Esprit des lois
1748

Care must be taken that laws do not offend against nature.
Il faut prendre garde que les lois soient concus de manière qu'elles ne choquent point la nature des choses.

Charles Louis de Montesquieu
De l'Esprit des lois
1748

Laws should not be changed without good reason.
Il ne faut point faire de changement dans une loi sans une raison suffisante.

Charles Louis de Montesquieu
De l'Esprit des lois
1748

The language of laws should be simple; directness is always better than elaborate wording.
Le style des lois doit être simple; l'expression directe s'entend toujours mieux que l'expression réfléchie.

Charles Louis de Montesquieu
De l'Esprit des lois
1748

Laws should not be subtle; they are designed for people of average understanding: they are not exercises in the art of logic but the simple reasoning of the head of the house.
Les lois ne doivent point être subtiles; elles sont faites pour des gens de médiocre entendement: elles ne sont point un art de logique, mais la raison simple d'un père de famille.

Charles Louis de Montesquieu
De l'Esprit des lois
1748

Just as useless laws weaken necessary ones, those that can be evaded weaken all legislation.
Comme les lois inutiles affaiblissent les lois nécessaires, celles qu'on peut éluder affaiblissent la législation.

Charles Louis de Montesquieu
De l'Esprit des lois
1748

Laws too gentle are seldom obeyed; too severe, seldom executed.

Benjamin Franklin
Poor Richard's Almanack
1732-57

The first of all laws is to respect the laws: the severity of penalties is only a vain resource, invented by little minds in order to substitute terror for that respect which they have no means of obtaining.

Jean Jacques Rousseau
A Discourse on Political Economy
1758

Good laws lead to the making of better ones; bad ones bring about worse.
Les bonnes lois en font faire de meilleures, les mauvaises en amènent de pires.

Jean Jacques Rousseau
The Social Contract
1762

Oliver Goldsmith *The Traveller* 1765	Laws grind the poor, and rich men rule the law.
1st Earl of Mansfield *Jones* v. *Randall* 1774	Whatever is contra bonos mores et decorum the principles of our laws prohibit and the King's Court as the general censor and guardian of the public morals is bound to restrain and punish.
Edmund Burke speech, "On Conciliation with the American Colonies" Mar 22, 1775	It is not, what a lawyer tells me I may do; but what humanity, reason, and justice tell me I ought to do.
George Washington letter to Colonel Vanneter 1781	Laws made by common consent must not be trampled on by individuals.
Immanuel Kant *Grundlagen zur Metaphysik der Sitten* 1785	There is, therefore, only one categorical imperative. It is: Act only according to that maxim by which you can at the same time will that it should become a universal law.
Samuel Johnson quoted by Hester Lynch Piozzi *Anecdotes of Samuel Johnson* 1786	The law is the last result of human wisdom acting upon human experience for the benefit of the public.
Alexander Hamilton *The Federalist* Dec 1, 1787	Government implies the power of making laws. It is essential to the idea of a law, that it be attended with a sanction; or, in other words, a penalty or punishment for disobedience.
Thomas Jefferson letter to M. Limozin Dec 22, 1787	Ignorance of the law is no excuse in any country. If it were, the laws would lose their effect, because it can be always pretended.
Thomas Jefferson letter to William Carmichael May 27, 1788	It is more dangerous that even a guilty person should be punished without the forms of law than that he should escape.
Thomas Jefferson letter to Abbé Arnond May 27, 1789	The execution of the laws is more important than the making of them.
Edmund Burke debate in the House of Commons on the impeachment of Warren Hastings May 28, 1794	There is but one law for all, namely, that law which governs all law, the law of our Creator, the law of humanity, justice, equity— the law of nature, and of nations.
Samuel Horsley speech in the House of Lords 1795	The mass of the people have nothing to do with the laws but to obey them.
Denis Diderot *Supplement to Bougainville's "Voyage"* 1796	Anyone who takes it upon himself, on his private authority, to break a bad law, thereby authorizes everyone else to break the good ones.

Men have feelings but the law does not.
L'homme a des entrailles et la loi n'en a pas.

Napoleon I
attributed remark in the
Council of State by Pelet
de la Lozère
*Opinions de a sur divers
sujets de politique et
d'administration*
1833

Laws and institutions must go hand in hand with the progress of the human mind.

Thomas Jefferson
letter to Samuel
Kercheval
Jul 12, 1816

Laws are made for men of ordinary understanding, and should therefore be construed by the ordinary rules of common sense. Their meaning is not to be sought for in metaphysical subtleties, which may make anything mean everything or nothing, at pleasure.

Thomas Jefferson
letter to Judge William
Johnson
Jun 12, 1823

The victim to too severe a law is considered as a martyr rather than a criminal.

Charles Caleb Colton
Lacön
1825

I will not say with Lord Hale, that "The Law will admit of no rival" . . . but I will say that it is a jealous mistress, and requires a long and constant courtship. It is not to be won by trifling favors, but by lavish homage.

Joseph Story
speech, "The Value and
Importance of Legal
Studies"
Aug 5, 1829

If a law commands me to sin I will break it; if it calls me to suffer, I will let it take its course unresistingly. The doctrine of blind obedience and unqualified submission to any human power, whether civil or ecclesiastical, is the doctrine of despotism, and ought to have no place among Republicans and Christians.

Angelina Grimké
"Appeal to the Christian
Women of the South"
*The Anti-Slavery
Examiner*
Sep, 1836

"If the law supposes that," said Mr. Bumble, . . . "the law is a ass—a idiot. If that's the eye of the law, the law is a bachelor; and the worst I wish the law is that his eye may be opened by experience—by experience."

Charles Dickens
Oliver Twist
1837-39

Our written law is often difficult to understand, but anyone can read it. There is nothing, on the other hand, more obscure for the ordinary person and less in his grasp than a legal system based on precedent. The need for the student of the law in England and the United States, the high esteem in which his talent is held, separates him more and more from the people, and finally puts him in a class apart.
Nos lois écrites sont souvent difficiles à comprendre, mais chacun peut y lire; il n'y a rien, au contraire, de plus obscur pour le vulgaire et de moins à sa portée qu'une législation fondée sur des précédents. Ce besoin qu'on a du légiste en Angleterre et aux Etats-Unis, cette haute idée qu'on se forme de ses lumières, le sépare de plus en plus du peuple, et achève de le mettre dans une classe à part.

**Alexis, Comte de
Tocqueville**
Democracy in America
1835-39

Good men must not obey the laws too well.

Ralph Waldo Emerson
"Politics"
Essays: Second Series
1844

Ralph Waldo Emerson "Politics" *Essays: Second Series* 1844	The form of government which prevails is the expression of what cultivation exists in the population which permits it. The law is only a memorandum.
Henry David Thoreau *Civil Disobedience* 1849	I think that we should be men first, and subjects afterward. It is not desirable to cultivate a respect for the law, so much as for the right.
Henry David Thoreau *Civil Disobedience* 1849	The lawyer's truth is not Truth, but consistency or a consistent expediency.
Wendell Phillips speech Apr 12, 1852	The best use of good laws is to teach men to trample bad laws under their feet.
Walter Savage Landor "Diogenes and Plato" *Imaginary Conversations* 1824-53	Many laws as certainly make bad men, as bad men make many laws.
Ulysses S. Grant first inaugural address Mar 4, 1869	I know no method to secure the repeal of bad or obnoxious laws so effective as their stringent execution.
Prince Otto von Bismarck speech in the Prussian Chamber of Deputies Mar 6, 1872	Laws are like medicine; they generally cure an evil by a lesser or a passing evil. *Gesetze sind wie Arzeneien, sie sind gewöhnlich nur Heilung einer Krankheit durch eine geringere oder vorübergehende Krankheit.*
James A. Garfield *Maxims* 1880	Coercion is the basis of every law in the universe—Human or Divine. A law is no law without coercion behind it.
Oliver Wendell Holmes Jr. *The Common Law* 1881	The law embodies the story of a nation's development through many centuries, and it cannot be dealt with as if it contained only the axioms and corollaries of a book of mathematics.
Henry Ward Beecher *Proverbs from Plymouth Pulpit* 1887	It usually takes a hundred years to make a law, and then, after it has done its work, it usually takes a hundred years to get rid of it.
Henry Ward Beecher *Proverbs from Plymouth Pulpit* 1887	Riches without law are more dangerous than is poverty without law.
James Bryce *The American Commonwealth* 1888	Law will never be strong or respected unless it has the sentiment of the people behind it. If the people of a state make bad laws, they will suffer for it. They will be the first to suffer. Suffering, and nothing else, will implant that sentiment of responsibility which is the first step to reform.
Benjamin Harrison speech in Indianapolis, Indiana Jul 12, 1888	To the law we bow with reverence. It is the one king that commands our allegiance. We will change our king when his rule is oppressive.

No good cause can be promoted upon the lines of lawlessness. Mobs do not discriminate, and the punishments inflicted by them have no repressive or salutary influence.

Benjamin Harrison
acceptance of
renomination for
presidency
Sep 3, 1892

Liberty, my fellow citizens, is responsibilty, and responsibilty is duty, and that duty is to preserve the exceptional liberty we enjoy within the law and for the law and by the law.

William McKinley
speech in Cleveland, Ohio
Jul 4, 1894

Law is merely the expression of the will of the strongest for the time being, and therefore laws have no fixity, but shift from generation to generation.

Brooks Adams
The Law of Civilization and Decay
1895

Law is largely crystallized custom, largely a mass of remedies which have been slowly evolved to meet the wrongs with which humanity has become thoroughly familiar.

Theodore Roosevelt
annual message as governor, Albany, New York
Jan 3, 1900

So long as governments set the example of killing their enemies, private individuals will occasionally kill theirs.

Elbert G. Hubbard
Contemplations
1902

Every new time will give its law.

Maxim Gorky
The Lower Depths
1903

Today there's law and order in everything. You can't beat anybody for nothing. If you do beat anyone, it's got to be for the sake of order.

Maxim Gorky
The Lower Depths
1903

No man is above the law and no man is below it; nor do we ask any man's permission when we ask him to obey it.

Theodore Roosevelt
speech
Jan, 1904

Great cases like hard cases make bad law.

Oliver Wendell Holmes Jr.
Northern Securities Company v. *United States*
1904

Laws are sand, customs are rock. Laws can be evaded and punishment escaped, but an openly transgressed custom brings sure punishment.

Mark Twain
The Gorkey Incident
1906

It cannot be helped, it is as it should be, that the law is behind the times.

Oliver Wendell Holmes Jr.
speech in New York City
Feb 15, 1913

After all, that is what laws are for, to be made and unmade.

Emma Goldman
"The Social Aspects of Birth Control"
Mother Earth
Apr, 1916

The common law is not a brooding omnipresence in the sky but the articulate voice of some sovereign or quasi sovereign that can be identified.

Oliver Wendell Holmes Jr.
Southern Pacific Co. v. *Jensen*
1917

Mohandas K. Gandhi
lecture to the Bombay
Provincial Cooperative
Conference
Sep 17, 1917

As in law so in war, the longest purse finally wins.

Hermann Hesse
Demian
1919

Those who are too lazy and comfortable to think for them-selves and be their own judges obey the laws. They have it easy. Others sense their own laws within them.

Wer zu bequem ist, um selber zu denken und selber sein Richter zu sein, der fügt sich eben in die Verbote, wie sie nun einmal sind. Er hat es leicht. Andere spüren selber Gebote in sich.

Calvin Coolidge
acceptance speech as
Republican vice-
presidental nominee
Jul 27, 1920

One with the law is a majority.

Roscoe Pound
*Introduction to the
Philosophy of Law*
1922

The law must be stable, but it must not stand still.

Louis D. Brandeis
dissenting opinion
Olmstead v. *United States*
1928

Decency, security and liberty alike demand that government officials shall be subjected to the same rules of conduct that are commands to the citizen. In a government of laws, existence of the government will be imperilled if it fails to observe the law scrupulously.

Bertolt Brecht
The Threepenny Opera
1928

The law is simply and solely made for the exploitation of those who do not understand it or of those, who out of naked need, cannot obey it.

Das Gesetz ist einzig und allein gemacht zur Ausbeutung derer, die es nicht verstehen oder die es aus nackter Not nicht befolgen können.

Learned Hand
speech in Washington,
D.C.
May 11, 1929

The language of the law must not be foreign to the ears of those who are to obey it.

James Truslow Adams
The Adams Family
1930

It will be of little avail to the people, that the laws are made by men of their own choice, if the laws be so voluminous that they cannot be read, or so incoherent that they cannot be understood.

Jean Anouilh
Antigone
1942

Nobody has a more sacred obligation to obey the law than those who make the law.

Felix Frankfurter
concurring opinion
United States v. *Mine
Workers*
1946

If one man can be allowed to determine for himself what is law, every man can. That means first chaos, then tyranny. Legal process is an essential part of the democratic process.

Mohandas K. Gandhi
*Non-Violence in Peace
and War*
1948

An unjust law is itself a species of violence. Arrest for its breach is more so.

Government can easily exist without law, but law cannot exist without government.

Bertrand Russell
"Ideas That Have Helped Mankind"
Unpopular Essays
1950

Every so often, we pass laws repealing human nature.

Howard Lindsay
quoted by John Crosby
New York Herald Tribune
Nov 21, 1954

Time and again a number of people—I, among them—have argued that you cannot change people's hearts merely by laws. Laws presumably express the conscience of a nation and its determination or will to do something.

Dwight D. Eisenhower
news conference
Sep 3, 1957

We are going to have to decide what kind of people we are— whether we obey the law only when we approve of it or whether we obey it no matter how distastful we may find it.

Harry Ashmore
on integration of Little Rock High School
Arkansas Gazette
Sep 4, 1957

Common sense often makes good law.

William O. Douglas
in court ruling
Mar 25, 1957

There is no person in this room whose basic rights are not involved in any successful defiance to the carrying out of court orders.

Dwight D. Eisenhower
on Arkansas' refusal to accept the Supreme Court's school desegregation ruling
May 14, 1958

We have never stopped sin by passing laws; and in the same way, we are not going to take a great moral ideal and achieve it merely by law.

Dwight D. Eisenhower
news conference
May 13, 1959

The police must obey the law while enforcing the law.

Earl Warren
unanimous opinion
Jun 22, 1959

Life and liberty can be as much endangered from illegal methods used to convict those thought to be criminals as from the actual criminals themselves.

Earl Warren
unanimous opinion
Jun 22, 1959

Fragile as reason is and limited as law is as the institutionalized medium of reason, that's all we have standing between us and the tyranny of mere will and the cruelty of unbridled, undisciplined feeling.

Felix Frankfurter
Felix Frankfurter Reminisces
1960

The law is a causeway upon which, so long as he keeps to it, a citizen may walk safely.

Robert Bolt
A Man for All Seasons
1962

Our nation is founded on the principle that observance of the law is the eternal safeguard of liberty and defiance of the law is the surest road to tyranny.

John F. Kennedy
televised speech
Sep 30, 1962

In civilized life, law floats in a sea of ethics.

Earl Warren
The New York Times
Nov 12, 1962

Martin Luther King Jr. *Wall Street Journal* Nov 13, 1962	It may be true that the law cannot make man love me, but it can keep him from lynching me, and I think that's pretty important.
Martin Luther King Jr. *Strength to Love* 1963	Morality cannot be legislated, but behavior can be regulated. Judicial decrees may not change the heart, but they can restrain the heartless.
John F. Kennedy televised speech Jun 11, 1963	Law alone cannot make men see right.
Roscoe Pound *Christian Science Monitor* Apr 24, 1963	Law is experience developed by reason and applied continually to further experience.
Martin Luther King Jr. *Why We Can't Wait* 1964	An individual who breaks a law that conscience tells him is unjust, and who willingly accepts the penalty of imprisonment in order to arouse the conscience of the community over its injustice, is in reality expressing the highest respect for the law.
Potter Stewart concurring opinion *Jacobellis* v. *Ohio* Jun 22, 1964	I shall not today attempt further to define the kinds of material . . . but I know it when I see it.
Hubert H. Humphrey speech in Williamsburg, Virginia May 1, 1965	There are not enough jails, not enough policemen, not enough courts to enforce a law not supported by the people.
Earl Warren majority opinion *Miranda* v. *Arizona* Jun 13, 1966	Prior to any questioning, the person must be warned that he has a right to remain silent, that any statement he does make may be used as evidence against him and that he has a right to the presence of an attorney, either retained or appointed.
Morton Irving Seiden *The Paradox of Hate: A Study in Ritual Murder* 1967	One can always legislate against specific acts of human wickedness; but one can never legislate against the irrational itself.
Harold Faber *The New York Times Magazine* Mar 17, 1968	If there isn't a law, there will be.
David Frost and Anthony Jay *The English* 1968	This is what has to be remembered about the law: Beneath that cold, harsh, impersonal exterior there beats a cold, harsh, impersonal heart.
William T. Gossett speech Aug 11, 1969	The rule of law can be wiped out in one misguided, however well-intentioned, generation.
Diane B. Schulder "Does the Law Oppress Women?" *Sisterhood Is Powerful* 1970	Law is a reflection and a source of prejudice. It both enforces and suggests forms of bias.

Through the centuries, men of law have been persistently concerned with the resolution of disputes . . . in ways that enable society to achieve its goals with a minimum of force and maximum of reason.

Archibald Cox
The New York Times
Dec 30, 1973

The states are not free, under the guise of protecting maternal health or potential life, to intimidate women into continuing pregnancies.

Harry A. Blackmun
majority opinion
Roe v. *Wade; Doe* v. *Bolton*
Jan 22, 1973

All laws are an attempt to domesticate the natural ferocity of the species.

John W. Gardner
San Francisco Chronicle
Jul 3, 1974

It is quite obvious that there are certain inherently governmental actions which, if undertaken by the sovereign in protection of . . . the nation's security, are lawful, but which if undertaken by private citizens are not.

Richard M. Nixon
Wall Street Journal
Mar 12, 1976

There are times when national interest is more important than the law.

Henry A. Kissinger
New York Times Magazine
Oct 31, 1976

(I am) appalled at the ethical bankruptcy of those who preach a right to life that means a bare existence in utter misery for so many.

Thurgood Marshall
Time
Jul 4, 1977

I have spent all my life under a Communist regime, and I will tell you that a society without any objective legal scale is a terrible one indeed. But a society with no other scale but the legal one is not quite worthy of man either.

Alexander Solzhenitsyn
commencement address at Harvard Univ. on "The Exhausted West"
Jun 8, 1978

Things in law tend to be black and white. But we all know that some people are a little bit guilty, while other people are guilty as hell.

Donald R. Cressey
Center Magazine
May/Jun, 1978

Abortion is inherently different from other medical procedures because no other procedure involves the purposeful termination of a potential life.

Potter Stewart
majority opinion
Harris v. *McRae*
Jun 30, 1980

We have the means to change the laws we find unjust or onerous. We cannot, as citizens, pick and choose the laws we will or will not obey.

Ronald Reagan
speech to the United Brotherhood of Carpenters and Joiners
Sep 3, 1981

There is far too much law for those who can afford it and far too little for those cannot.

Derek Bok
report to the Board of Overseers of Harvard Univ.
Apr 21, 1983

(Law is) vulnerable to the winds of intellectual or moral fashion, which it then validates as the commands of our most basic concept.

Robert H. Bork
The New York Times
Jan 4, 1985

Newton Minow *Time* Mar 18, 1985	In Germany, under the law everything is prohibited except that which is permitted. In France, under the law everything is permitted except that which is prohibited. In the Soviet Union, everything is prohibited, including that which is permitted. And in Italy, under the law everything is permitted, especially that which is prohibited.
Ronald D. Dworkin *Law's Empire* 1986	Law's empire is defined by attitude, not territory or power or process.
Ronald D. Dworkin *Law's Empire* 1986	Moral principle is the foundation of law.
Byron R. White majority opinion *Bowers* v. *Hardwick* Jun 30, 1986	The law . . . is constantly based on notions of morality, and if all laws representing essentially moral choices are to be invalidated under the due process clause, the courts will be very busy indeed.
Warren E. Burger quoted by Charlotte Saikowski, "The Power of Judicial Review" *Christian Science Monitor* Feb 11, 1987	Judges . . . rule on the basis of law, not public opinion, and they should be totally indifferent to pressures of the times.
Lawrence Gibbs *Wall Street Journal* Mar 3, 1987	A taxpaying public that doesn't understand the law is a taxpaying public that can't comply with the law.
Antonin Scalia concurring opinion Apr 21, 1987	A law can be both economic folly and constitutional.

Leadership/Statesmanship

Homer *Iliad* ca. 700 B.C.	To be both a speaker of words and a doer of deeds.
Homer *Iliad* ca. 700 B.C.	It is not possible to fight beyond your strength, even if you strive.
Confucius *The Analects* ca. 480 B.C.	He who exercises government by means of his virtue may be compared to the north polar star, which keeps its place and all the stars turn towards it.
Aeschylus *Prometheus Bound* ca. 478 B.C.	Every ruler is harsh whose rule is new.
Aristotle *Politics* 343 B.C.	They should rule who are able to rule best.

The man who commands efficiently must have obeyed others in the past, and the man who obeys dutifully is worthy of being some day a commander.

Nam et quit bene imperat, paruerit aliquando necesse est, et qui modeste paret, videtur, qui aliquando imperet, dignus esse.

Marcus Tullius Cicero
De Legibus
ca. 52 B.C.

But the actions of those who hold great power, and pass their lives in a lofty status, are known to all men. Therefore, in the highest position there is the least freedom of action.

Qui magno imperio praediti in excelso aetatem agunt, eorum facta cuncti mortales novere. Ita in maxima fortuna minima licentia est.

**Sallust
(Gaius Sallustius Crispus)**
The War with Catiline
ca. 40 B.C.

The foremost art of kings is the power to endure hatred.
Ars prima regni est posse invidiam pati.

Seneca (the Younger)
Hercules Furens
ca. 50

From this arises the question whether it is better to be loved rather than feared, or feared rather than loved. It might perhaps be answered that we should wish to be both: but since love and fear can hardly exist together, if we must choose between them, it is far safer to be feared than loved.

Nasce da questo una disputa: s'elli è meglio essere amato che temuto, o e converso. Respondesi, che si vorebbe essere l'uno e l'altro; ma, perché elli è difficile accozzarli insieme, è molto più sicuro essere temuto che amato, quando si abbia a mancare del'uno de' dua.

Niccolò Machiavelli
Il Principe
1532

He will act like prudent archers, who, seeing that the mark they plan to hit is too far away and knowing what space can be covered by the power of their bows, take an aim much higher than their mark, not in order to reach with their arrows so great a height, but to be able, with the aid of so high an aim, to attain their purpose.

Fare come gli arcieri prudenti, a' quali, parendo el loco dove disegnano ferire troppo lontano, e conoscendo fino a quanto va la virtù del loro arco, pongono la mira assai più alta che il loco destinato, non per aggiugnere con la loro freccia a tanta altezza, ma per potere con l'aiuto di sì alta mira pervenire al disegno loro.

Niccolò Machiavelli
Il Principe
1532

There is nothing more difficult to take in hand, more perilous to conduct, or more uncertain in its success, than to take the lead in the introduction of a new order of things.

E debbasi considerare, come non è cosa più difficile a trattare, né più dubia a riuscire, né più periculosa a maneggiare, che farsi capo a introdurre nuovi ordini.

Niccolò Machiavelli
Il Principe
1532

A prince being thus obliged to know well how to act as a beast must imitate the fox and the lion, for the lion cannot protect himself from traps, and the fox cannot defend himself from wolves. One must therefore be a fox to recognize traps, and a lion to frighten wolves.

Essendo adunque un principe necessitato sapere bene usare la bestia, debbe di quella pigliare la volpe ed il lione: perché il lione non si difenda da' lacci; la volpe non se difende da' lupi. Bisogna adunque essere volpe a conoscere i lacci, e lione a sbigottire i lupi.

Niccolò Machiavelli
Il Principe
1532

Niccolò Machiavelli *Il Principe* 1532	A man who wishes to act virtuously in every way necessarily comes to grief among so many who are not virtuous. Therefore if a prince wishes to maintain his rule he must learn how not to be virtuous, and to make use of this knowledge or not according to his need. *Perché uno uomo, che voglia fare in tutte le parte professione di buono, conviene ruini infra tanti che non sono buoni. Onde è necessario a uno principe, volendosi mantenere, imparare a potere essere non buono, e usarlo e non l'usare secondo la necessità.*
Michel de Montaigne "Nos affections s'emportent au-delà de nous" *Essais* 1580-88	We owe subjection and obedience to all our kings, whether good or bad, alike, for that has respect unto their office; but as to esteem and affection, these are only due to their virtue. *Nous devons la sujétion et l'obéissance également à tous Rois, car elle regarde leur office; mais l'estimation, non plus que l'affection, nous ne la devons qu'à leur vertu.*
Edmund Spenser *The Faerie Queene* 1596	Ill can he rule the great that cannot reach the small.
Elizabeth I *The Golden Speech* 1601	Though God hath raised me high, yet this I count the glory of my crown: that I have reigned with your loves.
William Shakespeare *Twelfth Night* 1601	Be not afraid of greatness: some are born great, some achieve greatness, and some have greatness thrust upon them
Ben Jonson *Sejanus* 1603	Whom hatred frights,/ Let him not dream on sovereignty.
William Shakespeare *Measure for Measure* 1604-05	No ceremony that to great ones 'longs,/ Not the king's crown, nor the deputed sword,/ The marshal's truncheon, nor the judge's robe,/ Become them with one half so good a grace/ As mercy does.
William Shakespeare *Othello* 1604-05	We cannot all be masters, nor all masters / Cannot be truly followed.
William Shakespeare *King Lear* 1605-06	Ay, every inch a king.
William Shakespeare *Macbeth* 1605-06	If chance will have me king, why, chance may crown me,/ Without my stir.
William Shakespeare *King Henry the Eighth* 1613	I would not be a queen/ For all the world.
Sir Francis Bacon "Of Cunning" *Essays* 1625	Nothing doth more hurt in a state than that cunning men pass for wise.
Sir Francis Bacon "Of Great Place" *Essays* 1625	Men in great places are thrice servants: servants of the sovereign or state, servants of fame, and servants of business.

All rising to great place is by a winding stair.

Sir Francis Bacon
"Of Great Place"
Essays
1625

He that would govern others, first should be/ Master of himself.

Philip Massinger
The Bondman
1629

Many punishments sometimes, and in some cases, as much discredit a prince as many funerals a physician.

Ben Jonson
"Of Statecraft"
Timber; or Discoveries
1640

I am one of those whose heart God hath drawn out to wait for some extraordinary dispensations, according to those promises that He hath held forth of things to be accomplished in the later time, and I cannot but think that God is beginning of them.

Oliver Cromwell
the army debates at
Putney, England
Nov 1, 1647

The renown of great men should always be measured by the means which they have used to acquire it.
La gloire des grands hommes se doit toujours mesurer aux moyens dont ils se sont servis pour l'acquérir.

Francois, Duc de La Rochefoucauld
Réflexions, ou Sentences et maximes morales
1665

The world usually rewards the appearance of ability rather than ability itself.
Le monde récompense plus souvent les apparences du mérite que le mérite même.

Francois, Duc de La Rochefoucauld
Réflexions, ou Sentences et maximes morales
1665

The mercy of princes is often just a way of gaining the affection of the people.
La clémence des princes n'est souvent qu'une politique pour gagner l'affection des peuples.

Francois, Duc de La Rochefoucauld
Réflexions, ou Sentences et maximes morales
1665

Those who spend their time on small things usually become incapable of large ones.
Ceux qui s'appliquent trop aux petites choses deviennent ordinairement incapables de grandes.

Francois, Duc de La Rochefoucauld
Réflexions, ou Sentences et maximes morales
1665

Even though men usually flatter themselves on their great deeds, but they are not often the results of a great design, but simply the results of chance.
Quoique les hommes se flattent de leurs grandes actions, elles ne sont pas souvent les effets d'un grand dessein, mais les effets du hasard.

Francois, Duc de La Rochefoucauld
Réflexions, ou Sentences et maximes morales
1665

The captain of a ship is not chosen from those of the passengers who comes from the best family.
On ne choisit pas pour gouverner un vaisseau celui des voyageurs qui est de la meilleure maison.

Blaise Pascal
Pensées
1670

Not the least of the qualities that go into the making of a great ruler is the ability of letting others serve him.
Etre capable de se laisser servir n'est pas une des moindres qualités, que puisse avoir un grand Roi.

Cardinal Richelieu
Political Testament part I, chap. 6
1687

Jean de La Bruyère
"De la cour"
Les Caractères
1688

The slave has only one master; the ambitious man has as many as there those who can help his career.

L'esclave n'a qu'un maître; l'ambitieux en a autant qu'il y a des gens utiles à sa fortune.

Jonathan Swift
Thoughts on Various Subjects
1706

Ambition often puts Men upon doing the meanest offices; so climbing is performed in the same position with creeping.

Joseph Addison
The Spectator
1711

If men of eminence are exposed to censure on one hand, they are as much liable to flattery on the other. If they receive reproaches which are not due to them, they likewise receive praises which they do not deserve.

Thomas Fuller
Gnomologia
1732

Great and good are seldom the same man.

Thomas Fuller
Gnomologia
1732

If you command wisely, you'll be obeyed cheerfully.

Thomas Fuller
Gnomologia
1732

The subject's love is the king's best guard.

Marquis de Vauvenargues
Réflexions et maximes
1746

One is not born for glory unless he is aware of the pace of time.

On n'est pas né pour la gloire lorsqu'on ne connaît pas le pas du temps.

4th Earl of Chesterfield
Letters to His Son
Dec 5, 1749

Those who see and observe kings, heroes, and statesmen, discover that they have headaches, indigestion, humors and passions, just like other people; every one which in their turns determine their wills in defiance of their reason.

Voltaire
Le Siècle de Louis XIV
1751

The history of the world's great leaders is often the story of human folly.

L'histoire des plus grands princes est souvent le récit des fautes des hommes.

Voltaire
Le Siècle de Louis XIV
1751

While taking his leave of the king to go off and command the army, Marshall Villars said so that all the court could hear: "Sire, I am going to fight Your Majesty's enemies, and I leave you here in the midst of mine."

Le maréchal de Villars dit un jour au roi devant toute la cour, lorsqu'il prenait congé pour aller commander l'armée: "Sire, je vais combattre les ennemis de Votre Majesté, et je vous laisse au milieu des miens."

**William Pitt
1st Earl of Chatham**
reported remarks to the
Duke of Devonshire,
quoted by Peter Douglas
Brown
William Pitt, Earl of Chatham
1978

I know that I can save this country and that no one else can.

No man was ever great by imitation.

Samuel Johnson
Rasselas
1759

The strongest is never strong enough to be always the master, unless he transforms strength into right, and obedience into duty.
Le plus fort n'est jamais assez fort pour être toujours le maître, s'il ne transforme sa force en droit et l'obéissance en devoir.

Jean Jacques Rousseau
The Social Contract
1762

Men may be popular without being ambitious; but there is rarely an ambitious man who does not try to be popular.

Frederick North 8th Baron North
speech in the House of Commons
March, 1769

My rule, in which I have always found satisfaction, is, never to turn aside in public affairs through views of private interest; but to go straight forward in doing what appears to me right at the time, leaving the consequences with Providence.

Benjamin Franklin
letter to Mrs. Jane Mecom
Dec 30, 1770

We must not in the course of public life expect immediate approbation and immediate grateful acknowlegment of our services. But let us persevere through abuse and even injury. The internal satisfaction of a good conscience is always present, and time will do us justice in the minds of the people, even those at present the most prejudiced against us.

Benjamin Franklin
letter to Joseph Galloway
Dec 2, 1772

Great men are the guide-posts and landmarks in the state.

Edmund Burke
speech in the House of Commons
Apr 19, 1774

If we do not lay out ourselves in the service of mankind whom should we serve?

Abigail Adams
letter to John Thaxter
Sep 29, 1778

Great offices will have great talents.

William Cowper
"The Winter Evening"
The Task
1785

A disposition to preserve, and an ability to improve, taken together, would be my standard of a statesman.

Edmund Burke
Reflections on the Revolution in France
1790

One can't reign and be innocent.
On ne peut régner innocemment.

Louis Antoine Léon de Saint-Just
speech to the National Convention
Nov 13, 1792

No one can rule guiltlessly.

Louis Antoine Léon de Saint-Just
speech to the National Convention
Nov 13, 1792

Edmund Burke
Letters on a Regicide Peace
1796-97

It is undoubtedly the business of ministers very much to consult the inclinations of the people, but they ought to take great care that they do not receive that inclination from the few persons who may happen to approach them.

Georg Wilhelm Friedrich Hegel
The German Constitution
1802

Herein lies political genius, in the identification of an individual with a principle.

Napoleon I
reported remark

In a narrow sphere great men are blunderers.
Dans une sphère étroite, les grands hommes sont des brouillons.

Napoleon I
letter to Louis Bonaparte, King of Holland
Dec 15, 1806

You cannot accomplish good for the people unless you face up to the weak and the foolish.
On ne fait le bien des peuples qu'en bravant l'opinion des faibles et des ignorants.

Napoleon I
letter to his brother, the King of Naples
Jul 30, 1806

You do not inspire confidence, you are too good.
Vous n'inspirez pas de confiance; vous êtes trop bon.

Napoleon I
letter to Louis Bonaparte, King of Holland
Apr 19, 1807

A leader of whom it is said, "he's a nice man," is lost.
Un prince dont on dit, c'est un bon homme, est un roi perdu.

Thomas Jefferson
letter to Albert Gallatin
Sep 20, 1808

Were we to act but in cases where no contrary opinion of a lawyer can be had, we should never act.

Napoleon I
letter to Louis Bonaparte, King of Holland
Aug 13, 1809

It is not by whining that one carries out the job of king.
Ce n'est pas en se plaignant qu'on fait le métier de roi.

Napoleon I
letter to M. Champagny, duc de Cadore
Jan 9, 1810

It is not with the words and explanations of theory that nations are governed.
Ce n'est point avec des mots et des exposés de principes qu'on gouverne les nations.

Thomas Jefferson
letter to John Adams
Oct 28, 1813

There is a natural aristocracy among men. The grounds of this are virtue and talent.

Napoleon I
quoted by Emmanuel de Las Cases
Mémorial de Ste. Hélène
Nov 18-19, 1816

The heart of a statesman must be in his head.
Le coeur d'un homme d'Etat doit être dans sa tête.

Percy Bysshe Shelley
Prometheus Unbound
1818–19

To know nor faith, nor love, nor law; to be/ Omnipotent but friendless is to reign.

In the council, there were men possessed of much more eloquence than I was: I always defeated them by this simple argument—two and two make four.

Napoleon I
attributed by Count
Charles-Tristan de
Montholon
*History of the Captivity of
Napoleon at St. Helena*
1847

To govern you do not follow any more or less good theory, you build with the materials you have at hand; you have to do what is necessary and make the best of it.
Il ne s'agit pas, pour gouverner, de suivre une théorie plus ou moins bonne, mais de bâtir avec les matériaux qu'on a sous la main; il faut savoir subir les necessités et en profiter.

Napoleon I
quoted by Count Charles-
Tristan de Montholon
*Histoire de la captivité de
Ste. Hélène*
1846

No man is truly great who is great only in his lifetime. The test of greatness is the page of history.

William Hazlitt
"The Indian Jugglers"
Table Talk
1821–22

He (Martin Van Buren) rowed to his object with muffled oars.

**John Randolph of
Roanoke**
quoted by W. Cabell
Bruce
*John Randolph of
Roanoke, 1773–1833*
1922

I consider myself stronger than most of my contemporaries, because I have an invincible hatred of words and empty phrases and my instinct is always towards action.

**Prince Clemens von
Metternich**
letter to Friedrich
von Gentz
Aug 5, 1825

He who comes up to his own idea of greatness must always have had a very low standard of it in his mind.

William Hazlitt
"Whether Genius Is Con-
scious of Its Powers?"
The Plain Speaker
1826

It was the boast of Augustus that he found Rome of brick and left it of marble. But how much nobler will be the sovereign's boast when he shall have it to say that he found law dear and left it cheap; found it a sealed book and left it a living letter; found it the patrimony of the rich and left it the inheritance of the poor; found it the two-edged sword of craft and oppression and left it the staff of honesty and the shield of innocence.

Henry Brougham
speech "On the Present
State of the Law"
Feb 7, 1828

One must be something, in order to do something.
Mann muss etwas sein, um etwas zu machen.

**Johann Wolfgang von
Goethe**
quoted by Johann Peter
Eckermann
Conversations with Goethe
Oct 20, 1828

A statesman should be possessed of good sense, a primary political quality; and its fortunate possessor needs a second quality—the courage to show that he has it.

(Louis) Adolphe Thiers
speech to the Chamber of
Deputies
May 6, 1834

William Hazlitt "On Great and Little Things" *Literary Remains* 1836	If you think you can win, you can win. Faith is necessary to victory.
Alexis, Comte de Tocqueville *Democracy in America* 1839	A man who raises himself by degrees to wealth and power, contracts, in the course of this protracted labor, habits of prudence and restraint which he cannot afterwards shake off. A man cannot gradually enlarge his mind as he does his house. *Un homme qui s'élève par degrés vers la richesse et le pouvoir, contracte, dans ce long travail, des habitudes de prudence et de retenue dont il ne peut ensuite se départir. On n'élargit pas graduellement son âme comme sa maison.*
Ralph Waldo Emerson "Self-Reliance" *Essays: First Series* 1841	It is easy in the world to live after the world's opinion; it is easy in solitude to live after our own; but the great man is he who in the midst of the crowd keeps with perfect sweetness the independence of solitude.
Ralph Waldo Emerson "Self-Reliance" *Essays: First Series* 1841	A foolish consistency is the hobgoblin of little minds, adored by little statesmen and philosophers and divines. . . . Speak what you think today in hard words and tomorrow speak what tomorrow thinks in hard words again, though it contradicts everything you said today.
Ralph Waldo Emerson "Self-Reliance" *Essays: First Series* 1841	To be great is to be misunderstood.
Thomas Carlyle *On Heroes, Hero-Worship, and the Heroic in History* 1841	No great man lives in vain. The history of the world is but the biography of great men.
Joseph Joubert *Pensées* 1842	You have to be like the pebble in the stream, keeping the grain, and rolling along without being dissolved or dissolving anything else. *Il faut etre caillou dans le torrent, garder ses veines, et rouler sans être ni dissous, ni dissolvant.*
Joseph Joubert *Pensées* 1842	Princes are more sensitive to any offense that tends to diminish their authority than to any service that tends to reinforce it. *Les princes sont plus sensibles aux offenses qui tendent à leur ôter l'autorité qu'aux services qui la leur donnent.*
Benjamin Disraeli *Coningsby* 1844	Man is only truly great when he acts from the passions.
Henry David Thoreau attributed by Arthur Samuel Jones *Thoreau's Incarceration As Told by His Jailer* Jul 23/24, 1846	Mr. Emerson visited Thoreau at the jail, and the meeting between the two philosophers must have been interesting and somewhat dramatic. The account of was told me by (Thoreau's aunt)—"Henry, why are you here?" "Waldo, why are you not here?"
Karl Marx *The German Ideology* 1846	The philosophers have only interpreted the world differently, the point is to change it.

Great events make me quiet and calm; it is only trifles that irritate my nerves.

Victoria
letter to King Leopold I of Belgium
Apr 4, 1848

Any man more right than his neighbors constitutes a majority of one.

Henry David Thoreau
Civil Disobedience
1849

The difference between a politician and a statesman is: a politician thinks of the next election and a statesman thinks of the next generation.

James Freeman Clarke

Every step of progress the world has made has been from scaffold to scaffold, and from stake to stake.

Wendell Phillips
speech in Worcester, Massachusetts
Oct 15, 1851

There are a thousand hacking at the branches of evil to one who is striking at the root.

Henry David Thoreau
"Economy"
Walden
1854

The rarity of great political oratory arises in great measure from this circumstance. Only those engaged in the jar of life have the material for it; only those withdrawn into a brooding imagination have the faculty for it.

Walter Bagehot
"Mr. Gladstone"
National Review
Jul, 1857

A constitutional statesman is in general a man of common opinions and uncommon abilities.

Walter Bagehot
"The Character of Sir Robert Peel"
National Review
Jul, 1857

With public sentiment, nothing can fail; without it, nothing can succeed. Consequently he who molds public sentiment goes deeper than he who enacts statutes or pronounces decisions.

Abraham Lincoln
speech at Ottawa, Illinois
Jul 31, 1858

Fame usually comes to those who are thinking about something else.

Oliver Wendell Holmes Sr.
The Autocrat of the Breakfast Table
1858

I hear many condemn these men because they were so few. When were the good and the brave ever in a majority?

Henry David Thoreau
A Plea for Captain John Brown
1859

Be ashamed to die until you have won some victory for humanity.

Horace Mann
commencement address at Antioch College
1859

There are men, who, by their sympathetic attractions, carry nations with them, and lead the activity of the human race.

Ralph Waldo Emerson
"Power"
The Conduct of Life
1860

John Stuart Mill *Considerations on Repre- sentative Government* 1861	A great statesman is he who knows when to depart from traditions, as well as when to adhere to them.
John Stuart Mill *Considerations on Repre- sentative Government* 1861	One person with a belief is a social power equal to ninety-nine who have only interests.
Abraham Lincoln letter to Zachariah Chandler Nov 20, 1863	I hope to "stand firm" enough not to go backward, and yet not go forward fast enough to wreck the country's cause.
Abraham Lincoln reply to the Missouri Committee of Seventy 1864	I desire so to conduct the affairs of this administration that if at the end, when I come to lay down the reins of power, I have lost every friend on earth, I shall at least have one friend left, and that friend shall be down inside me.
Abraham Lincoln letter to A.G. Hodges Apr 4, 1864	I claim not to have controlled events, but confess plainly that events have controlled me.
Abraham Lincoln speech in Washington, D.C. Apr 11, 1865	Important principles may and must be inflexible.
Prince Otto von Bismarck ɪuoted by Charles Lowe *Bismarck's Table Talk* 1895	When I wish to estimate the danger that is likely to accrue to me from any adversary, I first of all subtract the man's vanity from his other qualities.
Benjamin Disraeli speech Jun 24, 1872	The secret of success is constancy to purpose.
Oliver Wendell Holmes Sr. *The Poet at the Breakfast Table* 1872	Reason may be the lever, but sentiment gives you the fulcrum and the place to stand on if you want to move the world.
Frederic Harrison *Order and Progress* 1875	What makes a man minister? Debating power. And what makes a man Premier? Debating power. And what good is debating power to you? What has it ever done for you or for England? It bears the same relation to governing that tournaments did to fighting.
Havelock Ellis introduction to Joris Karl Huysman *Against the Grain* 1884	To be a leader of men one must turn one's back on men.
Friedrich Nietzsche "The Stillest Hour" *Thus Spoke Zarathustra* 1883-85	To do great things is difficult; but to command great things is more difficult. *Grosses vollführen ist schwer: aber das Schwerere ist, Grosses befehlen.*

Whoever fights monsters should see to it that in the process he does not become a monster.
Wer mit Ungeheuern kämpft, mag zusehn, dasz er nicht dabei zum Ungeheuer wird.

Friedrich Nietzsche
Beyond Good and Evil
1886

Public men are bees working in a glass hive; and curious spectators enjoy themselves in watching every secret movement, as if it were a study in natural history.

Henry Ward Beecher
Proverbs from Plymouth Pulpit
1887

What is the use of being elected or re-elected unless you stand for something?

Grover Cleveland
reported remarks to a political adviser
1887

We are all in the gutter, but some of us are looking at the stars.

Oscar Wilde
Lady Windermere's Fan
1892

In statesmanship get formalities right, never mind about the moralities.

Mark Twain
Following the Equator
1897

We do not admire a man of timid peace.

Theodore Roosevelt
speech in Chicago, Illinois
Apr 10, 1899

If a had been as intelligent as Spinoza, he would have written four volumes in an attic.
Si a avait été aussi intelligent que Spinoza, il aurait écrit quatre volumes dans une mansarde.

Anatole France
Monsieur Bergeret à Paris
1900

Some men owe most of their greatness to the ability of detecting in those they destine for their tools the exact quality of strength that matters for their work.

Joseph Conrad
Lord Jim
1900

I sometimes think that great men are like great mountains: one cannot realize their greatness till one stands at some distance from them.

Joseph Chamberlain
quoted by Austen Chamberlain
Down the Years
1935

For the present, at any rate, I must proceed alone. I must plough my own furrow alone, but before I get to the end of that furrow it is possible that I may not find myself alone.

5th Earl of Rosebery
speech to the City of London Liberal Club on being out of government
Jul 19, 1901

A great man's failures to understand define him.
On peut même dire que ses incompréhensions font la définition du grand homme.

Andre Gide
"Concerning Influence in Literature"
Pretexts
1903

It is at night that faith in light is admirable.
C'est la nuit qu'il est beau de croire a la lumière.

Edmond Rostand
Chantecler
1907

Alfred, 1st Viscount Milner speech in Glasgow, Scotland Nov 26, 1909	If we believe a thing to be bad, and if we have a right to prevent it, it is our duty to try to prevent it, and to damn the consequences.
Andrew Bonar Law reported conversation on becoming leader of Conservative party Nov 13, 1911	If I am a great man, then a good many great men must have been frauds.
Joseph Conrad *A Personal Record* 1912	All ambitions are lawful except those which climb upward on the miseries or credulities of mankind.
Woodrow Wilson campaign speech in New York City Oct 31, 1912	There is no cause half so sacred as the cause of a people. There is no idea so uplifting as the idea of the service of humanity.
Woodrow Wilson speech Oct 3, 1912	A man is not as big as his belief in himself; he is as big as the number of persons who believe in him.
Woodrow Wilson speech in Denver, Colorado Oct 7, 1912	It is harder for a leader to be born in a palace than to be born in a cabin.
Woodrow Wilson speech in Chester, Pennsylvania Oct 28, 1912	Every country is renewed out of the unknown ranks and not out of the ranks of those already famous and powerful and in control.
Theodore Roosevelt *Autobiography* 1913	The unforgivable crime is soft hitting. Do not hit at all if it can be avoided.
Woodrow Wilson speech in Philadelphia, Pennsylvania Oct 25, 1913	If you think too much about being re-elected, it is very difficult to be worth re-electing.
Woodrow Wilson speech on "The New Freedom" 1913	The man who is swimming against the stream knows the strength of it.
Miguel de Unamuno "Don Quixote Today" *Tragic Sense of Life in Men and Nations* 1913	The greatest height of heroism to which an individual, like a people, can attain is to know how to face ridicule. *El mas alto heroísmo para un individuo, como para un pueblo, es saber afrontar el ridículo*
Herbert Asquith 1st Earl of Oxford in conversation with his wife Jul 31, 1914	In public politics as in private life, character is better than brains, and loyalty more valuable then either; but, I shall have to work with the material that has been given to me.
W. Somerset Maugham *Of Human Bondage* 1915	Like all weak men he laid an exaggerated stress on not changing one's mind.

One cool judgment is worth a thousand hasty counsels. The thing to be supplied is light, not heat.

Woodrow Wilson
speech in Pittsburgh, Pennsylvania
Jan 29, 1916

Blessed is he whose fame does not outshine his truth.

Sir Rabindranath Tagore
Stray Birds
1916

Great political and social changes begin to be possible as soon as men are not afraid to risk their lives.

Thomas Masaryk
letter to R. Seton-Watson
Mar 16, 1917

It is unfortunate, considering that enthusiasm moves the world, that so few enthusiasts can be trusted to speak the truth.

Arthur Balfour
letter to Mrs. Drew
1918

There is something better, if possible, that a man can give than his life. That is his living spirit to a service that is not easy, to resist counsels that are hard to resist, to stand against purposes that are diffcult to stand against.

Woodrow Wilson
speech
May 30, 1919

Great men are but life-sized. Most of them, indeed, are rather short.

Sir Max Beerbohm
"A Point to Be Remembered by Very Eminent Men"
And Even Now
1920

To rule over oneself is the first condition for one who would rule over others.
Ser emperador de sí mismo es la primera condición para imperar a los demás.

Jose Ortega y Gasset
Invertebrate Spain
1922

The tragedy of life is not that man loses but that he almost wins.

Heywood Broun
"Sport for Art's Sake"
Pieces of Hate, and Other Enthusiasms
1922

The efficiency of the truly national leader consists primarily in preventing the division of the attention of a people, and always in concentrating it on a single enemy.
Überhaupt besteht die Kunst aller wahrhaft grossen Volksführer zu allen Zeiten in erster Linie mit darin, die Aufmerksamkeit eines Volkes nicht zu zersplittern, sondern immer auf einen einzigen Gegner zu konzentrieren.

Adolf Hitler
Mein Kampf
1924

You cannot choose your battlefield,/ The gods do that for you,/ But you can plant a standard/ Where a standard never flew.

Nathalia Crane
The Colors
ca. 1925

Statesmen must learn to live with scientists as the Medici once lived with artists.

Sir Oswald Mosley
quoted by Robert Skidelsky
Oswald Mosley
1975

Elbert G. Hubbard *The Note Book* 1927	Some men succeed by what they know; some by what they do; and a few by what they are.
Elbert G. Hubbard *The Note Book* 1927	An ounce of loyalty is worth a pound of cleverness.
Aldous Huxley *Proper Studies* 1927	Those who believe that they are exclusively in the right are generally those who achieve something.
Knut Rockne quoted *Argosy* Nov, 1976	You show me a good and gracious loser, and I'll show you a failure!
(James) Ramsay **MacDonald** reported conversation with Harold Nicolson and Vita Sackville-West Oct, 1930	If God were to come to me and say, "Ramsay, would you rather be a country gentleman than a Prime Minister?," I should reply, "Please, God, a country gentleman."
José Ortega y Gasset *The Revolt of the Masses* 1930	The truth is that you don't rule with the fist. And ruling is not the act of taking power, but exercising power in tranquillity. Actually, ruling is staying seated. *La verdad es que no se manda con los jenízaros. . . . Y mandar no es gesto de arrebatar el poder, sino tranquilo ejercicio de él. En suma: mandar es sentarse.*
Herbert Hoover in 1931, as quoted *Memoirs* 1952	One who brandishes a pistol must be prepared to shoot.
Franklin D. Roosevelt speech in San Francisco, California Sep 23, 1932	Government includes the art of formulating a policy, and using the political technique to attain so much of that policy as will receive general support; persuading, leading, sacrificing, teaching always, because the greatest duty of any statesman is to educate.
Franklin D. Roosevelt speech in New York City Nov 5, 1932	The fate of America cannot depend on any one man. The greatness of America is grounded in principles and not on any single personality.
Charles De Gaulle *Le Fil de l'épée* 1934	Authority must be accompanied by prestige and prestige comes only from distance. *L'autorité ne va pas sans prestige, ni le prestige sans l'éloignement.*
Charles De Gaulle *Le Fil de l'épée* 1934	The great leaders have always stage-managed their effects.
Jean Giraudoux *Tiger at the Gates* 1935	The privilege of the great is to see catastrophes from the terrace.
Ignazio Silone *The School for* *Dictatorships* 1939	The king presupposes subjects; the leader, followers. *Il re presuppone i sudditi, il dirigente i seguaci.*

The future lies with those wise political leaders who realize that the great public is interested more in government than in politics.

Franklin D. Roosevelt
speech in Washington, D.C.
Jan 8, 1940

I am fighting, as I have always fought, for the rights of the little man as well as for the big man—for the weak as well as the strong. . . . I am fighting to defend them against the power and might of those who rise up to challenge them. And I will not stop fighting.

Franklin D. Roosevelt
speech in Brooklyn, New York
1940

Glory is only given to those who have always dreamed of it.
La gloire se donne seulement à ceux qui l'ont toujours rêvée.

Charles De Gaulle
Vers l'armée de métier
1940

The only guide to a man is his conscience; the only shield to his memory is the rectitude and sincerity of his actions. It is very imprudent to walk through life without this shield, because we are so often mocked by the failure of our hopes and the upsetting of our calculations; but with this shield, however the fates may play, we march always in the ranks of honor.

Sir Winston S. Churchill
tribute in the House of Commons to Neville Chamberlain, following his death
Nov 12, 1940

I do not resent criticism, even when, for the sake of emphasis, it parts for the time with reality.

Sir Winston S. Churchill
speech in the House of Commons
Jan 22, 1941

No man is great enough or wise enough for any of us to surrender our destiny to. The only way in which anyone can lead us is to restore to us the belief in our own guidance.

Henry Miller
"The Alcoholic Veteran with the Washboard Cranium"
The Wisdom of the Heart
1941

The real leader has no need to lead—he is content to point the way.

Henry Miller
"The Wisdom of the Heart"
The Wisdom of the Heart
1941

I have not become the King's First Minister in order to preside over the liquidation of the British Empire.

Sir Winston S. Churchill
speech at the Lord Mayor's luncheon, London
Nov 10, 1942

A chief is a man who assumes responsibility. He says, "I was beaten." He does not say, "My men were beaten." Thus speaks a real man.
Le chef est celui qui prend tout en charge. Il dit: J'ai été battu. Il ne dit pas: Mes soldats ont été battus. L'homme véritable parle ainsi.

Antoine de Saint-Exupéry
Pilote de guerre
1942

Heroes are created by popular demand, sometimes out of the scantiest materials, or none at all.

Gerald White Johnson
American Heroes and Hero-Worship
1943

Unlucky the country that needs a hero.
Unglucklich das Land, das Helden nötig hat.

Bertolt Brecht
Leben des Galilei
1943

George S. Patton
letter to Cadet George S.
Patton, Jr.
Jun 6, 1944

Take calculated risks. That is quite different from being rash.

Franklin D. Roosevelt
fourth inaugural address
Jan 20, 1945

We may make mistakes—but they must never be mistakes which result from faintness of heart or abandonment of moral principle.

Walter Lippmann
"Roosevelt Has Gone"
New York Herald Tribune
Apr 14, 1945

The final test of a leader is that he leaves behind him in other men the conviction and the will to carry on.

Sir Max Beerbohm
"T. Fenning Dodworth"
Mainly on the Air
1946

Men prominent in life are mostly hard to converse with. They lack small-talk, and at the same time one doesn't like to confront them with their own great themes.

Harry S Truman
remarks in Winslow,
Arizona
Jun 15, 1948

You know, the greatest epitaph in the country is here in Arizona. It's in Tombstone, Ariz., and this epitaph says, "Here lies Jack Williams. He done his damndest." I think that is the greatest epitaph a man could have. Whenever a man does the best he can, then that is all he can do; and that is what your President has been trying to do for the last 3 years for this country.

Herbert Hoover
remarks
Nov 11, 1948

We believe in equal opportunity for all, but we know that this includes the opportunity to rise to leadership, to be uncommon! The great human advances have not been brought about by mediocre men and women.

Harry S Truman
quoted
Time
Nov 8, 1976

You know what makes leadership? It is the ability to get men to do what they don't want to do, and like it.

Brooks Atkinson
"January 27"
Once Around the Sun
1951

We need supermen to rule us—the job is so vast and the need for wise judgment is so urgent. But, alas, there are no supermen.

E.M. Forster
"What I Believe"
Two Cheers for Democracy
1951

I distrust Great Men. They produce a desert of uniformity around them and often a pool of blood too, and I always feel a little man's pleasure when they come a cropper.

Aneurin Bevan
In Place of Fear
1952

The first function of a political leader is advocacy. It is he who must make articulate the wants, the frustration, and the aspiration of the masses.

A.J.P. Taylor
"William Cobbett"
New Statesman
1953

There is nothing more agreeable in this life than to make peace with the Establishment—and nothing more corrupting.

Elmer Davis
But We Were Born Free
1954

This Republic was not established by cowards; and cowards will not preserve it.

A great man's greatest good luck is to die at the right time.

Eric Hoffer
The Passionate State of Mind
1954

We will not be driven by fear into an age of unreason if we . . . remember that we are not descended from fearful men, not from men who feared to write, to speak, to associate and to defend causes which were, for the moment unpopular.

Edward R. Murrow
"See It Now"
television broadcast
Mar 7, 1954

In the face of great danger, salvation can only come through greatness.
Face aux grands périls, le salut n'est que la grandeur.

Charles De Gaulle
Mémoires de guerre: L'Appel
1955

The leader is always alone in times of doom.
Toujours, le Chef est seul en face du mauvais destin.

Charles De Gaulle
Mémoires de guerre: L'Appel
1955

Old age is a shipwreck.
La vieillesse est un naufrage.

Charles De Gaulle
Mémoires de guerre: L'Appel
1955

I spoke. I had to. It is action that puts fervor to work. But it is words that create it.
Je parle. Il le faut bien. L'action met les ardeurs en oeuvre. Mais c'est la parole qui les suscite.

Charles De Gaulle
Mémoires de guerre: L'Appel
1955

To act coolly, intelligently and prudently in perilous circumstances is the test of a man—and also a nation.

Adlai E. Stevenson Jr.
The New York Times
Apr 11, 1955

A decision is the action an executive must take when he has information so incomplete that the answer does not suggest itself.

Adm. Arthur W. Radford
Time
Feb 25, 1957

The difference between being an elder statesman/ And posing successfully as an elder statesman/ Is practically negligible.

T.S. Eliot
The Elder Statesman
1958

At home, you always have to be a politician; when you're abroad, you almost feel yourself a statesman.

Harold Macmillan
Look
Apr 15, 1958

Difficulty is the excuse history never accepts.

Edward R. Murrow
on President John F. Kennedy's inaugural address
Oct 19, 1959

No one has a finer command of language than the person who keeps his mouth shut.

Sam Rayburn
quoted
Lawrence Daily Journal–World
Aug 29, 1978

Some men can make decisions and some cannot. Some men fret and delay under criticism. I used to have a saying that applies here, and I note that some people have picked it up, "If you can't stand the heat, get out of the kitchen."

Harry S Truman
Mr. Citizen
1960

Paul Goodman
Growing Up Absurd
1960

Few great men could pass Personnel.

Charles De Gaulle
Mémoires de guerre: Le Salut
1960

As for me, I know only too well my limits and weaknesses, and I also know that no man can take the place of a whole people. That is why I wanted to inspire their souls with the conviction that filled me.

Quant à moi, qui ne connais que trop mes limites et mon infirmité et qui sais bien qu'aucun homme ne peut se substituer à un peuple, comme je voudrais faire entrer dans les âmes la conviction qui m'anime!

Sir Basil Liddell Hart
Deterrent or Defense: Advice to Statesmen
1960

Keep strong, if possible. In any case, keep cool. Have unlimited patience. Never corner an opponent, and always assist him to save his face. Put yourself in his shoes—so as to see things through his eyes. Avoid self-righteousness like the devil— nothing so self-blinding.

Eleanor Roosevelt
letter to Peter Kamitchis
Oct 21, 1960

To say he (John F. Kennedy) would not make mistakes would be silly. Anyone would make mistakes with the problems that lie ahead of us.

Sam Rayburn
attributed
The Leadership of Sam Rayburn, Collected Tributes of His Colleagues
1961

You cannot be a leader, and ask other people to follow you, unless you know how to follow, too.

Barbara Ward
Saturday Review
Sep 30, 1961

The modern world is not given to uncritical admiration. It expects its idols to have feet of clay, and can be reasonably sure that press and camera will report their exact dimensions.

George F. Kennan
Russia and the West under Lenin and Stalin
1961

If we are to regard ourselves as a grown-up nation—and anything else will henceforth be mortally dangerous—then we must, as the Biblical phrase goes, put away childish things; and among these childish things the first to go, in my opinion, should be self-idealization and the search for absolutes in world affairs: for absolute security, absolute amity, absolute harmony.

John F. Kennedy
closed-circuit television broadcast
Nov 29, 1962

I am certain that after the dust of centuries has passed over our cities, we, too, will be remembered not for victories or defeats in battle or politics, but for our contribution to the human spirit.

Richard M. Nixon
press conference following defeat in California gubernatorial election
Nov 7, 1962

As I leave you I want you to know—just think how much you're going to be missing. You won't have Nixon to kick around anymore because, gentlemen, this is my last press conference.

Louis Nizer
My Life in Court
1962

I know of no higher fortitude than stubbornness in the face of overwhelming odds.

Martin Luther King Jr.
speech in Detroit, Michigan
Jun 23, 1963

If a man hasn't discovered something that he will die for, he isn't fit to live.

A nation reveals itself not only by the men it produces but also by the men it honors, the men it remembers.

John F. Kennedy
speech at Amherst College, Amherst, Massachusetts
Oct 26, 1963

There are things a man must not do even to save a nation.

Murray Kempton
"To Save a Nation"
America Comes of Middle Age
1963

I like to operate like a submarine on sonar. When I am picking up noise from both the left and right, I know my course is correct.

Gustavo Diaz Ordaz
while campaigning for presidency of Mexico
US News & World Report
Jul 13, 1964

The leader must know, must know he knows, and must be able to make it abundantly clear to those about him that he knows.

Clarence B. Randall
Making Good in Management
1964

A political leader must keep looking over his shoulder all the time to see if the boys are still there. If they aren't still there, he's no longer a political leader.

Bernard Baruch
quoted
The New York Times
Jun 21, 1965

Only he deserves power who every day justifies it.

Dag Hammarskjold
"1951"
Markings
1965

When I want to know what France thinks, I ask myself.

Charles De Gaulle
Time
Dec 17, 1965

I have against me the bourgeois, the military and the diplomats, and for me, only the people who take the Metro.

Charles De Gaulle
The New York Times
Dec 17, 1965

It's never the right time to take a particular stand.

Adam Clayton Powell Jr.
"One Must Die for Many"
Keep the Faith, Baby
1967

I respect only those who resist me, but I cannot tolerate them.

Charles De Gaulle
quoted
The New York Times Magazine
May 12, 1968

When statesmen forsake their own private conscience for the sake of their public duties . . . they lead their country by a short route to chaos.

Robert Bolt
A Man for All Seasons
1968

There are some people, you know, they think the way to be a big man is to shout and stomp and raise hell—and then nothing ever really happens. I'm not like that . . . I never shoot blanks.

Richard M. Nixon
Look
Oct 19, 1971

Richard M. Nixon
CBS-TV
Jan 2, 1972

My strong point is not rhetoric, it isn't showmanship, it isn't big promises—those things that create the glamour and the excitement that people call charisma and warmth. My strong point, if I have a strong point, is performance. I always do more than I say. I always produce more than I promise.

Golda Meir
Ms.
Apr, 1973

It's no accident many accuse me of conducting public affairs with my heart instead of my head. Well, what if I do?. . . . Those who don't know how to weep with their whole heart don't know how to laugh either.

Henry A. Kissinger
Ms.
Oct, 1975

We are not going around looking for opportunities to prove our manhood.

Charles M. Mathias Jr.
Time
Dec 8, 1975

People tend to want to follow the beaten path. The difficulty is that the beaten path doesn't seem to be leading anywhere.

Barbara Jordan
quoted in "Barbara Jordan" by Charles L. Sanders
Ebony
Feb, 1975

If I have anything special that makes me "influential" I simply don't know how to define it. If I knew the ingredients I would bottle them, package them and sell them, because I want everyone to be able to work together in a spirit of cooperation and compromise and accommodation without, you know, any caving in or anyone being woefully violated personally or in terms of his principles.

Mao Tse-tung
quoted
Time
Sep 20, 1976

The most important thing is to be strong. With strength, one can conquer others, and to conquer others gives one virtue.

Henry A. Kissinger
Time
Nov 8, 1976

A statesman who too far outruns the experience of his people will fail in achieving a domestic consensus, however wise his policies. (On the other hand), a statesman who limits his policies to the experience of his people is doomed to sterility.

Mao Tse-tung
quoted
Time
Sep 20, 1976

I am alone with the masses.

Kevin White
Time
Feb 9, 1976

Charismatic leadership is hungered for, but at the same time we fear it.

Elizabeth II
in Philadelphia, Pennsylvania, during American bicentennial celebrations
Newsweek
Jul 17, 1976

We lost the American colonies because we lacked the statesmanship to know the right time and the manner of yielding what is impossible to keep.

Bill Cosby
Ebony
Jun, 1977

I don't know the key to success, but the key to failure is trying to please everybody.

Richard M. Nixon
Dallas Times–Herald
Dec 10, 1978

If an individual wants to be a leader and isn't controversial, that means he never stood for anything.

If you don't stand for something, you will stand for anything.

Ginger Rogers
Parade
Jun 18, 1978

It's the orders you disobey that make you famous.

Douglas MacArthur
Time
Sep 11, 1978

Too bad that all the people who know how to run the country are busy driving taxicabs and cutting hair.

George Burns
Life
Dec, 1979

One had the sense that if (Charles De Gaulle) moved to a window, the center of gravity might shift, and the whole room might tilt everybody into the garden.

Henry A. Kissinger
Time
Oct 15, 1979

Competing pressures tempt one to believe that an issue deferred is a problem avoided: more often it is a crisis invited.

Henry A. Kissinger
Time
Oct 15, 1979

High office teaches decision making, not substance. It consumes intellectual capital; it does not create it.

Henry A. Kissinger
Time
Oct 15, 1979

The world is divided into those who want to become someone and those who want to accomplish something.

Jean Monnet
Time
Mar 26, 1979

A leader should not get too far in front of his troops or he will be shot in the ass.

Joseph Clark
Washingtonian
Nov, 1979

Men of power have no time to read; yet the men who do not read are unfit for power.

Michael Foot
Debts of Honour
1980

To those waiting with bated breath for that favourite media catch-phrase, the U-turn, I have only one thing to say: you turn if you want to. The lady's not turning.

Margaret Thatcher
speech to the Conservative party annual conference
Oct, 1980

The statesman's duty is to bridge the gap between his nation's experience and his vision.

Henry A. Kissinger
Years of Upheaval
1982

To have striven so hard, to have moulded a public personality out of so amorphous an identity, to have sustained that superhuman effort only to end with every weakness disclosed and every error compounding the downfall—that was a fate of biblical proportions. Evidently the Deity would not tolerate the presumption that all can be manipulated; an object lesson of the limits of human presumption was necessary.

Henry A. Kissinger
on the resignation of Richard Nixon
Years of Upheaval
1982

For some days, people thought that India was shaking. But there are always tremors when a great tree falls.

Rajiv Gandhi
speech following his mother's assassination
The New York Times
Nov 20, 1984

Indira Gandhi handwritten statement found after her death Oct 31, 1984	If I die a violent death, as some fear and a few are plotting, I know that the violence will be in the thought and the action of the assassins, not in my dying.
Desmond Tutu *Christian Science Monitor* Dec 20, 1984	I am a leader by default, only because nature does not allow a vacuum.
Margaret Thatcher on reference to her as the Iron Lady *Daily Telegraph* Mar 21, 1986	If you lead a country like Britain, a strong country, a country which has taken a lead in world affairs in good times and in bad, a country that is always reliable, then you have to have a touch of iron about you.
Margaret Thatcher *Daily Telegraph* Mar 21, 1986	I do not know anyone who has got to the top without hard work. That is the recipe. It will not always get you to the top, but should get you pretty near.
Margaret Thatcher *Parade* Jul 13, 1986	What is success? I think it is a mixture of having a flair for the thing that you are doing; knowing that it is not enough, that you have got to have hard work and a certain sense of purpose.
Margaret Thatcher on the Falklands War *New Yorker* Feb 10, 1986	It was sheer professionalism and inspiration and the fact that you really cannot have people marching into other people's territory and staying there.
Helmut Kohl *The New York Times* Jan 25, 1987	I have been underestimated for decades. I've done very well that way.
Jesse Jackson "Meet the Press," NBC-TV Jun 12, 1988	There's nothing wrong with having a big ego. It's all right to a have a Rolls Royce ego so long as you don't have a bicycle brain. If they coordinate, you can work it out pretty well.
Henry Kissinger remarks on a Mideast crisis, quoted in *Newsweek* Oct 22, 1990	The statesman must weigh the rewards of success against the penalties of failure. And he is permitted only one guess.
Henry Kissinger quoted in *Newsweek* Dec 10, 1990	One cannot combine the benefits of every course of action. And if one goes down a certain road, at some point one has to face the consequences that this road implies.

Legislatures and Legislation

Edmund Burke speech to the electors of Bristol Nov 3, 1774	Parliament is not a congress of ambassadors from different and hostile interests; which interests each must maintain, as an agent and advocate, against other agents and advocates; but parliament is a deliberative assembly of one nation, with one interest, that of the whole.

To render it (legislation) agreeable to good policy, three things are requisite. First, that the necessity of the times requires it; secondly, that it be not the probable source of greater evils than those it pretends to remedy; and lastly, that it have a probability of success.

Alexander Hamilton
"A Full Vindication"
Dec 15, 1774

The Commons, faithful to their system, remained in a wise and masterly inactivity.

Sir James Mackintosh
Vindiciae Gallicae
1791

Take a single step beyond the boundaries . . . specially drawn around the powers of Congress, is to take possession of a boundless field of power, no longer susceptible of any definition.

Thomas Jefferson
"Opinion on the Constitu-
tionality of the Bill for
Establishing a National
Bank"
Feb 15, 1791

Only make wise and moderate laws. But have them carried out with force and vigor.
Ne faites que les lois sages et modérées. Faites-les éxécuter avec force et énergie.

Napoleon I
letter to the provisional
government of the
Ligurian Republic
Nov 11, 1797

Legislation is not changed every day.
On ne change pas la législation tous les jours.

Napoleon I
decision
Sep 18, 1805

All the public business in Congress now connects itself with intrigues, and there is great danger that the whole government will degenerate into a struggle of cabals.

John Quincy Adams
Diary
Jan, 1819

When no limits are set to representative authority, the representatives of the people are not defenders of liberty but candidates for tyranny.

**Benjamin Constant de
Rebecque**
*Course of Constitutional
Politics*
1817-20

That 150 lawyers should do business together is not to be expected.

Thomas Jefferson
on the functioning of
Congress
Autobiography
Jan 6, 1821

The science of legislation is like that of medicine in one respect: that it is far more easy to point out what will do harm than what will do good.

Charles Caleb Colton
Lacön
1825

We ought to observe that practice which is the hardest of all—especially for young physicians—we ought to throw in no medicine at all—to abstain—to observe a wise and masterly inactivity.

**John Randolph of
Roanoke**
speech in the U.S. Senate
Jan 25, 1828

The great problem of legislation is, so to organize the civil government of a community . . . that in the operation of human institutions upon social action, self-love and social may be made the same.

John Quincy Adams
"Society and Civilization"
American Review
Jul, 1845

That a Parliament, especially a Parliament with Newspaper Reporters firmly established in it, is an entity which by its very nature cannot do work, but can do talk only.

Thomas Carlyle
Latter-Day Pamphlets
1850

<table>
<tr><td>

Thomas Carlyle
Latter-Day Pamphlets
1850

</td><td>

Parliament will train you to talk; and above all things to hear, with patience, unlimited quantities of foolish talk.

</td></tr>
<tr><td>

3rd Viscount Palmerston
letter to William Gladstone
May 16, 1861

</td><td>

The House of Commons allows itself to be led, but does not like to be driven, and is apt to turn upon those who attempts to drive it.

</td></tr>
<tr><td>

Anonymous
quoted by Gideon J. Tucker
New York Surrogate Reports
1866

</td><td>

No man's life, liberty or property are safe while the Legislature is in session.

</td></tr>
<tr><td>

Sir William Harcourt
letter to Charles Dilke
1870

</td><td>

Let us give our Republic not the best possible laws but the best which they will bear. This is the essence of politics; all the rest is speculation.

</td></tr>
<tr><td>

Benjamin Disraeli
speech in the House of Commons
Jun 18, 1875

</td><td>

Permissive legislation is the characteristic of a free people.

</td></tr>
<tr><td>

Lord Acton
letter to Mary Gladstone
Apr 24, 1881

</td><td>

If there is a free contract, in open market, between capital and labour, it cannot be right that one of the two contracting parties should have the making of the laws.

</td></tr>
<tr><td>

Mark Twain
Following the Equator
1897

</td><td>

It could probably be shown by facts and figures that there is no distinctly native American criminal class except Congress.

</td></tr>
<tr><td>

Oliver Wendell Holmes Jr.
Missouri, Kansas and Texas Railway Company v. May
1904

</td><td>

It must be remembered that legislatures are ultimate guardians of the liberties and welfare of the people in quite as great a degree as the courts.

</td></tr>
<tr><td>

Finley Peter Dunne
"The Vice-President"
Dissertations by Mr. Dooley
1906

</td><td>

It is his jooty to rigorously enforce th' rules iv th' Sinit. There ar're none. Th' Sinit is ruled be courtesy, like th' longshoreman's union.

</td></tr>
<tr><td>

Woodrow Wilson
address to the nation
Mar 4, 1917

</td><td>

A little group of wilful men (filibustering senators) representing no opinion but their own have rendered the great government of the United States helpless and contemptible.

</td></tr>
<tr><td>

"Kin" Hubbard
saying

</td><td>

Now and then an innocent man is sent to the legislature.

</td></tr>
<tr><td>

Joseph G. Cannon
quoted on his retirement
The Baltimore Sun
Mar 4, 1923

</td><td>

Nearly all legislation is the result of compromise.

</td></tr>
<tr><td>

John Sharp Williams
retirement speech
Mar 4, 1923

</td><td>

I may have grown cynical from long service, but . . . I sometimes think I'd rather be a dog and bay at the moon than stay in the Senate another six years and listen to it.

</td></tr>
</table>

When not realities but words are to be discussed Parliament wakes up. Then we are back in the comfortable pre-war world of make-believe. Politics are safe again; hairs are to be split, not facts to be faced. Hush! Do not awaken the dreamers. Facts will waken them in time with a vengeance.

Sir Oswald Mosley
Birmingham Town Crier
Dec 23, 1929

There is good news from Washington today. The Congress is deadlocked and can't act.

Will Rogers
quoted
Newsweek
Jun 9, 1975

The legislature, like the executive, has ceased to be even the creature of the people: it is the creature of pressure groups, and most of them, it must be manifest, are of dubious wisdom and even more dubious honesty.

H.L. Mencken
"The Library"
The American Mercury
May 1930

If today our action employs among its different weapons that of parliament, that is not to say that parliamentary parties exist only for parliamentary ends. For us parliament is not an end in itself, but merely a means to an end.

Adolf Hitler
speech in Munich
Sep 23, 1930

"Do you pray for the Senators, Dr. Hale?" someone asked the chaplain. "No, I look at the Senators and pray for the country."

Edward Everett Hale
quoted by Van Wyck
Brooks
New England: Indian Summer, 1865–1915
1940

One thing the House will NEVER forgive and that is if a Minister misleads it. If you find you have given an answer that isn't true, acknowledge it at once and express your regret.

Stanley Baldwin
letter to Sir John Reith
Jan 31, 1940

The only way to do anything in the American government is to bypass the Senate.

Franklin D. Roosevelt
quoted, on his return
from the Yalta Conference
Chicago Tribune
May 29, 1977

The great executives have given inspiration and push to the advancement of human society, but it is the legislator who has given stability and continuity to that slow and painful progress.

J. William Fulbright
speech at Univ. of
Chicago
1946

In one sense the House of Commons is the most unrepresentative of representative assemblies. It is an elaborate conspiracy to prevent the real clash of opinion which exists outside from finding an appropriate echo within its walls. It is a social shock absorber placed between privilege and the pressure of popular discontent.

Aneurin Bevan
In Place of Fear
1952

Parliament has joined the monarchy as a dignified, not an effective, element in the Constitution.

Richard Crossman
Diary
Mar 19, 1959

Legislators represent people, not trees or acres. Legislators are elected by voters, not farms or cities or economic interests.

Earl Warren
Reynolds v. *Sims*
Jun 15, 1964

If Moses had gone to Harvard Law School and spent three years working on the Hill, he would have written the Ten Commandments with three exceptions and a savings clause.

Charles Morgan Jr.
Rolling Stone
Jan 15, 1976

Betty Talmadge *The Reader* Nov 25, 1977	If you love the law and you love good sausage, don't watch either of them being made.
Hubert H. Humphrey quoted *Newsweek* Jan 23, 1978	The Senate is a place filled with goodwill and good intentions, and if the road to hell is paved with them, then it's a pretty good detour.
Barber B. Conable Jr. *Time* Oct 22, 1984	(Congress is) functioning the way the Founding Fathers intended—not very well. They understood that if you move too quickly, our democracy will be less responsible to the majority.
Barber B. Conable Jr. *Time* Oct 22, 1984	Exhaustion and exasperation are frequently the handmaidens of legislative decision.
Barber B. Conable Jr. *Time* Oct 22, 1984	I don't think it's the function of Congress to function well. It should drag its heels on the way to decision.
Barney Frank remarks on an anti-drug bill passed by the U.S. House of Representatives *The New York Times* Sep 12, 1986	This bill is the legislative equivalent of crack. It yields a short-term high but does long-term damage to the system and it's expensive to boot.
Edward I. Koch on budget of New York City *The New York Times* Jun 27, 1986	We're in the hands of the state legislature and God, but at the moment, the state legislature has more to say than God.

Liberalism

Johann Wolfgang von Goethe quoted by Johann Peter Eckermann *Conversations with Goethe* Feb 30, 1830	I am a moderate liberal, as all rational people are and ought to be, and it is in this spirit that I have tried to act throughout a long life. *Ein gemässigter Liberale, wie es alle vernünftigen Leute sind und sein sollen, und wie ich selber es bin und in welchem Sinne zu wirken ich während eines langen Lebens micht bemüht habe.*
William Ewart Gladstone speech in Plumstead, England 1878	Liberalism is trust of the people tempered by prudence; Conservatism is distrust of the people tempered by fear.
Friedrich Nietzsche "Skirmishes in a War with the Age" *Twilight of the Idols* 1888	Liberal institutions straightway cease from being liberal the moment they are soundly established. *Die liberalen Institutionen hören alsbald auf, liberal zu sein, sobald sie erreicht sind.*
Leo XIII letter to Archbishop of Bogotá Apr 6, 1900	The main principle and foundation of liberalism is the rejection of the divine law. . . . It rejects and destroys all authority and divine law.

A liberal mind is a mind that is able to imagine itself believing anything.

Max Eastman
Masses
Sep, 1917

A Liberal is a man who uses his legs and his hands at the behest—at the command—of his head.

Franklin D. Roosevelt
radio address
Oct 26, 1939

It is the duty of the liberal to protect and to extend the basic democratic freedoms.

Chester Bowles
New Republic
Jul 22, 1946

Political liberalism should also be defined in terms of objectives. A major objective is the protection of the economic work and doing it within the framework of a private economy. The liberal, emphasizing the civil and property rights of the individual, insists that the individual must remain so supreme as to make the state his servant.

Wayne Lyman Morse
New Republic
Jul 22, 1946

The essence of the Liberal outlook lies not in what opinions are held, but in how they are held: instead of being held dogmatically, they are held tentatively, and with a consciousness that new evidence may at any moment lead to their abandonment.

Bertrand Russell
"Philosophy and Politics"
Unpopular Essays
1950

We who are liberal and progressive know that the poor are our equals in every sense except that of being equal to us.

Lionel Trilling
"The Princess
Casamassima"
The Liberal Imagination
1950

A rich man told me recently that a liberal is a man who tells other people what to do with their money.

LeRoi Jones
"Tokenism: 300 years for
five cents"
Home
1966

The liberals in the House strongly resemble liberals I have known through the last two decades in the civil rights conflict. When it comes time to show on which side they will be counted, they suddenly excuse themselves.

Shirley Chisholm
Unbought and Unbossed
1970

Politics without ideology, and with a strong tendency towards autobiography, equals Liberalism.

Sir Stephen Spender
postscript
The Thirties and After
1978

There are no more liberals. . . . They've all been mugged.

James Q. Wilson
Time
Jan 21, 1985

Majority and Minorities

There is no maxim, in my opinion, which is more liable to be misapplied, and which, therefore, more needs elucidation, than the current one, that the interest of the majority is the political standard of right and wrong.

James Madison
letter to James Monroe
Oct 5, 1786

John Adams *A Defence of the Constitution of the Government of the United States* 1787–88	That the desires of the majority of the people are often for injustice and inhumanity against the minority, is demonstrated by every page of the history of the whole world.
James Madison speech to the Virginia Convention on the adoption of the U.S. Constitution Jun 5, 1788	On a candid examination of history, we shall find the turbulence, violence, and abuse of power, by the majority, trampling on the rights of the minority, have produced factions and commotions which, in republics, have, more frequently than any other cause, produced despotism.
Thomas Jefferson first inaugural address Mar 4, 1801	Though the will of the majority is in all cases to prevail, that will, to be rightful, must be reasonable. . . . The minority possess their equal rights, which equal laws must protect, and to violate which would be oppression.
James Madison speech to the Virginia constitutional convention, Richmond, Virginia Dec 2, 1829	In Republics, the great danger is, that the majority may not sufficiently respect the rights of the minority.
James Madison letter to Martin Van Buren Jul 5, 1830	The American people are too well schooled in the duty and practice of submitting to the will of the majority to permit any serious uneasiness on that account.
Lord John Russell speech in the House of Commons Oct 12, 1831	It is impossible that the whisper of a faction shall prevail against the voice of a nation.
Andrew Jackson letter to Gen. John Coffee Dec 14, 1832	When a faction in a state attempts to nullify a constitutional law of congress, or to destroy the union, the balance of the people composing this union have a perfect right to coerce them to obedience. This is my creed.
Alexis, Comte de Tocqueville *Democracy in America* 1835	The tyranny of the majority. *La tyrannie de la majorité.*
James K. Polk inaugural address Mar 4, 1845	The blessings of Liberty which our Constitution secures may be enjoyed alike by minorities and majorities.
John Stuart Mill *Principles of Political Economy* 1848	No society in which eccentricity is a matter of reproach, can be in a wholesome state.
Henry David Thoreau *Civil Disobedience* 1849	A wise man will not leave the right to the mercy of chance, nor wish it to prevail through the power of the majority. There is but little virtue in the action of masses of men.
Lord Macaulay letter to Henry Stephens Randall May 23, 1857	It is quite plain that your government will never be able to restrain a distressed and discontented majority. For with you the majority is the government, and has the rich, who are always a minority, absolutely at its mercy.

Governments exist to protect the rights of minorities. The loved and the rich need no protection: they have many friends and few enemies.

Wendell Phillips
speech in Boston,
Massachusetts
Dec 21, 1860

If by the mere force of numbers a majority should deprive a minority of any clearly written constitutional right, it might, in a moral point of view, justify revolution—certainly would if such a right were a vital one.

Abraham Lincoln
first inaugural address
Mar 4, 1861

The majority rules. If they want anything, they get it. If they want anything not right, they get it, too.

Sojourner Truth
speech in Rochester,
New York
1871

Let us not fall into the . . . pernicious error that multitude is divine because it is multitude.

James A. Garfield
speech at Hudson College
Jul 2, 1873

The most certain test by which we judge whether a country is really free is the amount of security enjoyed by minorities.

Lord Acton
lecture on "The History
of Freedom in Antiquity"
at Bridgnorth, England
Feb 26, 1877

The one pervading evil of democracy is the tyranny of the majority, or rather of that party, not always the majority, that succeeds, by force or fraud, in carrying elections.

Lord Acton
lecture on "The History
of Freedom in Antiquity"
at Bridgnorth, England
Feb 26, 1877

The minority is always right.
Minoriteten har altid retten.

Henrik Ibsen
An Enemy of the People
1882

In the majority beat many hearts, but it has no heart.
Die Majorität hat viele Herzen, aber ein Herz hat sie nicht.

**Prince Otto von
Bismarck**
speech in the Reichstag
Jun 12, 1882

Desperate courage makes One a majority.

Andrew Jackson
quoted by James Parton
*The Life of Andrew
Jackson*
1888

So long as a minority conforms to the majority, it is not even a minority. They must throw in their whole weight in the opposite direction.

Mohandas K. Gandhi
Indian Opinion
Sep 14, 1907

You can not have a decent, popular government unless the majority exercise the self-restraint that men with great power ought to exercise.

William Howard Taft
speech in Fresno,
California
Oct 10, 1909

Constitutions are checks upon the hasty action of the majority. They are the self-imposed restraints of a whole people upon a majority of them to secure sober action and a respect for the rights of the minority.

William Howard Taft
veto of Arizona
Enabling Act
Aug 22, 1911

Goldsworthy Lowes Dickinson
The Choice Before Us
1917

Government is everywhere to a great extent controlled by powerful minorities, with an interest distinct from that of the mass of the people.

Norman Douglas
South Wind
1917

No one can expect a majority to be stirred by motives other than ignoble.

Eugene V. Debs
speech at his trial in
Cleveland, Ohio
Sep 12, 1918

When great changes occur in history, when great principles are involved, as a rule the majority are wrong.

Joseph G. Cannon
quoted on his retirement
The Baltimore Sun
Mar 4, 1923

A majority can do anything.

José Ortega y Gasset
The Revolt of the Masses
1930

Society is always a dynamic interaction of two factors: minorities and the masses. Minorities are individuals or groups of individuals especially qualified. The masses are the collection of people not specially qualified.
La sociedad es siempre una unidad dinámica de dos factores: minorías y masas. Las minorías son individuos o grupos de individuos especialmente cualificados. La masa es el conjunto de personas no especialmente cualificadas.

Franklin D. Roosevelt
radio address
Mar 2, 1930

The moment a mere numerical superiority by either states or voters in this country proceeds to ignore the needs and desires of the minority, and for their own selfish purpose or advancement, hamper or oppress that minority, or debar them in any way from equal privileges and equal rights—that moment will mark the failure of our constitutional system.

Alfred M. Landon
Kansas Day address
Oct, 1936

A government is free in proportion to the rights it guarantees to the minority.

Claude McKay
A Long Way From Home
1937

It is hell to belong to a suppressed minority.

Franklin D. Roosevelt
letter to the National Association for the Advancement of Colored People
Jun 25, 1938

No democracy can long survive which does not accept as fundamental to its very existence the recognition of the rights of minorities.

James Reston
Sketches in the Sand
1967

A resolute minority has usually prevailed over an easygoing or wobbly majority whose prime purpose was to be left alone.

Jesse Jackson
interview
Playboy
Nov, 1969

I hear that melting pot stuff a lot, and all I can say is that we haven't melted.

Eleanor Holmes Norton
The New York Post
Mar 28, 1970

Being black has made me sensitive to any group who finds limitations put on it.

There can be no assumption that today's majority is "right" and the Amish and others like them are "wrong." A way of life that is odd or even erratic but interferes with no right or interests of others is not to be condemned because it is different.

Warren E. Burger
majority opinion
Wisconsin v. *Yoder*
May 15, 1972

Looking around the House, one realises that we are all minorities now—indeed, some more than others.

Jeremy Thorpe
speech in House of Commons after 1974 election when no party gained majority
Mar 6, 1974

We are of course a nation of differences. Those differences don't make us weak. They're the source of our strength.

Jimmy Carter
speech at Al Smith Dinner in New York City
Oct 21, 1976

America is not like a blanket—one piece of unbroken cloth, the same color, the same texture, the same size. America is more like a quilt—many patches, many pieces, many colors, many sizes, all woven and held together by a common thread.

Jesse Jackson
speech to the Democratic National Convention in San Francisco
Jul 17, 1984

Our flag is red, white and blue, but our nation is a rainbow—red, yellow, brown, black and white—and we're all precious in God's sight.

Jesse Jackson
speech to the Democratic National Convention in San Francisco
Jul 17, 1984

It is precisely because the issue raised by this case touches the heart of what makes individuals what they are that we should be especially sensitive to the rights of those whose choices upset the majority.

Harry A. Blackmun
dissenting opinion
Bowers v. *Hardwick*
Jun 30, 1986

Monarchy

A multitude of rulers is not a good thing. Let there be one ruler, one king.

Homer
Iliad
ca. 700 B.C.

The principal mark of a commonwealth, that is to say the existence of a sovereign power, can hardly be established except in a monarchy.

Jean Bodin
Six Books of the Commonwealth
1576

Not all the water in the rough rude sea/ Can wash the balm from an annointed king

William Shakespeare
King Richard II
1595

A good king will frame his actions to be according to the Law, yet he is not bound thereto but of his Good Will.

James I
The True Law of Free Monarchies
1598

Uneasy lies the head that wears a crown.

William Shakespeare
Henry IV, Part II
1597–98

James I speech to Parliament Mar 23, 1609	Kings are justly called Gods, for that they exercise a manner or resemblance of Divine power upon earth. For if you will consider the attributes of God, you shall see how they agree in the person of a king.
James I message to the House of Commons 1621	I will govern according to the common weal, but not according to the common will.
Sir Francis Bacon "Of Empire" *Essays* 1625	Princes are like to heavenly bodies, which cause good or evil times, and which have much veneration but no rest.
John Locke *First Tract on Government* 1660	Nor do men, as some fondly conceive, enjoy any greater share of this freedom in a pure commonwealth, if anywhere to be found, than in an absolute monarchy, the same arbitrary power being there in the assembly (which acts like one person) as in a monarch.
Earl of Rochester **(John Wilmot)** written on the bedcham- ber door of Charles II ca. 1670	Here lies our sovereign lord the King,/ Whose promise none relies on;/ He never said a foolish thing,/ Nor ever did a wise one.
Charles II reply to Lord Rochester ca. 1670	This is very true: for my words are my own, and my actions are my ministers.
Sir Robert Filmer *Patriarcha, Or the* *Natural Power of* *Kings Asserted* 1680	Men are not born free, and therefore could never have the liberty to choose either Governors, or Forms of Government. Princes have their Power Absolute, and by Divine Right, for Slaves could never have a Right to Compact of Consent. Adam was an absolute Monarch, and so are all Princes ever since.
John Dryden *Absalom and Achitophel* 1681	Kings are the publick Pillars of the State, Born to sustain and prop the Nations weight.
Jean de La Bruyère "Du Souverain ou de la république" *Les Caractères* 1688	If it is too much to have to take care of a family, if it's enough just to have to worry about yourself, think of the weight, of the burden, of a whole kingdom. *Si c'est trop de se trouver chargé d'une seule famille, si c'est assez d'avoir à répondre de soi seul, quel poids, quel accablement, que celui de tout un royaume.*
Matthew Prior *Solomon*	What is a King?—a man condemn'd to bear/ The public burden of the nation's care.
Daniel Defoe *The True-Born* *Englishman* 1701	When kings the sword of justice first lay down,/ They are no kings, though they possess the crown./ Titles are shadows, crowns are empty things,/ The good of subjects is the end of kings.
Alexander Pope *The Dunciad* 1728–43	The Right Divine of Kings to govern wrong.

He was the king's friend. Therefore, the king was the only monarch on earth who had a friend.

Il fut l'ami du roi, et le roi fut alors le seul monarque de la terre qui eût un ami.

Voltaire
(Francois Marie
Arouet)
"Les énigmes"
Zadig
1747

The prince is the first servant of his state.
Der Fürst ist der erste Diener seines Staates.

Frederick II
(the Great)
Memoirs of the House of Brandenburg
1758

The king never dies.

Sir William Blackstone
Commentaries on the Laws of England
1765

That the king can do no wrong, is a necessary and fundamental principle of the English constitution.

Sir William Blackstone
Commentaries on the Laws of England
1768

There is not a single crowned head in Europe whose talents or merit would entitle him to be elected a vestryman by the people of any parish in America.

Thomas Jefferson
letter to George Washington
May 2, 1788

A monarchy is a merchantman which sails well, but will sometimes strike on a rock, and go to the bottom; a republic is a raft which will never sink, but then your feet are always in the water.

Fisher Ames
speech in the House of Representatives
1795

Monarchy is only the string which ties the robbers' bundle.

Percy Bysshe Shelley
A Philosophical View of Reform
1819–20

Democracy is in every case a principle of dissolution, of decomposition. It tends to separate men, it loosens society. I am opposed to this because I am by nature and by habit constructive. That is why monarchy is the only government that suits my way of thinking. . . . Monarchy alone tends to bring men together, to unite them in compact, efficient masses, and to make them capable by their combined efforts of the highest degree of culture and civilization.

Prince Clemens von Metternich
reported conversation with George Ticknor
1835

Every noble crown is, and on earth will forever be, a crown of thorns.

Thomas Carlyle
Past and Present
1843

It is the misfortune of kings that they will not listen to the truth.

Johann Jacoby
letter to Frederick William II
Nov 2, 1848

Obedience to the laws and to the Sovereign, is obedience to a higher Power, divinely instituted for the good of the people, not of the Sovereign, who has equally duties & obligations.

Victoria
reported conversation with Lord John Russell
Aug 6, 1848

Prince Otto von Bismarck
reported conversation with a III of France
1862

In Prussia it is only kings who make revolutions.

Walter Bagehot
The English Constitution
1867

The sovereign has, under a constitutional monarchy such as ours, three rights - the right to be consulted, the right to encourage, the right to warn.

Walter Bagehot
The English Constitution
1867

So long as the human heart is strong and the human reason weak, Royalty will be strong because it appeals to diffused feeling, and the Republics weak because they appeal to the understanding.

Mark Twain
The Adventures of Huckleberry Finn
1884

All kings is mostly rapscallions.

Ludwig Fulda
Der Talisman
1893

You're still the king—even in your underwear.
Du bleibst der König—auch in Unterhosen.

Finley Peter Dunne
"Prince Henry's Reception"
Observations by Mr. Dooley
1902

A prince is a gr-reat man in th' ol' counthry, but he niver is as gr-reat over there as he is here (in America).

Ambrose Bierce
The Devil's Dictionary
1906

Absolute, adj. An absolute monarchy is one in which the sovereign does as he pleases so long as he pleases the assassins.

Woodrow Wilson
speech in Chattanooga, Tennessee
Aug 31, 1910

That a peasant may become king does not render the kingdom democratic.

William Ralph Inge
"Our Present Discontents"
Outspoken Essays: First Series
1919

A monarch frequently represents his subjects better than an elected assembly; and if he is a good judge of character he is likely to have more capable and loyal advisers.

Farouk I
Life
Apr 10, 1950

In a few years there will be only five kings in the world—the King of England and the four kings in a pack of cards.

Elizabeth II
first televised Christmas address
Dec 25, 1957

I cannot lead you into battle. I do not give you laws or administer justice but I can do something else—I can give my heart and my devotion to these old islands and to all the peoples of our brotherhood of nations.

Mohammed Reza Pahlevi
The New York Times
Oct 27, 1967

Let me tell you quite bluntly that this king business has given me personally nothing but headaches.

No medieval monarch in the whole of British history ever had such power as every modern British Prime Minister has in his or her hands. Nor does any American President have power approaching this.

Anthony Wedgwood Benn
Arguments for Socialism
1979

Something as curious as the monarchy won't survive unless you take account of people's attitudes. . . . After all, if people don't want it, they won't have it.

Prince Charles
quoted by Anthony Sampson
The Changing Anatomy of Britain
1983

Most of the monarchies of Europe were really destroyed by their greatest and most ardent supporters. It was the most reactionary people who tried to hold onto something without letting it develop and change.

Prince Philip
quoted by John Pearson
The Selling of the Royal Family
1986

Nationalism

Altogether, national hatred is something peculiar. You will always find it strongest and most violent where there is the lowest degree of culture.

Johann Wolfgang von Goethe
quoted by Johann Peter Eckermann
Conversations with Goethe
Mar 14, 1830

The worth of a State, in the long run, is the worth of the individuals composing it.

John Stuart Mill
On Liberty
1859

Individualities may form communities, but it is institutions alone that can create a nation.

Benjamin Disraeli
speech in Manchester, England
1866

Size is not grandeur, and territory does not make a nation.

Thomas Henry Huxley
"On University Education"
1876

The life of the nation is secure only while the nation is honest, truthful, and virtuous.

Frederick Douglass
speech on twenty-third anniversary of emancipation in the District of Columbia
Apr, 1885

The idea of a lawful separation between one nationality and the other . . . is a reactionary idea.

Vladimir Ilyich Lenin
Socialism and War
1915

Loyalty is a sentiment, not a law. It rests on love, not on restraint. The government of Ireland by England rests on restraint and not on law; and since it demands no love, it can evoke no loyalty.

Sir Roger Casement
at his trial for treason
Jul, 1916

Woodrow Wilson
speech in Washington, D.C.
Jun 5, 1917

There comes a time when it is good for a nation to know that it must sacrifice if need be everything that it has to vindicate the principles which it possesses.

Woodrow Wilson
speech to Congress
Feb 11, 1918

Self-determinism is not a mere phrase. It is an imperative principle of action, which statesmen will henceforth ignore at their peril.

Andre Gide
Journals
1918

The nationalist has a broad hatred and a narrow love. He cannot stifle a predilection for dead cities.

Theodore Roosevelt
speech in Saratoga, New York
Jul 19, 1918

There can be no fifty-fifty Americanism in this country. There is room here for only hundred per cent Americanism.

Albert Einstein
statement to G.S. Viereck
1921

Nationalism is an infantile disease. It is the measles of mankind.

José Ortega y Gasset
Invertebrate Spain
1922

Nations are formed and are kept alive by the fact that they have a program for tomorrow.
Las naciones se forman y viven de tener un programa para el mañana.

Stanley Baldwin
speech in London
Dec 4, 1934

There is a wind of nationalism and freedom blowing round the world, and blowing as strongly in Asia as elsewhere.

Franklin D. Roosevelt
message to Congress
Apr 14, 1938

The driving force of a nation lies in its spiritual purpose, made effective by free, tolerant but unremitting national will.

Joseph Stalin
reported conversation with Averell Harriman
Sep, 1941

We are under no illusion that they (the Russian people) are fighting for us (the Communist party). They are fighting for Mother Russia.

E.B. White
"Intimations"
One Man's Meat
1944

Nationalism has two fatal charms for its devotees: it presupposes local self-sufficiency, which is a pleasant and desirable condition, and it suggests, very subtly, a certain personal superiority by reason of one's belonging to a place which is definable and familiar, as against a place which is strange, remote.

Charles De Gaulle
Mémoires de guerre: L'Appel
1955

All my life I have held on to a certain idea of France.
Toute ma vie je me suis fait une certaine idée de la France.

Erich Fromm
The Sane Society
1955

Nationalism is our form of incest, is our idolatry, is our insanity. "Patriotism" is its cult.

Paul Valéry
"Extraneous Remarks"
Selected Writings
1964

All nations have present, or past, or future reasons for thinking themselves incomparable.

Patriotism is when love of your own people comes first; nationalism, when the hate for people other than your own comes first.

Charles De Gaulle
recalled on leaving the presidency
Life
May 9, 1969

To me the nation is the ultimate political reality. There is no political reality beyond it. But what it is cannot be determined scientifically; you cannot pick it up; you cannot measure it.

Enoch Powell
The Listener
May 28, 1981

Patriotism

The single best augury is to fight for one's country.

Homer
Iliad
ca. 700 B.C.

What a pity is it / That we can die but once to save our country!

Joseph Addison
Cato
1713

A patriot is a fool in ev'ry age.

Alexander Pope
"Epilogue to the Satires"
Imitations of Horace
1733–38

It is sad that being a good patriot often means being the enemy of the rest of mankind.
Il est triste que souvent, pour être bon patriote, on soit l'ennemi du reste des hommes.

Voltaire
"Patrie"
Dictionnaire philosophique
1764

Patriotism is the last refuge of the scoundrel.

Samuel Johnson
quoted by James Boswell
Life of Samuel Johnson
Apr 7, 1775

I only regret that I have but one life to lose for my country.

Nathan Hale
last words before being hanged by British
Sep 22, 1776

These are the times that try men's souls. The summer soldier and the sunshine patriot will, in this crisis, shrink from the service of his country; but he that stands it NOW deserves the love and thanks of man and woman.

Thomas Paine
The American Crisis
Sep 12, 1777

Everything belongs to the fatherland when the fatherland is in danger.

Georges Jacques Danton
speech to the National Convention
Aug 28, 1792

Breathes there the man, with soul so dead,/ Who never to himself hath said,/ This is my own, my native land!/ Whose heart hath ne'er within him burn'd,/ As home his footsteps he hath turn'd,/ From wandering on a foreign strand!

Sir Walter Scott
The Lay of the Last Minstrel
1805

Napoleon I
speech to Polish deputies
Jul 14, 1812

The love of country is the first virtue in a civilised man.

Stephen Decatur
toast at a dinner in
Norfolk, Virginia
Apr, 1816

Our country! In her intercourse with foreign nations may she always be in the right; but our country, right or wrong.

**Samuel Taylor
Coleridge**
"Political Knowledge"
The Friend
1818

Patriotism itself is a necessary link in the golden chains of our affections and virtues.

Ralph Waldo Emerson
Journals
1824

When a whole nation is roaring Patriotism at the top of its voice, I am fain to explore the cleanness of its hands and purity of its heart.

Henry Clay
speech in the U.S. Senate
1848

I have heard something said about allegiance to the South. I know no South, no North, no East, no West, to which I owe any allegiance. . . . The Union, sir, is my country.

Giuseppe Mazzini
speech in Milan
Jul 25, 1848

God has given you your country as cradle, and humanity as mother; you cannot rightly love your brethren of the cradle if you love not the common mother.

Lord Acton
"Nationality"
*The Home and Foreign
Review*
Jul, 1862

Patriotism is in political life what faith is in religion.

Robert E. Lee
letter to General P.G.T.
Beauregard
Oct 3, 1865

True patriotism sometimes requires of men to act exactly contrary, at one period, to that which it does at another, and the motive which impels them—the desire to do right— is precisely the same.

Henry James
The Portrait of a Lady
1881

I think patriotism is like charity—it begins at home.

Alfred, Lord Tennyson
The Charge of the Heavy
Brigade
1885

The song that nerves a nation's heart / Is in itself a deed.

Mark Twain
*A Connecticut Yankee at
King Arthur's Court*
1889

My kind of loyalty was loyalty to one's country, not to its institutions or its officeholders.

Carl Schurz
speech to the Anti-
Imperialistic Conference
in Chicago, Illinois
Oct 17, 1899

Our country, right or wrong. When right, to be kept right; when wrong, to be put right.

Mark Twain
Notebook
1935

Talking of patriotism, what humbug it is; it is a word which always commemorates a robbery. There isn't a foot of land in the world which doesn't represent the ousting and re-ousting of a long line of successive owners.

In the beginning of a change, the patriot is a scarce man, and brave, and hated and scorned. When his cause succeeds, the timid join him, for then it costs nothing to be a patriot.

Mark Twain
Notebook
1935

I realize that patriotism is not enough. I must have no hatred or bitterness towards anyone.

Edith Cavell
last words before being executed
Oct 12, 1915

The things that the flag stands for were created by the experiences of a great people. Everything that it stands for was written by their lives. The flag is the embodiment, not of sentiment, but of history.

Woodrow Wilson
speech
Jun 14, 1915

He who loves not his home and country which he has seen, how shall he love humanity in general which he has not seen?

William Ralph Inge
"Patriotism"
Outspoken Essays: First Series
1919

Patriotism is easy to understand in America. It means looking out for yourself by looking out for your country.

Calvin Coolidge
speech in Northampton, Massachusetts
May 30, 1923

Patriotism is a lively sense of responsibility. Nationalism is a silly cock crowing on its own dunghill.

Richard Aldington
The Colonel's Daughter
1931

Martyred many times must be/ Who would keep his country free.

Edna St. Vincent Millay
"To the Maid of Orleans"
Make Bright the Arrows
1940

Whenever you hear a man speak of his love for his country it is a sign that he expects to be paid for it.

H.L. Mencken
A Mencken Chrestomathy
1949

Patriotism is not a short and frenzied outburst of emotion but the tranquil and steady dedication of a lifetime.

Adlai E. Stevenson Jr.
speech to the American Legion Convention
Aug 30, 1952

To strike freedom of the mind with the fist of patriotism is an old and ugly subtlety.

Adlai E. Stevenson Jr.
speech in New York City
Aug 30, 1952

The military caste did not originate as a party of patriots, but as a party of bandits.

H.L. Mencken
Minority Report
1956

You're not supposed to be so blind with patriotism that you can't face reality. Wrong is wrong, no matter who does it or who says it.

Malcolm X
Malcolm X Speaks
1965

We will survive and become the stronger—not only because of a patriotism that stands for love of country, but a patriotism that stands for love of people.

Gerald R. Ford
speech in Grand Rapids, Michigan
Sep 7, 1968

Jacobo Timerman *Prisoner Without a Name, Cell Without a Number* 1981	The person who wants to fight senses his solitude and is frightened. Whereupon the silence reverts to patriotism. Fear finds its great moral revelation in patriotism.
Gary Hart television interview on "Nightline" after withdrawing from presidential race Sep 8, 1987	I think there is one higher office than president and I would call that patriot.

Political Campaigns

Woodrow Wilson campaign speech Sep 4, 1912	Prosperity is necessarily the first theme of a political campaign.
Woodrow Wilson acceptance at Sea Girt, New Jersey, of the nomination for presidency Aug 7, 1912	A Presidential campaign may easily degenerate into a mere personal contest, and so lose its real dignity.
Walter Lippmann "The Changing Focus" *A Preface to Politics* 1914	Football strategy does not originate in a scrimmage; it is useless to expect solutions in a political campaign.
James Harvey Robinson *The Human Comedy* 1937	Political campaigns are designedly made into emotional orgies which endeavor to distract attention from the real issues involved, and they actually paralyze what slight powers of cerebration man can normally muster.
Alben W. Barkley recalled on his death Apr 30, 1956	The best audience is intelligent, well-educated and a little drunk.
Dwight D. Eisenhower speech in Washington, D.C. Jun 7, 1957	There may be some cynics who think that a Platform is just a list of platitudes to lure the naive voter—a sort of facade behind which candidates sneak into power and then do as they please. I am not one of those.
Barry Goldwater slogan for presidential campaign 1964	In your heart, you know he's right.
Theodore H. White *The New York Times* Jan 5, 1969	The best time to listen to a politician is when he's on a stump on a street corner in the rain late at night when he's exhausted. Then he doesn't lie.
Ralph G. Martin *A Hero for Our Times* 1983	Handshaking is friendly until your hands bleed. Confetti looks festive until you're forced to spit out mouthfuls hurled directly into your face. Applause is wonderful until you can hardly hear yourself speak. A crush of screaming women is flattering until they tear your clothes.

The Kennedy organization doesn't run, it purrs.

Rowland Evans Jr.
quoted by Ralph G.
Martin
A Hero for Our Times
1983

The problems seem so easy out there on the stump. Deficits shrink with a rhetorical flourish.

Hugh Sidey
"Now Comes the
Hard Part"
Time
Nov 5, 1984

We love the blather and boast, the charge and countercharge of campaigning. Governing is a tougher deal.

Hugh Sidey
"Now Comes the
Hard Part"
Time
Nov 5, 1984

You can campaign in poetry. You govern in prose.

Mario Cuomo
New Republic
Apr 8, 1985

There is no excitement anywhere in the world, short of war, to match the excitement of an American presidential campaign.

Theodore H. White
interview
May 15, 1986

We were told our campaign wasn't sufficiently slick. We regard that as a compliment.

Margaret Thatcher
The New York Times
Jun 12, 1987

Our debates have been like the mating of pandas in the zoo— the expectations are high, there's a lot of fuss and commotion, but there's never any kind of result.

Bruce Babbitt
presidential primary cam-
paign speech in Des
Moines, Iowa
Jan 4, 1988

Senator, I served with Jack Kennedy. I knew Jack Kennedy. Jack Kennedy was a friend of mine. Senator, you're no Jack Kennedy.

Lloyd Bentsen
on Senator Dan Quayle's
self-comparison to
John F. Kennedy;
televised debate
Oct 5, 1988

One of the rules of the business is somebody gets to fill up the cup. If you want to be successful, you have to fill it up first.

John Sasso
remarks concerning
Dukakis's campaign
quoted in
Time
Nov 21, 1988

The most statesmanlike thing to do in politics is to tell the truth *during* a campaign. After you've concluded that you can't win that way, the second most statesmanlike thing is to borrow from Earl Long and tell the people you lied.

J. Bennett Johnston
remarks quoted in
Time
Nov 28, 1988

Until the big guns decide whether to uncap, no one else shoots.

Michael McCurry
remarks on an absence of
declared Democratic
presidential hopefuls,
quoted in
Newsweek
Nov 12, 1990

Mario Cuomo
explaining his intentions to
run for the US presidency
in 1992, quoted in
Newsweek
Nov 12, 1990

I have no plans and no plans to have plans.

Political Parties

Aristotle
Politics
343 B.C.

Those who think that all virtue is to be found in their own party principles push matters to extremes; they do not consider that disproportion destroys a state.

Jean de La Bruyère
"De l'homme"
Les Caractères
1688

Party loyalty lowers the greatest men to the petty level of the masses.
L'esprit de parti abaisse les plus grands hommes jusques aux petitesses du peuple.

1st Marquess of Halifax
Political Thoughts and Reflections
1750

The best Party is but a kind of Conspiracy against the rest of the Nation.

Joseph Addison
Spectator
Jul 24, 1711

There cannot be a greater Judgement befall a Country than such a dreadful Spirit of Division as rends a Government into two distinct People, and makes them greater Strangers and more averse to one another, than if they were actually two different Nations.

Alexander Pope
letter to E. Blount
Aug 27, 1714

Party-spirit, which at best is but the madness of many for the gain of a few.

Alexander Pope
letter to E. Blount
Aug 27, 1714

I find myself . . . hoping a total end of all the unhappy divisions of mankind by party-spirit, which at best is but the madness of many for the gain of a few.

John Arbuthnot
epigram
ca. 1735

All political parties die at last of swallowing their own lies.

4th Earl of Chesterfield (Philip Stanhope)
Old England, or the Constitutional Journal
Feb 5, 1743

Ninety men out of one hundred, when they talk of forming principles, mean no more than embracing parties, and, when they talk of supporting their party, mean serving their friends; and the service of their friends implies no more than consulting self-interest. By this gradation, principles are fitted to party, party degenerates into faction, and faction is reduced to self.

Edmund Burke
Observations on the Present State of the Nation
1769

Party divisions, whether on the whole operating for good or evil, are things inseparable from free government.

Party is a body of men united, for promoting by their joint endeavours the national interest, upon some particular principle in which they are all agreed.

Edmund Burke
Thoughts on the Cause of the Present Discontents
1770

Parties must ever exist in a free country.

Edmund Burke
speech, "On Conciliation with the American Colonies"
Mar 22, 1775

The most common and durable source of faction has been the various and unequal distribution of property.

James Madison
The Federalist
Nov 22, 1787

By a faction, I understand a number of citizens, whether amounting to a majority or a minority of the whole, who are united and actuated by some common impulse of passion, or of interest, adverse to the rights of other citizens, or to the permanent and aggregate interests of the community.

James Madison
The Federalist
Nov 22, 1787

Liberty is to faction what air is to fire, an aliment without which it instantly expires. But it could not be less folly to abolish liberty, which is essential to political life, because it nourishes faction, than it would be to wish annihilation of air, which is essential to animal life, because it imparts to fire its destructive agency.

James Madison
The Federalist
Nov 22, 1787

No free Country has ever been without parties, which are a natural offspring of Freedom.

James Madison
note of ca. 1821 on a speech at the Constitutional Convention
1787

If I could not go to heaven with a party, I would not go there at all.

Thomas Jefferson
letter to Francis Hopkinson
Mar 13, 1789

Let me now . . . warn you in the most solemn manner against the baneful effects of the spirit of party.

George Washington
Farewell Address to the People of the United States
Sep 17, 1796

The spirit of party serves always to distract the public councils, and enfeeble the public administration. It agitates the community with ill-founded jealousies and false alarms; kindles the animosity of one part against another; foments occasional riot and insurrection.

George Washington
Farewell Address to the People of the United States
Sep 19, 1796

Your party man, however excellent his intentions may be, is always opposed to any limitation of sovereignty. He regards himself as the next in succession, and handles gently the property that is to come to him, even while his opponents are its tenants.

Benjamin Constant de Rebecque
Course in Constitutional Politics
1817-20

Party is in England a stronger passion than love, avarice, or ambition; it is often compounded of them, but is stronger than any of them individually.

John Wilson Croker
Diary
Jun 22, 1821

John Wilson Croker letter to a friend 1830	I am one of those who have always thought that party attachments and consistency are in the first class of a statesman's duties, because without them he must be incapable of performing any useful service to the country.
Ralph Waldo Emerson *Journals* 1831	A sect or party is an elegant incognito devised to save a man from the vexation of thinking.
John Wilson Croker letter to Lord Brougham Mar 14, 1839	There are two great antagonistic principles at the root of all government—stability and experiment. The former is Tory, and the latter Whig: and the human mind divides itself into these classes as naturally and as inconsiderately, as to personal objects, as it does into indolence and activity, obstinacy and indecision, temerity and versatility, or any other of the various different or contradictory moods of the mind.
Ralph Waldo Emerson lecture on "The Conservative" in Boston, Massachusetts Dec 9, 1841	The two parties which divide the state, the party of Conservatism and that of Innovation, are very old, and have disputed the possession of the world ever since it was made.
William Henry Harrison inaugural address Mar 4, 1841	If parties in a republic are necessary to secure a degree of vigilance sufficient to keep the public functionaries within the bounds of law and duty, at that point their usefulness ends.
14th Earl of Derby (Edward Stanley) speech in the House of Commons Jun 4, 1841	When I first came into parliament, Mr. Tierney, a great Whig authority, used always to say that the duty of an Opposition was very simple—it was, to oppose everything, and propose nothing.
2nd Viscount Melbourne letter to Queen Victoria Apr 6, 1842	Mr. Pulteney, afterwards Earl of Bath, is reported to have said that political parties were like snakes, guided not by their heads but by their tails. Lord Melbourne does not know whether this is true of the snake, but it is certainly so of the party.
Benjamin Disraeli *Coningsby* 1844	No government can be long secure without formidable opposition.
Benjamin Disraeli letter to Lord John Manners Dec 17, 1845	He (Peel) is so vain that he wants to figure in history as the settler of all the great questions; but a Parliamentary constitution is not favourable to such ambitions, things must be done by parties, not by persons using parties as tools.
Benjamin Disraeli speech in the House of Commons Jan 22, 1846	Above all, maintain the line of demarcation between parties; for it is only by maintaining the independence of party that you can maintain the integrity of public men, and the pwer and influence of Parliament itself.
1st Duke of Wellington letter to Lord Stanley 1846	I have invariably objected to all violent and extreme measures, which is not exactly the mode of acquiring influence in a political party in England, particularly one in opposition to Government.

You cannot choose between party government and Parliamentary government. I say you can have no Parliamentary government if you have no party government; and therefore when gentlemen denounce party government, they strike at the scheme of government which, in my opinion, has made this country great, and which, I hope, will keep it great.

Benjamin Disraeli
speech in the House of Commons
Aug 30, 1848

We have a country as well as a party to obey.

James K. Polk
Diary
Dec 12, 1848

All parties, without exception, in so far as they seek power, are varieties of absolutism.

Pierre Joseph Proudhon
Confessions of a Revolutionary
1849

There can be but two great political parties in this country.

Stephen A. Douglas
speech in Bloomington, Illinois
Jul 16, 1858

A party of order or stability, and a party of progress or reform, are both necessary elements of a healthy state of political life.

John Stuart Mill
On Liberty
1859

Party is organised opinion.

Benjamin Disraeli
speech in Oxford, England
Nov 25, 1864

It is one of the misfortunes of our political system that parties are formed more with reference to controversies that are gone by, than to the controversies which these parties have actually to decide.

3rd Marquess of Salisbury
"The Coming Session"
Quarterly Review
Jan, 1866

I had to prepare the mind of the country, and to educate—if it be not arrogant to use such a phrase—to educate our Party. It is a large Party, and requires its attention to be called to questions of this kind with some pressure.

Benjamin Disraeli
speech in Edinburgh, Scotland on the Reform Act of 1867
Oct 29, 1867

So long as we have government by party, the very notion of repose must be foreign to English politics. Agitation is, so to speak, endowed in this country.

3rd Marquess of Salisbury
"The Commune and the Internationale"
Quarterly Review
Oct, 1871

He serves his party best who serves his country best.

Rutherford B. Hayes
inaugural address
Mar 5, 1877

All free governments are party government.

James A. Garfield
speech to the House of Representatives
Jan 18, 1878

I have always believed that what was best for the entire country was going to help both political parties in the end; for we are citizens in common of one great nation.

Ulysses S. Grant
speech in Kansas City, Missouri
Jul 2, 1880

Friedrich Engels "A Working Man's Party" *Labour Standard* Jul 23, 1881	In England, a real, democratic party is impossible unless it be a working man's party.
Sir W.S. Gilbert *Iolanthe* 1882	I often think it's comical/ How Nature always does contrive/ That every boy and gal,/ That's born into the world alive,/ Is either a little Liberal/ Or else a little Conservative!
John Bengough *The Prohibition Aesop* ca. 1896	You cannot influence a Political Party to do Right, if you stick to it when it does wrong.
Woodrow Wilson speech in Atlantic City, New Jersey Sep 10, 1912	I wish that party battles could be fought with less personal passion and more passion for the common good. I am not interested in fighting persons . . . but in fighting things.
Woodrow Wilson speech at Williams Grove, Pennsylvania Aug 29, 1912	I thank God that we have lived to see a time when men are beginning to reason upon the facts and not upon party tradition. I believe in party tradition, but . . . only as it is founded upon eternal principles of justice.
Woodrow Wilson first inaugural address Mar 4, 1913	The success of a party means little except when the Nation is using the party for a large and definite purpose.
Woodrow Wilson speech in Richmond, Indiana Sep 4, 1919	What difference does party make when mankind is involved?
Will Rogers "Breaking into the Writing Game" *The Illiterate Digest* 1924	The more you read and observe about this Politics thing, you got to admit that each party is worse than the other. The one that's out always looks the best.
Joseph G. Cannon attributed by L. White Busby *Uncle Joe Cannon* 1927	It's a damned good thing to remember in politics to stick to your party and never attempt to buy the favor of your enemies at the expense of your friends.
Bertrand Russell "Freedom in Society" *Skeptical Essays* 1928	To prevent resentment, governments attribute misfortunes to natural causes; to create resentment oppositions attribute them to human causes.
Richard Tawney quoted *The Guardian* 1934	Talk is nauseous without practice. Who will believe that the Labour Party means business so long as some of its stalwarts sit up and beg for sugar-plums, like poodles in a drawing-room. . . . To kick over an idol, you must first get off your knees.
Stanley Baldwin quoted by K. Middlemas and J. Barnes *Baldwin* 1970	This is the most important lesson that a man can learn, that opinions are nothing but the mere result of chance and temperament; that no party is on the whole better than another.

The American people are quite competent to judge a political party that works both sides of a street.

Franklin D. Roosevelt
campaign speech in Boston
Nov 4, 1944

Political language—and with variations this is true of all political parties, from Conservatives to Anarchists—is designed to make lies sound truthful and murder respectable.

George Orwell
"Politics and the English Language"
Shooting an Elephant
1950

Even more important than winning the election is governing the nation. That is the test of a political party—the acid, final test.

Adlai E. Stevenson Jr.
acceptance speech as Democratic candidate for president
Jul 26, 1952

Under democracy one party always devotes its chief energies to trying to prove that the other party is unfit to rule—and both commonly succeed, and are right.

H.L. Mencken
Minority Report
1956

When the Tories are in trouble, they bunch together and cogger up. When we (Labor) get into trouble, we start blaming each other and rushing to the press to tell them all the terrible things that somebody else has done.

Richard Crossman
Diary
May 8, 1956

To me, party platforms are contracts with the people.

Harry S Truman
Memoirs
1955-56

In our (British) traditional cricket match the parties are strong and the best team wins; in the strip poker of American politics, the parties are weak and the best man wins.

Richard Crossman
"Roosevelt—Warts and All"
New Statesman
1957

Let us not seek the Republican answer or the Democratic answer, but the right answer.

John F. Kennedy
speech in Baltimore, Maryland
Feb 18, 1958

There is no Democratic or Republican way of cleaning the streets.

Fiorello LaGuardia
attributed by Murray W. Stand in Charles Garrett
The LaGuardia Years
1961

Sometimes party loyalty asks too much.

John F. Kennedy
attributed by Arthur M. Schlesinger, Jr.
A Thousand Days: John F. Kennedy in the White House
1979

The role of a minority party is to hammer out a program that will solve the problems of America—not just obstruct the work of the majority party.

Lyndon Baines Johnson
quoted by Henry A. Zeiger
Lyndon B. Johnson: Man and President
1963

Herbert Hoover quoted *Christian Science Monitor* May 21, 1964	Honor is not the exclusive property of any political party.
Margaret Chase Smith *Declaration of Conscience* 1972	There are enough mistakes of the Democrats for the Republicans to criticize constructively without resorting to political smears.
Eugene J. McCarthy *Chicago Tribune* Sep 10, 1978	The two-party system has given this country the war of Lyndon Johnson, the Watergate of Nixon, and the incompetence of Carter. Saying we should keep the two-party system simply because it is working is like saying the Titanic voyage was a success because a few people survived on life rafts.
Enoch Powell *The Listener* May 28, 1981	There is one thing you can be sure of with the Conservative Party, before anything else—they have a grand sense for where the votes are.
Ronald Reagan speech to British Parliament Jun 8, 1982	The Soviet Union would remain a one-party nation even if an opposition party were permitted—because everyone would join that party.
Sir Karl Popper "Popper on Democracy" *The Economist* Apr 23, 1988	While people and their opinions always deserve the greatest respect, the opinions adopted by parties (which are typically instruments of personal advancement and of power, with all the chances for intrigue which this implies) are not to be identifed with ordinary human opinions: they are ideologies.
Nelson Polsby remarks quoted in *Time* Nov 21, 1988	The only thing wrong with the Democratic Party is that they can't elect a President.
Buddy Roemer remarks quoted in *Time* Mar 25, 1991	The most important things in life have nothing to do with party.

Politicians and Public Officials

Aristotle *Politics* ca. 325 B.C.	Nowadays, for the sake of the advantage which is to be gained from the public revenues and from office, men want to be always in office.
Marcus Tullius Cicero *Epistulae ad Familiares* ca. 50 B.C.	Persistence in one opinion has never been considered a merit in political leaders. *Numquam enim in praestantibus in republica gubernanda viris laudata est in una sententia perpetua permansio.*
Seneca (the Younger) *Letters to Lucilius* ca. 50	No man in public life thinks of the many he has outstripped; he thinks rather of those who have outstripped him. *Quod nemo eorum, qui in re publica versantur, quot vincat, sed a quibus vincatur, aspicit.*

Get thee glass eyes;/ And, like a scurvy politician, seem/ To see the things thou dost not.

William Shakespeare
King Lear
1605-06

The State, in choosing men to serve it, takes no notice of their opinions. If they be willing faithfully to serve it, that satisfies.

Oliver Cromwell
speech before the Battle of Marston Moor
Jul 2, 1644

No man can be a politician, except he be first a historian or a traveller; for except he can see what must be, or what may be, he is no politician.

James Harrington
Oceana
1656

There is nothing so despicable and useless as someone at court who can't do anything to further your career; I'm surprised that they even dare to show their face.
Il n'y a rien à la cour de si méprisable et de si indigne qu'un homme qui ne peut contribuer en rien à notre fortune: je m'étonne qu'il ose se montrer.

Jean de La Bruyère
"De la cour"
Les Caractères
1688

A private Life is to be preferr'd; the Honour and Gain of publick Posts, bearing no proportion with the Comfort of it.

William Penn
Some Fruits of Solitude in Reflections and Maxims
1693

Censure is the tax a man pays to the public for being eminent.

Jonathan Swift
Thoughts on Various Subjects
1711

He that puts on a public gown must put off a private person.

Thomas Fuller
Gnomologia
1732

There are scarcely any men more sour than those who are forced to be nice out of interest.
Il n'y a guère de gens plus aigres que ceux qui sont doux par intérêt.

Marquis de Vauvenargues
Réflexions et maximes
1746

The sad knowledge of human nature, that always comes too late, led the king to say: "Every time I fill a vacancy, I create a hundred malcontents and one ingrate."
Cette connaissance malheureuse des hommes, qu'on acquiert trop tard, faisait dire le roi: "Toutes les fois que je donne une place vacante, je fais cent mécontents et un ingrat."

Voltaire
Le Siècle de Louis XIV
1751

It is easier for a camel to go through the eye of a needle, or for a rich man to enter the kingdom of heaven, than for a politician to lay aside disguise.

1st Earl of Charlemont (James Caulfeild)
letter to the Earl of Chatham
Jan, 1867

Your representative owes you, not his industry only, but his judgment; and he betrays, instead of serving you, if he sacrifices it to your opinion.

Edmund Burke
speech to the electors of Bristol
Nov 3, 1774

His crimes are the only great things about him, and these are contrasted by the littleness of his motives.

Richard Brinsley Sheridan
The Duenna
1775

John Adams
letter to Benjamin Rush
Feb 8, 1778

Patience. Patience. Patience! the first, and last, and the middle virtue of a politician.

Edmund Burke
debate in the House of
Commons on
impeachment of Warren
Hastings
Feb 15, 1788

There never was a bad man that had ability for good service.

William Cobbett
"Observations on the
Emigration of Dr.
Priestley"
1794

No man has a right to pry into his neighbour's private concerns; and the opinions of every man are his private concern, while he keeps them so. . . . But when he makes those opinions public; when he once attempts to make converts, whether it be in religion, politics, or anything else; when he once comes forward as a candidate for public admiration, esteem or compassion, his opinions, his principles, his motives, every action of his life, public or private, becomes the fair subject of public discussion.

George Washington
letter to Edward
Carrington
Oct 9, 1795

In the appointments to the great offices of the government, my aim has been to combine geographical situation, and sometimes other considerations, with abilities and fitness of known characters.

**Napoleon I
(Napoleon Bonaparte)**
letter to Citizen Carnot
Aug 9, 1796

The great art of governing consists in not letting men grow old in their jobs.
Ne pas laisser vieillir les hommes doit être le grand art du gouvernement.

Thomas Jefferson
letter to Tench Coxe
May 21, 1799

Offices are as acceptable here as elsewhere, and whenever a man has cast a longing eye on them, a rottenness begins in his conduct.

Thomas Jefferson
remark to Baron von
Humboldt
1807

When a man assumes a public trust, he should consider himself as public property.

Thomas Jefferson
letter to John McLish
Jan 13, 1813

An honest man can feel no pleasure in the exercise of power over his fellow citizens.

John Wilson Croker
letter to Lord Exmouth
Oct 23, 1816

I never have and never will (I hope) do anything for the sake of popularity; he that steers by any other compass than his own sense of duty may be a popular, but cannot be an honest, and I think not a useful public servant.

Martin Van Buren
letter to Dr. Graham A.
Worth
Apr 22, 1819

A man to be a sound politician and in any degree useful to his country must be governed by higher and steadier considerations than those of personal sympathy and private regard.

Andrew Jackson
Journal
May-Jun, 1829

Every man who has been in office a few years believes he has a life estate in it, a vested right. This is not the principle of our government. It is a rotation in office that will perpetuate our liberty.

Sir Robert Peel
speech in the House of
Commons
1831

We are here to consult the interests and not to obey the will of the people.

The art of governing is a great metier, requiring the whole man, and it is therefore not well for a ruler to have too strong tendencies for other affairs.

Johann Wolfgang von Goethe
quoted by Johann Peter Eckermann
Conversations with Goethe
Feb 18, 1831

The conduct and opinions of public men at different periods of their careers must not be curiously contrasted in a free and aspiring society.

Benjamin Disraeli
speech at High Wycombe, England
Dec 16, 1834

On my arrival in the United States, I was struck by the degree of ability among the governed and the lack of it among the governing.
A mon arrivée aux Etats-Unis, je fus frappe de surprise en découvrant à quel point le mérite était commun parmi les gouvernés, et combien il était peu chez les gouvernants.

Alexis, Comte de Tocqueville
Democracy in America
1835

Never with my consent shall an officer of the people, compensated for his services out of their pockets, become the pliant instrument of the Executive will.

William Henry Harrison
inaugural address
Mar 4, 1841

Timid and interested politicians think much more about the security of their seats than about the security of their country.

Lord Macaulay
speech in the House of Commons
May, 1842

So long as the people of any country place their hopes of political salvation in leadership of any description, so long will disappointment attend them.

William Lovett
"Public Letter to Daniel O'Connell"
1843

A man ain't got no right to be a public man, unless he meets the public views.

Charles Dickens
Martin Chuzzlewit
1844

The passion for office among members of Congress is very great, if not absolutely disreputable, and greatly embarrasses the operations of the Government.

James K. Polk
Diary
Jun 22, 1846

I'm not a politician and my other habits are good. I've no enemys to reward, nor friends to sponge. But I'm a Union man.

Artemus Ward (Charles Farrar Browne)
speech in Weathersfield, Connecticut
Jul 4, 1859

You can always get the truth from an American statesman after he has turned seventy, or given up all hope of the Presidency.

Wendell Phillips
speech
Nov 7, 1860

An honest politician is one who, when he is bought, will stay bought.

Simon Cameron
reported remark
1860

Politicians are like the bones of a horse's fore-shoulder—not a straight one in it.

Wendell Phillips
speech
Jul, 1864

Abraham Lincoln quoted *Everyday Life* 1865	A fellow once came to me to ask for an appointment as a minister abroad. Finding he could not get that, he came down to some more modest position. Finally, he asked to be made a tidewaiter. When he saw he could not get that, he asked me for an old pair of trousers. It is sometimes well to be humble.
Benjamin Disraeli speech in the House of Commons Feb, 1866	I trust that the time may never come when the love of fame shall cease to be the sovereign passion of our public men.
Rutherford B. Hayes letter to General E.A. Merritt Feb 4, 1879	Let appointments and removals be made on business principles, and by fixed rules. . . . Let no man be put . . . out or in merely because he is our friend.
Grover Cleveland on acceptance of Democratic nomination for governor of New York Oct, 1882	Public officers are the servants and agents of the people, to execute the laws which the people have made.
Matthew Stanley Quay speech 1886	If you have a weak candidate and a weak platform, wrap yourself up in the American flag and talk about the Constitution.
Lord Acton letter to Bishop Mandell Creighton Apr 5, 1887	There is no worse heresy than that the office sanctifies the holder of it.
Lord Acton letter to Bishop Mandell Creighton Apr 5, 1887	No public character has ever stood the revelation of private utterance and correspondence.
Rutherford B. Hayes letter to William McKinley Jun 27, 1888	Men in political life must be ambitious.
Theodore Roosevelt *Thomas Hart Benton* 1897	He (John Tyler) has been called a mediocre man; but this is unwarranted flattery. He was a politician of monumental littleness.
5th Earl of Rosebery *Sir Robert Peel* 1899	There are two supreme pleasures in life. One is ideal, the other real. The ideal is when a man receives the seals of office from his Sovereign. The real pleasure comes when he hands them back.
William Allen White *Emporia Gazette* Oct 25, 1901	Tinhorn politicians.
George Bernard Shaw "The Revolutionist's Handbook" *Man and Superman* 1902	The politician who once had to learn to flatter Kings has now to learn how to fascinate, amuse, coax, humbug, frighten, or otherwise strike the fancy of the electorate.
George Bernard Shaw *Major Barbara* 1905	He knows nothing and he thinks he knows everything. That points clearly to a political career.

Politician, n. An eel in the fundamental mud upon which the superstructure of organized society is reared. When he wriggles he mistakes the agitation of his tail for the trembling of the edifice. As compared with the statesman, he suffers the disadvantage of being alive.

Ambrose Bierce
The Devil's Dictionary
1906

Nominee, n. A modest gentleman shrinking from the distinction of private life and diligently seeking the honorable obscurity of public office.

Ambrose Bierce
The Devil's Dictionary
1906

I hear our countrymen abroad saying: "you mustn't judge us by our politicians." I always want to interrupt and answer: "you must judge us by our politicians." We pretend to be the masters—we, the people—and if we permit ourselves to be ill served, to be served by corrupt and incompetent and inefficient men, then on our own head must the blame rest.

Theodore Roosevelt
speech at the Pacific Lutheran Theological Seminary
1911

Politicians are to serve the people, not to direct them.

Woodrow Wilson
speech in Pittsburgh, Pennsylvania
Oct 18, 1912

The perfection of Parliamentary style is to utter cruel platitudes with a grave and informing air; and, if a little pomposity be superadded, the House will instinctively recognize the speaker as a Statesman.

George William Erskine Russell
One Look Back
1912

Once you touch the biographies of human beings, the notion that political beliefs are logically determined collapses like a pricked ballon.

Walter Lippmann
A Preface to Morals
1913

Politicians tend to live "in character," and many a public figure has come to imitate the journalism which describes him.

Walter Lippmann
"The Changing Focus"
A Preface to Politics
1914

Most of the errors of public life . . . come, not because men are morally bad, but because they are afraid of somebody.

Woodrow Wilson
speech to the Princeton Univ. class of 1879
Jun 13, 1914

The best servants of the people, like the best valets, must whisper unpleasant truths in the master's ear. It is the court fool, not the foolish courtier, whom the king can least afford to lose.

Walter Lippmann
"Some Necessary Iconoclasm"
A Preface to Politics
1914

Every man who takes office in Washington either grows or swells. . . . When I give a man an office, I watch him carefully to see whether he is swelling or growing. The mischief of it is when they swell they do not swell enough to burst.

Woodrow Wilson
speech in Washington, D.C.
May 16, 1916

The proper memory for a politician is one that knows what to remember and what to forget.

John Morley
Recollections
1917

Beatrice Webb *Diary* Jun 7, 1917	The Trade Union Movement has become, like the hereditary peerage, an avenue to political power through which stupid untrained persons may pass up to the highest office if only they have secured the suffrages of the members of a large union. One wonders when able rascals will discover this open door to remunerative power.
Nancy Astor **Viscountess Astor** speech in Plymouth, England 1919	I am a Virginian, so naturally I am a politician.
James Bryce remark to Owen Wister 1921	A political career brings out the basest qualities in human nature.
George Bernard Shaw *Back to Methuselah* 1921	The nauseous sham goodfellowship our democratic public men get up for shop use.
Maurice Barrès *Mes cahiers* 1923	The politician is an acrobat. He keeps his balance by saying the opposite of what he does.
Beatrice Webb *Diary* Apr 7, 1924	Are all Cabinets congeries of little autocrats with a super-autocrat presiding over them?
Beatrice Webb *Diary* Nov 10, 1925	The middle man governs, however extreme may seem to be the men who sit on the Front Bench, in their reactionary or revolutionary opinions.
Andre Gide Second Notebook *Journal of the* *Counterfeiters* Mar 29, 1925	The public always prefers to be reassured. There are those whose job this is. There are only too many.
Sir Oswald Mosley quoted by Robert Skidelsky *Oswald Mosley* 1975	Faced with the alternative of saying good-bye to the gold standard, and therefore to his own employment, and good-bye to other people's employment, Mr. Churchill characteristically selected the latter course.
Bertrand Russell "Freedom in Society" *Skeptical Essays* 1928	Politicians, who have not time to become acquainted with human nature, are peculiarly ignorant of the desires that move ordinary men and women. Any political party whose leaders knew a little psychology could sweep the country.
Calvin Coolidge *Autobiography* 1929	What we need in appointive positions is men of knowledge and experience who have sufficient character to resist temptations.
Will Rogers quoted *Rocky Mountain News* May 28, 1980	The trouble with practical jokes is that very often they get elected.
Boies Penrose *Collier's Weekly* Feb 14, 1931	Public office is the last refuge of the scoundrel.

There is just one rule for politicians all over the world. Don't say in Power what you say in Opposition; if you do, you only have to carry out what the other fellows have found impossible.

John Galsworthy
Maid in Waiting
1931

The public official must pick his way nicely, must learn to placate though not to yield too much, to have the art of honeyed words but not to seem neutral, and above all to keep constantly audible, visible, likable, even kissable.

Learned Hand
speech in Washington, D.C.
Mar 8, 1932

did you ever/ notice that when/ a politician/ does get an idea/ he usually/ gets it all wrong.

Don Marquis
Archy's Life of Mehitabel
1933

A politician will do anything to keep his job—even become a patriot.

William Randolph Hearst
editorial
San Francisco Examiner
Aug 28, 1933

In our democracy officers of the government are the servants, and never the masters of the people.

Franklin D. Roosevelt
speech in Hollywood, California
Feb 27, 1941

How different the new order would be if we could consult the veteran instead of the politician.

Henry Miller
"The Alcoholic Veteran with the Washboard Cranium"
The Wisdom of the Heart
1941

When the political columnists say "Every thinking man" they mean themselves, and when the candidates appeal to "Every intelligent voter" they mean everybody who is going to vote for them.

Franklin P. Adams
Nods and Becks
1944

The trouble with this country is that there are too many politicians who believe, with a conviction based on experience, that you can fool all the people all of the time.

Franklin P. Adams
Nods and Becks
1944

Politicians are ambitious not to make important decisions but to say important things.

Richard Crossman
"Amery and Fisher"
New Statesman
1947

The necessary and wise subordination of the military to civil power will be best sustained when life-long professional soldiers abstain from seeking high political office.

Dwight D. Eisenhower
letter to Harry S Truman
Jan, 1948

A Lobbyist is a person that is supposed to help a Politician to make up his mind, not only help him but pay him.

Will Rogers
The Autobiography of Will Rogers
1949

Politicians, after all, are not over a year behind Public Opinion.

Will Rogers
The Autobiography of Will Rogers
1949

Will Rogers
The Autobiography of
Will Rogers
1949

A Congressman is never any better than his roads, and sometimes worse.

Will Rogers
The Autobiography of
Will Rogers
1949

There is a hundred things to single you out for promotion in party politics besides ability.

Earl Long
quoted
New Yorker
Jun 4, 1960

The kind of thing I'm good at is knowing every politician in the state and remembering where he itches.

Richard Crossman
Diary
Nov 13, 1951

One of the difficulties of politics is that politicians are shocked by those who are really prepared to let their thinking reach any conclusion. Political thinking consists in deciding upon the conclusion first and then finding good arguments for it. An open mind is considered irresponsible—and perhaps it really is.

Dean Acheson
on retiring to private life
Time
Dec 22, 1952

I will undoubtedly have to seek what is happily known as gainful employment, which I am glad to say does not describe holding public office.

Adlai E. Stevenson Jr.
speech in Los Angeles,
California
Sep 11, 1952

Your public servants serve you right; indeed often they serve you better than your apathy and indifference deserve.

Walter Lippmann
The Public Philosophy
1955

Successful democratic politicians are insecure and intimidated men. They advance politically only as they placate, appease, bribe, seduce, bamboozle, or otherwise manage to manipulate the demanding and threatening elements in their constituencies.

Richard M. Nixon
speech in New York City
Sep 14, 1955

There is no such thing as a nonpolitical speech by a politician.

Walter Lippmann
The Public Philosophy
1955

In government offices which are sensitive to the vehemence and passion of mass sentiment public men have no sure tenure. They are in effect perpetual office seekers, always on trial for their political lives, always required to court their restless constitutents.

John F. Kennedy
speech to the Harvard
Alumni Association
Jun 14, 1956

"Don't teach my boy poetry," an English mother recently wrote the Provost of Harrow. " Don't teach my boy poetry; he is going to stand for Parliament." Well, perhaps she was right—but if more politicians knew poetry, and more poets knew politics, I am convinced the world would be a little better place to live on this Commencement Day of 1956.

H.L. Mencken
Minority Report
1956

When I hear a man applauded by the mob I always feel a pang of pity for him. All he has to do to be hissed is to live long enough.

Harry S Truman
Memoirs
1955-56

A good politician with nerve and a program that is right can win in the face of the stiffest opposition.

The distinction between a statesman and a politician is that the former imposes his will and his ideas on his environment while the latter adapts himself to it.

Richard Crossman
"Roosevelt—Warts and All"
New Statesman
1957

A politician is a man who understands government, and it takes a politician to run a government. A statesman is a politician who's been dead 10 or 15 years.

Harry S Truman
New York World Telegram & Sun
Apr 12, 1958

A candidate for office can have no greater advantage than muddled syntax; no greater liability than a command of language.

Marya Mannes
More in Anger
1958

McCarthy invented the multi Lie—the lie with so many tiny gears and fragile connecting rods that reason exhausted itself in the effort to combat it.

Richard H. Rovere
"The Frivolous Demagogue"
Esquire
Jun, 1958

The politician is . . . trained in the art of inexactitude. His words tend to be blunt or rounded, because if they have a cutting edge they may later return to wound him.

Edward R. Murrow
speech at Guildhall in London
Oct 19, 1959

The politician in my country seeks votes, affection and respect, in that order. . . . With few notable exceptions, they are simply men who want to be loved.

Edward R. Murrow
speech at Guildhall in London
Oct 19, 1959

Politicians are the same all over. They promise to build a bridge even where there is no river.

Nikita S. Khrushchev
comments to the press on visit to United States
Oct, 1960

No government is better than the men who compose it.

John F. Kennedy
campaign speech at Wittenberg College, Springfield, Ohio
Oct 17, 1960

Public officials are not a group apart. They evitably reflect the moral tone of the society in which they live.

John F. Kennedy
message to Congress
Apr 27, 1961

They may be just as intelligent as you say. But I'd feel a helluva lot better if just one of them had ever run for sheriff.

Sam Rayburn
to Lyndon Johnson on advisers to President Kennedy, quoted by David Halberstam
The Best and the Brightest
1972

Since a politician never believes what he says, he is surprised when others believe him.

Charles De Gaulle
quoted
Newsweek
Oct 1, 1962

Idealism is the noble toga that political gentlemen drape over the will to power.

Aldous Huxley
recalled on his death
New York Herald Tribune
Nov 24, 1963

As the master politician navigates the ship of state, he both creates and responds to public opinion. Adept at tacking with the wind, he also succeeds, at times, in generating breezes of his own.

Stewart L. Udall
The Quiet Crisis
1963

A professional politician's first duty is to appeal to the forces that unite us, and to channel the forces that divide us into paths where a democratic solution is possible. It is our obligation to resolve issues—not to create them.

Lyndon Baines Johnson
Life
Nov 29, 1963

One has to be a lowbrow, a bit of a murderer, to be a politician, ready and willing to see people sacrificed, slaughtered, for the sake of an idea, whether a good one or a bad one.

Henry Miller
quoted by George Plimpton
Writers at Work
1963

The biggest danger for a politician is to shake hands with a man who is physically stronger, has been drinking and is voting for the other guy.

William Proxmire
New York Herald Tribune
Feb 16, 1964

He (Richard Nixon) is the kind of politician who would cut down a redwood tree, then mount the stump and make a speech for conservation.

Adlai E. Stevenson Jr.
recalled on his death
Jul 14, 1965

I once said cynically of a politician, "He'll double-cross that bridge when he comes to it."

Oscar Levant
The Memoirs of an Amnesiac
1965

Hyperbole was to Lyndon Johnson what oxygen is to life.

Lance Morrow
The New York Times
Apr 3, 1966

Probably the most distinctive characteristic of the successful politician is selective cowardice.

Richard Harris
"Annals of Legislation"
The New Yorker
Dec 14, 1968

He (Richard Nixon) is like a good prewar house—solidly built. They don't build them that way anymore. He's also been repainted several times.

Theodore H. White
on Richard M. Nixon's decision to run for president
Time
Feb 16, 1968

If people want a sense of purpose they should get it from their archbishop. They should certainly not get it from their politicians.

Harold Macmillan Earl of Stockton
quoted by Henry Fairlie
The Life of Politics
1969

Politicians trim and tack in their quest for power, but they do so in order to get the wind of votes in their sails.

Sir Ian Gilmour
The Body Politic
1969

In Pierre Elliott Trudeau Canada has at last produced a political leader worthy of assassination.

Irving Layton
"Obo II"
The Whole Bloody Bird
1969

Some members of congress are the best actors in the world.

Shirley Chisholm
Unbought and Unbossed
1970

I remember when I first came to Washington. For the first six months you wonder how the hell you ever got here. For the next six months you wonder how the hell the rest of them ever got here.

Harry S Truman
recalled on his death
Dec 26, 1972

Reading about one's failings in the daily papers is one of the privileges of high office in this free country of ours.

Nelson A. Rockefeller
speech in Syracuse, New York
Nov 29, 1972

Before you can become a statesman you first have to get elected, and to get elected you have to be a politician pledging support for what the voters want.

Margaret Chase Smith
Declaration of Conscience
1972

A passion for politics stems usually from an insatiable need, either for power, or for friendship and adulation, or a combination of both.

Fawn M. Brodie
Thomas Jefferson
1974

A politician ought to be born a foundling and remain a bachelor.

Claudia ("Lady Bird") Johnson
Time
Dec 1, 1975

Most politicians have a right to feel morally superior to their constituencies.

Daniel P. Moynihan
Rolling Stone
Aug 12, 1976

A boss is a political leader who is on somebody else's side.

Morris K. Udall
"Issues and Answers,"
ABC-TV
Apr 25, 1976

The main essentials of a successful prime minister (are) sleep and a sense of history.

Harold Wilson
The Government of Britain
1977

Every public official should be recycled occasionally.

John V. Lindsay
Chicago Tribune
Jan 22, 1978

Everybody in government is like a bunch of ants on a log floating down a river. Each one thinks he is guiding the log, but it's really just going with the flow.

Robert S. Strauss
Time
Apr 17, 1978

I'd rather keep my promises to other politicians than to God. God, at least, has a degree of forgiveness.

Anonymous
Washington Post
Jun 9, 1978

Politicians fascinate because they constitute such a paradox: they are an elite that accomplishes mediocrity for the public good.

Garry Wills
Time
Apr 23, 1979

The politician who will refuse the Foreign Office is not yet born.

Michael Stewart
Life and Labour
1980

A populist politician is a politician who says things because he believes them to be popular. At least that is my understanding of the term. I have never been that. My worst enemies couldn't say that.

Enoch Powell
The Listener
May 28, 1981

Katharine Hepburn fundraising letter for the Planned Parenthood Federation Nov, 1981	Most politicians will not stick their necks out unless they sense grass-roots support. . . . Neither you nor I should expect someone else to take our responsibility. If we remain passive, they will surely win.
Millicent Fenwick "60 Minutes," CBS-TV Feb 1, 1981	The curious fascination in this job is the illusion that either you are being useful or you could be—and that's so tempting.
Andy Rooney "60 Minutes," CBS-TV Oct 7, 1984	The only people who say worse things about politicians than reporters do are other politicians.
Charles Krauthammer "Pietygate: School for Scandal" *Time* Sep 10, 1984	If we insist that public life be reserved for those whose personal history is pristine, we are not going to get paragons of virtue running our affairs. We will get the very rich, who contract out the messy things of life; the very dull, who have nothing to hide and nothing to show; and the very devious, expert at covering their tracks and ambitious enough to risk their discovery.
Jesse Jackson speech to the Democratic National Convention in San Francisco Jul 17, 1984	I am not a perfect servant. I am a public servant doing my best against the odds.
Margaret Truman speech to joint session of Congress on 100th anni- versary of her father's birth May 8, 1984	He loved politicians—even Republicans.
Dean Rusk quoted *The New York Times* May 6, 1985	Give a member of Congress a junket and a mimeograph machine and he thinks he is secretary of state.
James C. Wright Jr. *The New York Times* Dec 9, 1986	Here is an animal (the rhinoceros) with a hide two feet thick, and no apparent interest in politics. What a waste.
Ronald Reagan interview with Barbara Walters, ABC-TV Mar 24, 1986	I've often wondered how some people in positions of this kind . . . manage without having had any acting experience.
Len Deighton *Mexico Set* 1986	In Mexico an air conditioner is called a politician because it makes a lot of noise but doesn't work very well.
Robertson Davies *The Papers of Samuel Marchbanks* 1986	The average politician goes through a sentence like a man exploring a disused mine shaft—blind, groping, timorous and in imminent danger of cracking his shins on a subordinate clause or a nasty bit of subjunctive.
Ann F. Lewis *The New York Times* Sep 24, 1986	Politicians have the same occupational hazard as generals— focusing on the last battle and overreacting to that.

I heard his library burned down and that both books were destroyed—and one of them hadn't even been colored in yet.

John Dawkins
quoted remarks on a political colleague
Wall Street Journal
Nov 14, 1986

I'm a participant in the doctrine of constructive ambiquity.

Vernon A. Walters
Christian Science Monitor
Sep 18, 1986

She (Gladys Kinnock) is said to be inclined to cough noisily when he goes on too long at the rostrum: but this is a traditional prerogative of the political wife, and rather more necessary in this instance than in most.

George Hill
London Times
Feb 19, 1987

When things haven't gone well for you, call in a secretary or a staff man and chew him out. You will sleep better and they will appreciate the attention.

Lyndon Baines Johnson
quoted
People
Feb 2, 1987

The CIA is made up of boys whose families sent them to Princeton but wouldn't let them into the family brokerage business.

Lyndon Baines Johnson
quoted
People
Feb 2, 1987

We (non-candidates) don't have to do what the candidates do—talk about huge issues in 30 seconds in a field somewhere, trying to make sure cows don't urinate on our shoes.

Mario Cuomo
quoted by A.M. Rosenthal
The New York Times
Mar 18, 1988

(The representative's) duty is to represent the interests of all those people whom he represents to the best of his ability. These interests will in almost all cases be identical with those of all the citizens of the country, of the nation. These are the interests he must pursue to the best of his knowledge. He is personally responsible to persons.

Sir Karl Popper
"Popper on Democracy"
The Economist
Apr 23, 1988

Politics

Man is by nature a political animal.

Aristotle
Politics
343 B.C.

Many have imagined republics and principalities which have never been seen or known to exist in reality; for how we live is so far removed from how we ought to live, that he who abandons what is done for what ought to be done, will rather bring about his own ruin than his preservation.

E molti si sono imaginati republiche e principati che non si sono mai visti né conosciuti essere in vero: perché egli è tanto discosto da come si vive a come si doverebbe vivere, che colui che lascia quello che si fa per quello che si doverrebbe fare impara piuttosto la ruina che la preservazione sua.

Niccolò Machiavelli
Il Principe
1532

Sir Francis Bacon *Advancement of Learning* 1605	We are much beholden to Machiavel and others, that write what men do, and not what they ought to do.
Jean de La Bruyère "Des jugements" *Les Caractères* 1688	The favor of princes does not exclude merit, but then neither is it based on it. *La faveur des princes n'exclut pas le mérite, et ne le suppose pas aussi.*
Marquis de Vauvenargues *Réflexions et maximes* 1746	The wicked are always surprised to find ability in the good. *Les méchants sont toujours surpris de trouver de l'habileté dans les bons.*
4th Earl of Chesterfield *Letters to His Son* Oct 22, 1750	In our Parliamentary government, connections are absolutely necessary; and, if prudently formed, ably maintained, the success of them is infallible.
William Pitt 1st Earl of Chatham quoted by John Morley *Walpole* 1909	I borrowed the Duke of Newcastle's majority to carry on the public business.
Jean Jacques Rousseau *Emile* 1762	Those people who treat politics and morality separately will never understand either of them.
Samuel Johnson reported conversation Apr 18, 1775	Politics are now nothing more than a means of rising in the world.
John Adams letter to Horatio Gates Mar 23, 1776	I agree with you that in politics the middle way is none at all.
John Adams letter to Robert R. Livingston Jan 23, 1783	I have lived long enough, and have experience enough of the conduct of governments and people, nations, and courts, to be convinced that gratitude, friendship, and unsuspecting confidence, and all the amiable passions of human nature, are the most dangerous guides in politics.
Maximilien Robespierre speech to the National Assembly May, 1791	In politics nothing is just save what is honest; nothing is useful except what is just.
Fisher Ames "No Revolutions" *Palladium* Nov, 1801	The agents that move politicks, are the popular passions; and those are ever, from the very nature of things, under the command of the disturbers of society.
Fisher Ames *The Dangers of American Liberty* 1805	It is indeed a law of politicks as well as of physicks, that a body in action must overcome an equal body at rest.
Sir Robert Peel letter to Henry Goulburn Sep 23, 1822	What is right must unavoidably be politic.

In politics as in religion, it so happens that we have less charity for those who believe the half of our creed, than for those that deny the whole of it.

Charles Caleb Colton
Lacön
1825

I find the remark, "'Tis distance lends enchantment to the view" is no less true of the political than of the natural world.

Franklin Pierce
letter
1832

The pendulum swung furiously to the left, because it had been drawn too far to the right.

Lord Macaulay
"Sir James Mackintosh"
Edinburgh Review
Jul, 1835

Gratitude is not an active sentiment in politics. It is a mistake to take account of it.

Prince Clemens von Metternich
letter to Esterhazy
Mar 18, 1841

Politics is the art of knowing and leading a multitude or a plurality; its glory is to lead them not where they want to go but where they should go.
La politique est l'art de connaître et de mener la multitude ou la pluralité; sa gloire est de la mener, non pas ou elle veut, mais ou elle doit aller.

Joseph Joubert
Pensées
1842

In politics you should always leave an old bone behind for the critics to chew on.
En politique, il faut toujours laisser un os à rongé aux frondeurs.

Joseph Joubert
Pensées
1842

There seem to me very few facts, at least ascertainable facts, in politics.

Sir Robert Peel
letter to Lord Brougham
1846

Great public measures cannot be carried by the influence of mere reason.

Sir Robert Peel
letter to Lord Radnor
1846

I have always considered politics in the presence of social dangers to be a luxury.

Prince Clemens von Metternich
letter to the
Archduchess Sophie
Mar 31, 1848

I have always noticed in politics how often men are ruined by having too good a memory.

Alexis, Comte de Tocqueville
Recollections
1893

He (Tom Brown) never wants anything but what's right and fair; only when you come to settle what's right and fair, it's everything he wants, and nothing you want. And that's his idea of a compromise.

Thomas Hughes
Tom Brown's Schooldays
1856

Finality is not the language of politics.

Benjamin Disraeli
speech in the House of Commons
Feb 28, 1859

Artemus Ward
"The Crisis"
Artemus Ward, His Book
1862

My pollertics, like my religion, being of an exceeding' accommodatin' character.

Prince Otto von Bismarck
speech to Prussian legislature
Dec 18, 1863

Politics is not an exact science.
Die Politik ist keine exakte Wissenschaft.

Prince Otto von Bismarck
speech in the Prussian House of Deputies
Dec 18, 1863

Let us learn to respect sincerity of conviction in our opponents.
Lernen wir Überzeugungstreue an den Gegnern achten.

Prince Otto von Bismarck
conversation with Meyer von Waldeck
Aug 11, 1867

Politics is the art of the possible.
Die Politik ist die Lehre von Möglichen.

Walter Bagehot
The English Constitution
1867

The whole life of English politics is the action and reaction between the Ministry and the Parliament.

Prince Otto von Bismarck
quoted by Charles Lowe
Bismarck's Table Talk
1895

To rule with the help of one's enemies is ever the worst kind of policy.

August Bebel
speech to the Reichstag
Jul 3, 1871

All political questions, all matters of right, are at bottom only questions of might.

Charles Dudley Warner
"Fifteenth Week"
My Summer in a Garden
1871

Politics makes strange bed-fellows.

Michael Bakunin
"A Circular Letter to My Friends in Italy"
1871

Idealism is the despot of thought, just as politics is the despot of will.

Michael Bakunin
The Knouto-Germanic Empire and the Social Revolution
1871

To exploit and to govern mean the same thing. . . . Exploitation and government are two inseparable expressions of what is called politics.

3rd Marquess of Salisbury
"The Position of Parties"
Quarterly Review
Oct, 1872

The optimist view of politics assumes that there must be some remedy for every political ill, and rather than not find it, it will make two hardships to cure one.

James A. Garfield
speech at Hudson College
Jul 2, 1873

We are apt to be deluded into false security by political catch-words, devised to flatter rather than instruct.

In politics one must take nothing tragically and everything seriously.

(Louis) Adolphe Thiers
speech to the Chamber of Deputies
May 24, 1873

The political spirit is the great force in throwing love of truth and accurate reasoning into a secondary place.

John Morley
On Compromise
1874

Those who would treat politics and morality apart will never understand the one or the other.

John Morley
Rousseau
1876

The commonest error in politics is sticking to the carcass of dead policies.

3rd Marquess of Salisbury
letter to Bulwer-Lytton
1878

Nothing is so dull as political agitation.

William Ewart Gladstone
speech at Glasgow Univ.
Dec 5, 1879

Politics are vulgar when they are not liberalised by history, and history fades into mere literature when it loses sight of its relation to practical politics.

Sir John Seely
The Expansion of England
1883

Politics is not a science, as many professors imagine, but an art.
Die Politik ist keine Wissenschaft, wie viele der Herren Professoren sich einbilden, sondern eine Kunst.

Prince Otto von Bismarck
speech in the Reichstag
Mar 15, 1884

In politics there is no use looking beyond the next fortnight.

Joseph Chamberlain
conversation with Arthur Balfour
Mar 22, 1886

It were not best that we should all think alike; it is difference of opinion that makes horse races.

Mark Twain
"Pudd'nhead Wilson's Calendar"
Pudd'nhead Wilson
1894

I ain't never seen no head so level that it could bear the lettin' in of politics. It makes a fool of a man and a worse fool of a fool.

Ellen Glasgow
The Voice of the People
1900

The most practical kind of politics is the politics of decency.

Theodore Roosevelt
remarks in Oyster Bay, New York
Jun, 1901

Beware of the man who does not return your blow: he neither forgives you nor allows you to forgive yourself.

George Bernard Shaw
"Maxims for Revolutionists"
Man and Superman
1902

Politics, as a practice, whatever its professions, has always been the systematic organization of hatreds.

Henry Adams
The Education of Henry Adams
1906

Ambrose Bierce *The Devil's Dictionary* 1906	Politics, n. A strife of interests masquerading as a contest of principles.
Ambrose Bierce *The Devil's Dictionary* 1906	Administration, n. An ingenious abstraction in politics, designed to receive the kicks and cuffs due to the premier or president.
Henry Adams *The Education of Henry Adams* 1906	Knowledge of human nature is the beginning and end of political education.
Henry Adams *The Education of Henry Adams* 1906	Practical politics consists in ignoring facts.
Henry Adams *The Education of Henry Adams* 1906	Modern politics is, at bottom, a struggle not of men but of forces.
August Bebel speech to the annual congress of the German Social Democratic Party 1906	The field of politics always presents the same struggle. There are the Right and the Left, and in the middle is the Swamp.
Ambrose Bierce *The Devil's Dictionary* 1906	Opposition, n. In politics the party that prevents the Government from running amuck by hamstringing it.
Sir Henry Campbell-Bannerman speech in Plymouth, England Jun 7, 1907	The people of this country are a straightforward people. They like honesty and straightforwardness of purpose. They may laugh at it and they may be amused by it and they may in a sense admire it, but they do not like cleverness. You may be too clever by half.
G.K. Chesterton *What's Wrong with the World* 1910	Compromise used to mean that half a loaf was better than no bread. Among modern statesmen it really seems to mean that half a loaf is better than a whole loaf.
Theodore Roosevelt announcement of candidacy for president 1912	My hat's in the ring. The fight is on and I'm stripped to the buff.
George William Erskine Russell *One Look Back* 1912	When the Government of the day and the Opposition of the day take the same side, one can be almost sure that some great wrong is at hand.
Thomas Masaryk memorandum on an "Independent Bohemia" Apr, 1915	In politics habits, and not only good ones, but bad ones just as well, rule humanity.
Sir Winston S. Churchill Remark ca. 1920	Politics are almost as exciting as war, and quite as dangerous. In war you can only be killed once, but in politics many times.

The whole aim of practical politics is to keep the populace alarmed (and hence clamorous to be led to safety) by menacing it with an endless series of hobgoblins, all of them imaginary.

H.L. Mencken
"Women as Outlaws"
The Smart Set
Dec, 1921

The instinctive appeal of every successful political movement is to envy, rivalry or hate, never to the need for co-operation.

Bertrand Russell
presidential address to the Students Union, London School of Economics
Oct 10, 1923

Politics, which, the planet over, are the fly in the amber, the worm in the bud . . . had, with great suddenness, deprived Wharton Cameron of a job.

Katherine Gerould
Conquistador
1923

Politics, as hopeful men practice it in the world, consists mainly of the delusion that a change in form is a change in substance.

H.L. Mencken
Prejudices: Fourth Series
1924

The friend of humanity cannot recognize a distinction between what is political and what is not. There is nothing that is not political.
Der Menschenfreund kann den Unterschied von Politik und Nichtpolitik überhaupt nicht anerkennen. Es gibt keine Nichtpolitik. Alles ist politik.

Thomas Mann
The Magic Mountain
1924

More men have been elected between Sundown and Sunup than ever were elected between Sunup and Sundown.

Will Rogers
"Mr. Ford and Other Political Self-Starters"
The Illiterate Digest
1924

Politics is not an art, but a means. It is not a product, but a process.

Calvin Coolidge
quoted by Edward E. Whiting
Calvin Coolidge: His Ideals of Citizenship
1924

In the field of politics, force and consent are correlative terms, and one does not exist without the other. The objection will be raised that this is a "forced" consent. But every consent is more or less forced . . . in the most liberal State as is the most oppressive tyranny there is always a consent, and it is always forced, conditioned, changeable.

Benedetto Croce
Elements of Politics
1925

The more cant there is in politics the better. Cant is nothing in itself; but attached to even the smallest quantity of sincerity, it serves like a nought after a numeral, to multiply whatever of geniune good-will may exist.

Aldous Huxley
Jesting Pilate
1926

Nobuddy ever fergits where he buried a hatchet.

"Kin" Hubbard
Abe Martin's Broadcast
1930

Political principles resemble military tactics; they are usually designed for a war which is over.

Richard Tawney
Equality
1931

Will Rogers syndicated newspaper article Jun 28, 1931	Politics has got so expensive that it takes lots of money to even get beat with.
Herbert Hoover press conference May 27, 1932	Our nation was not founded on the pork barrel, and it has not become great by political log-rolling.
Franklin D. Roosevelt quoted *Oui* May, 1978	Nothing just happens in politics. If something happens you can be sure it was planned that way.
Franklin D. Roosevelt speech in Winter Park, Florida Mar 23, 1936	The science of politics . . . may properly be said to be in large part the science of the adjustment of conflicting group interests.
Harold Lasswell book title 1936	Politics: Who Gets What, When, How.
Mao Tse-tung "On Protracted War" May, 1938	Politics is war without bloodshed while war is politics with bloodshed.
Walter Lippmann "The Indispensable Opposition" *Atlantic Monthly* Aug, 1939	The opposition is indispensable. A good statesman, like any other sensible human being, always learns more from his opponents than from his fervent supporters.
Mao Tse-tung "Interview with Three Correspondents" Sep 16, 1939	We should support whatever the enemy opposes and oppose whatever the enemy supports.
Ignazio Silone *The School for Dictatorships* 1939	A declining political class has all the infirmities of old age, including deafness. *Una classe politica in declino ha tutti gli acciacchi della vecchiaia, compresa la sordità.*
Arthur Koestler *Darkness at Noon* 1940	Politics can be relatively fair in the breathing spaces of history; at its critical turning points there is no other rule possible than the old one, that the end justifies the means.
Sir Stephen Spender "A Look at the Worst" *Horizon* Sep, 1940	By comparison with the greatest subjects of art . . . all politics seem like provincial struggles for booty between dusky tribes.
Albert Camus *Cahiers, 1935-1942* 1962	Politics, and the fate of mankind, are shaped by men without ideals and without greatness.
Paul Valéry *Tel quel* 1943	Politics is the art of preventing people from taking part in affairs which properly concern them.

You will find in politics that you are much exposed to the attribution of false motives. Never complain and never explain.

Stanley Baldwin
recorded in Harold Nicolson
Diary
Jul 21, 1943

Politics is the science of who gets what, when, and why.

Sidney Hillman
Political Primer for All Americans
1944

In politics, as in other things, there is no such thing as one getting something for nothing. The payoff may involve compromises of various types that may strike at the ideals and principles one has held dear all his life.

A. Philip Randolph
"Why I Can't Run for Congress on the Old Party Ticket"
The Call
Apr 28, 1944

Power politics is the diplomatic name for the law of the jungle.

Ely Culbertson
Must We Fight Russia?
1946

When I am abroad, I always make it a rule never to criticize or attack the government of my own country. I make up for lost time when I come home.

Sir Winston S. Churchill
speech in the House of Commons
Apr, 1947

If you ever injected truth into politics you have no politics.

Will Rogers
The Autobiography of Will Rogers
1949

In our time, political speech and writing are largely the defense of the indefensible.

George Orwell
"Politics and the English Language"
Shooting an Elephant
1950

People who think the mighty in Washington can be persuaded, or corrupted, if you will, by anything less than votes just don't understand what it's all about and never will. They don't know what Washington juice is made of.

George E. Allen
Presidents Who Have Known Me
1950

Honest difference of views and honest debate are not disunity. They are the vital process of policy among free men.

Herbert Hoover
speech in New York City
Dec 20, 1950

Power-worship blurs political judgment because it leads, almost unavoidably, to the belief that present trends will continue. Whoever is winning at the moment will always seem to be invincible.

George Orwell
"Second Thoughts on James Burnham"
Shooting an Elephant
1950

What is politics but persuading the public to vote for this and support that and endure these for the promise of those?

Gilbert Highet
"The Art of Persuasion"
Vogue
Jan 1951

Why is it that when political ammunition runs low, inevitably the rusty artillery of abuse is always wheeled into action?

Adlai E. Stevenson Jr.
speech in New York City
Sep 22, 1952

Harry S Truman
quoted by William Hillman
Mr. President
1952

Our American political situation is about the same from generation to generation. The main difficulty is that the rising generation never knows about the acts of the previous one—most people think it too much trouble to find out.

Alben W. Barkley
That Reminds Me
1954

"How can you think of voting for my opponent?" I exhorted. . . . "Surely you remember all these things I have done for you?" "Yeah," he said, "I remember. But what in hell have you done for me lately?"

Robert Louis Stevenson
quoted
Rocky Mountain News
Sep 3, 1979

Politics is perhaps the only profession for which no preparation is thought necessary.

Adlai E. Stevenson III
Time
Feb 26, 1979

I don't think ideas are incompatible with political reality.

Adlai E. Stevenson Jr.
quoted
Kansas City Star
Jan 30, 1977

Good government cannot exist side by side with bad politics: the best government is the best politics.

Agnes Sligh Turnbull
The Golden Journey
1955

Defeat in itself was part and parcel of the great gambling game of politics. A man who could not accept it and try again was not of the stuff of which leaders are made.

Agnes Sligh Turnbull
The Golden Journey
1955

The older you get the more you realize that gray isn't such a bad color. And in politics you work with it or you don't work at all.

Christabel Pankhurst
Unshackled
1959

Never lose your temper with the Press or the public is a major rule of political life.

James Joll
Three Intellectuals in Politics
1960

The tragedy of all political action is that some problems have no solution; none of the alternatives are intellectually consistent or morally uncompromising; and whatever decision is taken will harm somebody.

Willy Brandt
Mein Weg nach Berlin
1960

What we need is a synthesis of practical thoughts and idealistic aspirations.
Was wir brauchen, ist die Synthese von praktischem Denken und idealistischem Streben.

Bertrand de Jouvenel
The Pure Theory of Politics
1963

Politics is a systematic effort to move other men in the pursuit of some design.

Dwight D. Eisenhower
Time
Oct 25, 1963

(I despise people who) go to the gutter on either the right or the left and hurl rocks at those in the center.

Harold Macmillan
Wall Street Journal
Aug 13, 1963

I have never found, in a long experience of politics, that criticism is ever inhibited by ignorance.

If you're in politics and you can't tell when you walk into a room who's for you and who's against you, then you're in the wrong line of work.

Lyndon Baines
Johnson
quoted by Boothe
Mooney
The Lyndon Johnson Story
1964

A rigged convention is one with the other man's delegates in control. An open convention is when your delegates are in control.

James A. Farley
quoted
Convention and Election Almanac
1964

Ideas are great arrows, but there has to be a bow. And politics is the bow of idealism.

Bill Moyers
Time
Oct 29, 1965

Insofar as it represents a genuine reconciliation of differences, a consensus is a fine thing; insofar as it represents a concealment of differences, it is a miscarriage of democratic procedure.

J. William Fulbright
speech in the U.S. Senate
Oct 22, 1965

I happen to think that American politics is one of the noblest arts of mankind; and I cannot do anything else but write about it.

Theodore H. White
The New York Times
Jun 22, 1965

An independent is the guy who wants to take the politics out of politics.

Adlai E. Stevenson Jr.
"The Art of Politics"
The Stevenson Wit
1966

In politics, it seems, retreat is honorable if dictated by military considerations and shameful if even suggested for ethical reasons.

Mary McCarthy
"Solutions"
Vietnam
1967

All politics are based on the indifference of the majority.

James Reston
The New York Times
Jun 12, 1968

Experience suggests that the first rule of politics is never to say never. The ingenious human capacity for maneuver and compromise may make acceptable tomorrow what seems outrageous or impossible today.

William V. Shannon
The New York Times
Mar 3, 1968

Political extremism involves two prime ingredients: an excessively simple diagnosis of the world's ills and a conviction that there are identifiable villains back of it all.

John W. Gardner
No Easy Victories
1968

Politics is not the art of the possible. It consists in choosing between the disastrous and the unpalatable.

John Kenneth
Galbraith
Ambassador's Journal
1969

Never forget posterity when devising a policy. Never think of posterity when making a speech.

Sir Robert G. Menzies
The Measure of the Years
1970

It (politics) is a beautiful fraud that has been imposed on the people for years, whose practitioners exchange gilded promises for the most valuable thing their victims own, their votes. And who benefits most? The lawyers.

Shirley Chisholm
Unbought and Unbossed
1970

Reinhold Niebuhr
quoted on his death
The New York Times
Jun 2, 1971

The whole art of politics consists in directing rationally the irrationalities of men.

Lester B. Pearson
"The Tenth Decade,"
CBC-TV
1972

Politics is the skilled use of blunt objects.

Gerald R. Ford
hearings in the House of
Representatives on his
nomination as vice-
president
Nov 15, 1973

Truth is the glue that holds governments together. Compromise is the oil that makes governments go.

Richard M. Nixon
Time
Aug 19, 1974

There is one thing solid and fundamental in politics—the law of change. What's up today is down tomorrow.

Anaïs Nin
"Letter to Geismar"
The Diary of Anaïs Nin
1974

We cannot cure the evils of politics with politics. . . . Fifty years ago if we had gone the way of Freud (to study and tackle hostility within ourselves) instead of Marx, we might be closer to peace than we are.

Reinhold Niebuhr
quoted by Jimmy Carter
Why Not the Best?
1975

The sad duty of politics is to establish justice in a sinful world.

Lawrence Welk
Time
Apr 14, 1975

Politics, like music and golf, is best learned at an early age.

Barbara Castle
Castle Diaries
Apr 18, 1975

In politics, guts is all.

Groucho Marx
recalled on his death
Aug 19, 1977

Politics is the art of looking for trouble, finding it everywhere, diagnosing it incorrectly and applying the wrong remedies.

Richard M. Nixon
television interview with
David Frost
May 4, 1977

It's a piece of cake until you get to the top. You find you can't stop playing the game the way you've always played it. So you are lean and mean and resourceful and you continue to walk on the edge of the precipice because over the years you have become fascinated by how close you can walk without losing your balance.

Ronald Reagan
Los Angeles Herald–
Examiner
Mar 3, 1978

Politics I supposed to be the second-oldest profession. I have come to realize that it bears a very close resemblance to the first.

Robert S. Strauss
Texas Monthly
Feb, 1978

If you're in politics, you're a whore anyhow. It doesn't make any difference who you sleep with.

Peter Thorneycroft
Lord Thorneycroft
London Sunday Telegraph
Feb 11, 1979

The choice in politics isn't usually between black and white. It's between two horrible shades of gray.

Washington has no memory.

James Reston
The Observer
Sep 9, 1979

Politics is motion and excitement.

John Sears
Time
Nov 12, 1979

The best politics is no politics.

Henry M. Jackson
speech to the American
Bar Association
Feb 3, 1980

You never really win anything in politics. All you get is a chance to play for higher stakes and perform at a higher level.

John Sears
Time
Jan 21, 1980

We are not a cynical people. The will to believe lingers on. We like to think that heroes can emerge from obscurity, as they sometimes do; that elections do matter, even though the process is at least part hokum: that through politics we can change our society and maybe even find a cause to believe in.

Ronald Steel
"The Vanishing Campaign
Biography"
The New York Times
Aug 5, 1984

He (Dwight Eisenhower) wasn't used to being criticized, and he never did get it through his head that's what politics is all about. He was used to getting his ass kissed.

Harry S Truman
quoted on President
Dwight D. Eisenhower
The New York Times
Dec 2, 1984

In writing and politicking, it's best not to think about it, just do it.

Gore Vidal
quoted
*A Guide to the 99th
Congress*
1985

Nothing is so admirable in politics as a short memory.

John Kenneth
Galbraith
quoted
*A Guide to the 99th
Congress*
1985

Die-hard conservatives thought that if I couldn't get everything I asked for, I would jump off the cliff with the flag flying—go down in flames. No, if I can get 70 or 80 percent of what it is I'm trying to get . . . I'll take that and then continue to try to get the rest in the future.

Ronald Reagan
The New York Times
Oct 6, 1985

I seldom think of politics more than 18 hours a day.

Lyndon Baines
Johnson
quoted
*A Guide to the 99th
Congress*
1985

Politics in America is the binding secular religion.

Theodore H. White
Time
Dec 29, 1986

I always cheer up immensely if an attack is particularly wounding because I think, well, if they attack one personally, it means they have not a single political argument left.

Margaret Thatcher
Daily Telegraph
Mar 21, 1986

George P. Shultz *The New York Times* Dec 9, 1986	Nothing ever gets settled in this town (Washington) . . . a seething debating society in which the debate never stops, in which people never give up, including me. And so that's the atmosphere in which you administer.
Jimmy Breslin *Table Money* 1986	Politics, where fat, bald, disagreeable men, unable to be candidates themselves, teach a president how to act on a public stage.
Harriett Woods quoted by Steven V. Roberts in "Politicking Goes High-Tech" *The New York Times* Nov 2, 1986	The price of running for the Senate today is spending more time than you'd like to spend asking people for more money than they'd like to give.
George J. Mitchell at Iran–Contra hearings Jul 13, 1987	Although he's regularly asked to do so, God does not take sides in American politics.
Claiborne Pell *The New York Times* Feb 3, 1987	My opponent called me a cream puff. . . . Well, I rushed out and got the baker's union to endorse me.
William Safire "The Perfect Candidate" *The New York Times* Apr 16, 1987	Decide on some imperfect Somebody and you will win, because the truest truism in politics is: You can't beat Somebody with Nobody.
Lyndon Baines Johnson quoted *People* Feb 2, 1987	A man can take a little bourbon without getting drunk, but if you hold his mouth open an pour in a quart, he's going to get sick on it.
George Bush address to Congress Feb 9, 1989	The American people didn't send us here (Washington, D.C.) to bicker.
Henry Hyde remarks quoted in *Newsweek* Oct 15, 1990	Political courage reads well in editorials, but it doesn't translate into political reality.
a confidant of General Colin Powell reported remarks in *Newsweek* Mar 18, 1991	Politics isn't his [General Colin Powell's] thing. It's like a fancy suit. He can imagine trying it on, but it just doesn't fit.

Power

Herodotus *The Histories of Herodotus* ca. 430 B.C.	This is the bitterest pain among men, to have much knowledge but no power.
Sir Francis Bacon *Meditationes Sacrae* 1597	Knowledge is power. *Nam et ipsa scientia potestas est.*

In the first place, I put for a generall inclination of all mankind, a perpetuall and restlesse desire of Power after Power, that ceaseth onely in Death.

Thomas Hobbes
Leviathan
1651

Power is so apt to be insolent, and Liberty to be saucy, that they are very seldom upon good Terms.

1st Marquess of Halifax
Political Thoughts and Reflections
1750

Power and Liberty are like Heat and Moisture; where they are well mixt, everything prospers; where they are single, they are destructive.

1st Marquess of Halifax
Maxims of State
1700

Unlimited power is apt to corrupt the minds of those who possess it.

William Pitt
1st Earl of Chatham
speech in the House of Lords
Jan 9, 1770

The greater the power, the more dangerous the abuse.

Edmund Burke
speech, "On the Middlesex Election"
1771

As wealth is power, so all power will infallibly draw wealth to itself by some means or other.

Edmund Burke
speech in the House of Commons
Feb 11, 1780

One precedent in favor of power is stronger than an hundred against it.

Thomas Jefferson
Notes on the State of Virginia
1782

Neither philosophy, nor religion, nor morality, nor wisdom, nor interest will ever govern nations or parties against their vanity, their pride, their resentment or revenge, or their avarice or ambition. Nothing but force and power and strength can restrain them.

John Adams
letter to Thomas Jefferson
Oct 9, 1787

In the main it will be found that a power over a man's support is a power over his will.

Alexander Hamilton
The Federalist
Mar 21, 1788

What a perversion of the normal order of things! . . . to make power the primary and central object of the social system, and Liberty but its satellite.

James Madison
National Gazette
Dec 20, 1792

Power is not happiness.

William Godwin
An Enquiry Concerning Political Justice
1793

History has taught me that rulers are much the same in all ages, and under all forms of government; that they are as bad as they dare to be. The vanity of ruin and the curse of blindness have clung to them like an hereditary leprosy.

Samuel Taylor Coleridge
letter to George Coleridge
Apr, 1798

William Hazlitt "Character of Mr. Fox" 1807	The love of fame is consistent with the steadiest attachment to principle and indeed strengthens and supports it; whereas the love of power, where this is the ruling passion, requires the sacrifice of principle at every turn, and is inconsistent even with the shadow of it.
Charles Caleb Colton *Lacön* 1825	The worst thing that can be said of the most powerful is that they can take your life; but the same thing can be said of the most weak.
Charles Caleb Colton *Lacön* 1825	To know the pains of power, we must go to those who have it; to know its pleasure, we must go to those who are seeking it.
John Randolph of Roanoke speech to the U.S. Senate 1826	You cannot divorce property from power. You can only make them change hands.
William Hazlitt "On Application to Study" *The Plain Speaker* 1826	Power is pleasure; and pleasure sweetens pain.
James Madison speech to Virginia constitutional convention, Richmond, Virginia Dec 2, 1829	The essence of Government is power; and power, lodged as it must be in human hands, will ever be liable to abuse.
Giuseppe Mazzini letter to King Carlo Alberto of Savoy 1831	The secret of power is the will. *Il segreto della potenza è nella volontà.*
Edward George Bulwer-Lytton *England and the English* 1833	Co-operation is power; in proportion as people combine, they know their strength; civilization itself is but the effect of combining.
Henry Clay speech in the U.S. Senate Mar 14, 1834	The arts of power and its minions are the same in all countries and in all ages. It marks its victim: denounces it; and excites the public odium and the public hatred, to conceal its own abuses and encroachments.
Alexis, Comte de Tocqueville *Etat social et politique de la France* 1834	When the reality of power has been surrendered, it's playing a dangerous game to seek to retain the appearance of it; the external aspect of vigor can sometimes support a debilitated body, but most often it manages to deal it the final blow.
William Henry Harrison speech during presidential campaign 1840	Power is insinuating. Few men are satisfied with less power than they are able to procure. . . . No lover is ever satisfied with the first smile of his mistress.
Joseph Joubert *Pensées* 1842	Power makes you attractive; it even makes women love old men. *Le pouvoir est une beauté; il fait aimer aux femmes la vieillesse meme.*

You shall have joy, or you shall have power, said God; you shall not have both.

Ralph Waldo Emerson
Journal
1842

The highest proof of virtue is to possess boundless power without abusing it.

Lord Macaulay
review of Lucy Aikin
Life and Writings of Addison
1843

Political power, properly so called, is merely the organized power of one class for oppressing another.

Karl Marx
The Communist Manifesto
1848

As a matter of fact and experience, the more power is divided the more irresponsible it becomes.

Woodrow Wilson
Congressional Government
1885

Power tends to corrupt and absolute power corrupts absolutely.

Lord Acton (Sir John E.E. Dalberg, 1st Baron Acton)
Life of Mandell Creighton
1904

Power when wielded by abnormal energy is the most serious of facts.

Henry Adams
The Education of Henry Adams
1906

Power consists in one's capacity to link his will with the purpose of others, to lead by reason and a gift of cooperation.

Woodrow Wilson
letter to Mary A. Hulbert
Sep 21, 1913

The only prize much cared for by the powerful is power. The prize of the general is not a bigger tent, but command.

Oliver Wendell Holmes Jr.
speech at the Harvard Law School Association of New York
Feb 15, 1913

Power takes as ingratitude the writhing of its victims.

Sir Rabindranath Tagore
Stray Birds
1916

All political structures are based on power.
Alle politischen Gebilde sind Gewaltgebilde.

Max Weber
Wirtschaft und Gesellschaft
1922

Next to enjoying ourselves, the next greatest pleasure consists in preventing others from enjoying themselves, or more generally, in the acquisition of power.

Bertrand Russell
"The Recrudescence of Puritanism"
Skeptical Essays
1928

More power than any good man should want, and more power than any other kind of man ought to have.

Daniel O. Hastings
speech in U.S. Senate
Mar 23, 1935

We thought, because we had power, we had wisdom.

Stephen Vincent Benét
Litany for Dictatorships
1935

Franklin D. Roosevelt
second inaugural address
Jan 20, 1937

As intricacies of human relationships increase, so power to govern them must increase—power to stop evil; power to do good. The essential democracy of our Nation and the safety of our people depend not upon the absence of power, but upon lodging it with those whom the people can change or continue at stated intervals through an honest and free system of elections.

A. Philip Randolph
speech at the National
Negro Congress, Philadel-
phia, Pennsylvania
Oct 15-17, 1937

True liberation can be acquired and maintained only when the Negro people possess power: and power is the product and flower of organization . . . of the masses.

Aneurin Bevan
quoted by Michael Foot
Aneurin Bevan, 1945–
1960
1962

The purpose of getting power is to be able to give it away.

Eric Hoffer
The Passionate State of
Mind
1954

It is when power is wedded to chronic fear that it becomes formidable.

Eric Hoffer
The Passionate State of
Mind
1954

Our sense of power is more vivid when we break a man's spirit than when we win his heart.

Walter Lippmann
The Public Philosophy
1955

The first principle of a civilized state is that power is legitimate only when it is under contract.

H.L. Mencken
Minority Report
1956

The urge to save humanity is almost always only a false-face for the urge to rule it.

Hugh MacLennan
MacLean's Magazine
Nov 5, 1960

Give me the writing of a nation's advertising and propaganda, and I care not who governs its politics.

John F. Kennedy
speech at Amherst Col-
lege, Amherst,
Massachusetts
Oct 26, 1963

When power corrupts, poetry cleanses for art establishes the basic human truths which must serve as the touch-stone of our judgment.

Robert F. Kennedy
"I Remember, I Believe"
The Pursuit of Justice
1964

The problem of power is how to achieve its responsible use rather than its irresponsible and indulgent use—of how to get men of power to live for the public rather than off the public.

Eric Hoffer
The Ordeal of Change
1964

Power, whether exercised over matter or over man, is partial to simplification.

Bayard Rustin
"From Protest to Politics"
Commentary
Feb, 1965

There is a strong moralistic strain in the civil rights movement that would remind us that power corrupts, forgetting that the absence of power also corrupts.

Power in defense of freedom is greater than power in behalf of tyranny and oppression.

Malcolm X
speech on "Prospects for Freedom" in New York City
1965

Power never takes a back step—only in the face of more power.

Malcolm X
Malcolm X Speaks
1965

We have, I fear, confused power with greatness.

Stewart L. Udall
commencement address at Dartmouth College, Hanover, New Hampshire
Jun 13, 1965

Power tends to confuse itself with virtue and a great nation is peculiarly susceptible to the idea that its power is a sign of God's favor. . . . Once imbued with the idea of a mission, a great nation easily assumes that it has the means as well as the duty to do God's work.

J. William Fulbright
speech in the U.S. Senate
Apr 21, 1966

Law not served by power is an illusion; but power not ruled by law is a menace which our nuclear age cannot afford.

Arthur J. Goldberg
commencement address at the Catholic University of America
Time
Jun 17, 1966

Power is always charged with the impulse to eliminate human nature, the human variable, from the equation of action. Dictators do it by terror or by the inculcation of blind faith; the miltary do it by iron discipline; and the industrial masters think they can do it by automation.

Eric Hoffer
"Automation, Leisure, and the Masses"
The Temper of Our Time
1967

Powerlessness frustrates; absolute powerlessness frustrates absolutely. Absolute frustration is a dangerous emotion to run a world with.

Russell Baker
The New York Times
May 1, 1969

Power is the great aphrodisiac.

Henry A. Kissinger
The New York Times
Jan 19, 1971

Power and violence are opposites; where the one rules absolutely, the other is absent.

Hannah Arendt
"On Violence"
Crisis of the Republic
1972

Nobody can overthrow me—I have the power.

Mohammed Reza Pahlevi
U.S. News & World Report
Jun 26, 1978

If power corrupts, being out of power corrupts absolutely.

Douglass Cater
Book Digest
Dec, 1979

Kenneth Kaunda
Kaunda on Violence
1980

Some people draw a comforting distinction between "force" and "violence". . . . I refuse to cloud the issue by such word-play. . . . The power which establishes a state is violence; the power which maintains it is violence; the power which eventually overthrows it is violence. . . . Call an elephant a rabbit only if it gives you comfort to feel that you are about to be trampled to death by a rabbit.

General George Patton
quoted in
Time
Mar 18, 1991

For over a thousand years, Roman conquerors returning from the wars enjoyed the honor of a triumph, a tumultuous parade . . . The conqueror rode in a triumphal chariot . . . A slave stood behind the conqueror holding a golden crown and whispering in his ear a warning that all glory is fleeting.

Henry Tizard
Sir
quoted in
Time
Mar 18, 1991

We are a great nation, but if we continue to behave like a great power, we shall soon cease to be a great nation.

Prejudice and Discrimination

William Hazlitt
"On the Tendency of Sects"
The Round Table
1817

There is no prejudice so strong as that which arises from a fancied exemption from all prejudice.

David Walker
"Walker's Appeal"
Sep 28, 1829

Treat us like men, and there is no danger but we will all live in peace and happiness together. For we are not like you, hard hearted, unmerciful, and unforgiving. What a happy country this will be, if the whites will listen.

William Hazlitt
"On Prejudice"
Sketches and Essays
1839

Prejudice is the child of ignorance.

William Hazlitt
"On Prejudice"
Sketches and Essays
1839

Prejudice is never easy unless it can pass itself off for reason.

Frederick Douglass
"The Destiny of Colored Americans"
The North Star
Nov 16, 1849

The white man's happiness cannot be purchased by the black man's misery.

Frederick Douglass
Proceedings of the Colored National Convention
July 6–8, 1853

Having despised us, it is not strange that Americans should seek to render us despicable; having enslaved us, it is natural that they should strive to prove us unfit for freedom; having denounced us as indolent, it is not strange that they should cripple our enterprises.

It is never too late to give up our prejudices.

Henry David Thoreau
"Economy"
Walden
1854

The prejudice against color, of which we hear so much, is no stronger than that against sex. It is produced by the same cause, and manifested very much in the same way. The Negro's skin and the woman's sex are both prima facie evidence that they were intended to be in subjection to the white Saxon man.

Elizabeth Cady Stanton
speech to the New York state legislature
Feb 18, 1860

In a republic where all are declared equal an ostracised class of half of the people, on the ground of a distinction founded in nature, is an anomalous position, as harassing to its victims as it is unjust, and as contradictory as it is unsafe to the fundamental principles of a free government.

Elizabeth Cady Stanton
History of Woman Suffrage
1881

We still wonder at the stolid incapacity of all men to understand that woman feels the invidious distinctions of sex exactly as the black man does those of color, or the white man the more transient distinctions of wealth, family, position, place, and power; that she feels as keenly as man the injustice of disfranchisement.

Elizabeth Cady Stanton
History of Woman Suffrage
1881

Labor in a white skin cannot be free so long as labor in a black skin is branded.

Karl Marx
Das Kapital
1867-83

Anti-semitism is the socialism of fools.

August Bebel
Anti-semitism and Social Democracy
1893

After all there is but one race—humanity.

George Moore
The Bending of the Bough
1900

Cannot the nation that has absorbed ten million foreigners into its political life without catastrophe absorb ten million Negro Americans into that same political life at less cost than their unjust and illegal exclusion will involve?

W.E.B. Du Bois
"No Cowards or Trucklers"
In Their Own Words: 1865–1916
1966

Race prejudice decreases values both real estate and human; crime, ignorance and filth decrease values.

W.E.B. Du Bois
"What Would You Do?"
The Crisis
Nov, 1925

Persecution was at least a sign of personal interest. Tolerance is composed of nine parts of apathy to one of brotherly love.

Frank Moore Colby
"Trials of an Encyclopedist"
The Colby Essays
1926

The tendency of the casual mind is to pick out or stumble upon a sample which supports or defies its prejudices, and then to make it the representative of a whole class.

Walter Lippmann
Public Opinion
1929

No one can make you feel inferior without your consent.

Eleanor Roosevelt
This Is My Story
1937

Felix Frankfurter *Lane v. Wilson* 1939	The (Fifteenth) Amendment nullifies sophisticated as well as simple-minded modes of discrimination.
Richard Wright *Native Son* 1940	Injustice which lasts for three long centuries and which exists among millions of people over thousands of square miles of territory, is injustice no longer; it is an accomplished fact of life.
Pearl S. Buck *What America Means* *to Me* 1943	It is not healthy when a nation lives within a nation, as colored Americans are living inside America. A nation cannot live confident of its tomorrow if its refugees are among its citizens.
Pearl S. Buck *What America Means* *to Me* 1943	Race prejudice is not only a shadow over the colored—it is a shadow over all of us, and the shadow is darkest over those who feel it least and allow its evil effects to go on.
Max Lerner "We Teach What We Are" *Actions and Passions* 1949	In the end, as any successful teacher will tell you, you can only teach the things that you are. If we practice racism then it is racism that we teach.
Sir Isaiah Berlin *Political Ideas in the* *Twentieth Century* 1950	Conformities are called for much more eagerly today than yesterday; loyalties are tested far more severely; sceptics, liberals, individuals with a taste for private life and their own inner standards of behaviour, are objects of fear or derision and targets of persecution for either side, execrated or despised by all the embattled parties in the great ideological wars of our time.
Alan Barth *The Loyalty of Free Men* 1951	If tolerance of diversity involves an admitted element of risk to national unity, intolerance involves a certainty that unity will be destroyed.
Murray Kempton "George" *Part of Our Time* 1955	It is a measure of the Negro's circumstance that, in America, the smallest things usually take him so very long, and that, by the time he wins them, they are no longer little things: they are miracles.
Edward R. Murrow television broadcast Dec 31, 1955	Everyone is a prisoner of his own experiences. No one can eliminate prejudices—just recognize them.
Earl Warren unanimous opinion *"Brown II"* May 31, 1955	All provisions of federal, state or local law requiring or permitting discrimination in public education must yield.
Charles P. Curtis *A Commonplace Book* 1957	There are only two ways to be quite unprejudiced and impartial. One is to be completely ignorant. The other is to be completely indifferent. Bias and prejudice are attitudes to be kept in hand, not attitudes to be avoided.
John F. Kennedy *A Nation of Immigrants* 1958	Only in the case of the Negro has the melting pot failed to bring a minority into the full stream of American life.
Michael Harrington *The Other America* 1962	To be a Negro is to participate in a culture of poverty and fear that goes far deeper than any law for or against discrimination.

The American economy, the American society, the American unconscious are all racist.

Michael Harrington
The Other America
1962

So, let us not be blind to our differences—but let us also direct attention to our common interests and to the means by which those differences can be resolved. And if we cannot end now our differences, at least we can help make the world safe for diversity.

John F. Kennedy
commencement address
at The American Univ.
Jun 10, 1963

One hundred years ago, the slave was freed. One hundred years later, the Negro remains in bondage to the color of his skin.

Lyndon Baines Johnson
speech in Gettysburg,
Pennsylvania
May 30, 1963

No one has been barred on account of his race from fighting or dying for America—there are no "white" or "colored" signs on the foxholes or graveyards of battle.

John F. Kennedy
message to Congress on
his proposed
civil rights bill
Jun 19, 1963

The good neighbor looks beyond the external accidents and discerns those inner qualities that make all men human and, therefore, brothers.

Martin Luther King Jr.
Strength to Love
1963

To the average white man, a courthouse even in Mississippi is a place where justice is dispensed. To me, the black man, it is a place where justice is dispensed with.

John Oliver Killens
"Explanation of the Black Psyche"
The New York Times
Jun 7, 1964

Unfortunately many Americans live on the outskirts of hope— some because of their poverty, some because of their color, and all too many because of both. Our task is to help replace their despair with opportunity.

Lyndon Baines Johnson
first State of the Union
message
Jan 8, 1964

It will be helpful in our mutual objective to allow every man in America to look his neighbor in the face and see a man—not a color.

Adlai E. Stevenson Jr.
The New York Times
Jun 22, 1964

For the white man to ask the black man if he hates him is just like the rapist asking the raped, or the wolf asking the sheep, "Do you hate me?" The white man is in no moral position to accuse anyone else of hate!

Malcolm X
Autobiography of Malcolm X
1965

If you are black the only roads into the mainland of American life are through subservience, cowardice, and loss of manhood. These are the white man's roads.

LeRoi Jones
"Black Is a Country"
Home
1966

Unless man is committed to the belief that all of mankind are his brothers, then he labors in vain and hypocritically in the vineyards of equality.

Adam Clayton Powell Jr.
"Black Power: A Form of Godly Power"
Keep the Faith, Baby!
1967

Bayard Rustin "The Premise of the Stereotype" *Amsterdam News* Apr 8, 1967	Its birthplace is the sinister back room of the mind where plots and schemes are hatched for the persecution and oppression of other human beings.
Martin Luther King Jr. speech to the Southern Christian Leadership Conference Aug 16, 1967	Discrimination is a hellhound that gnaws at Negroes in every waking moment of their lives to remind them that the lie of their inferiority is accepted as truth in the society dominating them.
Otto Kerner Jr. *Report of the National Advisory Commission on Civil Disorders* 1968	Our nation is moving toward two societies, one black, one white—separate and unequal.
George C. Wallace 1963 inaugural address as governor of Alabama *Life* Dec 26, 1969	I draw the line in the dust and toss the gauntlet before the feet of tyranny, and I say segregation now, segregation tomorrow, segregation forever.
Steve Biko speech in Cape Town 1971	The myth of integration as propounded under the banner of the liberal ideology must be cracked because it makes people believe that something is being achieved when in reality the artificially integrated circles are a soporific to the blacks while salving the consciences of the few guilt-stricken whites.
Lyndon Baines Johnson remarks at a civil rights symposium at the Univ. of Texas Dec 12, 1972	I believe that the essence of government lies with unceasing concern for the welfare and dignity and decency and innate integrity of life for every individual. I don't like to say this and I wish I didn't have to add these words to make it clear but I will—regardless of color, creed, ancestry, sex or age.
William O. Douglas dissenting opinion *DeFunis* v. *Odegaard* Apr 23, 1974	If discrimination based on race is constitutionally permissible when those who hold the reins can come up with "compelling" reasons to justify it, then constitutional guarantees acquire an accordionlike quality.
Steve Biko quoted *Boston Globe* Oct 25, 1977	So as a prelude whites must be made to realize that they are only human, not superior. Same with blacks. They must be made to realize that they are also human, not inferior.
Thurgood Marshall *Time* Dec 4, 1978	The Ku Klux Klan never dies. They just stop wearing sheets because sheets cost too much.
William J. Brennan Jr. dissenting opinion Jun 28, 1978	We cannot . . . let colorblindness become myopia which masks the reality that many "created equal" have been treated within our lifetimes as inferior both by law and by their fellow citizens.
Ronald Reagan press conference Mar 13, 1981	This administration is totally colorblind.
Desmond Tutu *The New York Times* Jan 3, 1985	For goodness sake, will they hear, will white people hear what we are trying to say? Please, all we are asking you to do is to recognize that we are humans, too.

All I was doing was trying to get home from work.

Rosa Parks
on refusing to move to
the back of the bus, interview on NBC-TV
Dec 1, 1985

Presidency

You are apprehensive of monarchy; I, of aristocracy. I would therefore have given more power to the President and less to the Senate.

John Adams
letter to Thomas Jefferson
Dec 6, 1787

The process of election (by the electoral college) affords a moral certainty that the office of President will never fall to the lot of any man who is not in an eminent degree endowed with the requisite qualifications.

Alexander Hamilton
The Federalist
Mar 12, 1788

In executing the duties of my present important station, I can promise nothing but purity of intentions, and, in carrying these into effect, fidelity and diligence.

George Washington
message to Congress
Jul 9, 1789

My country has in its wisdom contrived for me the most insignificant office (the vice-presidency) that ever the invention of man contrived or his imagination conceived.

John Adams
letter to Abigail Adams
Dec 19, 1793

No man will ever carry out of the Presidency the reputation which carried him into it.

Thomas Jefferson
letter to Edward Rutledge
1796

I am tired of an office where I can do no more good than many others, who would be glad to be employed in it. To myself, personally, it brings nothing but unceasing drudgery and daily loss of friends.

Thomas Jefferson
letter to John Dickenson
Jan 13, 1807

I had rather be right than be President.

Henry Clay
letter to Senator Preston
of South Carolina
1839

No candidate for the Presidency ought ever to remain in the Cabinet. He is an unsafe advisor.

James K. Polk
Diary
Feb 21, 1848

You have heard the story, haven't you, about the man who was tarred and feathered and carried out of town on a rail? A man in the crowd asked him how he liked it. His reply was that if it was not for the honor of the thing, he would much rather walk.

Abraham Lincoln
response to a friend when
asked how he liked being
president
1861

As President, I have no eyes but constitutional eyes; I cannot see you.

Abraham Lincoln
reply to a South Carolina
commission
ca. 1861

Everything I say, you know, goes into print. If I make a mistake it doesn't merely affect me, or you, but the country. I, therefore, ought at least try not to make mistakes.

Abraham Lincoln
to a crowd gathered be-
fore the White House
Apr 10, 1865

Ulysses S. Grant annual message to Congress Dec 5, 1876	History shows that no Administration from the time of Washington to the present has been free from . . . mistakes. But I leave comparisons to history, claiming only that I have acted in every instance from a conscientious desire to do what was right, constitutional, within the law, and for the very best interests of the whole people.
Grover Cleveland letter to William F. Vilas Apr 19, 1889	And still the question, "What shall be done with our ex-Presidents?" is not laid at rest; and I sometimes think (one) solution of it, "Take them out and shoot them," is worthy of attention.
Oscar Wilde "The Soul of Man Under Socialism" *Fortnightly Review* Feb, 1891	In America the President reigns for four years, and Journalism governs for ever and ever.
Ambrose Bierce *The Devil's Dictionary* 1906	Presidency, n. The greased pig in the field game of American politics.
Finley Peter Dunne "The Vice-President" *Dissertations by Mr. Dooley* 1906	Th' prisidincy is th' highest office in th' gift iv th' people. Th' vice-prisidincy is th' next highest an' the lowest. It isn't a crime exactly. Ye can't be sint to jail f'r it, but it's a kind iv a disgrace.
Woodrow Wilson *Constitutional Government* 1908	The President is at liberty, both in law and and conscience, to be as big a man as he can.
Theodore Roosevelt speech in Binghamton, New York Oct 24, 1910	They talk of my power: my power vanishes into thin air the instant that my fellow citizens who are straight and honest cease to believe theat I represent them and fight for what is straight and honest; tht is all the strength I have.
William Howard Taft speech at the Univ. of Virginia, Charlottesville Jan, 1915	It is an old maxim that there are other ways of killing a cat than by choking it with butter, and it is a great deal easier . . . to use one's influence with the legislators to prevent objectionable bills passing than it is to wait until they do pass and then veto them.
William Howard Taft *Our Chief Magistrate and His Powers* 1916	The President can exercise no power which cannot be fairly and reasonably traced to some specific grant of power . . . in the Federal Constitution or in an act of Congress passed in pursuance thereof. There is no undefined residuum of power which he can exercise because it seems to be in the public interest.
Calvin Coolidge reported remark to Ethel Barrymore *Time* May 16, 1955	I think the American public wants a solemn ass as a President and I think I'll go along with them.
Calvin Coolidge reported remarks to Herbert Hoover 1928	You have to stand three or four hours a day of visitors (to the White House). Nine-tenths of them want something they ought not have. If you keep dead-still they will run down in three or four minutes. If you even cough or smile they will start up all over again.

An examination of the records of those Presidents who have served eight years will disclose in most every instance the latter part of their term has shown very little in the way of constructive accomplishment.

Calvin Coolidge
Autobiography
1929

The President cannot, with success, constantly appeal to the country. After a time he will get no response.

Calvin Coolidge
Autobiography
1929

The Presidency is not merely an administrative office. . . . It is pre-eminently a place of moral leadership. All our great Presidents were leaders of thought at times when certain historic ideas in the life of the nation had to be clarified.

Franklin D. Roosevelt
The New York Times
Sep 11, 1932

In the end the President has become increasingly the depository of all national ills, especially if things go wrong.

Herbert Hoover
in 1933, as quoted
Memoirs
1952

Theodore Roosevelt said, "sometimes I wish I could be President and Congress too." Well, I suppose if the truth were told, he is not the only President that has had that idea.

Franklin D. Roosevelt
remarks in Dallas, Texas
June 12, 1936

I should like to have it said of my first Administration that in it the forces of selfishness and of lust for power met their match. I should like to have it said of my second Administration that in it these forces met their master.

Franklin D. Roosevelt
speech at Madison Square
Garden in New York City
Oct 31, 1936

I would dare to dispute the integrity of the President on any occasion my country's welfare demanded it. . . . After all, the President of the United States is neither an absolute monarch or a descendant of a sun goddess.

Harold L. Ickes
Time
Mar 11, 1946

My God, this is a hell of a job! I have no trouble with my enemies. I can take care of them right now. But my damn friends, my god-damn friends, White, they're the ones that keep me walking the floor nights!

Warren G. Harding
quoted by William Allen
White
Autobiography
1946

In America any boy may become President and I suppose it's just one of the risks he takes.

Adlai E. Stevenson Jr.
speech in Indianapolis,
Indiana
Sep 26, 1952

You know how it is in an election year. They pick a president and then for four years they pick on him.

Adlai E. Stevenson Jr.
speech
Aug 28, 1952

Any man who has had the job I've had and didn't have a sense of humor wouldn't still be here.

Harry S Truman
The New York Times
Apr 19, 1955

The President is the only lobbyist that one hundred and fifty million americans have. The other twenty million are able to employ people to represent them—and that's all right, it's the exercise of the right of petition—but someone has to look out after the interests of the one hundred and fifty million that are left.

Harry S Truman
speech in San Francisco,
California
Oct 25, 1956

Most of the problems a President has to face have their roots in the past.

Harry S Truman
Memoirs
1955–56

Harry S Truman *Memoirs* 1955–56	The official position of the United States . . . is defined by decisions and declarations of the President. There can be only one voice in stating the position of this country in the field of foreign relations. This is of fundamental constitutional significance.
Harry S Truman *Memoirs* 1955–56	To be President of the United States is to be lonely, very lonely at times of great decisions.
Harry S Truman *Memoirs* 1955–56	Jefferson . . . was a master politician, and this helped make him a great leader. A President has to be a politician in order to get the majority to go along with him on his program.
Harry S Truman *Memoirs* 1955–56	A President needs political understanding to run the government, but he may be elected without it.
Harry S Truman *Memoirs* 1955–56	A President cannot always be popular.
Dwight D. Eisenhower quoted by a friend *Parade* Feb 2, 1958	This desk of mine is one at which a man may die, but from which he cannot resign.
Dwight D. Eisenhower *The New York Post* Oct 26, 1959	Oh, that lovely title, ex-president.
Harry S Truman lecture at Columbia Univ. Apr 27, 1959	The President is the representative of the whole nation and he's the only lobbyist that all the 160 million people in this country have.
Harry S Truman quoted by Richard E. Neustadt *Presidential Power, the Politics of Leadership* 1960	He'll (Dwight D. Eisenhower) sit here, and he'll say, "Do this! Do that!" And nothing will happen. Poor Ike—it won't be a bit like the Army. He'll find it very frustrating.
John F. Kennedy campaign speech, Crestwood, Missouri Oct 22, 1960	The function and responsibility of the President is to set before the American people the unfinished business, the things we must do if we are going to succeed as a nation.
Eleanor Roosevelt on campaign behavior for first ladies *The New York Times* Nov 11, 1962	Always be on time. Do as little talking as humanly possible. Remember to lean back in the parade car so everybody can see the president. Be sure not to get too fat, because you'll have to sit there in the back seat.
Dwight D. Eisenhower quoted by John F. Kennedy *Parade* Apr 8, 1962	No easy problems ever come to the President of the United States. If they are easy to solve, somebody else has solved them.
John F. Kennedy news conference Jun 14, 1962	I know that when things don't go well they like to blame the Presidents, and that is one of the things which Presidents are paid for.

I will do my best. That is all I can do. I ask for your help—and God's.

Lyndon Baines Johnson
following assassination of
John F. Kennedy
Nov 22, 1963

In the White House, the future rapidly becomes the past; and delay is itself a decision.

Theodore Sorensen
Nation's Business
Jun, 1963

Extremism in the pursuit of the Presidency is an unpardonable vice, Moderation in the affairs of the nation is the highest virtue.

Lyndon Baines Johnson
speech in New York in
reply to Barry Goldwater
Oct 31, 1964

A President's hardest task is not to do what is right, but to know what is right.

Lyndon Baines Johnson
State of the Union
Message
Jan 4, 1965

The American Presidency, it occurs to us, is merely a way station en route to the blessed condition of being an ex-President.

John Updike
"Eisenhower's Eloquence"
Assorted Prose
1965

"Why would anyone want to be President today?" the answer is not one of glory, or fame; today the burdens of the office outweigh its privileges. It's not because the President offers a chance to be somebody, but because it offers the chance to do something.

Richard M. Nixon
television
campaign speech
Sep 19, 1968

What we won when all of our people united . . . must not be lost in suspicion and distrust and selfishness and politics. . . . Accordingly, I shall not seek, and I will not accept, the nomination of my party for another term as president.

Lyndon Baines Johnson
televised speech
Mar 31, 1968

The first lady is, and always has been, an unpaid public servant elected by one person, her husband.

Claudia ("Lady Bird") Johnson
quoted
US News & World Report
Mar 9, 1987

The presidency has made every man who occupied it, no matter how small, bigger than he was: and no matter how big, not big enough for its demands.

Lyndon Baines Johnson
The New York Times
Mar 26, 1972

If I were to make public these tapes, containing blunt and candid remarks on many different subjects, the confidentiality of the office of the president would always be suspect.

Richard M. Nixon
televised speech
Aug 15, 1973

I began by telling the president that there was a cancer growing on the presidency and that if the cancer was not removed . . . the president himself would be killed by it.

John Dean
testimony to the Senate
Watergate hearings
Jul 25, 1973

Being president is like being a jackass in a hailstorm. There's nothing to do but stand there and take it.

Lyndon Baines Johnson
recalled on his death
Jan 22, 1973

Richard M. Nixon interview following his second inauguration Jan 22, 1973	I believe in the battle—whether it's the battle of a campaign or the battle of this office, which is a continuing battle.
Richard M. Nixon 60th birthday interview Jan 9, 1973	The presidency has many problems, but boredom is the least of them.
Sam Ervin at Senate Watergate hearings *Washington Post* Jul 12, 1973	There is nothing in the Constitution that authorizes or makes it the official duty of a president to have anything to do with criminal activities.
George S. McGovern on impeachment of Richard Nixon *San Francisco Examiner* Nov 29, 1973	When people ask if the United States can afford to place on trial the president, if the system can stand impeachment, my answer is, "Can we stand anything else?"
Pat Nixon interview in Monrovia, Liberia Mar 15, 1972	Being first lady is the hardest unpaid job in the world.
Howard H. Baker Jr. question to presidential counsel John Dean at the Watergate hearings Jun 28, 1973	The central question is simply put: What did the president know and when did he know it?
Harry S Truman quoted by Merle Miller *Plain Speaking: Conversa- tions with Harry S Truman* 1974	When you get to be President, there are all those things, the honors, the twenty-one gun salutes, all those things. You have to remember it isn't for you. It's for the Presidency.
Gerald R. Ford on succeeding Richard Nixon as president Aug 9, 1974	I am acutely aware that you have not elected me as your president by your ballots, so I ask you to confirm me with your prayers.
Richard M. Nixon televised speech Aug 8, 1974	I have never been a quitter. To leave office before my term is completed is opposed to every instinct in my body. But as president I must put the interests of America first. . . . Therefore, I shall resign the presidency effective at noon tomorrow.
John J. Sirica ruling on obtaining Watergate tapes from President Nixon *Christian Science Monitor* Sep 15, 1974	In all candor, the Court fails to perceive any reason for suspending the power of courts to get evidence and rule on questions of privilege in criminal matters simply because it is the president of the United States who holds the evidence.
Warren E. Burger unanimous opinion *U.S. v. Nixon* Jul 24, 1974	The president's need for complete candor and objectivity from advisers calls for great deference from the courts. However, when the privilege depends solely on the broad, undifferentiated claim of public interest in the confidentiality of such conversations, a confrontation with other values arises.

You really have to experience the feeling of being with the president in the Oval Office. . . .It's a disease I came to call Ovalitis.

John Dean
after conviction for his role in the Watergate coverup
Jan 1, 1975

The Presidency is no place for on-the-job training. I've always advocated the politics of substance, not the politics of style.

Frank Church
Encore American & Worldwide News
Jun, 1976

I think the President is the only person who can change the direction or attitude of our nation.

Jimmy Carter
Encore American & Worldwide News
Jun 21, 1976

There is no inherent Constitutional authority for the President or any intelligence agency to violate the law.

Select Committee on Intelligence Oper. U.S. Senate
The New York Times
May 2, 1976

I am against vice in every form, including the Vice Presidency.

Morris K. Udall
on being asked if he would accept vice presidential nomination
The New York Times
Apr 1, 1976

When the President does it, that means that it is not illegal.

Richard M. Nixon
television interview with David Frost
May 19, 1977

It isn't wisdom or intelligence that influences a President, it's opportunity.

Bill Moyers
Newsweek
Apr 17, 1978

Old men running for the Presidency of the United States are like old men who take young brides. It's an exciting idea for a while but it seldom works.

James Reston
"Scotty"
The New York Times
Jan 26, 1979

If Nixon is not forced to turn over tapes of his conversations with the ring of men who were conversing on their violations of the law, then liberty will soon be dead in this nation.

Earl Warren
quoted by William O. Douglas
The Court Years, 1939-75
1980

History buffs probably noted the reunion at a Washington party a few weeks ago of three ex-presidents; Carter, Ford and Nixon— See No Evil, Hear No Evil and Evil.

Robert J. Dole
to Washington Gridiron Club dinner
Mar 26, 1983

The first ladyship is the only federal office in which the holder can neither be fired nor impeached.

William Safire
The New York Times
Aug 16, 1984

Once a president gets to the White House, the only audience that is left that really matters is history. They all start competing against Lincoln as the greatest president. And the (library) building becomes the symbol, the memorial to that dream.

Doris Kearns Goodwin
on presidential libraries
The New York Times
Oct 13, 1985

Mario Cuomo *The New York Times* Feb 12, 1985	I said I didn't want to run for president. I didn't ask you to believe me.
Deng Xiaoping quoted by John F. Burns *The New York Times* Jan 2, 1985	The United States brags about its political system, but the president says one thing during the election, something else when he takes office, something else a midterm and something else when he leaves.
Edward M. Kennedy speech to Washington Gridiron Club Mar 22, 1986	Frankly, I don't mind not being president. I just mind that someone else is.
Ronald Reagan interview with Hugh Sidey *Time* Apr 7, 1986	I think the presidency is an institution over which you have temporary custody.
Ronald Reagan interview with Barbara Walters, ABC-TV Mar 24, 1986	I have come to the conclusion that the 22nd Amendment (limiting a president to two terms) was a mistake. Shouldn't the people have the right to vote for someone as many times as they want to vote for him?
Donald T. Regan *For the Record* 1988	Of all the inherent duties of an American President, the duty to say no on matters of principle is among the most important.
George Bush quoted in *Time* Nov 21, 1988	To those who supported me, I will try to be worthy of your trust, and to those that did not, I will try to earn it, and my hand is out to you, and I want to be your President too.

Public Opinion

Thomas Jefferson letter to Edward Carrington Jan 16, 1787	The basis of our government (is) the opinion of the people.
James Madison *National Gazette* Dec 19, 1791	Public opinion sets bounds to every government, and is the real sovereign in every free one.
Napoleon I letter to Citizen Melzi Nov 25, 1803	A government is based on public opinion and must keep in step with what public opinion decides, which considers and calculates everything. *Un gouvernement se forme de l'opinion publique, et marche avec ce qu'impose l'opinion publique, qui raisonne et calcule tout.*
William Hazlitt "Characteristics" *The Literary Examiner* 1823	Public opinion is the mixed result of the intellect of the community acting upon general feeling.
John Wilson Croker *Quarterly Review* Feb, 1835	No minister ever stood, or could stand, against public opinion.

In Democracies there is a besetting disposition to make publick opinion stronger than the law. This is the particular form in which tyranny exhibits itself in a popular government.

James Fenimore Cooper
The American Democrat
1838

The Government must always be in advance of public opinion.
Die Regierung muss der Bewegung immer um einen Schritt voraus sein.

Count Adolf Heinrich Arnim-Boytzenburg
speech to the United Landtag
April 2, 1848

A universal feeling, whether well or ill founded, cannot be safely disregarded.

Abraham Lincoln
speech in Peoria, Illinois
Oct 16, 1854

Public opinion is a weak tyrant compared with our own private opinion. What a man thinks of himself, that is which determines, or rather, indicates, his fate.

Henry David Thoreau
"Economy"
Walden
1854

Our government rests in public opinion. Whoever can change public opinion can change the government practically just so much.

Abraham Lincoln
speech in Chicago, Illinois
Dec 10, 1856

Public opinion in this country is everything.

Abraham Lincoln
speech in Columbus, Ohio
Sep 16, 1859

The press is not public opinion.
Die Presse ist nicht die öffentliche Meinung.

Prince Otto von Bismarck
speech in the Prussian Chamber of Deputies
Sep 30, 1862

In the modern world the intelligence of public opinion is the one indispensable condition of social progress.

Charles William Eliot
inaugural address as president of Harvard Univ.
1869

Public opinion is stronger than the legislature, and nearly as strong as the ten commandments.

Charles Dudley Warner
"Sixteenth Week"
My Summer in a Garden
1871

Public opinion, the fear of losing public confidence, apprehension of censure by the press make all men in power conservative and safe.

Rutherford B. Hayes
Diary
Oct 22, 1876

What we call public opinion is generally public sentiment.

Benjamin Disraeli
speech
Aug 3, 1880

Lincoln said in his homely way that he wanted "to take a bath in public opinion." I think I have a right to take a bath before I do much talking.

James A. Garfield
letter to Burke A. Hinsdale
Nov 17, 1880

William Ewart Gladstone speech at East Calder, Scotland Apr 2, 1880	The nation is a power hard to rouse, but when roused harder still and more hopeless to resist.
Henry Ward Beecher *Proverbs from Plymouth Pulpit* 1887	There is nothing that makes more cowards and feeble men than public opinion.
Henry Ward Beecher *Proverbs from Plymouth Pulpit* 1887	Public sentiment is to public officers what water is to the wheel of the mill.
Benjamin Harrison speech in Detroit, Michigan Feb 22, 1888	Public opinion is the most potent monarch this world knows.
Mark Twain "Corn Pone Opinions" *Europe and Elsewhere* 1925	Its name is Public Opinion. It is held in reverence. It settles everything. Some think it is the voice of God.
Carrie Chapman Catt testimony at U.S. Senate hearing Feb 13, 1900	No written law has ever been more binding than unwritten custom supported by popular opinion.
Theodore Roosevelt seventh annual message to Congress Dec 3, 1907	There must be public opinion back of the laws or the laws themselves will be of no avail.
O. Henry (William Sydney Porter) "A Ruler of Men" *Rolling Stones* 1912	A straw vote only shows which way the hot air blows.
Walter Lippmann "Revolution and Culture" *A Preface to Politics* 1914	Social movements are at once the symptoms and the instruments of progress. Ignore them and statesmanship is irrelevant; fail to use them and it is weak.
Robert M. LaFollette Sr. "Fooling the People as a Fine Art" *LaFollette's Magazine* Apr, 1918	Where public opinion is free and uncontrolled, wealth has a wholesome respect for the law.
William Ralph Inge "Our Present Discontents" *Outspoken Essays: First Series* 1919	Public opinion, a vulgar, impertinent, anonymous tyrant who deliberately makes life unpleasant for anyone who is not content to be the average man.

We are ruled by Public Opinion, not by Statute-law.

Elbert G. Hubbard
The Note Book
1927

Government, in the last analysis, is organized opinion. Where there is little or no public opinion, there is likely to be bad government, which sooner or later becomes autocratic government.

William Lyon Mackenzie King
Message of the Carillon
1927

One should respect public opinion in so far as is necessary to avoid starvation and to keep out of prison, but anything that goes beyond this is voluntary submission to an unnecessary tyranny.

**Bertrand Russell
3rd Earl Russell**
The Conquest of Happiness
1930

There is no group in America that can withstand the force of an aroused public opinion.

Franklin D. Roosevelt
on signing the National Industrial Recovery Act
Jun 16, 1933

A government can be no better than the public opinion that sustains it.

Franklin D. Roosevelt
speech in Washington, D.C.
Jan 8, 1936

The whole structure of democracy rests on public opinion.

Franklin D. Roosevelt
speech to the Institute of Human Relations
Aug 20, 1937

Nothing is more dangerous in wartime than to live in the temperamental atmosphere of a Gallup Poll, always feeling one's pulse and taking one's temperature.

Sir Winston S. Churchill
speech in the House of Commons
Sep 30, 1941

I see that a speaker at the week-end said that this was a time when leaders should keep their ears to the ground. All I can say is that the British nation will find it very hard to look up to leaders who are detected in that somewhat ungainly posture.

Sir Winston S. Churchill
speech in the House of Commons
Sep 30, 1941

People on the whole are very simple-minded, in whatever country one finds them. They are so simple as to take literally, more often than no, the things their leaders tell them.

Pearl S. Buck
What America Means to Me
1943

It isn't polls or public opinion alone of the moment that counts. It is right and wrong, and leadership—men with fortitude, honesty and a belief in the right that make epochs in the history of the world.

Harry S Truman
interview
1946

When distant and unfamiliar and complex things are communicated to great masses of people, the truth suffers a considerable and often a radical distortion. The complex is made over into the simple, the hypothetical into the dogmatic, and the relative into an absolute.

Walter Lippmann
The Public Philosophy
1955

What the lawmaker has to ascertain is not the true belief but the common belief.

Patrick Devlin
The Enforcement of Morals
1965

Ilya Ehrenburg
"What I Have Learned"
Saturday Review
Sep 30, 1967

It is far more difficult to change the mentality of the people than it is to change a country's political order or even its economy.

George H. Gallup
The New York Times
Dec 1, 1979

Polling is merely an instrument for gauging public opinion. When a president or any other leader pays attention to poll results, he is, in effect, paying attention to the views of the people. Any other interpretation is nonsense.

Mario Cuomo
keynote address to
Democratic National Con-
vention in San Francisco
Jul 16, 1984

We must get the American public to look past the glitter, beyond the showmanship, to the reality, the hard substance of things. And we'll do it . . . not so much with speeches that will bring people to their feet as with speeches that bring people to their senses.

Reform

Sir Francis Bacon
"Of Seditions and
Troubles"
Essays
1625

To give moderate liberty for griefs and discontentments to evaporate . . . is a safe way. For he that turneth the humours back, and maketh the wound bleed inwards, endangereth malign ulcers and pernicious impostumations.

Molière
The Misanthrope
1666

It is a folly second to none,/ To try to improve the world.
Et c'est une folie à nulle autre seconde/ De vouloir se mêler de corriger le monde.

Thomas Jefferson
letter to James Madison
Jun 20, 1787

The hole and the patch should be commensurate.

Edmund Burke
*Reflections on the Revolu-
tion in France*
1790

A state without some means of change is without the means of its conservation.

Sir James Mackintosh
Vindicae Gallicae
1791

Power vegetates with more vigour after these gentle prunings. A slender reform amuses and lulls the people: the popular enthusiasm subsides; and the moment of effectual reform is irretrievably lost. No important political improvement was ever obtained in a period of tranquility.

Thomas Jefferson
letter to Walter Jones
Mar 31, 1801

When we reflect how difficult it is to move or deflect the great machine of society, how impossible to advance the notions of a whole people suddenly to ideal right, we see the wisdom of Solon's remark, that no more good must be attempted than the nation can bear.

Thomas Jefferson
letter to James Ogilvie
Aug 4, 1811

Politics, like religion, hold up torches of martyrdom to the reformers of error.

**Samuel Taylor
Coleridge**
Biographia Literaria
1817

Every reform, however necessary, will by weak minds be carried to an excess, that itself will need reforming.

Know you not that, as in the case of the body natural, so in the case of the body politic, when motion ceases, the body dies?

Jeremy Bentham
Plan of Parliamentary Reform
1817

The population of this country with regard to some important improvement in their government may be compared to a vessel of water exposed to a temperature of 32x. Leave it perfectly still, and the water will remain uncongealed; shake it a little, and it shoots into ice immediately. All great changes are easily effected, when the time is come. Was it not an individual, without fortune, without name, and in fact without talents, who produced the reformation?

James Mill
letter to David Ricardo
Sep 23, 1818

Attempts at reform, when they fail, strengthen despotism, as he that struggles tightens those cords he does not succeed in breaking.

Charles Caleb Colton
Lacön
1825

I was . . . a great reformist; but never suspected that the people in power were against reform. I supposed they only wanted to know what was good in order to embrace it.

Jeremy Bentham
written fragment
Feb 2, 1827

The voice of great events is proclaiming to us, Reform, that you may preserve.

Lord Macaulay
speech on parliamentary reform
Mar 2, 1831

Reform, that you may preserve.

Lord Macaulay
House of Commons debate on the First Reform Bill
Mar 2, 1831

Conservatism goes for comfort, reform for truth.

Ralph Waldo Emerson
lecture on "The Conservative" in Boston, Massachusetts
Dec 9, 1841

If anything ail a man, so that he does not perform his functions, if he have a pain in his bowels even,—for that is the seat of sympathy,—he forthwith sets about reforming the world.

Henry David Thoreau
"Economy"
Walden
1854

Cautious, careful people, always casting about to preserve their reputation and social standing, never can bring about a reform. Those who are really in earnest must be willing to be anything or nothing in the world's estimation.

Susan B. Anthony
speaking on the need to reform divorce law
1860

Experience has two things to teach: the first is that we must correct a great deal; the second, that we must not correct too much.
Il y a deux choses que l'expérience doit apprendre: la première, c'est qu'il faut beaucoup corriger; la seconde, c'est qu'il ne faut pas trop corriger.

Eugene Delacroix
Journal
Mar 8, 1860

Reformers can be as bigoted and sectarian and as ready to malign each other, as the Church in its darkest periods has been to persecute its dissenters.

Elizabeth Cady Stanton
speech on "The Kansas Campaign of 1867"
1867

5th Earl of Rosebery (Archibald Primrose)
speech to the Working Men's Club and Institute Union
Jul 17, 1875

I believe that the labour of those who would ameliorate the conditions of the working classes is slower and more imperceptible than that of the insect which raises the coral reef from the bed of the ocean.

Friedrich Nietzsche
The Dawn
1881

If we wish a change to be as radical as possible, we have to apply the remedy in small doses, but unremittingly, for long periods. Can a great action be accomplished all at once?
Soll eine Veränderung möglichst in die Tiefe gehen, so gebe man das Mittel in den kleinsten Dosen, aber unablässig auf weite Zeitstrecken hin! Was ist Grosses auf einmal zu schaffen?

Henrik Ibsen
An Enemy of the People
1882

You should never wear your best trousers when you go out to fight for freedom and truth.
En skulde aldrig ha' sine bedste buxer på når en er ude og strider for frihed og sandhed.

Oscar Wilde
"The Soul of Man Under Socialism"
Fortnightly Review
Feb, 1891

What is said by great employers of labour against agitators is unquestionably true. Agitators are a set of interfering, meddling people, who come down to some perfectly contented class of the community, and sow the seeks of discontent amongst them. That is the reason why agitators are so absolutely necessary.

Mark Twain
"Pudd'nhead Wilson's Calendar"
Pudd'nhead Wilson
1894

Nothing so needs reforming as other people's habits.

Elizabeth Cady Stanton
The Woman's Bible
1895

Reformers who are always compromising, have not yet grasped the idea that truth is the only safe ground to stand upon.

Mary Elizabeth Lease
attributed

Kansas had better stop raising corn and begin raising hell.

Finley Peter Dunne
"Casual Observations"
Mr. Dooley's Opinions
1900

A man that'd expict to thrain lobsters to fly in a year is called a loonytic; but a man that thinks men can be tu'rrned into angels be an iliction is called rayformer an' remains at large.

George Moore
The Bending of the Bough
1900

All reformers are bachelors.

Finley Peter Dunne
"Reform Administration"
Observations by Mr. Dooley
1902

(Th' rayformer) don't undherstand that people wud rather be wrong an' comfortable thin right in jail.

Ambrose Bierce
The Devil's Dictionary
1906

Radicalism, n. The conservatism of to-morrow injected into the affairs of to-day.

Reform must come from within, not without. You cannot legislate for virtue.

James Cardinal Gibbons
speech in Baltimore, Maryland
Sep 13, 1909

Every man is a reformer until reform tramps on his toes.

Edgar Watson Howe
Country Town Sayings
1911

Standpatism is just as impossible in modern conditions as it is impossible for a thin crust of the earth to keep its place above the force of a volcano. All the blood in this nation is now running into the vital courses of reform, and the men who stand against reform are standing against nature, standing against all the impulses, all the energies, all the hopes, all the ambitions of America.

Woodrow Wilson
speech in Burlington, New Jersey
Oct 30, 1912

Every reform movement has a lunatic fringe.

Theodore Roosevelt
speech
1913

Unless the reformer can invent something which substitutes attractive virtues for attractive vices, he will fail.

Walter Lippmann
"The Taboo"
A Preface to Politics
1914

Hunger does not breed reform; it breeds madness and all the angry distempers that make an ordered life impossible.

Woodrow Wilson
speech to Congress
Nov 11, 1918

As soon as the people fix one Shame of the World, another turns up.

Edgar Watson Howe
Ventures in Common Sense
1919

Laws do not make reforms, reforms make laws.

Calvin Coolidge
quoted by Edward E. Whiting
Calvin Coolidge: His Ideals of Citizenship
1924

Nobody expects to find comfort and companionability in reformers.

Heywood Broun
"Whims"
New York World
Feb 6, 1928

The desire to understand the world and the desire to reform it are the two great engines of progress, without which human society would stand still or retrogress.

Bertrand Russell
"The Place of Sex Among Human Values"
Marriage and Morals
1929

If you try to make a big reform you are told you are doing too much, and if you make a modest contribution you are told you are only tinkering with the problem.

A.P. (Sir Alan Patrick) Herbert
speech in the House of Commons
Feb 3, 1939

The man who is forever disturbed about the condition of humanity either has no problems of his own or has refused to face them.

Henry Miller
Sunday after the War
1944

Franklin D. Roosevelt press conference May 30, 1944	You sometimes find something good in the lunatic fringe. In fact, we have got as part of our social and economic government today a whole lot of things which in my boyhood were considered lunatic fringe, and yet they are now part of everyday life.
Eric Hoffer *The True Believer* 1951	A mass movement attracts and holds a following not because it can satisfy the desire for self-advancement, but because it can satisfy the passion for self-renunciation.
Eric Hoffer *The True Believer* 1951	Mass movements can rise and spread without belief in a God, but never without belief in a devil.
Eleanor Roosevelt *On My Own* 1958	You can't move so fast that you try to change the mores faster than people can accept it. That doesn't mean you do nothing but it means that you do the things that need to be done according to priority.
Martin Luther King Jr. *Why We Can't Wait* 1964	Nonviolent action, the Negro saw, was the way to supplement, not replace, the process of change. It was the way to divest himself of passivity without arraying himself in vindictive force.
Alan Paton "The Challenge of Fear" *Saturday Review* Sep 9, 1967	To give up the task of reforming society is to give up one's responsibility as a free man.
Anonymous quoting a student at the University of Nanterre, France, following 1968 upheaval *The Economist* May 14, 1988	To achieve reforms, you have sometimes to try to make the revolution.
Whitney Moore Young Jr. recalled on his death Mar 11, 1971	Personally, I am not nonviolent, but I'm not a fool either. I can count.
Whitney Moore Young Jr. recalled on his death Mar 11, 1971	Should I . . . stand on 125th Street cussing out Whitey to show I am tough? Or should I go downtown and talk to an executive of General Motors about 20,000 jobs for unemployed Negroes?
Irving Kristol *Esquire* May 23, 1978	Many middle-class reformers will find to their surprise, that the populace is going to be quick to bite the hand that aims to feed it. The populace doesn't want to be fed; it wants more freedom to graze on its own.
Jimmy Carter speech to the Future Farmers of America in Kansas City Nov 9, 1978	If you fear making anyone mad, then you ultimately probe for the lowest common denominator of human achievement.

Religion and the State

Aristotle *Politics* 343 B.C.	If men think that a ruler is religious and has a reverence for the Gods, they are less afraid of suffering injustice at his hands.

Render therefore unto Caesar the things which are Caesar's; and unto God the things that are God's.

Bible
Matthew
ca. 90

The doctrine of persecution for cause of conscience is most evidently and lamentably contrary to the doctrine of Christ Jesus the Prince of Peace.

Roger Williams
The Bloudy Tenant of Persecution for Cause of Conscience
1644

A sanctimonious man is one who under an atheist king would be atheist.
Un dévot est celui qui sous un roi athée serait athée.

Jean de La Bruyère
"De la mode"
Les Caractères
1688

All religions must be tolerated. . .every man must go to heaven in his own way.
Die Religionen müssen alle toleriert werden . . . denn hier muss ein jeder nach seiner Fasson selig werden.

Frederick the Great
note to the Religious Department
Jun 22, 1740

That religion, or the duty which we owe to our Creator, and the manner of discharging it, can be directed only by reason and conviction, not by force or violence; and therefore all men are equally entitled to the free exercise of religion, according to the dictates of conscience.

Patrick Henry
Virginia Bill of Rights
Jun 12, 1776

That to compel a man to furnish contributions of money for the propagation of opinions which he disbelieves and abhors, is sinful and tyrannical.

Thomas Jefferson
"A Bill for Establishing Religious Freedom"
1779

It does me no injury for my neighbor to say there are twenty gods, or no God. It neither picks my pocket nor breaks my leg.

Thomas Jefferson
Notes on the State of Virginia
1782

It behoves every man who values liberty of conscience for himself, to resist invasions of it in the case of others; or their case may, by change of circumstances, become his own.

Thomas Jefferson
letter to Benjamin Rush
Apr 21, 1803

Are not Religion & Politics the Same Thing? Brotherhood is Religion.

William Blake
Jerusalem
1804

All religions united with government are more or less inimical to liberty. All separated from government, are compatible with liberty.

Henry Clay
speech in the House of Representatives
Mar 24, 1818

Civil liberty can be established on no foundation of human reason which will not at the same time demonstrate the right to religious freedom.

John Quincy Adams
letter to Richard Anderson
May 27, 1823

Samuel Taylor Coleridge
On the Constitution of the Church and State
1830

Religion, true or false, is and ever has been the centre of gravity in a realm, to which all other things must and will accommodate themselves.

Angelina Grimké
Letters to Catherine Beecher
1836

I recognize no rights but human rights—I know nothing of men's rights and women's rights; for in Christ Jesus there is neither male nor female. It is my solemn conviction that, until this principal of equality is recognized and embodied in practice, the church can do nothing effectual for the permanent reformation of the world.

Karl Marx
A Contribution to the Critique of Hegel's Philosophy of Right: Introduction
1844

Religion is the sigh of the oppressed creatures, the heart of a heartless world, just as it is the soul of soulless conditions. It is the opium of the people.

Die Religion ist der Seufzer der bedrängten Kreatur, das Gemüt einer herzlosen Welt, wie sie der Geist geistloser Zustände ist. Sie ist das Opium des Volkes.

Karl Marx
The Communist Manifesto
1848

Christian socialism is but the holy water with which the priest consecrates the heart-burnings of the aristocrat.

William Ewart Gladstone
letter to Cardinal Manning
Apr, 1850

Politics would become an utter blank to me were I to make the discovery that we were mistaken in maintaining their association with religion.

Ralph Waldo Emerson
Journals
1872

The religions are obsolete when the reforms do not proceed from them.

Robert G. Ingersoll
Prose-Poems and Selections
1884

In all ages, hypocrites, called priests, have put crowns upon the heads of thieves, called kings.

Thomas Masaryk
The Spirit of Russia
1913

The way in which, amid the political and social unrest of his time, Christ keeps aloof from politics, is truly sublime.

Agnes Maude Royden
speech at the City Temple, London
1917

The Church should no longer be satisfied to represent only the Conservative Party at prayer.

Franklin D. Roosevelt
speech to the Federal Council of Churches of Christ
Dec 6, 1933

If I were asked to state the great objective which Church and State are both demanding for the sake of every man and woman and child in this country, I would say that that great objective is "a more abundant life."

Joseph Stalin
reported conversation with Pierre Laval
May 13, 1935

The Pope! How many divisions has he got?

Mohandas K. Gandhi
Non-Violence in Peace and War
1948

I could not be leading a religious life unless I identified myself with the whole of mankind, and that I could not do unless I took part in politics.

The day that this country ceases to be free for irreligion, it will cease to be free for religion.

Robert H. Jackson
dissenting opinion
Zorach v. *Clausor*
Apr 7, 1952

I hope that no American . . . will waste his franchise and throw away his vote by voting either for me or against me solely on account of my religious affiliation. It is not relevant.

John F. Kennedy
Time
Jul 25, 1960

Tolerance implies no lack of commitment to one's own beliefs. Rather it condemns the oppression or persecution of others.

John F. Kennedy
letter to the National Conference of Christians and Jews
Oct 10, 1960

The church must be reminded that it is not the master or the servant of the state, but rather the conscience of the state.

Martin Luther King Jr.
Strength to Love
1963

If we get the federal government out of the classroom, maybe we'll get God back in.

Ronald Reagan
Washingtonian
Jul, 1976

I think the government ought to stay out of the prayer business.

Jimmy Carter
The New York Times
Apr 8, 1979

The government must pursue a course of complete neutrality toward religion.

John Paul Stevens
majority opinion
Wallace v. *Jaffree*
Jun 4, 1985

Republican Party

I knew that however bad the Republican party was, the Democratic party was much worse. The elements of which the Republican party was composed gave better ground for the ultimate hope of the success of the colored man's cause than those of the Democratic party.

Frederick Douglass
Life and Times of Frederick Douglass
1881

I recognize the Republican party as the sheet anchor of the colored man's political hopes and the ark of his safety.

Frederick Douglass
letter to men of Petersburg, Virginia
Aug 15, 1888

Th' raypublican party broke ye, but now that ye're down we'll not turn a cold shoulder to ye. Come in an' we'll keep ye—broke.

Finley Peter Dunne
"Mr. Dooley Discusses"
Mr. Dooley's Opinion
1900

The trouble with the Republican Party is that it has not had a new idea in 30 years. I am not speaking as a politician; I am speaking as an historian.

Woodrow Wilson
speech in Indianapolis, Indiana
Jan 8, 1915

Indeed there are some Republicans I would trust with anything—anything, that is, except public office.

Adlai E. Stevenson Jr.
campaign speech in Springfield, Illinois
Aug 14, 1952

Adlai E. Stevenson Jr. *The New York Times* Nov 15, 1952	It (the Republican Party) is an ancient political vehicle, held together by soft soap and hunger and with front-seat drivers and back-seat drivers contradicting each other in a bedlam of voices, shouting "go right" and "go left" at the same time.
Adlai E. Stevenson Jr. quoted *Human Behavior* May, 1978	I have been tempted to make a proposal to our Republican friends: that if they stop telling lies about us, we would stop telling the truth about them.
Adlai E. Stevenson Jr. "The Art of Politics" *The Stevenson Wit* 1966	The elephant has a thick skin, a head full of ivory, and as everyone who has seen a circus parade knows, proceeds best by grasping the tail of his predecessor.
Walter Lippmann recalled on his death Dec 14, 1974	Brains, you know, are suspect in the Republican Party.
Nelson A. Rockefeller *Time* Nov 17, 1975	I think the Republican Party is only going to be an effective party if it reflects the best interests of the American people, and traditionally that is in the center. That is where our country has always been. That is where the Republican Party has won.
Walter F. Mondale *Rolling Stone* Nov 4, 1976	For a workingman or woman to vote Republican this year is the same as a chicken voting for Colonel Sanders.
Dixy Lee Ray *Wall Street Journal* Mar 15, 1976	My answer to why did I choose the Democratic Party is that I spent three years in Washington under a Republican administration.
Richard Scammon *Guardian Weekly* Nov 12, 1978	There's nothing wrong with the Republican Party that double-digit inflation won't cure.
Jimmy Carter *Time* Jul 28, 1980	(Republicans are) men of narrow vision who are afraid of the future and whose leaders are inclined to shoot from the hip.
Ronald Reagan *Time* Jul 28, 1980	Thou shalt not criticize other Republicans.
Ronald Reagan remarks at a Republican fundraising dinner in Washington, D.C. May 4, 1982	We're the party that wants to see an America in which people can still get rich.
Ronald Reagan *The New York Times* Oct 10, 1984	Republicans believe every day is the Fourth of July, but Democrats believe every day is April 15.

Revolution

Bible *1 Samuel* ca. 800 B.C.	Rebellion is as the sin of witchcraft.

Is it not a simple fact that in any form of government revolution always starts from the outbreak of internal dissension in the ruling class? The constitution cannot be upset so long as that class is of one mind, however small it may be.

Plato
The Republic
ca. 390 B.C.

A desperate disease requires a dangerous remedy.

Guy Fawkes
to James I
Nov 5, 1605

The surest way to prevent seditions . . . is to take away the matter of them. For if there be fuel prepared, it is hard to tell whence the spark shall come that shall set it on fire.

Sir Francis Bacon
"Of Seditions and Troubles"
Essays
1625

When the people are in movement, it's not possible to see how calm will be restored; when they're quiet, you can't see how the calm will be destroyed.
Quand le peuple est en mouvement, on ne comprend pas par où le calme peut y entrer; et quand il est paisible, on ne voit pas par où le calme peut en sortir.

Jean de La Bruyère
"Du souverain ou de la république"
Les Caractères
1688

If the abuse be enormous, nature will rise up, and claiming her original rights, overturn a corrupt political system.

Samuel Johnson
quoted by James Boswell
Life of Samuel Johnson
Jul 6, 1763

The spirit of resistance to government is so valuable on certain occasions, that I wish it to be always kept alive. It will often be exercised when wrong but better so than not be exercised at all. I like a little rebellion now and then. It is like a storm in the atmosphere.

Thomas Jefferson
letter to Abigail Adams
Feb 22, 1787

I hold it, that a little rebellion now and then, is a good thing, and as necessary in the political world as storms in the physical. . . . It is a medicine for the sound health of government.

Thomas Jefferson
letter to James Madison
Jan 30, 1787

Insurrection is the most sacred of duties.

Marie Joseph, Marquis de Lafayette
speech to the National Assembly
Feb 20, 1790

Every successful revolt is termed a revolution, and every unsuccessful one a rebellion.

Joseph Priestly
letter to Edmund Burke
1791

The tree of liberty grows only when watered by the blood of tyrants.
L'arbre de la liberté ne croit qu'arrosé par le sang des tyrans.

Bertrand Barère de Vieuzac
speech to the National Assembly
1792

Let the law be ruthless and order will be restored.
Que la loi soit terrible et tout rentrera dans l'ordre.

Georges Jacques Danton
speech to the National Convention
Sep 22, 1792

Bertrand Barère de Vieuzac speech to the National Convention 1793	Let us make terror the order of the day.
Henry Clay speech in the House of Representatives Mar 4, 1818	An oppressed people are authorized whenever they can to rise and break their fetters.
Johann Wolfgang von Goethe quoted by Johann Peter Eckermann *Conversations with Goethe* Jan 4, 1824	A great revolution is never the fault of the people, but of the government.
Charles Caleb Colton *Lacön* 1825	If we trace the history of most revolutions, we shall find that the first inroads upon the laws have been made by the governors, as often as by the governed.
Prince Clemens von Metternich letter to Count d'Apponyi Oct 28, 1829	When the ground shakes under governments it is no good their trying to sit still; nature will not allow it!
Francois Guizot speech in Paris Dec 29, 1830	The spirit of revolution, the spirit of insurrection, is a spirit radically opposed to liberty.
Prince Clemens von Metternich letter to Esterhazy Mar 17, 1831	In revolutions those who want everything always get the better of those who want only a certain amount.
1st Duke of Wellington reported conversation with Lord Mahon Nov 2, 1831	I always had a horror of revolutionising any country for a political object. I always said, if they rise of themselves, well and good, but do not stir them up—it is a fearful responsibility.
Giuseppe Mazzini *Manifesto of Young Italy* 1831	Great revolutions are the work rather of principles than of bayonets, and are achieved first in the moral, and afterwards in the material sphere. *Le grandi rivoluzioni si compiono piú coi principii, che colle baionette: dapprima nell'ordine morale, poi nel materiale.*
Giuseppe Mazzini *General Instructions for the Members of Young Italy* 1831	Insurrection—by means of guerrilla bands—is the true method of warfare for all nations desirous of emancipating themselves from a foreign yoke. *La guerra d'insurrezione per bande è la guerra di tutte le Nazioni che s'emancipano da un conquistatore straniero.*
Andrew Jackson "Proclamation to the People of South Carolina" Dec 10, 1832	Secession, like any other revolutionary act, may be morally justified by the extremity of oppression; but to call it a constitutional right is confounding the meaning of the term.

Moderation is fatal to factions, just as it is the vital principle of established power. To ask malcontents to be moderate is like asking them to destroy the foundations of their existence.

Prince Clemens von Metternich
letter to Count d'Apponyi
Feb 6, 1834

There is no grievance that is a fit object of redress by mob law.

Abraham Lincoln
speech in Springfeld, Illinois
Jan 27, 1838

Every revolution was first a thought in one man's mind, and when the same thought occurs to another man, it is the key to that era.

Ralph Waldo Emerson
"History"
Essays: First Series
1841

The world is always childish, and with each new gewgaw of a revolution or new constitution that it finds, thinks it shall never cry any more.

Ralph Waldo Emerson
Journals
1847

When a sixth of the population of a nation which has undertaken to be the refuge of liberty are slaves, and a whole country (Mexico) is unjustly overrun and conquered by a foreign army, and subjected to military law, I think that it is not too soon for honest men to rebel and revolutionize. What makes this duty the more urgent is the fact that the country so overrun is not our own, but ours is the invading army.

Henry David Thoreau
Civil Disobedience
1849

Better to perish with the revolution than to seek refuge in the almshouse of reaction.

Alexander Ivanovich Herzen
introduction, "To My Son Alexander"
From The Other Shore
1848-49

All men recognize the right of revolution; that is, the right to refuse allegiance to, and to resist, the government, when its tyranny or its inefficiency are great and unendurable. But almost all say that such is not the case now.

Henry David Thoreau
Civil Disobedience
1849

If powerful men will not write justice with black ink, on white paper, ignorant and violent men will write it on the soil, in letters of blood, and illuminate their rude legislation with burning castles, palaces, and towns.

Theodore Parker
quoted by Daniel Aaron
Men of Good Hope
1951

Revolutions are not made; they come. A revolution is as natural a growth as an oak. It comes out of the past. Its foundations are laid far back.

Wendell Phillips
speech
Jan 8, 1852

Revolutions never go backward.

Wendell Phillips
speech
Feb 17, 1861

Old forms of government finally grow so oppressive that they must be thrown off even at the risk of reigns of terror.

Herbert Spencer
"On Manners and Fashion"
Essays on Education
1861

Lord Acton "Nationality" *The Home and Foreign Review* Jul, 1862	Two forces which are the worst enemies of civil freedom are the absolute monarchy and the revolution.
Victor Hugo *Les Misérables* 1862	Would you realize what Revolution is, call it Progress; and would you realize what Progress is, call it Tomorrow. *Voulez-vous vous rendre compte de ce que la révolution, appelez-la Progrès; et voulez-vous vous rendre compte de ce que c'est que le progrès, appelez-le Demain.*
Edward George Bulwer-Lytton 1st Baron Lytton speech, House of Commons 1866	A reform is a correction of abuses; a revolution is a transfer of power.
Edmond & Jules de Goncourt *Journal* Jul 12, 1867	There are only two great currents in the history of mankind: the baseness which makes conservatives and the envy which makes revolutionaries. *Il n'y a que deux courants dans l'histoire de l'humanité: la bassesse qui fait les conservateurs et l'envie qui fait les révolutionnaires.*
Michael Bakunin letter to Nechayev 1870	A revolutionary idea is revolutionary, vital, real and true only because it expresses and only so far as it forms popular instincts which are the result of history.
Michael Bakunin letter to Nechayev 1870	It is impossible to arouse the people artificially. People's revolutions are born from the course of events.
Michael Bakunin *God and the State* 1882	There are but three ways for the populace to escape its wretched lot. The first two are by the route of the wineshop or the church; the third is by that of the social revolution.
Leo XIII encyclical *Immortale Dei* 1885	To despise legitimate authority, in whomsoever vested, is unlawful, as a rebellion against the Divine Will; and whoever resists that rushes wilfully to destruction.
Thomas Masaryk *The Foundations of Marxist Theory* 1899	Revolution or dictatorship can sometimes abolish bad things, but they can never create good and lasting ones. Impatience is fatal in politics.
Vladimir Ilyich Lenin *What Is To Be Done?* 1902	Without a revolutionary theory there can be no revolutionary movement.
George Bernard Shaw *Man and Superman* 1902	Any person under the age of thirty who, having knowledge of the existing social order, is not a revolutionist, is an inferior. And yet Revolutions have never lightened the burden of tyranny, they have only shifted it to another shoulder.

Only on the bones of the oppressors can the people's freedom be founded—only the blood of the oppressors can fertilize the soil for the people's self-rule.

Joseph Stalin
appeal written for the Tbilisi Social Democratic Committee
1905

Revolution, n. In politics, an abrupt change in the form of misgovernment.

Ambrose Bierce
The Devil's Dictionary
1906

Insurrection, n. An unsuccessful revolution. Disaffection's failure to substitute misrule for bad government.

Ambrose Bierce
The Devil's Dictionary
1906

Rebel, n. A proponent of a new misrule who has failed to establish it.

Ambrose Bierce
The Devil's Dictionary
1906

We have learned that it is pent-up feelings that are dangerous, whispered purposes that are revolutionary, covert follies that warp and poison the mind.

Woodrow Wilson
Consitutional Government
1908

You can never have a revolution in order to establish a democracy. You must have a democracy in order to have a revolution.

G.K. Chesterton
Tremendous Trifles
1909

The right of revolution is the inherent right of a people to cast out their rulers, change their policy, or effect radical reforms in their system of government or institutions, by force or a general uprising, when the legal and constitutional methods of making such changes have proved inadequate, or are so obstructed as to be unavailable.

Henry Campbell Black
Constitutional Law
1910

Jefferson's Declaration of Independence is a practical document for the use of practical men. It is not a thesis for philosophers, but a whip for tyrants; it is not a theory of government, but a program of action.

Woodrow Wilson
speech in Indianapolis, Indiana
Apr 13, 1911

There is something that governments care far more for than human life, and that is the security of property, and so it is through property that we shall strike the enemy.

Emmeline Pankhurst
speech, "I Incite This Meeting to Rebellion"
Oct 17, 1912

An agitation to attain a political or economic end must rest upon an implied willingness and ability to use force. Without that it is mere wind and attitudinizing.

James Connolly
Forward
Mar 14, 1914

The revolution is incapable either of regretting or of burying its dead.

Joseph Stalin
quoted by Isaac Deutscher
Stalin, A Political Biography
1967

Thinkers prepare the revolution; bandits carry it out.

Mariano Azuela
The Flies
1918

Woodrow Wilson seventh annual message to Congress Dec 2, 1919	The seed of revolution is repression.
William Ralph Inge "Our Present Discontents" *Outspoken Essays: First Series* 1919	If there is one safe generalisation in human affairs, it is that revolutions always destroy themselves.
Leon Trotsky *Where is Britain Going?* 1926	Revolutions are as a rule not made arbitrarily. If it were possible to map out the revolutionary road beforehand and in a rational way, then it would probably also be possible to avoid the revolution altogether. Revolution is an expression of the impossibility of reconstructing class society by rational methods.
Suzanne LaFollette "The Beginnings of Emancipation" *Concerning Women* 1926	People never move towards revolution; they are pushed towards it by intolerable injustices in the economic and social order under which they live.
Suzanne LaFollette "The Beginning of Emancipation" *Concerning Women* 1926	The revolutionists did not succeed in establishing human freedom; they poured the new wine of belief in equal rights for all men into the old bottle of privilege for some; and it soured.
Louis D. Brandeis concurring opinion *Whitney v. California* 1927	Those who won our independence by revolution were not cowards. They did not fear political change. They did not exalt order at the cost of liberty.
Mao Tse-tung "Report on an Investigation of the Peasant Movement in Hunan" Mar, 1927	A revolution is not a dinner party, or writing an essay, or painting a picture, or doing embroidery; it cannot be so refined, so leisurely and gentle, so temperate, kind, courteous, restrained and magnanimous.
Madame Sun Yat-sen (Sung Ching-ling) *People's Tribune* Jul 14, 1927	In the last analysis, all revolutions must be social revolutions, based upon fundamental changes in society; otherwise it is not revolution, but merely a change of government. . . .
Jose Ortega y Gasset *Revolt of the Masses* 1930	A revolution only lasts fifteen years, a period which coincides with the effectiveness of a generation. *Una revolución no dura más de quince años, período que coincide con la vigencia de una generación.*
Mao Tse-tung "Be Concerned with the Well-Being of the Masses . . ." Jan 27, 1934	The revolutionary war is a war of the masses; it can be waged only by mobilizing the masses and relying on them.
Carl Sandburg *The People, Yes* 1936	Revolt and terror pay a price. / Order and law have a cost.

Under fully developed Capitalism civilization is always on the verge of revolution. We live as in a villa on Vesuvius.

George Bernard Shaw
The Intelligent Woman's Guide to Socialism, Capitalism, Sovietism and Fascism
1937

If you rebel against high-heeled shoes, take care to do it in a very smart hat.

George Bernard Shaw
The Intelligent Woman's Guide to Socialism, Capitalism, Sovietism and Fascism
1937

A revolutionary party is a contradiction in terms.

Richard Crossman
"Mussolini and Coolidge"
New Statesman
1939

Fascism was a counter-revolution against a revolution that never took place.
Il fascismo è stata una controrivoluzione contro una rivoluzione che hon ha avuto luogo.

Ignazio Silone
The School for Dictatorships
1939

Though a revolution may call itself "national," it always marks the victory of a single party.

Andre Gide
Journals
Oct 17, 1941

The successful revolutionary is a statesman, the unsuccessful one a criminal.

Erich Fromm
Escape from Freedom
1941

Martyrs are needed to create incidents. Incidents are needed to create revolutions. Revolutions are needed to create progress.

Chester Bomar Himes
"Negro Martyrs are Needed"
Crisis
May, 1944

Everything reactionary is the same; if you don't hit it, it won't fall. This is also like sweeping the floor; as a rule, where the broom does not reach, the dust will not vanish of itself.

Mao Tse-tung
"The Situation and Our Policy After the Victory in the War Against Japan"
Aug 13, 1945

The revolutionary wants to change the world; he transcends it and moves toward the future, towards an order of values which he himself invents. The rebel is careful to preserve the abuses from which he suffers so that he can go on rebelling against them.

Jean-Paul Sartre
Baudelaire
1947

A non-violent revolution is not a program of seizure of power. It is a program of transformation of relationships, ending in a peaceful transfer of power.

Mohandas K. Gandhi
Non-Violence in Peace and War
1948

Every revolutionary ends by becoming either an oppressor or a heretic.
Tout révolutionnaire finit en oppresseur ou en hérétique.

Albert Camus
The Rebel
1951

When hopes and dreams are loose in the streets, it is well for the timid to lock doors, shutter windows and lie low until the wrath has passed.

Eric Hoffer
The True Believer
1951

Adlai E. Stevenson Jr. speech in Los Angeles, California Sep 9, 1952	The time to stop a revolution is at the beginning, not the end.
Murray Kempton "Father and Sons" *Part of Our Time* 1955	Every social war is a battle between the very few on both sides who care and who fire their shots across a crowd of spectators.
Robert Lindner "The Instinct of Rebellion" *Must You Conform?* 1956	As a dimension of man, rebellion actually defines him.
Nikita S. Khrushchev speech to the Supreme Soviet *Pravda* May 8, 1957	Revolutions are the locomotives of history.
Walter Lippmann "For Charles De Gaulle" *From Today and Tomorrow* Jun 5, 1958	A regime, an established order, is rarely overthrown by a revolutionary movement; usually a regime collapses of its own weakness and corruption and then a revolutionary movement enters among the ruins and takes over the powers that have become vacant.
Fidel Castro *The New York Times* Apr 22, 1959	I began revolution with 82 men. If I had to do it again, I'd do it with 10 or 15 and absolute faith. It does not matter how small you are if you have faith and a plan of action.
Ernesto Guevara "Che" *Guerrilla Warfare, A Method* 1961	A revolution that does not continue to grow deeper is a revolution that is retreating.
John F. Kennedy speech to Latin American diplomats Mar 12, 1962	Those who make peaceful revolution impossible will make violent revolution inevitable.
Malcolm X speech in New York City Nov, 1963	If violence is wrong in America, violence is wrong abroad. If it is wrong to be violent defending black women and black children and black babies and black men, then it is wrong for America to draft us, and make us violent abroad in defense of her. And if it is right for America to draft us, and teach us how to be violent in defense of her, then it is right for you and me to do whatever is necessary to defend our own people right here in this country.
Malcolm X speech in New York City Dec 1, 1963	The Negro revolution is controlled by foxy white liberals, by the Government itself. But the Black Revolution is controlled only by God.
Malcolm X speech in New York City Dec, 1963	Revolutions are never peaceful.

Revolutions are never waged singing "We Shall Overcome." Revolutions are based upon bloodshed.

Malcolm X
speech in New York City
Apr, 1964

Not actual suffering but the hope of better things incites people to revolt.

Eric Hoffer
The Ordeal of Change
1964

If you feed the people just with revolutionary slogans they will listen today, they will listen tomorrow, they will listen the day after tomorrow, but on the fourth day they will say, "To hell with you."

Nikita S. Khrushchev
quoted
The New York Times
Oct 4, 1964

In a nonviolent movement there must be a latent threat of eruption, a dormant possibility of sudden and violent action if concessions are to be won, respect gained, and the established order altered.

George Jackson
letter to his mother from
Soledad prison
Mar, 1967

We used to think that revolutions are the cause of change. Actually it is the other way around: change prepares the ground for revolution.

Eric Hoffer
"A Time of Juveniles"
The Temper of Our Time
1967

The duty of every revolutionary is to make a revolution.

Fidel Castro
quoted by Herbert
Matthews
Castro
1969

The most radical revolutionary will become a conservative the day after the revolution.

Hannah Arendt
New Yorker
Sep 12, 1970

We must realize that today's Establishment is the new George III. Whether it will continue to adhere to his tactics, we do not know. If it does, the redress, honored in tradition, is also revolution.

William O. Douglas
Points of Rebellion
1970

The surest guide to the correctness of the path that women take is joy in the struggle. Revolution is the festival of the oppressed.

Germaine Greer
"Revolution"
The Female Eunich
1970

I suggested that we use the panther as our symbol and call our political vehicle the Black Panther Party. The panther is a fierce animal, but he will not attack until he is backed into a corner; then he will strike out.

Huey Newton
Revolutionary Suicide
1973

Revolution is a drama of passion. We did not win the People over by appealing to reason but by developing hope, trust, fraternity.

Mao Tse-tung
quoted
Time
Sep 20, 1976

It takes a revolution to make a solution.

Bob Marley
To the Point International
Sep 12, 1977

It is easier to run a revolution than a government.

Ferdinand E. Marcos
Time
Jun 6, 1977

Bernard-Henri Lévy *Time* Sep 12, 1977	The only successful revolution of this century is totalitarianism.

Rights/Human Rights

William Shakespeare *Henry V* 1598-1600	Every subject's duty is the king's; but every subject's soul is his own.
Thomas Jefferson *Declaration of* *Independence* Jul 4, 1776	We hold these truths to be self-evident, that all men are created equal, that they are endowed by their creator with certain inalienable Rights, that among these are Life, Liberty and the pursuit of happiness.
Thomas Jefferson referring to slavery *Notes on the State of* *Virginia* 1782	I tremble for my country when I reflect that God is just; that his justice cannot sleep forever.
Sir William Blackstone *Commentaries on the* *Laws of England* 1783	The public good is in nothing more essentially interested, than in the protection of every individual's private rights.
Thomas Jefferson letter to James Madison Mar 15, 1787	If we cannot secure all our rights, let us secure what we can.
Thomas Jefferson letter to James Madison Dec 20, 1787	A bill of rights is what the people are entitled to against every government on earth, general or particular, and what no just government hould refuse, or rest in inferences.
Thomas Paine *The Rights of Man* 1791	Man did not enter into society to become worse than he was before, nor to have fewer rights than he had before, but to have those rights better secured.
James Madison "Property" *National Gazette* Mar 29, 1792	As a man is said to have a right to his property, he may be equally said to have a property in his rights.
Mary Wollstonecraft "Dedication" *A Vindication of the Rights* *of Woman* 1792	If the abstract rights of man will bear discussion and explanation, those of woman, by a parity of reasoning, will not shrink from the same test: though a different opinion prevails in the country.
James Madison speech to the Virginia constitutional convention, Richmond, Virginia Dec 2, 1829	The personal right to acquire property, which is a natural right, gives to property, when acquired, a right to protection, as a social right.
Samuel Taylor **Coleridge** *Table-Talk* Nov 20, 1831	Rights! There are no rights whatever without corresponding duties . . . you will find nowhere in our parliamentary records the miserable sophism of the Rights of Man.

We first crush people to the earth, and then claim the right of trampling on them forever, because they are prostrate.

Lydia Maria Child
An Appeal on Behalf of That Class of Americans Called Africans
1833

Human beings have rights, because they are moral beings: the rights of all men grow out of their moral nature; and as all men have the same moral nature, they have essentially the same rights.

Jeanne-Françoise Deroin
Letters to Catherine Beecher
1836

The people know their rights, and they are never slow to assert and maintain them, when they are invaded.

Abraham Lincoln
speech in Springfield, Illinois
Jan, 1837

They have rights who dare maintain them.

James Russell Lowell
"The Present Crisis"
1844

The true Republic: men: their rights and nothing more; women: their rights and nothing less.

Susan B. Anthony
motto of her newspaper
The Revolution

That . . . man . . . says women can't have as much rights as man, cause Christ wasn't a woman. Where did your Christ come from? . . . From God and a woman. Man had nothing to do with it.

Sojourner Truth
speech at the Women's Rights Convention in Akron, Ohio
1851

Many Abolitionists have yet to learn the ABC of woman's rights.

Susan B. Anthony
Journal
Jun, 1860

The rights and interests of every or any person are only secure from being disregarded, when the person interested is himself able, and habitually disposed, to stand up for them.

John Stuart Mill
Considerations on Representative Government
1861

The destiny of the colored American . . . is the destiny of America.

Frederick Douglass
speech at the Emancipation League, Boston, Massachusetts
Feb 12, 1862

If slavery is not wrong, nothing is wrong.

Abraham Lincoln
letter to A.G. Hodges
Apr 4, 1864

There is a great stir about colored men getting their rights, but not a word about colored women; and if colored men get their rights, and not colored women theirs, you see, the colored men will be masters over the women and it will be as bad as before. So I am for keeping the thing going while things are stirring, because if we wait till it is still, it will take a great while to get it going again.

Sojourner Truth
speech to the annual meeting of the Equal Rights Convention in New York City
May 9, 1867

The simplest truths often meet the sternest resistance and are slowest in getting general acceptance.

Frederick Douglass
"The Women's Suffrage Movement"
The New National Era
Oct 6, 1870

Susan B. Anthony
speech at her trial for
voting
1873

Here, in the first paragraph of the Declaration (of Independence), is the assertion of the natural right of all to the ballot; for how can "the consent of the governed" be given, if the right to vote be denied?

Lydia Maria Child
message to supporters of
women's suffrage
ca. 1875

Yours for the unshackled exercise of every faculty by every human being.

**Elizabeth Cady
Stanton**
*History of Woman
Suffrage*
1881

Like all disfranchised classes, they began by asking to have certain wrongs redressed, and not be asserting their own right to make laws for themselves.

Frederick Douglass
speech at Civil Rights
Mass Meeting,
Washington, D.C.
Oct 22, 1883

No man can put a chain about the ankle of his fellow man without at last finding the other end fastened about his own neck.

Frederick Douglass
speech in Louisville,
Kentucky
Sep, 1883

Human law may know no distinction among men in respect of rights, but human practice may.

Robert G. Ingersoll
*Prose-Poems and
Selections*
1884

I am the inferior of any man whose rights I trample under foot.

Alexander Crummell
speech to the Protestant
Episcopal Church
Congress, Buffalo,
New York
Nov 20, 1888

The race problem is a moral one. . . . Its solution will come especially from the domain of principles. Like all the other great battles of humanity, it is to be fought out with the weapons of truth.

Alexander Crummell
speech to the Protestant
Episcopal Church
Congress, Buffalo,
New York
Nov 20, 1888

This country should be agitated and even convulsed till the battle of liberty is won and every man in the land is guaranteed fully every civil and political right.

**William Lloyd
Garrison**
Life
1885-89

Wherever there is a human being, I see God-given rights inherent in that being whatever may be the sex or complexion.

Benjamin Harrison
acceptance of
renomination for the
Presidency
Sep 3, 1892

There is no security for the personal or political rights of any man in a community where any man is deprived of his personal or political rights.

José Martí
Mi Raza
1893

Men have no special right because they belong to one race or another: the word man defines all rights.

In view of the Constitution, in the eye of the law, there is in this country no superior, dominant, ruling class of citizens. There is no caste here. Our Constitution is color-blind, and neither knows nor tolerates classes among citizens. In respect of civil rights, all citizens are equal before the law. The humblest is the peer of the most powerful.

John Marshall Harlan
dissenting opinion
Plessy v. *Ferguson*
1896

In every civilized society property rights must be carefully safeguarded; ordinarily and in the great majority of cases, human rights and property rights are fundamentally and in the long run, identical; but when it clearly appears that there is a real conflict between them, human rights must have the upper hand; for property belongs to man and not man to property.

Theodore Roosevelt
speech at the Univ. of Paris
Apr 23, 1910

There is in this world no such force as the force of a man determined to rise. The human soul cannot be permanently chained.

W.E.B. Du Bois
speech to the Republican Club of New York
Mar 5, 1910

A right is worth fighting for only when it can be put into operation.

Woodrow Wilson
speech in Chattanooga, Tennessee
Aug 31, 1910

When a just cause reaches its flood tide . . . whatever stands in the way must fall before its overwhelming power.

Carrie Chapman Catt
speech, "Is Woman Suffrage Progressing?" in Stockholm, Sweden
1911

We are here to claim our rights as women, not only to be free, but to fight for freedom. It is our privilege, as well as our pride and our joy, to take some part in this militant movement, which, as we believe, means the regeneration of all humanity. Nothing but contempt is due to those people who ask us to submit to unmerited oppression. We shall not do it.

Christabel Pankhurst
speech
Mar 23, 1911

What I am interested in is having the government of the United States more concerned about human rights than about property rights. Property is an instrument of humanity; humanity isn't an instrument of property.

Woodrow Wilson
speech in Minneapolis, Minnesota
Sep 18, 1912

Next to the right of liberty, the right of property is the most important individual right guaranteed by the Constitution and the one which, united with that of personal liberty, has contributed more to the growth of civilization than any other institution established by the human race.

William Howard Taft
Popular Government
1913

The American people . . . believe that peace should rest upon the rights of peoples, not the rights of governments—the rights of peoples great or small, weak or powerful.

Woodrow Wilson
reply to the peace proposal of Pope Benedict XV
Aug 27, 1917

There is no right to strike against the public safety by anybody, anywhere, anytime.

Calvin Coolidge
telegram to the president of the American Federation of Labor
Sep 14, 1919

Calvin Coolidge acceptance speech as Republican vice-presidential nominee Jul 27, 1920	Men speak of natural rights, but I challenge any one to show where in nature any rights existed or were recognized until there was established for their declaration and protection a duly promulgated body of corresponding laws.
Clarence Day *This Simian World* 1920	It is fair to judge peoples by the rights they will sacrifice most for.
Suzanne LaFollette "The Beginnings of Emancipation" *Concerning Women* 1926	Most people, no doubt, when they espouse human rights, make their own mental reservations about the proper application of the word "human."
Suzanne LaFollette "What Is to Be Done" *Concerning Women* 1926	Rights that depend on the sufferance of the State are of uncertain tenure.
Emmeline Pankhurst press conference 1926	Of course we expected a great deal from our enfranchisement. But so did men when they fought for theirs. It is the only way—to keep fighting, to believe that the miracle is going to happen.
Adolf Hitler speech to Nazi party leaders in Munich Sep, 1928	There is only one right in the world and that right is one's own strength.
Louis D. Brandeis *Olmstead* v. *United States* 1928	They (the makers of the constitution) conferred, as against the Government, the right to be let alone—the most comprehensive of rights and the right most valued by civilized men.
Dolores Ibarruri "La Pasionaria" speech in Valencia, Spain 1936	Better to die on one's feet than to live on one's knees. *Mejor morir a pie que vivir en rodillas.*
A. Philip Randolph speech at the National Negro Congress, Philadelphia, Pennsylvania Oct 15-17, 1937	If Negroes secure their goals, immediate and remote, they must win them, and to win them they must fight, sacrifice, suffer, go to jail and, if need be, die for them.
Martin Niemoeller attributed	In Germany they came first for the Communists, and I didn't speak up because I wasn't a Communist. Then they came for the Jews, and I didn't speak up because I wasn't a Jew. Then they came for the trade unionists, and I didn't speak up because I wasn't a trade unionist. then they came for the Catholics, and I didn't speak up because I was a Protestant. Then they came for me and by that time no one was left to speak up.
Eleanor Roosevelt *The New York Times* Feb 4, 1947	It is not that you set the individual apart from society but that you recognize in any society that the individual must have rights that are guarded.
Hubert H. Humphrey speech to the Democratic national convention Aug, 1948	I say the time has come to walk out of the shadow of states' rights and into the sunlight of human rights.

Certain rights can never be granted to the government, but must be kept in the hands of the people.

Eleanor Roosevelt
The New York Times
May 3, 1948

In these days, it is doubtful that any child may reasonably be expected to succeed in life if he is denied the opportunity of an education. Such an opportunity, where the state has undertaken to provide it, is a right which must be made available to all on equal terms. Separate educational facilities are inherently unequal.

Earl Warren
unanimous opinion
Brown v. *Board of Education of Topeka, Kansas*
May 17, 1954

We conclude that in the field of public education the doctrine of "separate but equal" has no place.

Earl Warren
unanimous opinion
Brown v. *Board of Education of Topeka, Kansas*
May 17, 1954

"Freedom from fear" could be said to sum up the whole philosophy of human rights.

Dag Hammarskjold
on the 180th anniversary of the Virginia Declaration of Human Rights
May 20, 1956

What men value in this world is not rights but privileges.

H.L. Mencken
Minority Report
1956

It is my hope that as the Negro plunges deeper into the quest for freedom and justice he will plunge even deeper into the philosophy of non-violence. The Negro all over the South must come to the point that he can say to his white brother: "We will match your capacity to inflict suffering with our capacity to endure suffering. We will meet your physical force with soul force. We will not hate you, but we will not obey your evil laws. We will soon wear you down by pure capacity to suffer."

Martin Luther King Jr.
letter to Chester Bowles
Oct 28, 1957

Homosexual behavior between consenting adults in private should no longer be a criminal offense.

Sir John Frederick Wolfenden
Wolfenden Report
Sep 5, 1957

Where, after all, do universal human rights begin? In small places close to home—so close and so small that they cannot be seen on any map of the world. Yet they are the world of the individual person: the neighborhood he lives in; the school or college he attends; the factory, farm or office where he works. Such are the places where every man, woman and child seeks equal justice, equal opportunity, equal dignity without discrimination. Unless these rights have meaning there, they have little meaning anywhere.

Eleanor Roosevelt
remarks at the United Nations Commission on Human Rights
Mar 27, 1958

I want every American free to stand up for his rights, even if he has to sit down for them.

John F. Kennedy
campaign speech
Aug 3, 1960

The 4th Amendment and the personal rights it secures have a long history. At the very core stands the right of a man to retreat into his own home and there be free from unreasonable governmental intrusion.

Potter Stewart
unanimous opinion
Bartkus v. *Illinois; Abbate* v. *U.S.*
Mar 5, 1961

John F. Kennedy speech to Congress Jan 11, 1962	America stands for progress in human rights as well as economic affairs, and a strong America requires the assurance of full and equal rights to all its citizens, of any race of any color.
Hugo L. Black at the American Jewish Congress Apr 14, 1962	It is my belief that there are "absolutes" in our Bill of Rights, and that they were put there on purpose by men who knew what words meant and meant their prohibitions to be "absolutes."
John F. Kennedy speech on the 100th anniversary of the Emancipation Proclamation Sep 22, 1962	In giving rights to others which belong to them, we give rights to ourselves and to our country.
John F. Kennedy address to the nation on civil rights Jun 11, 1963	This Nation was founded by men of many nations and backgrounds. It was founded on the principle that all men are created equal, and that the rights of every man are diminished when the rights of one man are threatened.
Lyndon Baines Johnson speech to Congress Nov 27, 1963	We have talked long enough in this country about equal rights. We have talked for 100 years or more. Yet, it is time now to write the next chapter—and to write it in books of law.
Lyndon Baines Johnson address to Congress Nov 27, 1963	I urge you . . . to enact a civil rights law so that we can move forward to eliminate from this country every trace of discrimination and oppression based upon race or color. There could be no greater source of strength to this nation both at home and abroad.
John F. Kennedy televised speech Jun 11, 1963	One hundred years of delay have passed since President Lincoln freed the slaves, yet their heirs, their grandsons, are not fully free. They are not yet freed from the bonds of injustice; they are not yet freed from social and economic oppression. And this nation, for all its hopes and all its boasts, will not be fully free until all its citizens are free.
Lyndon Baines Johnson speech at Wayne State Univ., Detroit, Michigan Jan 6, 1963	Until justice is blind to color, until education is unaware of race, until opportunity ceases to squint its eyes at pigmentation of human complexions, emancipation will be a proclamation—but it will not be a fact.
Martin Luther King Jr. speech at the Civil Rights March on Washington, D.C. Aug 28, 1963	I say to you today even though we face the difficulties of today and tomorrow, I still have a dream. It is a dream that is deeply rooted in the American dream. I have a dream that one day this nation will rise up, live out the true meaning of its creed. We hold these truths to be self-evident, that all men are created equal. I have a dream that one day on the red hills of Georgia the sons of former slaves and the sons of former slave-owners will be able to sit down together at the table of brotherhood . . . I have a dream that one day every valley shall be exalted, every hill and mountain shall be made low. The rough places will be made plain and the crooked places will be made straight.
John F. Kennedy televised speech on civil rights Jun 11, 1963	Every American ought to have the right to be treated as he would wish to be treated, as one would wish his children to be treated. This in not the case.

I have a dream that my four little children will one day live in a nation where they will not be judged by the color of their skin, but by the content of their character.

Martin Luther King Jr. speech at the Civil Rights March on Washington, D.C. Aug 28, 1963

We are not fighting for integration, nor are we fighting for separation. We are fighting for recognition as human beings. We are fighting for . . . human rights.

Malcolm X speech on "Black Revolution" in New York City 1964

The political philosophy of black nationalism means that the black man should control the politics and the politicians in his own community; no more.

Malcolm X speech on "The Ballot or the Bullet" 1964

The Negro was willing to risk martyrdom in order to move and stir the social conscience of his community and the nation. . . . He would force his oppressor to commit his brutality openly, with the rest of the world looking on. . . . Nonviolent resistance paralyzed and confused the power structures against which it was directed.

Martin Luther King Jr. *Why We Can't Wait* 1964

Nonviolence is the answer to the crucial political and moral questions of our time; the need for man to overcome oppression and violence without resorting to oppression and violence.

Martin Luther King Jr. speech accepting the Nobel Peace Prize Dec 11, 1964

A rioter with a Molotov cocktail in his hands is not fighting for civil rights any more than a Klansman with a sheet on his back and mask on his face. They are both more or less what the law declares them: lawbreakers, destroyers of constitutional rights and liberties and ultimately destroyers of a free America.

Lyndon Baines Johnson remarks to a White House conference during riots in Los Angeles Aug 20, 1965

We deal with a right of privacy older than the Bill of Rights— older than our political parties, older than our school system.

William O. Douglas majority opinion *Griswold* v. *Connecticut* Jun 7, 1965

The Negro revolt is not aimed at winning friends but at winning freedom, not interpersonal warmth but institutional justice.

Harvey G. Cox Jr. *The Secular City* 1966

The greatest achievement of the civil rights movement is that it has restored the dignity of indignation.

Frederic Wertham *A Sign for Cain: An Exploration in Human Violence* 1966

Every man should know that his conversations, his correspondence, and his personal life are private. I have urged Congress—except when the Nation's security is at stake—to take action to that end.

Lyndon Baines Johnson remarks at swearing-in of Ramsey Clark as attorney general Mar 10, 1967

The man who walks alone is soon trailed by the F.B.I.

Wright Morris *A Bill of Rites, A Bill of Wrongs, A Bill of Goods* 1967

Herman Weinkrantz
ruling on harrassment of
"hippies"
The New York Times
Jul 1, 1968

This court will not deny the equal protection of the law to the unwashed, unshod, unkempt and uninhibited.

Potter Stewart
majority opinion
Jun 17, 1968

At the very least, the freedom that Congress is empowered to secure . . . includes the freedom to buy whatever a white man can buy, the right to live wherever a white man can live. If Congress cannot say that being a freeman means at least this much, then the 13th Amendment made a promise it cannot keep.

Edward Heath
speech at the Lord May-
or's banquet, London
Nov 16, 1970

Abhorrence of apartheid is a normal attitude, not a policy.

Whitney Moore Young Jr.
recalled on his death
Mar 11, 1971

There is no such thing as a moderate in the civil rights movement; everyone is a radical. The difference is whether or not one is all rhetoric or relevant.

A. Philip Randolph
quoted by Jervis
Anderson
*A. Philip Randolph, a
Biographical Portrait*
1972

Salvation for a race, nation, or class must come from within. Freedom is never granted; it is won. Justice is never given; it is exacted. Freedom and justice must be struggled for by the oppressed of all lands and races, and the struggle must be continuous, for freedom is never a final fact, but a continuing evolving process to higher and higher levels of human, social, economic, political and religious relationships.

Potter Stewart
majority opinion
Lynch v. *Household Fi-
nance Corp.*
Mar 23, 1972

The dichotomy between personal liberties and property rights is a false one. Property does not have rights. People have rights.

Potter Stewart
majority opinion
Lynch v. *Household
Finance Corp.*
Mar 23, 1972

In fact, a fundamental interdependence exists between the personal right to liberty and the personal right in property.

Louise Nevelson
quoted
AFTRA
1974

The freer that women become, the freer will men be. Because when you enslave someone—you are enslaved.

Steve Biko
statement at trial
May 3, 1976

The basic tenet of black consciousness is that the black man must reject all value systems that seek to make him a foreigner in the country of his birth and reduce his basic human dignity.

Potter Stewart
majority opinion
Runyon v. *McCrary,
Fairfax-Brewster School,
Inc.*
Jun 25, 1976

It may be assumed that parents have a 1st Amendment right to send their children to educational institutions that promote the belief that racial segregation is desirable, and that the children have an equal right to attend such institutions. But it does not follow that the practice of excluding racial minorities from such institutions is also protected by the same principle.

Ramsey Clark
The New York Times
Oct 2, 1977

A right is not what someone gives you; it's what no one can take from you.

We talk a lot about human rights, but I don't know of any human right that is more important than a job.

William Norris
Time
Apr 3, 1978

The rights of all persons are wrapped in the same constitutional bundle as those of the most hated member of the community.

Abraham Lincoln Wirin
Time
Feb 20, 1978

Human rights is the soul of our foreign policy, because human rights is the very soul of our sense of nationhood.

Jimmy Carter
speech on the 30th anniversary of UN Declaration of Human Rights
Dec 6, 1978

I loathe all manifestations of extremism and I believe we should strive, above all else, for the dignity and human rights of mankind, regardless of race, color and creed.

Lord Louis Mountbatten
recalled on his death
Time
Sep 10, 1979

My decision to register women . . . confirms what is already obvious throughout our society—that women are now providing all types of skills in every profession. The military should be no exception.

Jimmy Carter
on proposal to register women for the draft
Feb 8, 1980

The 4th Amendment protects the individual's privacy in a variety of settings. In none is the zone of privacy more clearly defined than when bounded by the unambiguous physical dimensions of an individual's home—a zone that finds its roots in clear and specific constitutional terms: "the right of the people to be secure in their . . . houses . . . shall not be violated."

John Paul Stevens
majority opinion
Peyton v. *New York;*
Riddick v. *New York*
Apr 15, 1980

America did not invent human rights. In a very real sense . . . human rights invented America.

Jimmy Carter
farewell address
Jan 14, 1981

This is a celebration of individual freedom, not of homosexuality. No government has the right to tell its citizens when or whom to love. The only queer people are those who don't love anybody.

Rita Mae Brown
speech in San Francisco, California
Aug 28, 1982

My belief has always been . . . that wherever in this land any individual's constitutional rights are being unjustly denied, it is the obligation of the federal government—at point of bayonet if necessary—to restore that individual's constitutional rights.

Ronald Reagan
press conference
May 17, 1983

A married woman has the same right to control her own body as does an unmarried woman.

Sol Wachtler
unanimous opinion, New York State Court of Appeals
Dec 20, 1984

America's view of apartheid is simple and straightforward: We believe it is wrong. We condemn it. And we are united in hoping for the day when apartheid will be no more.

Ronald Reagan
on sanctions against South Africa
Sep 9, 1985

I am not interested in picking up crumbs of compassion thrown from the table of someone who considers himself my master. I want the full menu of rights.

Desmond Tutu
"Today," NBC-TV
Jan 9, 1985

Sidney H. Asch majority opinion barring discrimination on basis of sexual orientation May 7, 1985	Where sexual proclivity does not relate to job function, it seems clearly unconstitutional to penalize an individual in one of the most imperative of life's endeavors, the right to earn one's daily bread.
Edward I. Koch on signing law barring discrimination on basis of sexual orientation *US News & World Report* Apr 14, 1986	You don't have to love them. You just have to respect their rights.
Harry A. Blackmun dissenting opinion *Bowers* v. *Hardwick* Jun 30, 1986	The right of an individual to conduct intimate relationships in the intimacy of his or her own home seems to me to be the heart of the Constitution's protection of privacy.
Harry A. Blackmun dissenting opinion *Bowers* v. *Hardwick* Jun 30, 1986	(Disapproval of homosexuality cannot justify) invading the houses, hearts and minds of citizens who choose to live their lives differently.
Harry A. Blackmun dissenting opinion *Bowers* v. *Hardwick* Jun 30, 1986	What the Court really has refused to recognize is the fundamental interest all individuals have in controlling the nature of their intimate associations.

Role of the State/of Government

Aristotle *Politics* 343 B.C.	A state is not a mere society, having a common place, established for the prevention of mutual crime and for the sake of exchange. . . . Political society exists for the sake of noble actions, and not of mere companionship.
Juvenal *Satires* ca. 125	Two things only the poeple anxiously desire, bread and the circus games. *Duas tantem res anxius optat,/ Panem et Circenses.*
Niccolò Machiavelli *Il Principe* 1532	When neither their property not their honor is touched, the majority of men live content. *Qualunque volta alle universalità degli uomini non si toglie né roba né onore, vivono contenti.*
Sir Francis Bacon *Advancement of Learning* 1605	Man seeketh in society comfort, use, and protection.
Sir Francis Bacon "Of Seditions and Troubles" *Essays* 1625	Above all things, good policy is to be used that the treasure and monies in a state be not gathered into a few hands. For otherwise a state may have a great stock and yet starve. And money is like muck, not good except it be spread.

The true aim of government is liberty.
Finis ergo reipublicae revera libertas est.

Baruch (Benedictus de) Spinoza
Tractatus Theologico-Politicus
1670

The ultimate aim of government is not to rule, or restrain, by fear, nor to exact obedience, but contrariwise, to free every man from fear, that he may live in all possible security; in other words, to strengthen his natural right to exist and work without injury to himself or others.
Finem ejus (reipublica) ultimum non esse dominari, nec homines metu retinere et alterius juris facere, sed contra, unumquemque metu liberare ut secure quoad ejus fieri potest vivat, hoc est, ut jus suum naturale ad existendum et operandum absque suo et alterius damno optime retineat.

Baruch (Benedictus de) Spinoza
Tractatus Theologico-Politicus
1670

The best condition of a commonwealth is easily discovered from the purpose of political order: which is simply peace and security of life.
Qualis autem cujuscunque imperii optimus sit status facile ex fine status civilis cognoscitur: qui scilicet nullus alius est quam pax vitaeque securitas.

Baruch (Benedictus de) Spinoza
Tractatus Politicus
1676

Government has no other end but the preservation of Property.

John Locke
The Second Treatise on Government
1690

The public must and will be served.

William Penn
Some Fruits of Solitude in Reflections and Maxims
1693

That action is best, which procures the greatest happiness for the greatest numbers.

Francis Hutcheson
Inquiry into the Original of our Ideas of Beauty and Virtue
1725

Whatever alms may be given to a beggar in the street, this does not fulfill the state's obligation, which owes to every citizen an assured subsistence, proper nourishment, suitable clothing, and a mode of life not incompatible with health.
Quelques aumônes que l'on fait à un homme nu dans les rues, ne remplissent point les obligations de l'Etat, qui doit à tous les citoyens une subsistance assurée, la nourriture, un vêtement convenable, et un genre de vie qui ne soit point contraire à la santé.

Charles Louis de Montesquieu
De l'Esprit des lois
1748

It should be remembered that the foundation of the social contract is property; and its first condition, that every one should be maintained in the peaceful possession of what belongs to him.

Jean Jacques Rousseau
A Discourse on Political Economy
1758

The good and happiness of the members, that is the majority of the members of any state, is the great standard by which every thing relating to that state must finally be determined.

Joseph Priestly
Essay on Government
1768

George Mason *Virginia Bill of Rights* Jun 12, 1776	Government is, or ought to be instituted for the common benefit, protection, and security of the people, nation, or community; of all the various modes and forms of government, that is best which is capable of producing the greatest degree of happiness and safety, and is most effectually secured against the danger of maladministration.
George Washington letter to David Stuart Jul 1, 1787	The primary cause of all our disorders lies in the different State Governments, and in the tenacity of that power which pervades the whole of their system. . . . Incompatibility in the laws of different States, and disrespect to those of the general government must render the situation of this great Country weak, inefficient and disgraceful.
James Madison *The Federalist* Jan 23, 1788	The safety and happiness of society are the objects at which all political institutions aim, and to which all such institutions must be sacrificed.
James Madison *Federalist* Feb 27, 1788	A good government implies two things: fidelity to the object of government, which is the happiness of the people; secondly, a knowledge of the means by which that object can be best attained.
James Madison *The Federalist* Feb 6, 1788	Justice is the end of government. It is the end of society.
James Madison *The Federalist* Feb. 12, 1788	Government is instituted no less for protection of the property, than of the persons of individuals.
James Monroe "Observations of the Federal Government" 1789	The best frame of government is that which is most likely to prevent the greatest sum of evil.
George Washington letter to the Count de Moustier Nov 1, 1790	The aggregate happiness of society, which is best promoted by the practice of a virtuous policy, is, or ought to be, the end of all government.
Thomas Paine *Declaration of the Friends* *of Universal Peace and* *Liberty* 1791	We hold the moral obligation of providing for old age, helpless infancy, and poverty, is far superior to that of supplying the invented wants of courtly extravagance.
Edmund Burke *Reflections on the Revolu-* *tion in France* 1791	Government is a contrivance of human wisdom to provide for human wants. Men have a right that these wants should be provided for by this wisdom.
James Madison *National Gazette* Mar 29, 1792	Government is instituted to protect property of every sort; as well that which lies in the various rights of individuals, as that which the term particularly expresses. This being the end of government, that alone is a just government, which impartially secures to every man, whatever is his own.

Government was intended to suppress injustice, but its effect has been to embody and perpetuate it.

William Godwin
"Summary of Principles"
An Enquiry Concerning Political Justice
1793

And having looked to the Government for bread, on the very first scarcity they will turn and bite the hand that fed them.

Edmund Burke
Thoughts and Details on Scarcity
1800

States do not prosper through ideology.
Les Etats ne prospèrent point par l'idéologie.

Napoleon I
letter to M. Cambacérès
Apr 24, 1805

Where the state is weak, the army rules.
Là où le gouvernement est faible, l'armée gouverne.

Napoleon I
remarks in the Council of State
Jan 9, 1808

The care of human life and happiness, and not their destruction, is the first and only legitimate object of good government.

Thomas Jefferson
letter to the Republican citizens of Maryland
Mar 31, 1809

The main objects of all science, the freedom and happiness of man . . . (are) the sole objects of all legitimate government.

Thomas Jefferson
letter to General Thaddeus Kosciusko
Feb 26, 1810

Were we directed from Washington when to sow, & when to reap, we should soon want bread.

Thomas Jefferson
Autobiography
1892

It is high time, My Lord, that the subjects of Christian Governments should be taught that neither historically or morally, in fact or by right, have men made the State; but that the State, and that alone, makes them men.

Samuel Taylor Coleridge
letter to Lord Liverpool
1817

It is an easy and a vulgar thing to please the mob, and not a very arduous task to astonish them; but essentially to benefit and improve them is a work fraught with difficulty and teeming with danger.

Charles Caleb Colton
Lacön
1825

The office of government is not to confer happiness, but to give men opportunity to work out happiness for themselves.

William Ellery Channing
Christian Examiner
Sep/Oct, 1827

The business of government is not directly to make the people rich, but to protect them in making themselves rich; and a government which attempts more than this is precisely the government which is likely to perform less. Governments do not and cannot support the people.

Lord Macaulay (Thomas Babington, 1st Baron Macaulay)
speech on parliamentary reform
Mar 2, 1831

All communities are apt to look to government too much. . . . The framers of our excellent Constitution . . . wisely judged that the less government interferes with private pursuits the better for the general prosperity.

Martin Van Buren
message to special session of Congress
Sep 4, 1837

Ralph Waldo Emerson
Journals
1839

Man exists for his own sake and not to add a laborer to the State.

2nd Viscount Melbourne
quoted by Lord David Cecil
Lord M.
1954

The whole duty of government is to prevent crime and to preserve contracts.

Pierre Joseph Proudhon
Qu'est-ce la propriété?
1840

As man seeks justice in equality, so society seeks order in anarchy.

Louis Blanc
The Organization of Work
1840

What the proletarian lack is capital, and the duty of the state is to see that he gets it. Were I to define the state, I should prefer to think of it as the poor man's bank.

Rufus Choate
speech in the U.S. Senate
Jul 2, 1841

The final end of government is not to exert restraint but to do good.

John Tyler
letter to Gov. Rufus King of Rhode Island
May 9, 1842

A government never loses anything by mildness and forbearance to its own citizens, more especially when the consequences of an opposite course may be the shedding of blood.

Thomas Carlyle
Past and Present
1843

"A fair day's wages for a fair day's work": it is as just a demand as governed men ever made of governing. It is the everlasting right of man.

Ralph Waldo Emerson
"Politics"
Essays: Second Series
1844

The less government we have, the better—the fewer laws, and the less confided power.

Walt Whitman
editorial
Brooklyn Eagle
Apr 4, 1846

It is only the novice in political economy who thinks it is the duty of government to make its citizens happy.—Government has no such office. To protect the weak and the minority from the impositions of the strong and the majority—to prevent any one from positively working to render the people unhappy . . . to do the labor not of an officious inter-meddler in the affairs of men, but of a prudent watchman who prevents outrage—these are rather the proper duties of a government.

Giuseppe Mazzini
Watchword for the Roman Republic
1849

Inexorable as to principles, tolerant and impartial as to persons.

Henry David Thoreau
Civil Disobedience
1849

The mass of men serve the state thus, not as men mainly, but as machines, with their bodies.

Abraham Lincoln
written fragment
Jul 1, 1854

The legitimate object of government, is to do for a community of people, whatever they need to have done, but can not do, at all, or can not, so well do, for themselves—in their separate, and individual capacities. In all that the people can individually do as well for themselves, government ought not to interfere.

I am for those means which will give the greatest good to the greatest number.

Abraham Lincoln
speech in Cincinnati, Ohio
Feb 12, 1861

The State . . . is the most flagrant negation, the most cynical and complete negation of humanity.

Michael Bakunin
Federalism, Socialism and Anti-Theologism
1868

A great scholar and a great wit, 300 years ago, said that, in his opinion, there was a great mistake in the Vulgate, which, as you all know, is the Latin translation of the Holy Scriptures, and that, instead of saying "Vanity of vanities, all is vanity"—Vanitas vanitatum, omnia vanitas—the wise and witty king really said, Sanitas sanitatum, omnia sanitas. Gentlemen, it is impossible to overrate the importance of the subject. After all, the first consideration of a Minister should be the health of the people.

Benjamin Disraeli
speech in Manchester, England
Apr 3, 1872

It is an old saying that, after all, the great end and aim of the British Constitution is to get twelve honest men into a box. That is really a very sensible way of putting the theory, that the first end of government is to give security to life and property, and to make people keep their contracts.

John Morley
speech to the Midland Institute in Birmingham, England
Oct 5, 1876

The health of the people is really the foundation upon which all their happiness and all their powers as a state depend.

Benjamin Disraeli
speech in the House of Commons
Jul 24, 1877

Is it not rooted in our entire moral relationships that the individual who comes before his fellow citizens and says, "I am physically fit, ready for work, but can find no job," is entitled to say, "Give me a job!" and the state is obliged to find a job for him?

Prince Otto von Bismarck
speech to the Reichstag
May 9, 1884

Good government . . . has for its objects the protection of every person within its care in the greatest liberty consistent with the good order of society, and his perfect security in the enjoyment of his earnings with the least possible diminution for public needs.

Grover Cleveland
second annual message to Congress
Dec 6, 1886

The government is not an almoner of gifts among the people, but an instumentality by which the people's affairs should be conducted upon business principles, regulated by the public needs.

Grover Cleveland
message to the House of Representatives
Feb 26, 1887

Prepare for war in time of peace. Not by fortifications, by navies, or by standing armies. But by policies which will add to the happiness and the comfort of all our people and which will tend to the distribution of intelligence and wealth equally among all. Our strength is a contented and intelligent community.

Rutherford B. Hayes
Diary
Jun 25, 1887

The state is like the human body. All of the functions it carries out are not noble ones.
L'Etat est comme le corps humain. Toutes les fonctions qu'il accomplit ne sont pas nobles.

Anatole France
Les Opinions de M. Jérôme Coignard

The lessons of paternalism ought to be unlearned and the better lesson taught that while the people should patriotically and cheerfully support their Government its functions do not include the support of the people.

Grover Cleveland
second inaugural address
Mar 4, 1893

Mark Twain *Notebook* 1935	That government is not best which best secures mere life and property—there is a more valuable thing—manhood.
Heinrich von Treitschke *Politics* 1897–1901	If the state has the power to send the flower of its manhood to die in thousands for the sake of the lives of the whole community, it would be absurd to deny it the right to put criminals to death if they are a danger to the public weal.
Theodore Roosevelt speech in Springfield, Illinois Jul 4, 1903	A man who is good enough to shed his blood for his country is good enough to be given a square deal afterwards. More than that no man is entitled to, and less than that no man shall have.
William Howard Taft acceptance of Republican nomination for president in Chicago, Illinois Jul 28, 1908	The administration of justice lies at the foundation of government.
Woodrow Wilson *The State: Elements of* *Historical and Practical* *Politics* 1911	Government should not be made an end in itself; it is a means only,—a means to be freely adapted to advance the best interests of the social organism. The State exists for the sake of Society, not Society for the sake of the State.
Woodrow Wilson speech in Fall River, Massachusetts Sep 26, 1912	We used to say that the ideal of government was for every man to be left alone and not interfered with, except when he interfered with somebody else; and that the best government was the government that did as little governing as possible. . . . But we are coming now to realize that life is so complicated that . . . the law has to step in and create new conditions under which we may live, the conditions which will make it tolerable for us to live.
Woodrow Wilson first inaugural address Mar 4, 1913	Our thought has been "Let every man look out for himself, let every generation look out for itself," while we reared giant machinery which made it impossible that any but those who stood at the levers of control should have a chance to look out for themselves.
Oliver Wendell **Holmes Jr.** *Pennsylvania Coal Company v. H.J. Mahon* 1922	The general rule, at least, is that while property may be regulated to a certain extent, if regulation goes too far it will be recognized as a taking.
Oliver Wendell **Holmes Jr.** *Tyson & Bro.* v. *Banton* 1927	But to many the superfluous is the necessary, and it seems to me that Government does not go beyond its sphere in attempting to make life livable for them.
Herbert Hoover speech at Palo Alto, California Aug 11, 1928	To me the foundation of American life rests upon the home and the family. I read into these great economic forces, these intricate and delicate relations of the government with business and with our political and social life, but one supreme end . . . that we strengthen the security, the happiness, and the independence of every home.
Benjamin N. Cardozo *Adler* v. *Deegan* 1929	If the moral and physical fibre of its manhood and its womanhood is not a state concern, the question is, what is?

Progress is born of cooperation in the community—not from government restraints.

Herbert Hoover
inaugural address
Mar 4, 1929

Nations have recently been led to borrow billions for war; no nation has ever borrowed largely for education. Probably, no nation is rich enough to pay for both war and civilization. We must make our choice; we cannot have both.

Abraham Flexner
Universities
1930

It is the purpose of the government to see that not only the legitimate interests of the few are protected but that the welfare and the rights of the many are conserved.

Franklin D. Roosevelt
speech in Portland,
Oregon
Sep 21, 1932

Government has the definite duty to use all its power and resources to meet new social problems with new social controls.

Franklin D. Roosevelt
quoted
Newsweek
Nov 27, 1978

It is customary in democratic countries to deplore expenditure on armaments as conflicting with the requirements of the social services. There is a tendency to forget that the most important social service that a government can do for its people is to keep them alive and free.

Sir John Cotesworth Slessor
Strategy for the West
1954

The government must be the trustee for the little man, because no one else will be. The powerful can usually help themselves—and frequently do.

Adlai E. Stevenson Jr.
quoted
Human Behavior
May, 1978

Chaos and ineptitude are anti-human; but so too is a superlatively efficient government equipped with all the products of a highly developed technology.

Aldous Huxley
Tomorrow and Tomorrow and Tomorrow
1956

Government should be concerned with anti-social conduct, not with utterances.

William O. Douglas
dissenting opinion
Roth v. *United States*
Jun 24, 1957

Too often our Washington reflex is to discover a problem and then throw money at it, hoping it will somehow go away.

Kenneth B. Keating
The New York Times
Dec 24, 1961

The state is the servant of the citizen, and not his master.

John F. Kennedy
State of the Union
address
Jan 11, 1962

The business of government is the business of the people.

John F. Kennedy
speech in New York City
May 20, 1962

Work for elimination of concrete evils rather than for the realisation of abstract goods. Do not aim at establishing happiness by political means. Rather, aim at the elimination of poverty by direct means.

Sir Karl Popper
"Utopia and Violence"
Conjecture and Refutation
1962

Wealth is the means, and people are the ends. All our material riches will avail us little if we do not use them to expand the opportunities of our people.

John F. Kennedy
State of the Union
message
Jan 11, 1962

John F. Kennedy
speech at Amherst
College, Amherst,
Massachusetts
Oct 26, 1963

I look forward to . . . a future in which our country will match its military strength with our moral restraint, its wealth with our wisdom, its power with our purpose.

Barry Goldwater
speech in West Chester,
Pennsylvania
Oct 21, 1964

A government that is big enough to give you all you want is big enough to take it all away.

Lyndon Baines Johnson
speech at the Univ. of
Michigan
May 22, 1964

The great society is a place where men are more concerned with the quality of their goals than the quantity of their goods.

William O. Douglas
dissenting opinion
Osborn v. *United States*
1966

We are rapidly entering the age of no privacy, where everyone is open to surveillance at all times; where there are no secrets from government.

Pierre Eliot Trudeau
The New York Times
Jun 16, 1968

The state has no business in the bedrooms of the nation.

Stanislaw Lec
More Unkempt Thoughts
1968

Prolong human life only when you can shorten its miseries.

Richard M. Nixon
televised speech on
welfare reform
Aug 8, 1969

If we take the route of the permanent handout, the American character will itself be impoverished.

Gerald R. Ford
address to Congress
Aug 12, 1974

The American wage earner and the American housewife are a lot better economists than most economists care to admit. They know that a government big enough to give you everything you want is a government big enough to take from you everything you have.

Henry A. Kissinger
Washington Post
Nov 25, 1975

We must resist the myth that government is a gigantic conspiracy. We cannot allow the intelligence services of the country to be dismantled.

Richard B. Cheney
Washington Post
Nov 6, 1975

I am skeptical about the ability of government to solve problems, and I have a healthy respect for the ability of people to solve problems on their own.

George F. Will
speech to Association of
American Publishers
Washingtonian
Jul, 1975

World War II was the last government program that really worked.

Jimmy Carter
speech to the California
State Senate in
Sacramento
May 20, 1976

All I want is the same thing you want. To have a nation with a government that is as good and honest and decent and competent and compassionate and as filled with love as are the American people.

Anything that the private sector can do, the government can do it worse.

Dixy Lee Ray
Mother Jones
May, 1977

It was once said that the moral test of government is how that government treats those who are in the dawn of life, the children; those who are in the twilight of life, the elderly; and those who are in the shadows of life—the sick, the needy and the handicapped.

Hubert H. Humphrey
speech at dedication of
Hubert H. Humphrey
building, Washington,
D.C.
Nov 4, 1977

Americans have always had an ambivalent attitude toward intelligence. When they feel threatened, they want a lot of it, and when they don't, they regard the whole thing as somewhat immoral.

Vernon A. Walters
Silent Missions
1978

I believe that we have an obligation to those in need, but that government should not be the provider of first resort for things that the private sector can produce better.

George Bush
address to Congress
Feb 9, 1989

Separation of Powers

A legislative, an executive, and a judicial power comprehend the whole of what is meant and understood by government. It is by balancing each of these powers against the other two, that the efforts in human nature towards tyranny can alone be checked and restrained, and any degree of freedom preserved in the constitution.

John Adams
letter to Richard Henry
Lee
Nov 15, 1775

In all tyrannical governments the supreme magistracy, or the right both of making and enforcing the laws, is vested in one and the same man, or one and the same body of men; and wherever these two powers are united together, there can be no public liberty.

Sir William Blackstone
*Commentaries on the
Laws of England*
1783

The accumulation of all powers legislative, executive, and judiciary in the same hands, whether of one, a few or many, and whether hereditary, self-appointed, or elective, may justly be pronounced the very definition of tyranny.

James Madison
The Federalist
Jan 30, 1788

With all the fanatical and preposterous theories about the rights of man (the theories, not the rights themselves, I speak of) there is nothing but power that can restrain power.

**John Randolph of
Roanoke**
speech, as quoted
Richmond Enquirer
Jun 4, 1824

Within these limits the power vested in the American courts of justice of pronouncing a statute to be unconstitutional forms one of the most powerful barriers that have ever been devised against the tyranny of political assemblies.

Resserré dans ses limites, le pouvoir accordé aux tribunaux américains de prononcer sur l'inconstitutionnalité des lois, forme encore une des plus puissantes barrières qu'on ait jamais élevées contre la tyrannie des assemblées politiques.

**Alexis, Comte de
Tocqueville**
Democracy in America
1835

Edward Gibbon *The History of the Decline and Fall of the Roman Empire* 1838	The principles of a free constitution are irrevocably lost, when the legislative power is nominated by the executive.
Louis D. Brandeis dissenting opinion *Myers* v. *United States* 1926	The doctrine of the separation of powers was adopted by the Convention of 1787, not to promote efficency but to preclude the exercise of arbitrary power. The purpose was, not to avoid friction, but, by means of the inevitable friction incident to the distribution of the governmental powers among three departments, to save the people from autocracy.
Franklin D. Roosevelt press conference Jul 23, 1937	It is the duty of the President to propose and it is the privilege of the Congress to dispose.
Richard M. Nixon White House statement Mar 12, 1973	Under the doctrine of separation of powers, the manner in which the president personally exercises his assigned executive powers is not subject to questioning by another branch of government.
Court of Appeals United States ruling that President Nixon had to turn over presidential tapes *The New York Times* Oct 14, 1973	Man has discovered no technique for long preserving free government except that the executive be under the law.
Frank Church *Washington Post* Feb 17, 1976	If we are to preserve freedom and keep constitutional government alive in America, it cannot be left to a President and his agents alone to decide what must be kept secret. Congress, if it is to check the abuse of executive power, must retain its right to inquiry and independent judgement.

Social Justice

William Shakespeare *Coriolanus* 1607–08	The gods sent not/ Corn for the rich men only.
John Locke *An Essay Concerning Human Understanding* 1690	Where there is no property there is no injustice.
Samuel Johnson quoted by James Boswell *Life of Samuel Johnson* 1770	A decent provision for the poor is the true test of civilization.
Henry David Thoreau *Civil Disobedience* 1849	Under a government which imprisons any unjustly, the true place for a just man is also a prison . . . the only house in a slave State in which a free man can abide with honor.

So we defend ourselves and our henroosts, and maintain slavery.

Henry David Thoreau
A Plea for Captain John Brown
1859

The strongest bond of human sympathy outside the family relation should be one uniting all working people of all nations and tongues and kindreds.

Abraham Lincoln
letter to New York Workingmen's Association
Mar 21, 1864

Property is the fruit of labor. Property is desirable, is a positive good in the world. Let not him who is homeless pull down the house of another, but let him work diligently and build one for himself, thus by example assuring that his own shall be safe from violence.

Abraham Lincoln
"Reply to New York Workingmen's Democratic Republican Association"
Mar 21, 1864

I am weary seeing our laboring classes so wretchedly housed, fed, and clothed, while thousands of dollars are wasted every year over unsightly statues. If these great men must have outdoor memorials let them be in the form of handsome blocks of buildings for the poor.

Elizabeth Cady Stanton
Diary
1880

When commerical capital occupies a position of unquestioned ascendancy, it everywhere constitutes a system of plunder.

Karl Marx
Das Kapital
1867-83

Lack of money is the root of all evil.

George Bernard Shaw
"Maxims for Revolutionists"
Man and Superman
1902

Security, the chief pretence of civilization, cannot exist where the worst of dangers, the danger of poverty, hangs over everyone's head.

George Bernard Shaw
preface
Major Barbara
1905

It is significant that whenever the public mind is to be diverted from a great social wrong, a crusade is inaugurated against indecency, gambling, saloons, etc.

Emma Goldman
"The Tragedy of Women's Emancipation"
Anarchism and Other Essays
1911

There never can be equality of awards or possessions so long as the human plan contains varied talents and differing degrees of industry and thrift, but ours ought to be a country free from the great blotches of distressed poverty.

Warren G. Harding
inaugural address
Mar 4, 1921

In every truth, the beneficiaries of a system cannot be expected to destroy it.

A. Philip Randolph
The Truth About Lynching
ca. 1922

Hungry men have no respect for law, authority or human life.

Marcus Moziah Garvey
Philosophy and Opinions
1923

The ultimate end of all revolutionary social change is to establish the sanctity of human life, the dignity of man, the right of every human being to liberty and well-being.

Emma Goldman
My Further Disillusionment in Russia
1924

Aldous Huxley *Jesting Pilate* 1926	A man may have strong humanitarian and democratic principles; but if he happens to have been brought up as a bath-taking, shirt-changing lover of fresh air, he will have to overcome certain physical repugnances before he can bring himself to put those principles into practice.
Franklin D. Roosevelt second inaugural address Jan 20, 1937	I see one-third of a nation ill-housed, ill-clad, ill-nourished. . . . The test of our progress is not whether we add more to the abundance of those who have much; it is whether we provide enough for those who have too little.
Joseph Schumpeter *Capitalism, Socialism,* *and Democracy* 1942	Capitalism inevitably and by virtue of the very logic of its civilization creates, educates and subsidizes a vested interest in social unrest.
Will Rogers *The Autobiography of* *Will Rogers* 1949	The Lord so constituted everybody that no matter what color you are you require the same amount of nourishment.
Harry S Truman speech in San Francisco, California Sep 4, 1951	I don't believe in government for special privilege. Our resources should be used for the benefit of all the people.
Adlai E. Stevenson Jr. speech in Columbus, Ohio Oct 3, 1952	Understanding human needs is half the job of meeting them.
John Kenneth **Galbraith** *The Affluent Society* 1958	Social imbalance reflects itself in inability to enforce laws, including significantly those which protect and advance basic social justice, and in failure to maintain and improve essential service.
Mary McCarthy "My Confession" *On the Contrary* 1961	An unrectified case of injustice has a terrible way of lingering, restlessly, in the social atmosphere like an unfinished question.
John W. Gardner *Excellence* 1961	For every talent that poverty has stimulated it has blighted a hundred.
John F. Kennedy speech to the United Nations General Assembly Sep 25, 1961	Political sovereignty is but a mockery without the means of meeting poverty and illiteracy and disease. Self-determination is but a slogan if the future holds no hope.
Michael Harrington *The Other America* 1962	One cannot raise the bottom of a society without benefiting everyone above.
Michael Harrington *The Other America* 1962	There is the fundamental paradox of the welfare state: that it is not built for the desperate, but for those who are already capable of helping themselves.
Lyndon Baines **Johnson** State of the Union address Jan 8, 1964	This administration today, here and now, declares unconditional war on poverty in America. I urge this Congress and all Americans to join with me in that effort.

The challenge of the next half-century is whether we have the wisdom to use wealth to enrich and elevate our national life—and to advance the quality of American civilization—for in your time we have the opportunity to move not only toward the rich society and the powerful society, but upward to the Great Society.

Lyndon Baines Johnson
speech at the Univ. of Michigan
May 22, 1964

Speaking like this doesn't mean that we're anti-white, but it does mean we're anti-exploitation, we're anti-degradation, we're anti-oppression.

Malcolm X
speech on "The Ballot or the Bullet"
1964

If freedom makes social progress possible, so social progress strengthens and enlarges freedom. The two are inseparable partners in the great adventure of humanity.

Robert F. Kennedy
"Berlin East and West"
The Pursuit of Justice
1964

Neither you nor I are willing to accept the tyranny of poverty, nor the dictatorship of ignorance, nor the despotism of ill health, nor the oppression of bias and prejudice and bigotry. We want change. We want progress. We want it both abroad and at home—and we aim to get it.

Lyndon Baines Johnson
speech to college students
Aug 4, 1965

The landscape should belong to the people who see it all the time.

LeRoi Jones
Home
1966

No poor, rural, weak, or black person should ever again have to bear the additional burden of being deprived of the opportunity for an education, a job, or simple justice.

Jimmy Carter
inaugural address as governor of Georgia in Atlanta
Jan 12, 1971

Senator, I am one of them. You do not seem to understand who I am. I am a black woman, the daughter of a dining-car worker. . . . If my life has any meaning at all, it is that those who start out as outcasts can wind up as being part of the system.

Patricia Roberts Harris
in testimony to the U.S. Senate
Newsweek
Jan 24, 1977

If you turn your back on these people, you yourself are an animal. You may be a well-dressed animal, but you are nevertheless an animal.

Edward I. Koch
calling for civic compassion for persons with AIDS
The New York Times
Jan 25, 1987

How do you argue with someone who states that the people who are sleeping on the grates of the streets of America "are homeless by choice"?

Patti Davis
remarks quoted in
Newsweek
Oct 1, 1990

Socialism

Property is theft.
La propriété, c'est le vol.

Pierre Joseph Proudhon
Qu'est-ce la propriété?
1840

Herbert Spencer
"The Coming Slavery"
The Contemporary Review
Apr, 1884

All socialism involves slavery. . . . That which fundamentally distinguishes the slave is that he labours under coercion to satisfy another's desires.

William Morris
written for "Justice"
1884

What I mean by Socialism is a condition of society in which there should be neither rich nor poor, neither master nor master's man, neither idle nor overworked, neither brain-sick brain workers nor heart-sick hand workers, in a word, in which all men would be living in equality of condition, and would manage their affairs unwastefully, and with the full consciousness that harm to one would mean harm to all—the realization at last of the meaning of the word commonwealth.

Henry George
Protection or Free Trade
1885

Labor may be likened to a man who as he carries home his earnings is waylaid by a series of robbers. One demands this much, and another that much, but last of all stands one who demands all that is left, save just enough to enable the victim to maintain life and come forth the next day to work. . . . And the robber that takes all that is left, is private property in land.

Eugene V. Debs
speech
Jan 1, 1897

The issue is Socialism versus Capitalism. I am for Socialism because I am for humanity.

Jules Renard
Journal
Aug, 1905

Socialism must come down from the brain and reach the heart.

Joseph Stalin
quoted by Isaac
Deutscher
*Stalin, A Political
Biography*
1924

Objectively, Social Democracy is the moderate wing of fascism.

Leon Blum
preface to French edition
of James Burnham
The Age of the Organisers

The revolutionary transformation of the regime of property and production is not an end in itself, but the necessary means and the indispensable condition of the liberation of the human being, which is an end in itself and is the final goal of socialism.
La transformation révolutionnaire du régime de propriété et de la production n'est pas une fin en soi, mais le moyen nécessaire et la condition indispensable de la libération de la personne humaine, qui est, elle, une fin en soi et la dernière du socialisme.

Stanley Baldwin
**1st Earl Baldwin of
Bewdley**
quoted by K. Middlemas
and J. Barnes
Baldwin

Socialism and laisser faire are like the north and south poles. They don't really exist.

Pius XI
encyclical
Quadragesimo Anno
1931

Whether considered as a doctrine, or as an historical fact, or as a movement, socialism, if it really remains socialism, cannot be brought into harmony with the dogmas of the Catholic Church. . . . Religious socialism, Christian socialism, are expressions implying a contradiction in terms.

Socialism means equality of income or nothing.

George Bernard Shaw
appendix
The Intelligent Woman's Guide to Socialism, Capitalism, Sovietism and Fascism
1937

The aim of Socialism is to set up a universal society founded on equal justice for all men and equal peace for all nations.

Leon Blum
For All Mankind
1941

As a matter of practical necessity, socialist democracy may eventually turn out to be more of a sham than capitalist democracy ever was.

Joseph Schumpeter
Capitalism, Socialism and Democracy
1942

The great corruption of Socialism which threatens us at present . . . calls itself Fascism in Italy, National Socialism (Nazi for short) in Germany, New Deal in the United States, and is clever enough to remain nameless in England; but everywhere it means the same thing: Socialist production and Unsocialist distribution.

George Bernard Shaw
Everybody's Political What's What?
1944

Unimaginative people disparage Socialism because it will, they fear, reduce life to a dead level. Never was an apprehension less plausible. Millions of well-fed bumptious citizens with plenty of leisure for argument will provide all the excitement the most restless spirits can desire.

George Bernard Shaw
Everybody's Politcal What's What?
1944

No socialist system can be established without a political police. . . . They would have to fall back on some form of Gestapo.

Sir Winston S. Churchill
BBC radio broadcast
Jun 4, 1945

Every reasonable human being should be a moderate Socialist.

Thomas Mann
The New York Times
Jun 18, 1950

The inherent vice of capitalism is the unequal sharing of blessings; the inherent virtue of socialism is the equal sharing of miseries.

Sir Winston S. Churchill
saying

I believe that for the past twenty years there has been a creeping socialism spreading in the United States.

Dwight D. Eisenhower
speech to Republican leaders, Custer State Park, South Dakota
Jun 11, 1953

If the Labour Party is not going to be a Socialist Party, I don't want to lead it. . . . When you join a team in the expectation that you are going to play rugger, you can't be expected to be enthusiastic if you are asked to play tiddly-winks.

Aneurin Bevan
speech in Manchester, England
Jan 26, 1956

Total abstinence and a good filing-system are not now the right sign-posts to the socialist Utopia; or at least, if they are, some of us will fall by the wayside.

Anthony Crosland
The Future of Socialism
1956

The two most important emotions of the Labour Party are a doctrinaire faith in nationalization, without knowing what it means, and a doctrinaire faith in pacifism, without facing its consequences.

Richard Crossman
Diary
Oct 4, 1957

Richard Crossman *Diary* Jul 3, 1959	The definition of the Left is a group of people who will never be happy unless they can convince themselves that they are about to be betrayed by their leaders.
Bernard-Henri Lévy *Time* Mar 13, 1978	Between the barbarity of capitalism, which censures itself much of the time, and the barbarity of socialism, which does not, I guess I might choose capitalism.

Taxation and Budgets

Plato *The Republic* ca. 390 B.C.	When there is an income tax, the just man will pay more and the unjust less on the same amount of income.
Jean Baptiste Colbert attributed ca. 1665	The art of taxation consists in so plucking the goose as to obtain the largest possible amount of feathers with the smallest possible amount of hissing.
Charles Pratt **Earl Camden** speech in the House of Lords 1765	The British Parliament has no right to tax the Americans. . . . Taxation and representation are inseparably united. God hath joined them; no British Parliament can put them asunder. To endeavour to do so is to stab our very vitals.
John Dickinson *Resolutions of the Stamp* *Act Congress* Oct 19, 1765	It is inseparably essential to the freedom of a people that no taxes be imposed on them but with their own consent, given personally or by their representatives.
Edmund Burke speech in the House of Commons Apr 19, 1774	To please universally was the object of his life; but to tax and to please, no more than to love and to be wise, is not given to men.
Alexander Hamilton letter to Robert Morris Apr 30, 1781	A national debt, if it is not excessive, will be to us a national blessing.
Thomas Jefferson letter to James Madison Oct 28, 1785	Another means of silently lessening the inequality of property is to exempt all from taxation below a certain point, and to tax the higher portions of property in geometric progression as they rise.
Benjamin Franklin letter to David Hartley Dec 4, 1789	Our Constitution is in actual operation; everything appears to promise that it will last; but nothing in this world is certain but death and taxes.
Edmund Burke *Letter to a Noble Lord* 1796	Mere parsimony is not economy. . . . Expense, and great expense, may be an essential part of true economy.
Thomas Jefferson first annual message to Congress Dec 8, 1801	Sound principles will not justify our taxing the industry of our fellow citizens to accumulate treasure for wars to happen we know not when, and which might not perhaps happen but from the temptations offered by that treasure.
Napoleon I decision Nov 15, 1804	Not one cent should be raised unless it is in accord with the law. *Il ne doit pas être levé un centime, si ce n'est en vertu d'une loi.*

And to preserve their independence, we must not let our rulers load us with perpetual debt. We must make our election between economy and liberty, or profusion and servitude.

Thomas Jefferson
letter to Samuel Kercheval
Jul 12, 1816

I, however, place economy among the first and most important of republican virtues, and public debt as the greatest of the dangers to be feared.

Thomas Jefferson
letter to William Plumer
Jul 21, 1816

That the power to tax involves the power to destroy . . . is not to be denied.

John Marshall
McCullough v. *Maryland*
1819

The greatest, the most important power entrusted to the government is the right to tax the citizens; it is from this right that all the others flow. Today, therefore, political science consists essentially in being able to draw up a good budget. Now, the ability to do this is an administrative ability, from which it follows that administrative ability is the principal ability needed in politics.

Claude Henri, Comte de Saint-Simon
Politics
1819

I am one of those who do not believe that a national debt is a national blessing . . . it is calculated to raise around the administraiton a moneyed aristocracy dangerous to the liberties of the country.

Andrew Jackson
letter to L.H. Colman
Apr 26, 1824

That most delicious of all privileges—spending other people's money.

John Randolph of Roanoke
quoted by W. Cabell Bruce
John Randolph of Roanoke, 1773–1833
1922

The wisdom of man never yet contrived a system of taxation that would operate with perfect equality.

Andrew Jackson
"Proclamation to the People of South Carolina"
Dec 10, 1832

Countries, therefore, when lawmaking falls exclusively to the lot of the poor cannot hope for much economy in public expenditure.
Les pays ou les pauvres seraient exclusivement chargés de faire la loi ne pourraient donc espérer une grande économie dans les dépenses publiques.

Alexis, Comte de Tocqueville
Democracy in America
1835

In other words, a democratic government is the only one in which those who vote for a tax can escape the obligation to pay it.
En d'autre termes, le gouvernement de la démocratie est le seul ou celui qui vote l'impôt puisse échapper à l'obligation de le payer.

Alexis, Comte de Tocqueville
Democracy in America
1835

As an individual who undertakes to live by borrowing, soon finds his original means devoured by interest, and next no one left to borrow from—so must it be with a government.

Abraham Lincoln
campaign circular
Mar 4, 1843

Of all debts men are least willing to pay the taxes. What a satire is this on government! Everywhere they think they get their money's worth, except for these.

Ralph Waldo Emerson
"Politics"
Essays: Second Series
1844

To tax the community for the advantage of a class is not protection: it is plunder.

Benjamin Disraeli
speech in the House of Commons
May 14, 1850

Prince Otto von Bismarck speech in the Prussian Chamber of Deputies Jun 1, 1865	People are glad to be defended, but they are not glad about paying for it. *Man lässt sich gern schützen, aber man zahlt nicht gern.*
Andrew Johnson first annual message to Congress Dec 4, 1865	The life of a republic lies certainly in the energy, virtue, and intelligence of its citizens; but it is equally true that a good revenue system is the life of an organized government.
Andrew Johnson first annual message to Congress Dec 4, 1865	No favored class should demand freedom from assessment, and the taxes should be so distributed as to not fall unduly on the poor, but rather on the accumulated wealth of the country.
Charles Dudley Warner "Sixteenth Week" *My Summer in a Garden* 1870	The thing generally raised on city land is taxes.
Grover Cleveland second annual message to Congress Dec 6, 1886	When more than the people's sustenance is exacted through the form of taxation than is necessary to meet the just obligations of Government and expenses of its economical administration, such exaction becomes ruthless extortion and a violation of the fundamental principles of a free Government.
Oliver Wendell Holmes Jr. *Compañía de Tabacos* v. *Collector* 1904	Taxes are what we pay for civilized society.
Ambrose Bierce *The Devil's Dictionary* 1906	Houseless, adj. Having paid all taxes on household goods.
Calvin Coolidge speech in Washington, D.C. Jun 30, 1924	The power to tax is the power to destroy. . . . A government which lays taxes on the people not required by urgent public necessity and sound public policy is not a protector of liberty, but an instrument of tyranny.
Will Rogers "Helping the Girls with Their Income Taxes" *The Illiterate Digest* 1924	The Income Tax has made more Liars out of the American people than golf has.
Calvin Coolidge inaugural address Mar 4, 1925	I favor the policy of economy, not because I wish to save money, but because I wish to save people. The men and women of this country who toil are the ones who bear the cost of the Government. Every dollar that we carelessly waste means that their life will be so much the more meager. Every dollar that we prudently saves means that their life will be so much the more abundant. Economy is idealism in its most practical form.
Calvin Coolidge inaugural address Mar 4, 1925	The collection of any taxes which are not absolutely required, which do not . . . contribute to the public welfare, is only a species of legalized larceny.

The power to tax is not the power to destroy while this Court sits.

Oliver Wendell Holmes Jr.
dissenting opinion
Panhandle Oil Company v. *Mississippi ex rel. Knox, Attorney General*
1928

Lord, the money we do spend on Government and it's not one bit better than the government we got for one-third the money twenty years ago.

Will Rogers
quoted by Paula McSpadden Love
The Will Rogers Book
1972

Too often in recent history liberal governments have been wrecked on rocks of loose fiscal policy.

Franklin D. Roosevelt
message to Congress
Mar 10, 1933

Taxes, after all, are the dues that we pay for the privileges of membership in an organized society.

Franklin D. Roosevelt
speech in Worcester, Massachusetts
Oct 21, 1936

Our national debt after all is an internal debt owed not only by the Nation but to the Nation. If our children have to pay interest on it they will pay that interest to themselves. A reasonable internal debt will not impoverish our children or put the Nation into bankruptcy.

Franklin D. Roosevelt
speech to the American Retail Federation
May 22, 1939

Noah must have taken into the Ark two taxes, one male and one female, and did they multiply bountifully! Next to guinea pigs, taxes must have been the most prolific animals.

Will Rogers
The Autobiography of Will Rogers
1949

When everybody has got money they cut taxes, and when they're broke they raise 'em. That's statesmanship of the highest order.

Will Rogers
The Autobiography of Will Rogers
1949

It's a terribly hard job to spend a billion dollars and get your money's worth.

George M. Humphrey
Look
Feb 23, 1954

The purpose is clear. It is safety with solvency. The country is entitled to both.

Dwight D. Eisenhower
on unification of the three military services
Apr 17, 1958

There is one difference between a tax collector and a taxidermist—the taxidermist leaves the hide.

Mortimer Caplin
Time
Feb 1, 1963

The Federal Government is the people and the budget is a reflection of their need.

John F. Kennedy
speech in Washington, D.C.
Apr 19, 1963

Government expands to absorb revenue and then some.

Tom Wicker
quoted by Harold Faber
The New York Times Magazine
Mar 17, 1968

Erving Goffman interview *The New York Times* Feb 12, 1969	Man is not like other animals in the ways that are really significant: animals have instincts, we have taxes.
Nelson A. Rockefeller letter to John V. Lindsay *The New York Times* Apr 25, 1971	There is no doubt that many expensive national projects may add to our prestige or serve science. But none of them must take precedence over human needs. As long as Congress does not revise its priorities, our crisis is not just material, it is a crisis of the spirit.
Herman E. Talmadge *American Legion* *Magazine* Aug, 1975	Virtually everything is under federal control nowadays except the federal budget.
David Muchow *Chicago Sun–Times* Nov 19, 1976	Budgeting is a black art practiced by bureaucratic magicians.
Russell B. Long *The New York Times* Dec 31, 1976	Tax reform means "Don't tax you, don't tax me, tax that fellow behind the tree."
Milton Friedman *U.S. News & World* *Report* Mar 7, 1977	There's only one place where inflation is made: that's in Washington . . . in response to pressures from the people at large. . . . The voting public . . . ask their Congressmen to enact goodies in the form of spending, but they are unhappy about having taxes raised to pay for those goodies.
Lane Kirkland *U.S. News & World* *Report* May 19, 1980	Any jackass can draw up a balanced budget on paper.
David Stockman "The Education of David Stockman," by William Greider *The Atlantic Monthly* Dec, 1981	None of us really understands what's going on with all these numbers.
Ronald Reagan *The New York Times* Mar 18, 1985	Someone must stand up to those who say, "Here's the key, there's the Treasury, just take as many of those hard-earned tax dollars as you want."
Ronald Reagan televised speech May 28, 1985	Most (tax revisions) didn't improve the system, they made it more like Washington itself; complicated, unfair, cluttered with gobbledygook and loopholes designed for those with the power and influence to hire high-priced legal and tax advisers.
Ronald Reagan speech in Independence, Missouri Sep 2, 1985	The current tax code is a daily mugging.
Les Aspin report on letter to the Secretary of Defense *The New York Times* Feb 5, 1985	Before we give you billions more, we want to know what you've done with the trillion you've got.

(A tax loophole is) something that benefits the other guy. If it benefits you, it is tax reform.

Russell B. Long
recalled on his retirement
Time
Nov 10, 1986

Read my lips: no new taxes.

George Bush
acceptance speech as
Republican nominee
for preseident
Aug 18, 1988

Read my hips.

George Bush
responding, while jogging,
to questions about pro-
posed tax hikes, quoted in
Newsweek
Oct 22, 1990

Over my dead veto.

George Bush
remarks expressing oppo-
sition to proposed income
tax hikes, reported in
Newsweek
Nov 19, 1990

Treason

Treason doth never prosper: what's the reason?/ For if it prosper, none dare call it treason.

Sir John Harington
"Of Treason"
Epigrams

Caesar had his Brutus, Charles the First, his Cromwell, and George the Third ("Treason!" cried the Speaker) may profit by their example. If this be treason, make the most of it.

Patrick Henry
speech to the Virginia
House of Representatives
1765

Traters, I will here remark, are a onfortnit class of peple. If they wasn't, they wouldn't be traters. They conspire to bust up a country—they fail, and they're traters. They bust her, and they become statesmen and heroes.

Artemus Ward
"The Tower of London"
Artemus Ward in London
1872

The fear of doing right is the grand treason in times of danger.

Henry Ward Beecher
*Proverbs from Plymouth
Pulpit*
1887

They talk of a man betraying his country, his friends, his sweetheart. There must be a moral bond first. All a man can betray is his conscience.

Joseph Conrad
Under Western Eyes
1911

If I had to choose between betraying my country and betraying my friend, I hope I should have the guts to betray my country.

E.M. Forster
"What I Believe"
Two Cheers for Democracy
1951

Ethel and Julius Rosenberg letter released by their attorney the day of execution for espionage Jun 19, 1953	We are the first victims of American fascism.
Kim (Harold) Philby *The New York Times* Dec 19, 1967	To betray you must first belong.

War and Peace

Homer *Iliad* ca. 700 B.C.	Victory shifts from man to man.
Aesop "The Town Mouse and the Country Mouse" *Fables* ca. 550 B.C.	Better beans and bacon in peace than cakes and ale in fear.
Lao-Tse *The Way of the Tao* 6th cent. B.C.	Stretch a bow to the very full,/ And you will wish you had stopped in time.
Confucius *The Analects* ca. 480 B.C.	To lead an uninstructed people to war is to throw them away.
Euripides *The Phoenician Women* ca. 411–409 B.C.	Dead men have no victory.
Aristotle *Nicomachean Ethics* ca. 325 B.C.	We make war that we may live in peace.
Bible *Isaiah* ca. 200 B.C.	And he shall judge among the nations, and shall rebuke many people: and they shall beat their swords into plowshares, and their spears into pruninghooks: nation shall not lift up sword against nation, neither shall they learn war any more.
Terence *Eunuchus* ca. 165 B.C.	He is wise who tries everything before arms. *Omnia prius experiri quam armis sapietem decet.*
Cicero *Pro T. Annio Milone oratio* 52 B.C.	Laws are silent in time of war. *Silent enim leges inter arma.*
Marcus Tullius Cicero *De Officiis* 44 B.C.	Let arms yield to the toga, the laurel crown to praise. *Cedant arma togae, concedat laurea laudi.*

Endless money forms the sinews of war.
Primum nervos belli, pecuniam infinitam.

Marcus Tullius Cicero
Philippics
44–43 B.C.

The name of peace is sweet and the thing itself good, but between peace and slavery there is the greatest difference.
Et nomen pacis dulce est et ipsa res salutaris, sed inter pacem et servitutem plurimum interest.

Marcus Tullius Cicero
Philippics
44–43 B.C.

Peace is liberty in tranquility; servitude the last of all evils, one to be repelled, not only by war but even by death.
Pax est tranquilla libertas, servitus postremum malorum omnium non modo bello, sed morte etiam repellendum.

Marcus Tullius Cicero
Philippics
44–43 B.C.

Certain peace is better and safer than anticipated victory.
Melior tutiorque est certa pax quam sperata victoria.

Livy
Ab Urbe Condita
ca. 29 B.C.

It is sweet and honorable to die for your country.
Dulce et decorum est pro patria mori.

**Horace
(Quintus Horatius Flaccus)**
Odes
23 B.C.

Of war men ask the outcome, not the cause.
Quaeritur belli exitus, non causa.

Seneca (the Younger)
Hercules Furens
ca. 50

Blessed are the peacemakers: for they shall be called the children of God.

Bible
Matthew
ca. 90

Where they make a desert, they call it peace.
Atque ubi solitudinem faciunt, pacem appellant.

Cornelius Tacitus
Agricola
ca. 98

The gods are on the side of the stronger.
Deos fortioribus adesse.

Cornelius Tacitus
Historiae
ca. 100

We are now suffering the evils of a long peace. Luxury, more deadly than war, broods over the city, and avenges a conquered world.
Nunc patimur longae pacis mala, saevior armis/ Luxuria incubuit victumque ulciscitur orbem.

Juvenal
Satires
ca. 115

Let him who desires peace prepare for war.
Qui desiderat pacem, praeparet bellum.

**Vegetius
(Flavius Vegetius Renatus)**
De Rei Militari
ca. 375

In order for a war to be just, three things are necessary. First, the authority of the sovereign. . . . Secondly, a just cause. . . . Thirdly . . . a rightful intention.
Dicendum quod ad hoc quod aliquod bellum sit justum, tria requiruntur. Primo quidem, auctoritas principis, cujus mandato bellum est gerendum. . . . Secundo, requiritur causa justa. . . . Tertio, requiritur ut sit intentio bellantium recta.

St. Thomas Aquinas
Summa Theologiae
1273

Desiderius Erasmus *Adagia* 1515	The most disadvantageous peace is better than the most just war.
Niccolò Machiavelli *Il Principe* 1532	A prince should therefore have no other aim or thought, nor take up any other thing for his study, but war and its organization and discipline, for that is the only art that is necessary to one who commands. *Debbe adunque uno principe non avere altro obietto né altro pensiero, né prendere cosa alcuna per sua arte, fuora della guerra e ordini e disciplina di essa; perché quella è sola arte che si espetta a chi comanda.*
Niccolò Machiavelli *Il Principe* 1532	Among other evils which being unarmed brings you, it causes you to be despised. *Perché intra le altre cagioni che ti arreca di male lo essere disarmato, ti fa contennendo.*
Theodore Beza *De Haereticis* 1554	Since the chief and ultimate end of human society is not that men should live together in peace, but that, living in peace, they should serve God, it is the function of the Magistrate to risk even this outward peace (if no otherwise may it be done) in order to secure and maintain in his land the true service of God in its purity.
Christopher Marlowe *Tamburlaine the Great* 1587	Accurst be he that first invented war.
Michel de Montaigne "Des mauvais moyens employés à bonne fin" *Essais* 1580–88	A foreign war is a lot milder than a civil war. *Une guerre étrangère est un mal bien plus doux que la civile.*
Michel de Montaigne "De l'incertitude de notre jugement" *Essais* 1580–88	It's not victory if it doesn't end the war. *Ce n'est pas victoire, si elle ne met fin à la guerre.*
Miguel de Cervantes *Don Quixote* 1605–15	There is nothing so subject to the inconstancy of fortune as war. *Las cosas de la guerra más que otras, están sujetas a continua mudanza.*
Sir Francis Bacon "Of the True Greatness of Kingdoms and Estates" *Essays* 1625	Nay, number itself in armies importeth not much, where the people is of weak courage; for as Virgil saith, "It never troubles the wolf how many the sheep be."
Sir Francis Bacon "Of the True Greatness of Kingdoms and Estates" *Essays* 1625	He that commands the sea is at great liberty, and may take as much and as little of the war as he will.

No body can be healthful without exercise, neither natural body or politic; and certainly to a kingdom or estate, a just and honourable war is the true exercise.

Sir Francis Bacon
"Of the True Greatness of Kingdoms and Estates"
Essays
1625

A just fear of an imminent danger, though there be no blow given, is a lawful cause of war.

Sir Francis Bacon
"Of Empire"
Essays
1625

One sword keeps another in the sheath.

George Herbert
Jacula Prudentum
1651

The condition of man . . . is a condition of war of everyone against everyone.

Thomas Hobbes
Leviathan
1651

Peace hath her victories no less renowned than war.

John Milton
Sonnet 16
1652

Peace is not the mere absence of war, but a virtue based on strength of character.
Pax enim non belli privatio, sed virtus est quae ex animi fortitudine oritur.

Baruch (Benedictus de) Spinoza
Tractatus Politicus
1677

Just as with the soldier who does not carry his sword at all times is subject to mishaps, so too the Kingdom that is not always prepared has much to fear.
Comme il arrive beaucoup d'inconvénients au soldat qui ne porte pas toujours son epée, le Royaume qui n'est pas toujours sur ses gardes . . . à beaucoup a craindre.

Cardinal Richelieu
Political Testament
1687

From hence, let fierce contending nations know/ What dire effects from civil discord flow.

Joseph Addison
Cato
1713

Ever since the invention of gunpowder . . . I continually tremble lest men should, in the end, uncover some secret which would provide a short way of abolishing mankind, of annihilating peoples and nations in their entirety.

Charles Louis de Montesquieu
Les Lettres persanes
1721

Better a lean peace than a fat victory.

Thomas Fuller
Gnomologia
1732

They may ring their bells now, before long they will be wringing their hands.

Sir Robert Walpole 1st Earl of Orford
speech in the House of Commons on celebrations at outbreak of war with Spain
Oct 19, 1739

The possession of battle-ready troops, a well-filled state treasury and a lively disposition, these were the real reasons which moved me to war.

Frederick the Great
on the invasion of Silesia
A History of My Times
1741

Voltaire
Le Siècle de Louis XIV
1751

A victorious general has no faults in the eye of the public, while a defeated general is always wrong no matter how wise his conduct may have been.

Un général victorieux n'a point fait de fautes aux yeux du public, de même que le general battu a toujours tort, quelque sage conduit qu'il ait eue.

Samuel Johnson
The Idler
Nov 11, 1758

Among the calamities of war, may be justly numbered the diminution of the love of truth, by the falsehoods which interest dictates, and credulity encourages.

Voltaire
Candide
1759

In this country it is considered wise to kill an admiral from time to time in order to encourage the others.

Dans ce pays-ci il est bon de tuer de temps en temps un amiral pour encourager les autres.

Jean Jacques Rousseau
The Social Contract
1762

The right of conquest has no foundation other than the right of the strongest.

A l'égard du droit de conquête, il n'a d'autre fondement que la loi du plus fort.

Benjamin Franklin
letter to Josiah Quincy
Sep 11, 1773

There never was a good war or a bad peace.

Patrick Henry
speech to the Virginia
Convention
Mar 23, 1775

The battle, sir, is not to the strong alone; it is to the vigilant, the active, the brave.

Peter Muhlenberg
sermon in Woodstock,
Virginia
Jan, 1776

There is a time for all things, a time to preach and a time to pray, but those times have passed away. There is a time to fight, and that time has now come.

George Washington
general orders
Jul 6, 1777

Nothing can be more hurtful to the service, than the neglect of discipline; for that discipline, more than numbers, gives one army the superiority over another.

Thomas Paine
The American Crisis
Sep 12, 1777

It is not a field of a few acres of ground, but a cause, that we are defending, and whether we defeat the enemy in one battle, or by degrees, the consequences will be the same.

Thomas Paine
The American Crisis
Mar 21, 1778

It is the object only of war that makes it honorable. And if there was ever a just war since the world began, it is this in which America is now engaged.

Thomas Paine
The American Crisis
1776-83

He who is the author of a war lets loose the whole contagion of hell and opens a vein that bleeds a nation to death.

Thomas Paine
Prospects on the Rubicon
1787

War involves in its progress such a train of unforeseen and unsupposed circumstances that no human wisdom can calculate the end. It has but one thing certain, and that is to increase taxes.

George Washington
first annual address to
Congress
Jan 8, 1790

To be prepared for War is one of the most effectual means of preserving peace.

A free people ought not only to be armed, but disciplined; to which end a uniform and well-digested plan is requisite.

George Washington
fifth annual message
to Congress
Jan 8, 1790

Whatever enables us to go to war, secures our peace.

Thomas Jefferson
letter to James Monroe
Jul 11, 1790

War contains so much folly, as well as wickedness, that much is to be hoped from the progress of reason; and if any thing is to be hoped, every thing ought to be tried.

James Madison
"Universal Peace"
National Gazette
Feb 2, 1792

Each generation should be made to bear the burden of its own wars, instead of carrying them on, at the expense of other generations.

James Madison
National Gazette
Feb 2, 1792

To make war upon those who trade with us is like setting a bulldog upon a customer at the shop-door.

Thomas Paine
The Age of Reason
1794

Avoiding occasions of expense by cultivating peace, we should remember also that timely disbursements to prepare for danger frequently prevent much greater disbursements to repel it.

George Washington
Farewell Address to the People of the United States
Sep 19, 1796

I venture to say no war can be long carried on against the will of the people.

Edmund Burke
Letters on a Regicide Peace
1796-97

If they want peace, nations should avoid the pinpricks that precede cannon shots.

Napoleon I
reported conversation
with Czar Alexander I at
Tilsit
Jun 22, 1807

In war one sees one's own difficulties, and does not take into account those of the enemy; one must have confidence in oneself.

Napoleon I
letter to Eugene
Beauharnais
Apr 30, 1809

In times of peace the people look most to their representatives; but in war, to the executive solely.

Thomas Jefferson
letter to Caesar A.
Rodney
Feb 10, 1810

May the pens of the diplomats not ruin again what the people have attained with such exertions.

Gebhard Leberecht von Blücher
words following the Battle
of Waterloo
1813

If ever there was a holy war, it was that which saved our liberties and gave us independence.

Thomas Jefferson
letter to John Wayles
Eppes
Nov 6, 1813

Nothing except a battle lost can be half so melancholy as a battle won.

1st Duke of Wellington
dispatch from Waterloo
Jun, 1815

Thomas Jefferson letter to Noah Worchester Nov 26, 1817	My views and feelings (are) in favor of the abolition of war . . . and I hope it is practicable, by improving the mind and morals of society, to lessen the disposition to war; but of its abolition I despair.
Charles Caleb Colton *Lacön* 1825	War is a game in which princes seldom win, the people never.
Karl von Clausewitz *War, Politics and Power* 1962	War is the province of chance. In no other sphere of human activity must such a margin be left for this intruder. It increases the uncertainty of every circumstance and deranges the course of events.
Karl von Clausewitz *On War* 1832	War therefore is an act of violence intended to compel our opponents to fulfil our will.
Karl von Clausewitz *On War* 1833	War is regarded as nothing but the continuation of state policy with other means. *Der Krieg ist nichts anderes als die Fortsetzung der Politik mit anderen Mitteln.*
Andrew Jackson farewell address Mar 4, 1837	We shall more certainly preserve peace when it is well understood that we are prepared for war.
3rd Viscount Palmerston letter to Lord Granville of France Jun 10, 1839	A quarter of a century of peace does not pass over a nation in vain.
Joseph Joubert *Pensées* 1842	The sound of the drum drives out thought; for that very reason it is the most military of instruments.
Andrew Jackson letter to James A. Polk May 2, 1845	War is a blessing compared with national degradation.
Heinrich Heine "Zwei Ritter" *Romancero* 1851	Living, just as much as dying/ For one's fatherland, is sweet. *Leben bleiben, wie das Sterben/ Für das Vaterland ist süss.*
Lord John Russell speech in Greenock, Scotland Sep 19, 1853	If peace cannot be maintained with honor, it is no longer peace.
John Greenleaf Whittier "The Hero" 1853	Peace hath higher tests of manhood/ Than battle ever knew.
John Bright speech in the House of Commons Mar 31, 1854	If this phrase of the "balance of Power?" is to be always an argument for war, the pretence for war will never be wanting, and peace can never be secure.

It is magnificent, but it is not war.
C'est magnifique, mais ce n'est pas la guerre.

Pierre Bosquet
reported remark on the
charge of the Light Bri-
gade at the Battle of
Balaclava
Oct 25, 1854

A nation will not count the sacrifice it make, if it supposes it is engaged in a struggle for its fame, its influence and its existence.

Benjamin Disraeli
speech on "Prosecution
of the War"
May 24, 1855

Still a Union that can only be maintained by swords and bayonets, and in which strife and civil war are to take the place of brotherly love and kindness, has no charm for me.

Robert E. Lee
letter to his son, George
Washington Custis Lee
Jan 23, 1861

There are good points about all . . . wars. People forget self. The virtues of magnanimity, courage, patiotism, etc., are called into life. People are more generous, more sympathetic, better, than when engaged in the more selfish pursuits of peace.

Rutherford B. Hayes
letter to S. Birchard
May 8, 1861

It is well that war is so terrible—we should grow too fond of it.

Robert E. Lee
to James Longstreet
Dec 13, 1862

War is an ugly thing, but not the ugliest of things: the decayed and degraded state of moral and patriotic feeling which thinks nothing worth a war, is worse.

John Stuart Mill
"The Contest in America"
Fraser's Magazine
Feb, 1862

No terms except an unconditional and immediate surrender can be accepted. I propose to move immediately upon your works.

Ulysses S. Grant
mesage to General S.B.
Buckner, Fort Donelson
Feb 16, 1862

You cannot qualify war in harsher terms than I will. War is cruelty, and you cannot refine it.

**William Tecumseh
Sherman**
letter to James M. Cal-
houn, mayor of Atlanta
Jul 12, 1864

I propose to fight it out on this line, if it takes all summer.

Ulysses S. Grant
dispatch from Spotsylvania
Court House, Virginia
May 11, 1864

With malice toward none; with charity for all; with firmness in the right, as God gives us to see the right, let us strive on to finish the work we are in; to bind up the nation's wounds; to care for him who shall have borne the battle, and for his widow, and his orphan— to do all which may achieve and cherish a just, and a lasting peace, among ourselves, and with all nations.

Abraham Lincoln
second inaugural address
Mar 4, 1865

The legitimate object of war is a more perfect peace.

**William Tecumseh
Sherman**
speech in St. Louis,
Missouri
Jul 20, 1865

Herman Melville
"The March into Virginia"
*Battlepieces and Aspects of
the War*
1866

All wars are boyish, and are fought by boys.

Michael Bakunin
*Federalism, Socialism and
Anti-Theologism*
1868

Every State must conquer or be conquered.

August Bebel
speech to the Reichstag
Nov, 1870

In time of war the loudest patriots are the greatest profiteers.

**3rd Marquess of
Salisbury**
"The Terms of Peace"
Quarterly Review
Oct, 1870

The first object of a treaty of peace should be to make future war improbable.

**Prince Otto von
Bismarck**
quoted by Charles Lowe
Bismarck's Table Talk
1895

He who has once gazed into the glazed eye of a dying warrior on the field of battle will think twice before beginning a war.

Friedrich Nietzsche
Human, All Too Human
1878

Against war it may be said that it makes the victor stupid and the vanquished revengeful.
Zuungunsten des Krieges kann man sagen: er macht den Sieger dumm, den Besiegten boshaft.

**William Tecumseh
Sherman**
speech in Columbus, Ohio
Aug 11, 1880

There is many a boy here to-day who looks on war as all glory, but, boys, it is all hell.

Helmut von Moltke
letter
1880

A war, even the most victorious, is a national misfortune.

Friedrich Nietzsche
*The Wanderer and His
Shadow*
1880

Rendering oneself unarmed when one had been the best-armed, out of a height of feeling—that is the means to real peace, which must always rest on a peace of mind.
Sich wehrlos machen, während man der Wehrhafteste war, aus einer Höhe der Empfindung heraus, —das ist das Mittel zum wirklichen Frieden welcher immer auf einem Frieden der Gesinnung ruhen muss.

Chester Alan Arthur
first annual message to
Congress
Dec 6, 1881

If we heed the teachings of history we shall not forget that in the life every nation emergencies may arise when a resort to arms can alone save it from dishonor.

**Elizabeth Cady
Stanton**
*History of Woman
Suffrage*
1881

War is not the normal state of the human family in its higher development, but merely a feature of barbarism lasting on through the transition of the race, from the savage to the scholar.

The real war will never get into the books.

Walt Whitman
"The Real War"
Specimen Days
1882

If you have a nation of men who have risen to that height of moral cultivation that they will not declare war or carry arms, for they have not so much madness left in their brains, you have a nation of lovers, of benefactors, of true, great, and able men.

Ralph Waldo Emerson
"War"
Miscellanies
1884

War educates the senses, calls into action the will, perfects the physical constitution, brings men into such swift and close collision in critical moments that man measures man.

Ralph Waldo Emerson
"War"
Miscellanies
1884

The word state is identical with the word war.

Prince Peter Kropotkin
Paroles d'un révolté
1885

It is not merely cruelty that leads men to love war, it is excitement.

Henry Ward Beecher
Proverbs from Plymouth Pulpit
1887

Let us ever remember that our interest is in concord not in conflict, and that our real eminence as a nation lies in the victories of peace, not those of war.

William McKinley
speech in Washington, D.C.
1890

As long as war is regarded as wicked, it will always have its fascination. When it is looked upon as vulgar, it will cease to be popular.

Oscar Wilde
"Intentions"
The Critic as Artist
1891

We are not interested in the possibilities of defeat.

Victoria
letter to Arthur J. Balfour
Dec, 1899

The wars of the people will be more terrible than those of the kings.

Sir Winston S. Churchill
speech in the House of Commons
May 12, 1901

Without war no state could exist. All those we know of arose through war. . . . War, therefore, will endure to the end of history, as long as there is a multiplicity of states.

Heinrich von Treitschke
Politics
1897-1901

A good navy is not a provocative of war. It is the surest guaranty of peace.

Theodore Roosevelt
second annual message to Congress
Dec 2, 1902

Capitalism carries within itself war, as clouds carry rain.

Jean Jaurès
Studies in Socialism
1902

Generally peace tells for righteousness; but if there is conflict between the two, then our fealty is due first to the cause of righteousness.

Theodore Roosevelt
fourth annual message to Congress
Dec 6, 1904

Ambrose Bierce *The Devil's Dictionary* 1906	War, n. A by-product of the arts of peace.
George Santayana *The Life of Reason:* *Reason in Society* 1905-06	To call war the soil of courage and virtue is like calling debauchery the soil of love.
George Santayana *The Life of Reason:* *Reason in Society* 1905-06	To delight in war is a merit in the soldier, a dangerous quality in the captain and a positive crime in the statesman.
Ambrose Bierce *The Devil's Dictionary* 1906	Battle, n. A method of untying with the teeth a political knot that would not yield to the tongue.
Theodore Roosevelt speech at Harvard Univ. Feb 23, 1907	A really great people, proud and high-spirited, would face all the disasters of war rather than purchase that base prosperity which is bought at the price of national honor.
David Lloyd George speech in Manchester, England Apr 21, 1908	The day will come when a nation that lifts up the sword against a nation will be put in the same felon category as the man who strikes his brother in anger.
Thomas Hardy *The Dynasts* 1904-08	War makes rattling good history; but Peace is poor reading.
William Howard Taft inaugural address Mar 4, 1909	A modern navy can not be improvised. It must be built and in existence when the emergency arises.
Theodore Roosevelt speech at the Univ. of Paris Apr 23, 1910	War is a dreadful thing, and unjust war is a crime against humanity. But it is such a crime because it is unjust, not because it is war.
Woodrow Wilson speech in Denver, Colorado May 7, 1911	No man can sit down and withhold his hands from the warfare against wrong and get peace from his acquiescence.
Theodore Roosevelt letter to Henry L. Stoddard Jul, 1912	You cannot fight hard unless you think you are fighting to win.
Karl Liebknecht speech at outbreak of World War I 1914	The main enemy is at home (is in our own camp). *Der Feind steht im eigenen Lager.*
Theodore Roosevelt *The New York Times* Nov 22, 1914	The navy of the United States is the right arm of the United States and is emphatically the peacemaker.
Romain Rolland "Inter arma caritas" *Journal de Genève* Oct 30, 1914	I find war detestable but those who praise it without participating in it even more so.

ı am proud of the fact that I never invented weapons to kill.

Thomas Alva Edison
The New York Times
Jun 8, 1915

There is a price which is too great to pay for peace, and that price can be put in one word. One cannot pay the price of self-respect.

Woodrow Wilson
speech in Des Moines, Iowa
Feb 1, 1916

The belief that public opinion or international public opinion, unbacked by force, had the slightest effect in restraining a powerful military nation in any course of action . . . has been shown to be a pathetic fallacy.

Theodore Roosevelt
Metropolitan
Feb, 1916

Only a peace between equals can last. Only a peace the very principle of which is equality and a common participation in a common benefit.

Woodrow Wilson
speech to the U.S. Senate
Jan 22, 1917

I want to stand by my country, but I cannot vote for war. I vote no.

Jeanette Rankin
casting her vote against declaration of war
Apr 6, 1917

All wars are wars among thieves who are too cowardly to fight and who therefore induce the young manhood of the whole world to do the fighting for them.

Emma Goldman
"Address to the Jury"
Mother Earth
Jul, 1917

The government will . . . go on in the highly democratic method of conscripting American manhood for European slaughter.

Emma Goldman
"Address to the Jury"
Mother Earth
Jul, 1917

The right is more precious than peace.

Woodrow Wilson
speech to Congress
Apr 2, 1917

This may be safely turned down. No sane enemy, acquainted with our institutions, would destroy the War Office.

Sir George Murray
comment on a World War I defence memo, quoted by Austen Chamberlain
Down the Years
1935

War is much too serious a matter to be left to generals.
La guerre est une chose beaucoup trop sérieuse pour être confiée à des généraux.

Georges Clemenceau
quoted
New York Times
Jul 14, 1944

My home policy? I wage war. My foreign policy? I wage war. Always, everywhere, I wage war.

Georges Clemenceau
speech to the Chamber of Deputies
Mar 8, 1918

It is far easier to make war than to make peace.

Georges Clemenceau
speech at Verdun, France
Jul 14, 1919

Injustice, arrogance, displayed in the hour of triumph will never be forgotten or forgiven.

David Lloyd George
memorandum written during the Paris peace conference
1919

A. Philip Randolph
"The Cause and Remedy
of Race Riots"
The Messenger
1919

Make wars unprofitable and you make them impossible.

Rosa Luxemburg
*The Crisis in the German
Social Democracy*
1919

Victory or defeat? It is the slogan of all-powerful militarism in every belligerent nation. . . . And yet, what can victory bring to the proletariat?

Woodrow Wilson
speech to veterans in St.
Louis, Missouri
Sep 5, 1919

Is there any man . . . who does not know that the seed of war in the modern world is industrial and commercial rivalry?

H.G. Wells
The Outline of History
1920

We want to get rid of the militarist not simply because he hurts and kills, but because he is an intolerable thick-voiced blockhead who stands hectoring and blustering in our way to achievement.

Warren G. Harding
address to the International Armaments Conference in Washington, D.C.
Feb 6, 1922

I once believed in armed preparedness. I advocated it. But I have come now to believe there is a better preparedness in a public mind and a world opinion made ready to grant justice precisely as it exacts it. And justice is better served in conferences of peace than in conflicts at arms.

A. Philip Randolph
The Truth About Lynching
ca. 1922

Violence seldom accomplishes permanent and desired results. Herein lies the futility of war.

Calvin Coolidge
radio broadcast
Dec 10, 1923

The only true and lasting peace (is) based on justice and right.

Calvin Coolidge
speech in Baltimore,
Maryland
Sep 6, 1924

Peace must have other guarantees than constitutions and covenants.Laws and treaties may help, but peace and war are attitudes of mind.

Adolf Hitler
Mein Kampf
1924

Mankind has grown strong in eternal struggles and it will only perish through eternal peace.
Im ewigen Kämpfe ist die Menschheit gross geworden—im ewigen Frieden geht sie zugrunde.

Calvin Coolidge
speech in Annapolis,
Maryland
Jun 3, 1925

If we are to promote peace on earth, we must have a great deal more than the power of the sword. We must call into action the spiritual and moral forces of mankind.

Adolf Hitler
speech in Kulmbach,
Germany
Feb, 1928

Struggle is the father of all things. . . . It is not by the principles of humanity that man lives or is able to preserve himself above the animal world but solely by means of the most brutal struggle.

Bertrand Russell
"Some Prospects: Cheerful and Otherwise"
Skeptical Essays
1928

Those who in principle oppose birth control are either incapable of arithmetic or else in favour of war, pestilence and famine as permanent features of human life.

War is not the continuation of policy. It is the breakdown of policy.

Hans von Seeckt
Thoughts of a Soldier
1929

Who would prefer peace to the glory of hunger and thirst, of wading through mud, and dying in the service of one's country?

Jean Giraudoux
Amphitryon 38
1929

The enemy advances, we retreat; the enemy camps, we harass; the enemy tires, we attack; the enemy retreats, we pursue.

Mao Tse-tung
letter
Jan 5, 1930

No soldier starts a war—they only give their lives to it. Wars are started by you and me, by bankers and politicians, excitable women, newspaper editors, clergymen who are ex-pacifists, and Congressmen with vertebrae of putty. The youngsters yelling in the streets, poor kids, are the ones who pay the price.

Father Francis P. Duffy
sermon, Marshall Joffre memorial service, New York City
Jan, 1931

There could be real peace only if everyone were satisfied. That means there is not often a real peace. There are only actual states of peace which, like wars, are mere expedients.
Il n'y aurait de paix véritable que si tout le monde était satisfait. C'est dire qu'il n'y a pas souvent de paix véritable. Il n'y a que des paix réelles, qui ne sont comme les guerres que les expédients.

Paul Valéry
"Greatness and Decadence of Europe"
Reflections on the World Today
1931

The only treaties that ought to count are those which would effect a settlement between ulterior motives.
Les seuls traités qui compteraient sont ceux qui conclueraient entre les arrière-pensées.

Paul Valéry
"Greatness and Decadence of Europe"
Reflections on the World Today
1931

Everyone knows that war can no longer be considered, even by the coldest calculator or the strongest nation, as a means of attaining, with any reasonable probability, a determined objective.
Tout le monde, par exemple, sait bien que la guerre ne peut plus être considérée, même par le calculateur le plus froid et par la nation la plus puissante, comme un moyen d'atteindre, avec une probabilité suffisante, un but determiné.

Paul Valéry
preface to a book by Mariano H. Carnejo
La Lutte pour la paix
Oct, 1933

Wars may be fought with weapons, but they are won by men. It is the spirit of the men who follow and of the man who leads that gains the victory.

George S. Patton
Cavalry Journal
Sep, 1933

Peace is indivisible.

Maxim Litvinov
speech to the League of Nations
1934

Everyone, when there's war in the air, learns to live in a new element: falsehood.

Jean Giraudoux
Tiger at the Gates
1935

During war we imprison the rights of man.

Jean Giraudoux
Tiger at the Gates
1935

Once blood is shed in a national quarrel reason and right are swept aside by the rage of angry men.

David Lloyd George
War Memoirs
1933–36

Joseph Goebbels speech in Berlin Jan 17, 1936	We can do without butter, but . . . not without guns. One cannot shoot with butter, but with guns.
Joseph Goebbels radio broadcast 1936	Guns will make us powerful; butter will only make us fat.
José Ortega y Gasset "En cuanto al pacifismo" 1937	War is not an instinct but an invention. *La guerra no es un instinto, sino un invento.*
Aldous Huxley *The Olive Tree* 1937	The most shocking fact about war is that its victims and its instruments are individual human beings, and that these individual beings are condemned by the monstrous conventions of politics to murder or be murdered in quarrels not their own.
Neville Chamberlain on his return from the Munich Conference Sep 30, 1938	This is the second time that there has come back from Germany to Downing Street peace with honour. I believe it is peace for our time.
Neville Chamberlian radio broadcast about Hitler's threatened invasion of Czechoslovakia Sep 27, 1938	How horrible, fantastic, incredible it is that we should be digging trenches and trying on gas-masks here because of a quarrel in a faraway country between people of whom we know nothing.
Sir Winston S. **Churchill** speech in the House of Commons on the Munich agreement Sep, 1938	England has been offered a choice between war and shame. She has chosen shame and will get war.
Sir Winston S. **Churchill** speech in the House of Commons on the Munich agreement Oct 5, 1938	All is over. Silent, mournful, abandoned, broken, Czechoslovakia recedes into darkness. . . . We have sustained a defeat without a war.
Mao Tse-tung "On Protracted War" May, 1938	History shows that wars are divided into two kinds, just and unjust. All wars that are progressive are just, and all wars that impede progress are unjust.
Mao Tse-tung "Problems of War and Strategy" Nov 6, 1938	War can be abolished only through war, and in order to get rid of the gun it is necessary to take up the gun.
Mao Tse-tung "Problems of War and Strategy" Nov 6, 1938	Weapons are an important factor in war, but not the decisive one; it is man and not materials that counts.

I tell you there's nothing to stop war from going on forever. . . . A slight case of negligence, and it's bogged down up to the axles. And then it's a matter of hauling the war out of the mud again. But emperor and kings and popes will come to its rescue.

Ich sag: dass der Krieg einmal aufhort, ist nicht gesagt. . . . Vielleicht ein Ubersehn, und das Schlamassel ist da. Und dann kann man den Krieg wieder aus dem Dreck ziehn! Aber die Kaiser und Konige und der Papst wird ihm zu Hilf kommen in seiner Not.

Bertolt Brecht
Mother Courage
1939

I hear the same talk about "sanctity of treaties," "law and order," "resisting agression" and "enforcement of morality." Such phrases have always been the stock in trade of those who have vested interests which they want to preserve against those in revolt against a rigid system.

John Foster Dulles
speech opposing U.S. entry into World War II, Detroit, Michigan
Oct 29, 1939

Victory at all costs, victory in spite of all terror, victory however long and hard the road may be; for without victory there is no survival.

Sir Winston S. Churchill
speech in the House of Commons
May 13, 1940

Never in the field of human conflict was so much owed by so many to so few.

Sir Winston S. Churchill
speech in the House of Commons on role of the R.A.F. during Battle of Britain
Aug 20, 1940

You ask, what is our policy? I will say, it is to wage war by sea, land, and air, with all our might and with all the strength that God can give us.

Sir Winston S. Churchill
speech in the House of Commons
May 13, 1940

We shall not flag or fail. We shall go on to the end. We shall fight in France, we shall fight on the seas and oceans, we shall fight with growing confidence and growing strength in the air, we shall defend our island, whatever the cost may be, we shall fight on the beaches, we shall fight on the landing grounds, we shall fight in the fields and in the streets, we shall fight in the hills; we shall never surrender.

Sir Winston S. Churchill
speech in the House of Commons following the Dunkirk evacuation
Jun 4, 1940

We cannot accept the doctrine that war must be forever a part of man's destiny.

Franklin D. Roosevelt
campaign speech in Cleveland, Ohio
Nov 2, 1940

War challenges virtually every other institution of society— the justice and equity of its economy, the adequacy of its political systems, the energy of its productive plant, the bases, wisdom and purposes of its foreign policy.

Walter Millis
The Faith of an American
1941

In the Soviet Army it takes more courage to retreat than to advance.

Joseph Stalin
reported conversation with Averell Harriman
Sep, 1941

Henry Miller
"The Alcoholic Veteran
with the Washboard
Cranium"
The Wisdom of the Heart
1941

We kill because we're afraid of our own shadow, afraid that if we used a little common sense we'd have to admit that our glorious principles were wrong.

**Sir Winston S.
Churchill**
speech in the House of
Commons
Nov 11, 1942

The problems of victory are more agreeable than those of defeat, but they are no less difficult.

Aneurin Bevan
debate in the House of
Commons
Jul 2, 1942

The Prime Minister wins debate after debate and loses battle after battle. The country is beginning to say that he fights debates like a war and a war like a debate.

**Sir Winston S.
Churchill**
speech in the House of
Commons
Jul 2, 1942

There is no working middle course in wartime.

**Antoine de Saint-
Exupéry**
Pilote de guerre
1942

War is not an adventure. It is a disease. It is like typhus.
La guerre n'est pas une aventure. La guerre est une maladie. Comme le typhus.

Albert Camus
Cahiers, 1935–1942
1962

We used to wonder where war lived, what it was that made it so vile. And now we realize that we know where it lives, that it is inside ourselves.

Charles Péguy
"The Rights of Man"
Basic Verities
1943

It is better to have a war for justice than peace in injustice.

Herbert Hoover
speech to the Republican
national convention in
Chicago, Illinois
Jun 27, 1944

Older men declare war. But it is youth that must fight and die. And it is youth who must inherit the tribulation, the sorrow, and the triumphs that are the aftermath of war.

Franklin D. Roosevelt
speech at the Foreign
Policy Association, New
York City
Oct 21, 1944

Peace, like war, can succeed only where there is a will to enforce it, and where there is available power to enforce it.

**Sir Winston S.
Churchill**
remarks to General Ismay
on V-E day
May 7, 1945

The eagle has ceased to scream, but the parrots will now begin to chatter. The war of the giants is over and the pigmies will now start to squabble.

Dwight D. Eisenhower
speech in Frankfurt,
Germany
Jun 10, 1945

We are going to have peace even if we have to fight for it.

As long as there are sovereign nations possessing great power, war is inevitable.

Albert Einstein
"Einstein on the Atomic Bomb"
Atlantic Monthly
Nov, 1945

If man does find the solution for world peace it will be the most revolutionary reversal of his record we have ever known.

George C. Marshall
Biennial Report of the Chief of Staff, United States Army
Sep 1, 1945

We live under a system by which the many are exploited by the few, and war is the ultimate sanction of that exploitation.

Harold Joseph Laski
Plan or Perish
1945

Since wars begin in the minds of men, it is in the minds of men that the defences of peace must be constructed.

UNESCO
Constitution
1946

I hate war as only a soldier who has lived it can, only as one who has seen its brutality, its futility, its stupidity. Yet there is one thing to say on its credit side—victory required a mighty manifestation of the most ennobling of the virtues of man— faith, courage, fortitude, sacrifice!

Dwight D. Eisenhower
speech in Ottawa, Canada
Jan 10, 1946

I have never met anybody who wasn't against war. Even Hitler and Mussolini were, according to themselves.

David Low
The New York Times
Feb 10, 1946

Wars occur because people prepare for conflict, rather than for peace.

Trygve Lie
Labor
Sep 6, 1947

I do not approve the extermination of the enemy; the policy of exterminating or, as it is barbarously said, liquidating enemies, is one of the most alarming developments of modern war and peace, from the point of view of those who desire the survival of culture. One needs the enemy.

T.S. Eliot
Notes Towards the Defir tion of Culture
1948

In War: Resolution. In Defeat: Defiance. In Victory:Magnanimity. In Peace: Good Will.

Sir Winston S. Churchill
The Second World War
1948

Morality is contraband in war.

Mohandas K. Gandhi
Non-Violence in Peace and War
1948

What difference does it make to the dead, the orphans and the homeless, whether the mad destruction is wrought under the name of totalitarianism or the holy name of liberty or democracy?

Mohandas K. Gandhi
Non-Violence in Peace and War
1948

War is an unmitigated evil. But it certainly does one good thing. It drives away fear and brings bravery to the surface.

Mohandas K. Gandhi
Non-Violence in Peace and War
1948

Sir Winston S. Churchill
The Second World War
1949

No one can guarantee success in war, but only deserve it.

I.F. Stone
quoted
The Truman Era
Jan 24, 1949

We Smiths want peace so bad we're prepared to kill every one of the Joneses to get it.

Max Lerner
"On Peacetime Military Training"
Actions and Passions
1949

The way to prevent war is to bend every energy toward preventing it, not to proceed by the dubious indirection of preparing for it.

Will Rogers
The Autobiography of Will Rogers
1949

Diplomats are just as essential to starting a war as Soldiers are for finishing it. You take Diplomacy out of war and the thing would fall flat in a week.

Dwight D. Eisenhower
speech at Columbia Univ.
Mar 23, 1950

Peace is more the product of our day-to-day living than of a spectacular program, intermittently executed.

Dwight D. Eisenhower
speech at Columbia Univ.
Mar 23, 1950

The pact of Munich was a greater blow to humanity than the atomic bomb at Hiroshima.

Omar N. Bradley
Military Review
Feb, 1950

In war there is no second prize for the runner-up.

Bertrand Russell
"Ideas That Have Harmed Mankind"
Unpopular Essays
1950

People who are vigorous and brutal often find war enjoyable, provided that it is a victorious war and that there is not too much interference with rape and plunder. This is a great help in persuading people that wars are righteous.

George Orwell
"Second Thoughts on James Burnham"
Shooting an Elephant
1950

The quickest way of ending a war is to lose it.

Douglas MacArthur
address to Congress
Apr 19, 1951

In war there is no substitute for victory.

Sir Winston S. Churchill
radio address
Oct 8, 1951

I do not hold that we should rearm in order to fight. I hold that we should rearm in order to parley.

Dwight D. Eisenhower
statement on learning that Pres. Truman had fired Gen. Douglas MacArthur
April 11, 1951

When you put on a uniform, there are certain inhibitions that you accept.

Eleanor Roosevelt
radio broadcast on the Voice of America
Nov 11, 1951

For it isn't enough to talk about peace. One must believe in it. And it isn't enough to believe in it. One must work at it.

After each war there is a little less democracy to save.

Brooks Atkinson
"January 7"
Once Around the Sun
1951

War is both the product of an earlier corruption and a producer of new corruptions.

Lewis Mumford
"The Challenge to Renewal"
The Conduct of Life
1951

To my mind, to kill in war is not a whit better than to commit ordinary murder.

Albert Einstein
speech in Tokyo
1952

The field of combat was a long, narrow, green-baize covered table. The weapons were words.

Adm. C. Turner Joy
commenting on truce talks with North Korea
The New York Times
Dec 31, 1952

I hate war. War destroys individuals and whole generations. It throws civilization into the dark ages. But there is only one kind of war the American people have any stomach for and that is a war against hunger and pestilence and disease.

Harry S Truman
quoted by William Hillman
Mr. President
1952

It is fatal to enter any war without the will to win it.

Douglas MacArthur
speech to the Republican National Convention
Jul 7, 1952

War is an invention of the human mind. The human mind can invent peace with justice.

Norman Cousins
Who Speaks for Man?
1953

In the final choice a soldier's pack is not so heavy a burden as a prisoner's chains.

Dwight D. Eisenhower
first inaugural address
Jan 20, 1953

History does not long entrust the care of freedom to the weak or the timid. We must acquire proficiency in defense and display stamina in purpose.

Dwight D. Eisenhower
first inaugural address
Jan 20, 1953

Every gun that is fired, every warship launched, every rocket fired signifies, in the final sense, a theft from those who hunger and are not fed, those who are cold and are not clothed. The world in arms is not spending money alone. It is spending the sweat of its labourers, the genius of its scientists, the hopes of its children.

Dwight D. Eisenhower
speech to the American Society of Newspaper Editors
Apr 16, 1953

If any foreign minister begins to defend to the death a "peace conference," you can be sure his government has already placed its orders for new battleships and airplanes.

Joseph Stalin
recalled on his death
Mar 5, 1953

The hand that signed the treaty bred a fever,/ And famine grew, and locusts came;/ Great is the hand that holds dominion over/ Man by scribbled name.

Dylan Thomas
"The Hand That Signed the Paper"
Collected Poems
1953

Sir Winston S. Churchill *The New York Times* Jun 27, 1954	To jaw-jaw always is better than to war-war.
Sir Winston S. Churchill 80th birthday address to Parliament Nov 30, 1954	I have never accepted what many people have kindly said—namely that I inspired the nation. Their will was resolute and remorseless, and as it proved, unconquerable. It fell to me to express it. It was the nation and the race dwelling all round the globe that had the lion's heart. I had the luck to be called upon to give the roar. I also hope that I sometimes suggested to the lion the right place to use his claws.
Jawaharlal Nehru *London Observer* Aug 29, 1954	The only alternative to coexistence is codestruction.
Dwight D. Eisenhower reported remarks Mar 17, 1954	The most terrible warfare is to be a second lieutenant leading a platoon when you are on the battlefield.
Charles De Gaulle *Mémoires de guerre: L'Appel* 1955	The war has started incredibly badly. Therefore, it must be continued. *La guerre commence infiniment mal. Il faut donc qu'elle continue.*
Capt. Robert Lewis comments on 10th anniversary of first nuclear bomb *Enola Gay* May 19, 1955	As the bomb fell over Hiroshima and exploded, we saw an entire city disappear. I wrote in my log the words: "My God, what have we done?"
Dwight D. Eisenhower letter to Everett E. Hazlett Aug 20, 1956	Some day there is going to be a man sitting in my present chair who has not been raised in the military services and who will have little understanding of where slashes in their estimates can be made with little or no damage. If that should happen while we still have the state of tension that now exists in the world, I shudder to think of what could happen in this country.
John Foster Dulles *Life* Jan 11, 1956	You have to take chances for peace, just as you must take chances in war. Some say that we were brought to the verge of war. The ability to get to the verge of war without getting into the war is the necessary art.
Harry S Truman *Memoirs* 1955-56	Warfare, no matter what weapons it employs, is a means to an end, and if that end can be achieved by negotiated settlements of conditional surrender, there is no need for war.
Gen. Nathan F. Twining *The New York Times* Mar 31, 1956	If our air forces are never used, they have achieved their finest goal.
Eleanor Roosevelt letter to Gus Ranis Jan 23, 1956	Mr. Dulles has just frightened most of our allies to death with a statement that there is an art in actually threatening war and coming to the brink but retreating from the brink.

I have always been opposed even to the thought of fighting a "preventive war." There is nothing more foolish than to think that war can be stopped by war. You don't "prevent" anything by war except peace.

Harry S Truman
Memoirs
1955-56

If you live among dogs, keep a stick. After all, this is what a hound has teeth for—to bite when he feels like it!

Nikita S. Khrushchev
interview in Japanese
newspaper
Jul 9, 1957

The more bombers, the less room for doves of peace.

Nikita S. Khrushchev
speech on Moscow radio
Mar 14, 1958

It is far more important to be able to hit the target than it is to haggle over who makes a weapon or who pulls a trigger.

Dwight D. Eisenhower
on unification of the three
military services
Apr 17, 1958

A general and a bit of shooting makes you forget your troubles . . . it takes your mind off the cost of living.

Brendan Behan
The Hostage
1958

A government needs one hundred soldiers for every guerrilla it faces.

Fulgencio Batista
telephone interview
El Caribe
Jan 1, 1959

I like to believe that people, in the long run, are going to do more to promote peace than our governments. Indeed, I think that people want peace so much that one of these days governments had better get out of the way and let them have it.

Dwight D. Eisenhower
radio and television broadcast, London, England
Aug 31, 1959

The new and terrible dangers which man has created can only be controlled by man.

John F. Kennedy
speech at the Univ. of
California
Nov 2, 1959

Youth is the first victim of war; the first fruit of peace. It takes twenty years or more of peace to make a man; it takes only twenty seconds of war to destroy him.

Baudouin I
address to joint session of
U.S. Congress
May 12, 1959

It is an unfortunate fact that we can secure peace only by preparing for war.

John F. Kennedy
campaign speech in
Seattle, Washington
Sep 6, 1960

The major deterrent (to war) is in a man's mind.

Adm. Arleigh Burke
US News & World Report
Oct 3, 1960

It would indeed be the ultimate tragedy if the history of the human race proved to be nothing more noble than the story of an ape playing with a box of matches on a petrol dump.

David Ormsby-Gore
Christian Science Monitor
Oct 25, 1960

In the councils of government, we must guard against the acquisition of unwarranted influence, whether sought or unsought, by the military-industrial complex. The potential for the disastrous rise of misplaced power exists and will persist.

Dwight D. Eisenhower
farewell address
Jan 17, 1961

John F. Kennedy speech to the United Nations General Assembly Sep 25, 1961	Let us call a truce to terror. Let us invoke the blessings of peace. And, as we build an international capacity to keep peace, let us join in dismantling the national capacity to wage war.
John F. Kennedy speech at the Univ. of North Carolina Oct 12, 1961	Peace and freedom do not come cheap, and we are destined— all of us here today—to live out most if not all of our lives in uncertainty and challenge and peril.
John F. Kennedy speech to the United Nations General Assembly Sep 25, 1961	Unconditional war can no longer lead to unconditional victory. . . . Mankind must put an end to war or war will put an end to mankind.
John F. Kennedy televised speech Jul 25, 1961	I hear it said that West Berlin is militarily untenable—and so was Bastogne, and so, in fact, was Stalingrad. Any danger spot is tenable if men—brave men—will make it so.
Anthony Eden *Facing the Dictators* 1962	There were two kinds of sanctions, effective and ineffective. To apply the latter was provocative and useless. If we were to apply the former, we ran the risk of war, and it would be dangerous to shut our eyes to the fact.
Douglas MacArthur speech at the U.S. Military Academy, West Point, New York May 12, 1962	The soldier, above all other people, prays for peace, for he must suffer and bear the deepest wounds and scars of war.
John F. Kennedy State of the Union message Jan 11, 1962	Arms alone are not enough to keep peace. It must be kept by men.
John F. Kennedy televised speech Oct 22, 1962	Aggressive conduct, if allowed to go unchecked and unchallenged, ultimately leads to war.
Charles De Gaulle *Time* Jul 12, 1963	Treaties are like roses and young girls. They last while they last.
John F. Kennedy commencement address at the American Univ. Jun 10, 1963	World peace, like community peace, does not require that each man love his neighbor—it requires only that they live together with mutual tolerance, submitting their disputes to a just and peaceful settlement.
Lyndon Baines Johnson speech to Congress Nov 27, 1963	In this age when there can be no losers in peace and no victors in war—we must recognize the obligation to match national strength with national restraint.
John F. Kennedy State of the Union address Jan 14, 1963	The mere absence of war is not peace.
John F. Kennedy speech to the United Nations General Assembly Sep 20, 1963	Peace is a daily, a weekly, a monthly process, gradually changing opinions, slowly eroding old barriers, quietly building new structures.

That's the way it is in war. You win or lose, live or die—and the difference is just an eyelash.

Douglas MacArthur
Reminiscences
1964

We are not about to send American boys nine or ten thousand miles away from home to do what Asian boys ought to be doing for themselves.

Lyndon Baines Johnson
televised speech
Oct 21, 1964

This is not a jungle war, but a struggle for freedom on every front of human activity.

Lyndon Baines Johnson
televised speech on the war in Vietnam
Aug 4, 1964

They call upon us to supply American boys to do the job that Asian boys should do.

Lyndon Baines Johnson
reported remarks
Aug 12, 1964

To insist on strength . . . is not war-mongering. It is peace-mongering.

Barry Goldwater
The New York Times
Aug 11, 1964

I was in the Victoria Library in Toronto in 1915, studying a Latin poet, and all of a sudden I thought, "War can't be this bad." So I walked out and enlisted.

Lester B. Pearson
quoted by Robinson Deal
The Pearson Phenomenon
1964

We did not choose to be the guardians of the gate, but there is no one else.

Lyndon Baines Johnson
televised speech
Jul 28, 1964

Could I have but a line a century hence crediting a contribution to the advance of peace, I would yield every honor which has been accorded by war.

Douglas MacArthur
recalled on his death
Apr 5, 1964

War is a poor chisel to carve out tomorrows.

Martin Luther King Jr.
television documentary
Dec, 1965

To tell you the truth, I thought of all the damned paperwork this was going to mean in the morning.

Gen. Walter Bedell Smith
on signing the armistice that ended World War II in Europe
The New York Times
May 8, 1965

Past experience provides little basis for confidence that reason can prevail in an atmosphere of mounting war fever. In a contest between a hawk and a dove the hawk has a great advantage, not because it is a better bird, but because it is a bigger bird with lethal talons and a highly developed will to use them.

J. William Fulbright
speech in the U.S. Senate
Apr 21, 1966

A riot is a spontaneous outburst. A war is subject to advance planning.

Richard M. Nixon
speech in New York City
Dec 8, 1967

Herbert Block
"Herblock"
Herblock Gallery
1968

This is particularly true of those bellicose Republican "conservatives" and Dixiecrats who are more ready to lay down lives than prejudices and who can hear the most distant drum more clearly than the cry of a hungry child in the street.

Will Durant
The Lessons of History
1968

Peace is an unstable equilibrium, which can be preserved only by acknowledged supremacy or equal power.

Dwight D. Eisenhower
news conference in Indio,
California
Mar 15, 1968

I say when you get into a war, you should win as quick as you can, because your losses become a function of the duration of the war. I believe when you get in a war, get everything you need and win it.

Robert McNamara
on the utility of nuclear
weapons
The Essence of Security
1968

One cannot fashion a credible deterrent out of an incredible action.

Lyndon Baines
Johnson
quoted
Time
Apr 15, 1985

I don't know what it will take out there—500 casualties maybe, maybe 500,000. It's the aughts that scare me.

Norman Thomas
recalled on his death
Dec 19, 1968

(President John F.) Kennedy said that if we had nuclear war we'd kill 300 million people in the first hour. (Secretary of Defense Robert) McNamara, who is a good businessman and likes to save, says it would be only 200 million.

Lyndon Baines
Johnson
quoted
Time
Apr 15, 1985

It is always a strain when people are being killed. I don't think anybody has held this job who hasn't felt personally responsible for those being killed.

Charles De Gaulle
quoted
The New York Times
Magazine
May 12, 1968

No country without an atom bomb could properly consider itself independent.

Richard M. Nixon
televised speech
Nov 3, 1969

North Vietnam cannot defeat or humiliate the United States. Only Americans can do that.

Richard M. Nixon
first inaugural address
Jan 20, 1969

The greatest honor history can bestow is the title of peacemaker. This honor now beckons America. . . . This is our summons to greatness.

Golda Meir
Life
Oct 3, 1969

We have always said that in our war with the Arabs we had a secret weapon—no alternative.

Gamal Abdel Nasser
speech to the National
Assembly
Jan 20, 1969

People do not want words—they want the sound of battle . . . the battle of destiny.

We don't thrive on military acts. We do them because we have to, and thank God we are efficient.

Golda Meir
Vogue
Jul, 1969

You will kill 10 of our men, and we will kill 1 of yours, and in the end it will be you who tire of it.

Ho Chi Minh
recalled on his death
Sep 3, 1969

It is not enough just to be for peace. The point is, what can we do about it?

Richard M. Nixon
interview with C.L.
Sulzberger
The New York Times
Mar 10, 1971

That was the order of the day.

William L. Calley Jr.
on killing Vietnamese civilians at My Lai in 1968
Feb 23, 1971

They were all enemy. They were all to be destroyed.

William L. Calley Jr.
on killing Vietnamese civilians at My Lai in 1968
Feb 23, 1971

If there is any one lesson to be plainly derived from the experiences we have had with disarmament in the past half-century, it is that armaments are a function and not a cause of political tensions and that no limitation of armaments on a multilateral scale can be effected as long as the political problems are not tackled and regulated in some realistic way.

George F. Kennan
Memoirs
1972

The sergeant is the Army.

Dwight D. Eisenhower
The New York Times
Dec 24, 1972

Not war but peace is the father of all things.
Nicht der Krieg, der Friede ist der Vater aller Dinge.

Willy Brandt
Über den Tag hinaus
1974

If the Third World War is fought with nuclear weapons, the fourth will be fought with bows and arrows.

Lord Louis Mountbatten
Maclean's
Nov 17, 1975

I don't think the contradictions between capitalism and socialism can be resolved by war. This is no longer the age of the bow and arrow. It's the nuclear age, and war can annihilate us all. The only way to achieve solutions seems to be for the different social systems to coexist.

Fidel Castro
Seven Days
Jun 20, 1977

A war regarded as inevitable or even probable, and therefore much prepared for, has a very good chance of eventually being fought.

George F. Kennan
The Cloud of Danger
1977

The superpowers have the privilege of being able to destroy our planet several times in rapid succession, and yet there are still those who try to score political points by declaring that one or other of them is lagging dangerously behind the other in potential for obliteration.

Peter Ustinov
Dear Me
1977

Muhammad Anwar El-Sadat speech in Cairo Mar 8, 1978	Peace is much more precious than a piece of land.
Ronald Reagan *The Observer* Jun 29, 1980	Of the four wars in my lifetime, none came about because the U.S. was too strong.
Kenneth Kaunda *Kaunda on Violence* 1980	Passive resistance is a sport for gentlemen (and ladies)—just like the pursuit of war, a heroic enterprise for the ruling classes but a grievous burden on the rest.
Kenneth Kaunda "On the State of South Africa" *Kaunda on Violence* 1980	The drama can only be brought to its climax in one of two ways—through the selective brutality of terrorism or the impartial horrors of war.
Kenneth Kaunda *Kaunda on Violence* 1980	War is just like bush-clearing—the moment you stop, the jungle comes back even thicker, but for a little while you can plant and grow a crop in the ground you have won at such a terrible cost.
Jimmy Carter televised address to the nation on the invasion of Afghanistan by the USSR Jan 4, 1980	Aggression unopposed becomes a contagious disease.
Max Cleland speech at the dedication of Vietnam Veterans Mem-orial, Washington D.C. *Time* Nov 22, 1982	Within the soul of each Vietnam veteran there is probably something that says "Bad war, good soldier." (It is time to) separate the war from the warrior.
Ernest F. Hollings on U.S. Marines in Lebanon *Time* Dec 26, 1983	If they've been put there to fight, there are far too few. If they've been put there to be killed, there are far too many.
Ronald Reagan speech to the United Nations General Assembly Sep 26, 1983	The awful truth is that the use of violence for political gain has become more, not less widespread in the last decade.
Ronald Reagan referring to veterans of the Vietnam War, at a press conference Nov 11, 1984	Some of your countrymen were unable to distinguish between their native dislike for war and the stainless patriotism of those who suffered its scars. But there has been a rethinking (and) now we can say to you, and say as a nation, thank you for your courage.
Ronald Reagan on the Unknown Soldier of the Vietnam War May 25, 1984	We pray for the wisdom that this hero be America's last unkown.
Gen. John W. Vessey Jr. *The New York Times* Jul 15, 1984	(My job is) to give the president and secretary of defense military advice before they know they need it.

The fact that the talk may be boring or turgid or uninspiring should not cause us to forget the fact that it is preferable to war.

Henry Cabot Lodge Jr.
on the United Nations, recalled on his death
Feb 27, 1985

You're not here to die for your country. You're here to make those so-and-sos die for theirs.

Gen. John Michaelis
to troops fighting in Korea, recalled on his death
Time
Nov 11, 1985

(This is) an era of violent peace.

Adm. James D. Watkins
quoted by Richard Halloran, "A Silent Battle Surfaces"
The New York Times
Dec 7, 1986

The more you sweat in peace, the less you bleed in war.

Hyman G. Rickover
1983 retirement speech, recalled on his death
Jul 8, 1986

Terrorism (takes) us back to ages we thought were long gone if we allow it a free hand to corrupt democratic societies and destroy the basic rules of international life.

Jacques Chirac
speech to the U.N. General Assembly
Sep 24, 1986

Terrorism has become the systematic weapon of a war that knows no borders or seldom has a face.

Jacques Chirac
speech to the U.N. General Assembly
Sep 24, 1986

The notion of a defense that will protect American cities is one that will not be achieved, but it is that goal that supplies the political magic, as it were, in the president's vision.

James R. Schlesinger
testimony to the Senate Foreign Relations Committee
The New York Times
Feb 7, 1987

There's nothing like a good war to make people feel important.

a Democratic House aide
quoted in
Newsweek
Sep 10, 1990

You shouldn't go to war unless you know what kind of peace you want.

a French diplomat
quoted in
Newsweek
Oct 29, 1990

War is not neat, it's not tidy, and once you resort to it, it's uncertain and it's a mess.

William Crowe Jr.
quoted in
Newsweek
Dec 10, 1990

Yours is a society which cannot accept 10,000 dead in one battle.

Saddam Hussein
remarks to US Ambassador April Glaspie in August, 1990, reported in
Newsweek
Jan 7, 1991

Patrick Leahy
remarks quoted in
Newsweek
Jan 14, 1991

I think for better or worse we've crossed the Rubicon. The question is not whether or not we have a war, it's when.

Bernard Shaw
CNN news report from
Baghdad, quoted in
Newsweek
Jan 28, 1991

Clearly I've never been there, but it feels like we are in the center of hell.

**General H. Norman
Schwarzkopf**
remarks at a press con-
ference quoted in
The New York Times
Feb 28, 1991

As far as Saddam Hussein being a great military strategist, he is neither a strategist, nor is he schooled in the operational art, nor is he a tactician, nor is he a general, nor is he a soldier. Other than that, he's a great military man—I want you to know that.

Women in Politics

Plato
The Republic
ca. 390 B.C.

There is no occupation concerned with the management of social affairs which belongs either to women or to men, as such . . . and every occupation is open to both.

John Knox
*First Blast of the Trumpet
Against the Monstrous
Regiment of Women*
1558

To promote a Woman to bear rule, superiority, dominion, or empire, above any Realm, Nation, or City, is repugnant to Nature; contumely to God, a thing most contrarious to his revealed will and approved ordinance; and finally it is the subversion of good Order, of all equity and justice.

**Jean Jacques
Rousseau**
Emile
1762

Women have, or ought to have, but little liberty; they are apt to indulge themselves excessively in what is allowed them.

Abigail Adams
letter to John Adams
Mar 31, 1776

If particular care is not paid to the ladies, we are determined to foment a rebellion, and will not hold ourselves bound by any laws in which we have no voice, no representation.

Mary Wollstonecraft
*A Vindication of the Rights
of Woman*
1792

When man, governed by reasonable laws, enjoys his natural freedom, let him despise woman, if she do not share it with him.

Washington Irving
*Knickerbocker's History
of New York*
1809

His wife "ruled the roast," and in governing the governor, governed the province, which might thus be said to be under petticoat government.

**Elizabeth Cady
Stanton**
First Woman's Rights
Convention, Seneca Falls,
New York
Jul 19–20, 1848

Resolved, That it is the duty of the women of this country to secure to themselves their sacred right to the elective franchise.

If the first woman God ever made was strong enough to turn the world upside down all alone, these together ought to be able to turn it back and get it right side up again, and now that they're asking to do it, the men better let them.

Sojourner Truth
speech to the Women's Rights Convention in Akron, Ohio
1851

Because the revolutionary tempest, in over-turning at the same time the throne and the scaffold, in breaking the chain of the black slave, forgot to break the chain of the most oppressed of all—of Woman, the pariah of humanity.

Jeanne-Françoise Deroin
letter from St. Lazare Prison
Jun 15, 1851

We have, moreover, the profound conviction that only by the power of association based on solidarity—by the union of the working classes of both sexes to organize labor—can be acquired, completely and pacifically, the civil and political equality of women, and the social right for all.

Jeanne-Françoise Deroin
letter from St. Lazare Prison
Jun 15, 1851

Women—one half the human race at least—care fifty times more for a marriage than a ministry.

Walter Bagehot
The English Constitution
1867

Women must not depend upon the protection of man, but must be taught to protect herself.

Susan B. Anthony
speech in San Francisco, California
Jul, 1871

The ignorance and indifference of the majority of women, as to their status as citizens of a republic, is not remarkable, for history shows that the masses of all oppressed classes, in the most degraded conditions, have been stolid and apathetic until partial success had crowned the faith and enthusiasm of the few.

Elizabeth Cady Stanton
History of Woman Suffrage
1881

The queens in history compare favorably with the kings.

Elizabeth Cady Stanton
History of Woman Suffrage
1881

But when at last woman stands on an even platform with man, his acknowledged equal everywhere, with the same freedom to express herself in the religion and government of the country, then, and not until then,. . . will he be able to legislate as wisely and generously for her as for himself.

Elizabeth Cady Stanton
History of Woman Suffrage
1881

Give women the vote, and in five years there will be a crushing tax on bachelors.

George Bernard Shaw
preface
Man and Superman
1902

We are here, not because we are lawbreakers; we are here in our efforts to become law-makers.

Emmeline Pankhurst
speech at her trial in London
Oct 21, 1908

True, the movement for women's rights has broken many old fetters, but it has also forged new ones.

Emma Goldman
"The Tragedy of Women's Emancipation"
Anarchism and Other Essays
1911

Emma Goldman
"The Tragedy of
Women's Emancipation"
*Anarchism and
Other Essays*
1911

There is no hope even that woman, with her right to vote, will ever purify politics.

Emmeline Pankhurst
My Own Story
1914

If we women are wrong in destroying private property in order that human values may be restored, then I say, in all reverence, that it was wrong for the Founder of Christianity to destroy private property, as He did when He lashed the money changers out the Temple and when He drove the Gadarene swine into the sea.

Emmeline Pankhurst
foreword
My Own Story
1914

The militancy of men, through all the centuries, has drenched the world with blood, and for these deeds of horror and destruction men have been rewarded with monuments, with great songs and epics. The militancy of women has harmed no human life save the lives of those who fought the battle of righteousness.

Nancy Astor
My Two Countries
1923

I can conceive of nothing worse than a man-governed world—except a woman-governed world.

Jeanette Rankin
quoted
Newsweek
Feb 14, 1966

We're half the people; we should be half the Congress.

Adolfo Lopez Mateos
Time
Oct 12, 1959

A woman is a citizen who works for Mexico. We must not treat her differently from a man, except to honor her more.

**Lyndon Baines
Johnson**
on appointing ten women
to top government
positions
Mar 4, 1964

I want to make a policy statement. I am unabashedly in favor of women.

**Lyndon Baines
Johnson**
on swearing-in of women
appointees
Apr 13, 1964

To conclude that women are unfitted to the task of our historic society seems to me the equivalent of closing male eyes to female facts.

Richard M. Nixon
speech to the League of
Women Voters,
Washington, D.C.
Apr 16, 1969

Certainly in the next 50 years we shall see a woman president, perhaps sooner than you think. A woman can and should be able to do any political job that a man can do.

Germaine Greer
"Revolution"
The Female Eunich
1970

Women's liberation, if it abolishes the patriarchal family, will abolish a necessary substructure of the authoritarian state, and once that withers away, Marx will have come true willy-nilly, so let's get on with it.

Shirley Chisholm
Unbought and Unbossed
1970

Of my two "handicaps," being female put many more obstacles in my path than being black.

Women have been and are prejudiced, narrowminded, reactionary, even violent. Some women. They, of course, have a right to vote and a right to run for office. I will defend that right, but I will not support them or vote for them.

One of the things being in politics has taught me is that men are not a reasoned or reasonable sex.

I am working for the time when unqualified blacks, browns and women join the unqualified men in running our government.

In politics women . . . type the letters, lick the stamps, distribute the pamphlets and get out the vote. Men get elected.

You can't have a Congress that responds to the needs of the workingman when there are practically no people here who represent him. And you're not going to have a society that understands its humanity if you don't have more women in government.

In politics if you want anything said, ask a man. If you want anything done, ask a woman.

If you had to work in the environment of Washington, D.C. as I do, and watch those men who are so imprisoned and so confined by their 18th-century thought patterns, you would know that if anybody is going to be liberated, it's men who must be liberated in this country.

There aren't many women now I'd like to see as President— but there are fewer men.

When men talk about defense, they always claim to be protecting women and children, but they never ask the women and children what they think.

Party organization matters. When the door of a smoke-filled room is closed, there's hardly ever a woman inside.

Toughness doesn't have to come in a pinstripe suit.

What has the women's movement learned from (Geraldine Ferraro's) candidacy for vice president? Never get married.

Bella Abzug
speech to the National
Women's Political Caucus,
Washington, D.C.
Jul 10, 1971

Margaret Thatcher
BBC-radio
Jan 14, 1972

Sissy Farenthold
quoted
The Los Angeles Times
Sep 18, 1974

Clare Boothe Luce
quoted
Saturday Review/World
Sep 15, 1974

Bella Abzug
quoted, "Impeachment?"
by Claire Safran
Redbook
Apr, 1974

Margaret Thatcher
People
Sep 15, 1975

Barbara Jordan
speech at the International Women's Year Conference, Austin, Texas
Nov 10, 1975

Clare Boothe Luce
Newsweek
Oct 22, 1979

Patricia Schroeder
*The New York Times
Book Review*
Feb 17, 1980

Millicent Fenwick
"60 Minutes," CBS-TV
Feb 1, 1981

Dianne Feinstein
Time
Jun 4, 1984

Gloria Steinem
quoted
Boston Globe
May 14, 1987

Author Index

Bacon, Sir Francis, 1st Viscount St. Albans, 1561–1626. English statesman & philosopher.
International Affairs/Diplomacy **139**
Judiciary and Judges **149**
Justice **153**
Leadership/Statesmanship **172, 173**
Monarchy **202**
Politics **232**
Power **244**
Reform **266**
Revolution **275**
Role of the State/of Government **294**
War and Peace **318, 319**

Bagehot, Walter, 1826–1877. British banker, editor & economist.
Democracy **31**
International Affairs/Diplomacy **141**
Leadership/Statesmanship **179**
Monarchy **204**
Politics **234**
Women in Politics **345**

Bailey, F. Lee, 1933– . American lawyer & author.
Constitution **22**

Baker, Howard H., Jr., 1925– . American politician; senator from Tennessee, 1966–85.
Presidency **260**

Baker, Russell, 1925– . American journalist & author.
Power **249**

Bakunin, Michael
Equality **66**
Freedom/Liberty **114**
Government and Business **137**
Politics **234**
Revolution **278**
Role of the State/of Government **299**
War and Peace **324**

Baldwin, James, 1924–1987. American author, dramatist, essayist.
Democracy **43**
Freedom/Liberty 125

Baldwin, Roger N., 1884–1981. American social reformer; a founder of the American Civil Liberties Union & director, 1920–50.
Democracy **43**

Baldwin, Stanley, 1st Earl Baldwin of Bewdley, 1867–1937. British politician; prime minister of the United Kingdom, 1923, 1924–29, 1935–37.
Education **61**
Freedom of the Press **103**
Legislatures and Legislation **195**
Nationalism **206**
Political Parties **216**
Politics **239**
Socialism **308**

Balfour, Arthur, 1st Earl of Balfour, 1848–1930. British politician; prime minister of the United Kingdom, 1902–06.
Democracy **35**
Leadership/Statesmanship **183**

Balzac, Honoré de, 1799–1850. French novelist.
Democracy **29**

Bancroft, George, 1800–1891. American historian.
Democracy **29**

Barère de Vieuzac, Bertrand, 1755–1841. French revolutionary.
Revolution **275, 276**

Barkley, Alben W., 1877–1956. American politician; vice-president of the United States, 1948–52.
Political Campaigns **210**
Politics **240**

Barrès, Maurice, 1896–1923. French author.
Politicians and Public Officials **224**

Barth, Alan, 1906– . American writer.
Prejudice and Discrimination **252**

Baruch, Bernard, 1870–1965. American businessman; adviser to presidents.
Dictatorship/Tyranny **54**
Elections and Voting **63**
Expressions and Phrases **86**
Government **136**
Leadership/Statesmanship **189**

Batista, Fulgencio, 1901–1973. Dictator of Cuba, 1952–59.
War and Peace **337**

Baudouin I, 1930– . King of the Belgians, 1951– .
War and Peace **337**

Beauvoir, Simone de, 1908–1986. French feminist & author.
Freedom/Liberty **121**

Bebel, August, 1840–1913. German socialist & writer.
Politics **234, 236**
Prejudice and Discrimination **251**
War and Peace **324**

Beecher, Henry Ward, 1813–1887. American clergyman & social reformer.
Conservatism **19**
Democracy **32**
Dictatorship/Tyranny **51**
Freedom/Liberty **115**
Government **134**
Law **164**
Leadership/Statesmanship **181**
Public Opinion **264**
Treason **315**
War and Peace **325**

Beerbohm, Sir Max, 1872–1956. English critic, essayist & novelist.
Justice **156**
Leadership/Statesmanship **183, 186**

Behan, Brendan, 1923–1964. Irish dramatist & author.
War and Peace **337**

Bellamy, Carol
Expressions and Phrases **95**

Benét, Stephen Vincent, 1898–1943. American poet & author.
Power **247**

Bengough, John, 1851–1923. Canadian poet & political cartoonist.
Political Parties **216**

Republican Party **274**
Rights/Human Rights **293**
Role of the State/of Government **302**
Social Justice **307**
War and Peace **342**

Casement, Sir Roger, 1864–1916. Irish nationalist.
Nationalism **205**

Castle, Barbara, 1911– . British politician; member of parliament, 1945–79.
Politics **242**

Castro, Fidel, 1926– . Cuban communist leader; premier of Cuba, 1959– .
International Affairs/Diplomacy **147**
Revolution **282, 283**
War and Peace **341**

Cater, Douglass, 1923– . American author, editor, educator.
Power **249**

Catt, Carrie Chapman, 1859–1947. American feminist; founder of League of Women Voters.
Public Opinion **264**
Rights/Human Rights **287**

Cavell, Edith, 1865–1915. English nurse; executed by Germans in World War I for helping Allied soldiers.
Patriotism **209**

Cavour, Camillo, Conte di, 1810–1861. Italian statesman; first premier of Italy.
Freedom/Liberty **113**

Cellini, Benvenuto, 1500–1571. Italian sculptor & author.
Dictatorship/Tyranny **46**

Cervantes, Miguel de, 1547–1616. Spanish poet & dramatist.
Law **160**
War and Peace **318**

Chaffee, Zechariah Jr., 1885–1957. American educator.
Constitution **22**
Freedom of the Press **103**

Chamberlain, Joseph, 1836–1914. English politician & social reformer.
Democracy **32**
Economics/The Economy **56**
Leadership/Statesmanship **181**
Politics **235**

Chamberlain, Neville, 1869–1940. British politician; prime minister of the United Kingdom, 1937–40.
War and Peace **330**

Chandler, A.B., ("Happy"), 1898– . American politician; governor of Kentucky, 1935–39, 1955–59.
Expressions and Phrases **93**

Channing, William Ellery, 1780–1842. American clergyman & abolitionist.
Role of the State/of Government **297**

Charlemont, 1st Earl of, (James Caulfeild), 1728–1779. Irish nationalist leader.
Politicians and Public Officials **219**

Charles, Prince, 1948– . Prince of Wales.
Monarchy **205**

Charles I, 1600–1649. King of Great Britain & Ireland, 1625–49.
Dictatorship/Tyranny **47**

Charles II, 1630–1685. King of Great Britain & Ireland, 1660–85.
Monarchy **202**

Chartier, Emile Auguste, ("Alain"), 1868–1951. French essayist, philosopher & educator.
Expressions and Phrases **83**
Freedom of Speech **98**

Chayefsky, Paddy, 1923–1981. American dramatist.
Democracy **43**

Cheney, Richard B. American politician; Secretary of Defense, 1989– .
Role of the State/of Government **302**

Chesterfield, 4th Earl of, (Philip Stanhope), 1694–1773. English author & politician.
Freedom/Liberty **106**
Leadership/Statesmanship **174**
Political Parties **212**
Politics **232**

Chesterton, G.K., 1874–1936. English poet, critic & essayist.
Class Divisions **8**
Politics **236**
Revolution **279**

Child, Lydia Maria, 1802–1880. American feminist & author.
Rights/Human Rights **285, 286**

Chiles, Lawton M. Jr., 1930– . American politician; senator from Florida, 1971–89.
Ethics in Politics **72**

Chirac, Jacques, 1932– . French politician; prime minister of France, 1974–76, 1986–88.
War and Peace **343**

Chisholm, Shirley, 1924– . American politician; congresswoman from New York, 1968–82.
Democracy **42**
Ethics in Politics **72**
Liberalism **197**
Politicians and Public Officials **228**
Politics **241**
Women in Politics **346**

Choate, Rufus, 1799–1859. American lawyer & politician.
Role of the State/of Government **298**

Chou En-lai, 1898–1976. Chinese communist leader; premier of China, 1949–76.
International Affairs/Diplomacy **144**

Church, Frank, 1924–1984. American politician; senator from Idaho, 1956–81.
Presidency **261**
Separation of Powers **304**

Churchill, Sir Winston S., 1874–1965. British statesman; prime minister of the United Kingdom, 1940–45, 1952–54.
Communism **14**
Conservatism **20**
Democracy **38, 39**
Dictatorship/Tyranny **53**

De Gaulle, Charles, 1890–1970. French military leader & statesman; president of France, 1959–69.
Expressions and Phrases **88, 91**
Government **136**
International Affairs/Diplomacy **145**
Leadership/Statesmanship **184, 185, 187, 188, 189**
Nationalism **206, 207**
Politicians and Public Officials **227**
War and Peace **336, 338, 340**

Dean, John, 1938– . American lawyer & public official; counsel to the president, 1971–73.
Presidency **259, 261**

Debray, Régis, 1940– . French author & public official.
Communism **16**

Debs, Eugene V., 1855–1926. American socialist leader.
Freedom/Liberty **118**
Majority and Minorities **200**
Socialism **308**

Decatur, Stephen, 1779–1820. American naval officer.
Patriotism **208**

Defoe, Daniel, 1661–1731. English author.
Dictatorship/Tyranny **47**
Monarchy **202**

Deighton, Len, 1929– . English novelist.
Politicians and Public Officials **230**

Delacroix, Eugene, 1798–1863. French artist.
Reform **267**

Deng Xiaoping, 1904– . Chinese political leader.
Communism **17**
Presidency **262**

Derby, 14th Earl of, (Edward Stanley), 1799–1869. British politician; prime minister of United Kingdom, 1852, 1858–59, 1866–68.
Expressions and Phrases **79**
International Affairs/Diplomacy **141**
Political Parties **214**

Deroin, Jeanne-Françoise, 1805–1894. French feminist.
Rights/Human Rights **285**
Women in Politics **345**

Devlin, Patrick, 1905– . British jurist.
Public Opinion **265**

Dewey, John, 1859–1952. American educator & philosopher.
Democracy **34**
Education **60**
Freedom/Liberty **119**

Diaz Ordaz, Gustavo, 1911–1979. Mexican politician; president of Mexico, 1964–70.
Leadership/Statesmanship **189**

Dickens, Charles, 1812–1870. English author.
Law **163**
Politicians and Public Officials **221**

Dickinson, Goldsworthy Lowes, 1862–1932. British essayist, pacifist & philosopher.
Majority and Minorities **200**

Dickinson, John, 1732–1808. American politician & revolutionary leader.
Freedom/Liberty **106**
Taxation and Budgets **310**

Diderot, Denis, 1713–1784. French philosopher & editor.
Dictatorship/Tyranny **48**
Expressions and Phrases **73**
Law **162**

Disraeli, Benjamin, 1st Earl of Beaconsfield, 1804–1881. British author & statesman; prime minister of the United Kingdom 1868, 1874–80.
Class Divisions **5**
Conservatism **18**
Democracy **28**
Education **60**
Elections and Voting **62**
Expressions and Phrases **76, 77, 78, 79**
Government **134**
International Affairs/Diplomacy **141**
Justice **155**
Leadership/Statesmanship **178, 180**
Legislatures and Legislation **194**
Nationalism **205**
Political Parties **214, 215**
Politicians and Public Officials **221, 222**
Politics **233**
Public Opinion **263**
Role of the State/of Government **299**
Taxation and Budgets **311**
War and Peace **323**

Djilas, Milovan, 1911– . Yugoslav Communist leader & writer.
Communism **15, 17**

Dole, Robert J., 1923– . American politician; senator from Kansas, 1968– .
Presidency **261**

Donnelly, Ignatius, 1831–1901. American politician & author.
Democratic Party **44**

Dostoevsky, Fyodor, 1821–1881. Russian novelist.
Dictatorship/Tyranny **50**

Douglas, Helen Gahagan, 1900–1980. American singer & politician; congresswoman from California, 1945–51.
Elections and Voting **63**

Douglas, Norman, 1868–1952. Scottish author.
Majority and Minorities **200**

Douglas, Stephen A., 1813–1861. American politician; senator from Illinois, 1847–61.
Political Parties **215**

Douglas, Thomas, 1904–1986. Canadian clergyman & politician; premier of Saskatchewan, 1944–61; leader, New Democrats, 1961–71.
Expressions and Phrases **91**

Douglas, William O., 1898–1980. American jurist; justice of Supreme Court, 1939–75.
Constitution **23**
Freedom of Speech **99, 100**
Freedom/Liberty **123, 127**
Judiciary and Judges **151**
Law **167**

Goodman, Paul, 1911–1972. American author & educator.
Leadership/Statesmanship **188**

Goodwin, Doris Kearns, 1943– . American political scientist & biographer.
Presidency **261**

Gorbachev, Mikhail S., 1931– . Russian communist leader; secretary general of Communist Party of the Soviet Union, 1985– .
Communism **17**
International Affairs/Diplomacy **149**

Gorky, Maxim, 1868–1936. Russian dramatist.
Communism **12**
Dictatorship/Tyranny **52**
Law **165, 168**

Gowon, Yakubu, 1934– . Nigerian military & political leader; head of state, 1966–75.
Dictatorship/Tyranny **55**

Grant, Ulysses S., 1822–1885. American military leader & politician; president of the United States, 1869–77.
Democracy **31**
Freedom/Liberty **113**
Law **164**
Political Parties **215**
Presidency **256**
War and Peace **323**

Gray, Lt. Gen. Alfred M.
Democracy **43**

Greene, Graham, 1904– . English author.
Communism **16**

Greer, Germaine, 1939– . Australian author & feminist.
Revolution **283**
Women in Politics **346**

Grenville, George, 1712–1770. British politician.
Government **129**

Grey, Edward, 1st Viscount Grey of Fallodon, 1862–1933. British politician; foreign secretary, 1905–16.
Expressions and Phrases **81**

Grimké, Angelina, 1805–1879. American abolitionist & feminist.
Dictatorship/Tyranny **49**
Law **163**
Religion and the State **272**

Grimond, Jo. British politician; leader of the Liberal Party, 1956–1967.
Expressions and Phrases **90**

Guevara, Ernesto, "Che," 1928–1967. Argentine revolutionary.
Revolution **282, 276**

Hague, Frank, 1896–1956. American politician; boss of Union County, New Jersey.
Freedom/Liberty **119**

Haile Selassie, 1892–1975. Emperor of Ethiopia, 1930–75.
International Affairs/Diplomacy **143**

Hailsham, Lord, (Quinton Hogg), 1907– . British politician.
Freedom/Liberty **121**

Hale, Edward Everett, 1822–1909. American clergyman and author; sometime chaplain of the United States Senate.
Legislatures and Legislation **195**

Hale, Nathan, 1755–1776. American Revolutionary spy.
Patriotism **207**

Halifax, 1st Marquess of, (George Savile), 1633–1695. English politician & author.
Expressions and Phrases **73**
Law **160**
Political Parties **212**
Power **245**

Hamer, Fannie Lou, 1917–1977. American political activist.
Expressions and Phrases **93**

Hamilton, Alexander, 1757–1804. American politician & author; secretary of the treasury, 1789–95.
Class Divisions **4**
Democracy **27**
Dictatorship/Tyranny **49**
Equality **65**
Government **130, 131**
Government and Business **137**
International Affairs/Diplomacy **139**
Law **162**
Legislatures and Legislation **193**
Power **245**
Presidency **255**
Taxation and Budgets **310**

Hammarskjold, Dag, 1905–1961. Swedish statesman; secretary general of the United Nations, 1953–61.
Expressions and Phrases **88, 89**
International Affairs/Diplomacy **144**
Leadership/Statesmanship **189**
Rights/Human Rights **289**

Hammurabi, 1955–1913 B.C. Babylonian king.
Justice **152**

Hand, Learned, 1872–1961. American jurist; judge, U.S. Court of Appeals, 1924–51.
Democracy **36**
Expressions and Phrases **90**
Freedom of Speech **99**
Freedom of the Press **103**
Freedom/Liberty **119, 121**
Justice **156**
Law **166**
Politicians and Public Officials **225**

Harcourt, Sir William, 1827–1904. British lawyer & politician; leader of the Liberal Party, 1893–98.
Conservatism **19**
Legislatures and Legislation **194**

Hardie, Keir, 1856–1915. Scottish labor leader; a founder of the Labour Party and its first candidate for parliament.
Class Divisions **8**
Freedom/Liberty **115**

Harding, Warren G., 1865–1923. American politician; president of the United States, 1920–23.
Democracy **35**
Expressions and Phrases **82**

Revolution **277**

Hesburgh, Theodore M., 1917– . American author & educator; president of Notre Dame Univ., 1952–86.
Elections and Voting **64**

Hesse, Hermann, 1877–1962. Swiss author.
Law **166**

Highet, Gilbert, 1906–1978. American author, educator & critic.
Politics **239**

Hightower, Jim. American public official; Texas state commissioner of agriculture.
Expressions and Phrases **96**
Government and Business **139**

Hill, George. British journalist.
Politicians and Public Officials **231**

Hillman, Sidney, 1887–1946. American labor leader.
Politics **239**

Himes, Chester Bomar, 1909–1984. American author.
Democracy **39**
Expressions and Phrases **85**
Freedom/Liberty **121**
Revolution **281**

Hitler, Adolf, 1889–1945. German dictator; leader of Germany, 1933–45.
Dictatorship/Tyranny **52**
Education **61**
Leadership/Statesmanship **183**
Legislatures and Legislation **195**
Rights/Human Rights **288**
War and Peace **328**

Ho Chi Minh, 1890–1969. Vietnamese national leader.
War and Peace **341**

Hobbes, Thomas, 1588–1679. English philospher & writer.
Power **245**
War and Peace **319**

Hobhouse, Leonard, 1864–1929. British journalist & social reformer.
Equality **67**

Hochhuth, Rolf, 1931– . German dramatist.
International Affairs/Diplomacy **147**

Hodges, Luther H., 1898–1974. American politician & public official.
Economics/The Economy **58**

Hoffer, Eric, 1902–1983. American author & philosopher.
Dictatorship/Tyranny **54, 55**
Equality **67**
Expressions and Phrases **86, 87**
Freedom/Liberty **126**
Government **136**
Leadership/Statesmanship **187**
Power **248, 249**
Reform **270**
Revolution **281, 283**

Hölderlin, Friedrich, 1770–1843. German poet.
Dictatorship/Tyranny **49**

Hollings, Ernest F., 1922– . American politician; senator from South Carolina, 1966– .
War and Peace **342**

Holmes, Oliver Wendell, Jr., 1841–1935. American jurist; justice of the Supreme Court, 1902–32.
Freedom of Speech **98**
Justice **156**
Law **164, 165**
Legislatures and Legislation **194**
Power **247**
Role of the State/of Government **300**
Taxation and Budgets **312, 313**

Holmes, Oliver Wendell, Sr., 1809–1894. American poet, author & essayist.
Class Divisions **8**
Freedom of Speech **97**
Leadership/Statesmanship **179, 180**

Homer, ca. 700 B.C. Greek poet.
Expressions and Phrases **72**
Leadership/Statesmanship **170**
Monarchy **201**
Patriotism **207**
War and Peace **316**

Hoover, Herbert, 1874–1964. American politician; president of the United States, 1929–1933.
Democracy **35**
Economics/The Economy **57**
Ethics in Politics **71**
Freedom of Speech **98**
Government **135**
International Affairs/Diplomacy **143**
Leadership/Statesmanship **184, 186**
Political Parties **218**
Politics **238, 239**
Presidency **257**
Role of the State/of Government **300, 301**
War and Peace **332**

Hopkins, Harry L., 1890–1946. American public official.
Expressions and Phrases **83**

Horace, (Quintus Horatius Flaccus), 65–8 B.C. Roman poet & satirist.
Justice **152**
War and Peace **317**

Horsley, Samuel, 1733–1806. English bishop.
Law **162**

Howe, Edgar Watson, 1853–1937. American editor and author.
Dictatorship/Tyranny **52**
Expressions and Phrases **81, 82**
Freedom of the Press **102**
Reform **269**

Howe, Louis McHenry, 1871–1920. American journalist; secretary to F.D. Roosevelt.
Ethics in Politics **71**

Howells, William Dean, 1837–1920. American novelist & editor.
Dictatorship/Tyranny **51**

Hubbard, "Kin," 1868–1930. American journalist & humorist.
Class Divisions **9**
Elections and Voting **63**

King, William Lyon Mackenzie, 1874–1950. Canadian politician; prime minister of Canada, 1921–30, 1935–48.
Public Opinion **265**

Kirkland, Lane, 1922– . American labor union official; president, AFL-CIO, 1979– .
Taxation and Budgets **314**

Kirkpatrick, Jeane J., 1926– . American diplomat.
Democratic Party **46**
Government **137**

Kissinger, Henry A., 1923– . American diplomat; Secretary of State, 1973–76.
Communism **17**
Expressions and Phrases **93, 94, 95**
International Affairs/Diplomacy **147, 148**
Law **169**
Leadership/Statesmanship **190, 191, 192**
Power **249**
Role of the State/of Government **302**

Knox, John, 1505–1572. Scottish religious leader & reformer.
Women in Politics **344**

Koch, Edward I., 1924– . American politician; mayor of New York City, 1981–89.
Ethics in Politics **72**
Expressions and Phrases **95**
Legislatures and Legislation **196**
Rights/Human Rights **294**
Social Justice **307**

Koestler, Arthur, 1905–1983. Hungarian author.
Politics **238**

Kohl, Helmut, 1930– . German politician; chancellor of Federal Republic of Germany, 1982– .
Leadership/Statesmanship **192**

Krauthammer, Charles, 1950– . American psychiatrist, journalist & author.
Politicians and Public Officials **230**

Kristol, Irving, 1920– . American editor & author.
Reform **270**

Kropotkin, Prince Peter, 1842–1921. Russian geographer & anarchist.
Freedom/Liberty **116**
War and Peace **325**

Krutz, Jerome
Ethics in Politics **72**

La Bruyère, Jean de, 1645–1696. French author & philosopher.
Dictatorship/Tyranny **47**
Judiciary and Judges **150**
Justice **153**
Leadership/Statesmanship **174**
Monarchy **202**
Political Parties **212**
Politicians and Public Officials **219**
Politics **232**
Religion and the State **271**
Revolution **275**

La Rochefoucauld, Francois, Duc de, 1613–180. French epigramist.
Expressions and Phrases **73**

Justice **153**
Leadership/Statesmanship **173**

Lafayette, Marie Joseph, Marquis de, 1757–1834. French military & political leader.
Revolution **275**

LaFollette, Robert M., Sr., 1855–1925. American politician & reform leader; congressman from Wisconsin, 1885–1891; senator, 1906–1925.
Public Opinion **264**

LaFollette, Suzanne, 1893– . American feminist & social reformer.
Conservatism **20**
Freedom/Liberty **118**
Revolution **280**
Rights/Human Rights **288**

LaGuardia, Fiorello, 1882–1947. American politician; mayor of New York, 1934–45.
Political Parties **217**

Landon, Alfred M., 1887– . American politician; Republican candidate for president, 1936.
Majority and Minorities **200**

Landor, Walter Savage, 1775–1864. English author & poet.
Class Divisions **6**
Dictatorship/Tyranny **50**
Expressions and Phrases **77**
Law **164**

Lao-Tse, 570–490 B.C. Chinese philosopher.
War and Peace **316, 333**

Lasswell, Harold, 1902– . American economist.
Politics **238**

Laurier, Sir Wilfrid, 1841–1919. Canadian politician; prime minister of Canada, 1896–1911.
Conservatism **20**

Law, Andrew Bonar, 1858–1923. British politician; prime minister of the United Kingdom, 1922–23.
Leadership/Statesmanship **182**

Lawrence, D.H., 1885–1930. English novelist & essayist.
Freedom/Liberty **119**

Layton, Irving, 1916– . Canadian author.
Politicians and Public Officials **228**

Lazarus, Emma, 1849–1887. American poet.
Freedom/Liberty **115**

Leahy, Patrick Joseph, 1940– . U.S. senator.
War and Peace **344**

Lease, Mary Elizabeth, 1853–1933. American populist & social reformer.
Reform **268**

Lec, Stanislaw, 1909–1966. Czech author.
Justice **157**
Role of the State/of Government **302**

Lee, Robert E., 1807–1870. American military leader.
Patriotism **208**
War and Peace **323**

Lenin, Vladimir Ilyich, 1870–1924. Russian revolutionary; head of U.S.S.R., 1917–24.
Communism **12, 13**
Democracy **34**

Minow, Newton, 1926– . American lawyer & public official.
Law **170**

Mirabeau, Honoré Gabriel, Comte de, 1749–1791. French revolutionary.
Class Divisions **5**
Expressions and Phrases **76**

Mitchell, George J., 1933– . American politician; senator from Maine, 1974– .
Politics **244**

Mitford, Nancy, 1904–1973. English author.
Class Divisions **10**

Molière, 1622–1673. French dramatist.
Reform **266**

Moltke, Helmut von, 1800–1891. German general & statesman.
War and Peace **324**

Mondale, Walter F., 1928– . American politician; senator from Minnesota, 1964–77; vice-president of the United States, 1977–81.
Republican Party **274**

Monnet, Jean, 1888–1979. French economist & diplomat; a founder of European Community.
Leadership/Statesmanship **191**

Monroe, James, 1758–1831. American politician; president of the United States, 1817–1825.
Education **59**
Role of the State/of Government **296**

Montaigne, Michel de, 1533–1592. French essayist.
Expressions and Phrases **73**
Government **128**
Justice **153**
Law **160**
Leadership/Statesmanship **172**
War and Peace **318**

Montesquieu, Charles Louis de, 1689–1755. French philosopher.
Freedom/Liberty **106**
Law **161**
Role of the State/of Government **295**
War and Peace **319**

Moore, George, 1873–1958. English philosopher.
Prejudice and Discrimination **251**
Reform **268**

Morgan, Charles, Jr., 1930– . American lawyer & author.
Legislatures and Legislation **195**

Morgan, J.P., 1837–1913. American financier.
Expressions and Phrases **83**

Morley, John, (1st Viscount Morley of Blackburn), 1838–1923. English author & politician.
Dictatorship/Tyranny **51, 52**
Ethics in Politics **70**
Politicians and Public Officials **223**
Politics **235**
Role of the State/of Government **299**

Morris, William, 1834–1896. English poet, author & craftsman.
Class Divisions **7**
Economics/The Economy **56**

Socialism **308**

Morris, Wright, 1910– . American author.
Rights/Human Rights **291**

Morrow, Lance, 1939– . American journalist & author.
Democratic Party **46**
Politicians and Public Officials **228**

Morse, Wayne Lyman, 1900–1974. American politician; senator from Oregon, 1945–69.
Liberalism **197**

Mosley, Sir Oswald, 1896–1980. British politician; founder of Union of Fascists.
Class Divisions **9**
Leadership/Statesmanship **183**
Legislatures and Legislation **195**
Politicians and Public Officials **224**

Mountbatten, Lord Louis, 1900–1979. British naval officer & member of royal family.
Rights/Human Rights **293**
War and Peace **341**

Moyers, Bill, 1934– . American political commentator.
Politics **241**
Presidency **261**

Moynihan, Daniel P., 1927– . American politician; senator from New York, 1976– .
Conservatism **20**
Expressions and Phrases **93**
Freedom of Speech **100**
Freedom of the Press **104**
Government **136**
Politicians and Public Officials **229**

Muchow, David
Taxation and Budgets **314**

Muhlenberg, Peter, 1746–1801. American religious leader & politician; congressman from Pennsylvania, 1789–91, 1793–95, 1799–1801.
War and Peace **320, 335**

Munro, Hector Hugh, (Saki), 1870–1916. English author.
Expressions and Phrases **83**

Munro, Ross H.
Communism **17**

Murray, Sir George, 1849–1938. British public official.
War and Peace **327**

Murrow, Edward R., 1908–1965. American broadcaster & political commentator.
Leadership/Statesmanship **187**
Politicians and Public Officials **227**
Prejudice and Discrimination **252**

Muskie, Edmund S., 1914– . American politician; senator from Maine, 1959–80; secretary of state, 1980–81.
Democracy **42**

Mussolini, Benito, 1883–1945. Italian political leader; fascist dictator of Italy, 1922–43.
Dictatorship/Tyranny **53**

Scott, Sir Walter, 1771–1832. Scottish poet, novelist, historian.
Patriotism **207**

Sears, John, 1940– . American lawyer & political strategist.
Politics **243**

Seeckt, Hans von, 1866–1936. German military leader.
International Affairs/Diplomacy **142**
War and Peace **329**

Seely, Sir John, 1834–1895. English historian.
Politics **235**

Seiden, Morton Irving, 1921– . American essayist & educator.
Law **168**

Seneca (the Elder), ca. 55 B.C.–40 A.D. Roman rhetorician.
Law **158**

Seneca (the Younger), Lucius Annaeus, 4 B.C.–65 A.D. Roman philosopher, statesman & dramatist.
Expressions and Phrases **73**
Freedom/Liberty **105**
Leadership/Statesmanship **171**
Politicians and Public Officials **218**
War and Peace **317**

Sevareid, Eric, 1912– . American broadcaster & political commentator.
Expressions and Phrases **94**

Seward, William H., 1801–1872. American politician & diplomat.
Constitution **22**

Shakespeare, William, 1564–1616. English dramatist & poet.
Democracy **25**
Dictatorship/Tyranny **46**
Freedom/Liberty **105**
Law **160**
Leadership/Statesmanship **172**
Monarchy **201**
Politicians and Public Officials **219**
Rights/Human Rights **284**
Social Justice **304**

Shannon, William V., 1927– . American diplomat & author; U.S. ambassador to Ireland, 1977–81.
Politics **241**

Shaw, Bernard, 1940– . American news correspondent.
War and Peace **344**

Shaw, George Bernard, 1856–1950. British dramatist & critic.
Class Divisions **9**
Communism **12, 13**
Democracy **33**
Dictatorship/Tyranny **51**
Ethics in Politics **70**
Expressions and Phrases **82**
Freedom/Liberty **116**
Politicians and Public Officials **222, 224**
Politics **235**
Revolution **278, 281**
Social Justice **305**
Socialism **309**

Women in Politics **345**

Shelley, Percy Bysshe, 1792–1822. English poet.
Dictatorship/Tyranny **49**
Expressions and Phrases **75**
Leadership/Statesmanship **176**
Monarchy **203**

Sheridan, Richard Brinsley, 1751–1816. Irish playwright & politician.
Ethics in Politics **69**
Freedom of the Press **101**
Justice **153**
Politicians and Public Officials **219**

Sherman, William Tecumseh, 1820–1891. American Civil War general.
Democracy **31**
Expressions and Phrases **80**
War and Peace **323, 324**

Shipler, David K., 1942– . American journalist.
International Affairs/Diplomacy **149**

Shultz, George P., 1920– . American diplomat; Secretary of State, 1982–1989.
Government and Business **139**
Politics **244**

Sidey, Hugh, 1927– . American journalist.
Political Campaigns **211**

Siéyès, Abbé (Emmanuel), 1748–1836. French clergyman, revolutionary & political leader.
Democracy **27, 37**

Silone, Ignazio, 1900–1978. Italian author.
Dictatorship/Tyranny **53**
Freedom/Liberty **123**
Leadership/Statesmanship **184**
Politics **238**
Revolution **281**

Simon, William E., 1927– . American public official & businessman; secretary of the treasury, 1974–77.
Elections and Voting **64**

Simpson, Alan K., 1936– . American politician; senator from Wyoming.
Freedom/Liberty **128**

Sinclair, Upton, 1878–1968. American author.
Dictatorship/Tyranny **52**

Sirica, John J., 1904– . American jurist.
Presidency **260**

Slessor, Sir John Cotesworth, 1897-? British military leader; promoted air-marshal, 1940; chief of the Air Staff, 1950–52.
Role of the State/of Government **301**

Smith, Adam, 1723–1790. Scottish political economist.
Class Divisions **4**
Economics/The Economy **56**

Smith, Alfred E., 1873–1944. American politician; Democratic candidate for president, 1928.
Democracy **36**

Smith, Gen. Walter Bedell, 1895–1961. American military leader.
War and Peace **339**

Stockman, David, 1946– . American public official; director, Office of Management and Budget,1981–85.
Taxation and Budgets **314**

Stone, I.F., 1907–1989. American journalist.
Freedom of the Press **104**
Freedom/Liberty **127**
War and Peace **334**

Story, Joseph, 1779–1845. American jurist; justice on the Supreme Court, 1811–45.
Law **163**

Strauss, Robert S., 1918– . American lawyer& politician; chairman of the Democratic Party, 1972–77.
Expressions and Phrases **94**
Politicians and Public Officials **229**
Politics **242**

Sumner, Charles, 1811–1874. American author.
Freedom/Liberty **114**

Sumner, William Graham, 1840–1910. American economist, educator & sociologist.
Equality **67**

Sun Yat-sen, Madame, (Sung Ching-ling), 1892–1981. Chinese social reformer & political leader.
Revolution **280**

Sutherland, George, 1862–1942. American politician & jurist; senator from Utah, 1905–17; justice ofthe Supreme Court, 1922–38.
Freedom of the Press **103**
Freedom/Liberty **119**

Swift, Jonathan, 1667–1745. English clergyman, satirist & author.
Law **160**
Leadership/Statesmanship **174**
Politicians and Public Officials **219**

Sylvester, Arthur. American government official; assistant secretary of defense during Kennedy administration.
Government **136**

Tacitus, Cornelius, 55–117. Roman historian & orator.
War and Peace **317**

Taft, William Howard, 1857–1930. American politician & jurist; president of the United States, 1909–13; chief justice, 1921–1930.
Freedom of Speech **98**
Freedom/Liberty **116**
Majority and Minorities **199**
Presidency **256**
Rights/Human Rights **287**
Role of the State/of Government **300**
War and Peace **326**

Tagore, Sir Rabindranath, 1861–1941. Indian poet.
Leadership/Statesmanship **183**
Power **247**

Talleyrand, Charles-Maurice de, 1754–1838. French statesman & diplomat.
Expressions and Phrases **75**

Talmadge, Betty
Legislatures and Legislation **196**

Talmadge, Herman E., 1913– . American politician; senator from Georgia, 1957–75.
Taxation and Budgets **314**

Tawney, Richard, 1880–1962. English economic historian.
Democracy **37**
Government and Business **138**
Political Parties **216**
Politics **237**

Taylor, A.J.P., 1906– . English historian.
Leadership/Statesmanship **186**

Tennyson, Alfred, Lord, 1809–1892. English poet.
Conservatism **19**
Patriotism **208**

Terence, ca. 185–159 B.C. Roman dramatist & poet.
Law **158**
War and Peace **316**

Thatcher, Margaret, 1925– . British politician; prime minister of the United Kingdom, 1979– .
Dictatorship/Tyranny **55**
Expressions and Phrases **95, 96**
International Affairs/Diplomacy **148, 149**
Leadership/Statesmanship **191, 192**
Political Campaigns **211**
Politics **243**
Women in Politics **347**

Thiers, (Louis) Adolphe, 1797–1877. French historian & politician; premier of France, 1836, 1840, 1870–71; president, 1871–73.
Leadership/Statesmanship **177**
Politics **235**

Thomas, Dylan, 1914–1953. Welsh poet & author.
War and Peace **335**

Thomas, Norman, 1884–1968. American socialist leader & author.
Democracy **44**
War and Peace **340**

Thomson, Roy Herbert, Lord Thomson of Fleet, 1894–1976. British press lord.
Conservatism **21, 18**

Thoreau, Henry David, 1817–1862. American author & philosopher.
Elections and Voting **62**
Expressions and Phrases **77**
Government **133, 134**
Government and Business **137**
Law **164**
Leadership/Statesmanship **178, 179**
Majority and Minorities **198**
Prejudice and Discrimination **251**
Public Opinion **263**
Reform **267**
Revolution **277**
Role of the State/of Government **298**
Social Justice **304, 305**

Thorneycroft, Peter, Lord Thorneycroft, 1909– . British politician; chancellor of the exchequer, 1957–58; chairman, Conservative Party, 1975–78.
Politics **242**

Thorpe, Jeremy, 1929– . British politician; head of Liberal Party, 1967–76.
Majority and Minorities **201**

POWER
NOTES

POWER
NOTES

POWER
NOTES

POWER
NOTES